G. P. R. (George Payne Rainsford) James

The Robber

A Tale

G. P. R. (George Payne Rainsford) James

The Robber
A Tale

ISBN/EAN: 9783337122270

Printed in Europe, USA, Canada, Australia, Japan

Cover: Foto ©ninafisch / pixelio.de

More available books at **www.hansebooks.com**

THE ROBBER,

A TALE.

BY

G. P. R. JAMES,

AUTHOR OF "RICHELIEU," "GIPSY," ETC.

"More should I question thee, and more I must—
Though more to know would not be more to trust—
From whence thou cam'st, how tended on. But rest
Unquestioned, welcome; and undoubted, blest."

A NEW EDITION.

LONDON:
GEORGE ROUTLEDGE AND SONS,
THE BROADWAY, LUDGATE.
NEW YORK: 416, BROOME STREET.

THE ROBBER.

CHAPTER I.

It was in the olden time of *merry England*—not at that far removed period when our native land first received its jocund name from the bowmen of Sherwood, and when the yeoman or the franklin, who had wandered after some knightly banner to the plains of the Holy Land, looked back upon the little island of his birth with forgetfulness of all but its cheerful hearths and happy days. Oh, no! it was in a far later age, when, notwithstanding wars and civil contentions not long past by, our country still deserved the name of merry England, and received it constantly amongst a class peculiarly its own. That class was the "good old country gentleman," an antediluvian animal swallowed up and exterminated by the deluge of modern improvements, and whose very bones are now being ground to dust by railroads and steam-carriages. Nevertheless, in that being there was much to wonder at as well as much to admire; and the inimitable song which commemorates its existence does not more than justice to the extinct race. It was in the days of Walton and Cotton, then or somewhere thereabouts (for it is unnecessary in a tale purely domestic, to fix the date to a year), that the events which we are about to narrate, took place, and the scene is entirely in *merry England*.

The court and the country were at that period—with the present we have nothing to do—two completely distinct and separate climates; and while the wits and the libertines, the fops and the soldiers, the poets and the philosophers, of the reigns of Charles, James, William, and Anne, formed a world in which debauchery, vice, strife, evil passion, rage, jealousy, and hatred, seemed the only occupations of genius, and the true sphere for talent; while Oxford and Cambridge had their contentions, and vied with the capital in nourishing feuds and follies of their own; there was a calm and quiet world apart, amidst the shady brooks and sunny fields and dancing streams of merry England; a world which knew but little of the existence of the other, except when the vices, or follies, or crimes of the world of the court called upon the world of the country to resist the encroachments of its neighbour, and defend its own quiet prosperity.

From the peasant who tilled the glebe, and whistled to outsing the lark over his happy toil, up to the lord of the manor, the knight whose many ancestors had all been knights before him, the countrymen of England mingled hardly, if at all, with the world of the metropolis and of the court; except, indeed, when some aspiring spirit, filled with good viands and a fair conceit, raised his wishes to be knight of the shire, and sit in parliament amongst the more courtly of the land; or else when some borough sent its representative to the senate to bring down strange tales of London life and fresh fashions for the wives and daughters.

There was, indeed, a connecting link between the two states of being we have described, afforded by the old hereditary nobility of the land, many members of which still lingered by the ancestral hall, as yet unallured from the calm delights of rural life, and the dignified satisfaction of *dwelling amongst their own people*, even by all the amusements or luxuries of the capital. An annual visit to London, an appearance in the court of the sovereign and the house of peers, at certain times, varied the existence of this class of men; and neither liking, comprehending, nor esteeming the wits and foplings of the metropolis, they returned well pleased to hold their ancient state in the country, bearing renewed importance amongst the country gentlemen around, from this fresh visit to the fountain of all honours and distinctions.

Great, indeed, was their importance amongst their neighbours at times—far greater than we in the present day can well picture to ourselves; for independent of the consequence acquired by spending large incomes within a limited sphere, the feeling of feudal influence was not extinct, though the fact had become a nonentity; and the tenantry on a great man's estate looked up to him in those days with the greater veneration and devotion, because they were not compelled to do so. Above the tenantry, again, the squire and the magistrate, who not only owed a great part of their comfort in the county, their consideration with their neighbours, and their estimation in their own eyes, to the degree of favour in which they stood with the earl, the marquis, or the duke, but who might at any time be rendered uncomfortable and persecuted, if not oppressed, in case they forfeited his good graces, failed not to show their reverence for him on every legitimate occasion—and sometimes, perhaps, went a little further.

Thus, of the little hierarchy of the county, there was generally some nobleman as the chief, and from him it descended through baronets, lords of the manor, knights, justices, squires, and many an *et cetera*, down to the lowest class of all, who still looked up to that chief, and would tell the passer-by, with much solemn truth, that "the earl was quite a king in his own part of the world."

Amongst such classes, in such scenes, and at such a period, took place the events about to be described.

At the door of a small, neat country inn stood gazing forth a traveller, one clear bright morning in the end of the month of May. The hour was early: the matutinal servants of the house were scarcely up; and Molly, with mop and pail, was busily washing out the passage which was soon to be thickly strewn with clean yellow sand. The scene before the traveller's eyes was one on which it is pleasant to dwell; the centre street of a small country town, many miles from a great city. There were a few light clouds in the sky, but they did not interrupt the rays of the great orb of light, who was yet low down in the heaven; and the shadows of the manifold white houses, with their peaked gables turned across the street, forming a fanciful pattern on the ground; the yellow sunshine and the blue shade lying clear and distinct, except where a little fountain burst forth half way down the town, and mingled the two together.

It was, as I have said, a cool and pleasant scene for the eye to rest upon; and even the casements of the houses opposite, shaded by the close-drawn white curtain, gave an idea of calm and happy repose. The world within were all yet asleep: the toil, the anxiety, the care, the strife of active life, had not yet began.

The eye of the traveller rested upon the picture apparently well pleased. It gazed contemplatively up the street to where the road had been made to take a turn, in order to avoid the brow of the gentle hill on which the town was built, and which, crowned with houses of pleasant irregularity, interrupted the further view in that direction; and then that eye turned downward to the place where the highway opened out into the country beyond, after passing over a small bright stream by a brick bridge of ancient date. Over the bridge was slowly wending at the same moment a long line of cattle, lowing as they went forth to pasture, with a herd following in tuneful mood, and neither hurrying himself nor them. The stranger's eye rested on them for a single moment, but then roved on to the landscape which was spread out beyond the bridge, and on it he gazed as curiously as if he had been a painter.

On it, too, we must pause, for it has matter for our consideration. The centre of the picture presented a far view over a bright and smiling country, with large masses of woodland, sloping up in blue lines to some tall brown hills at the distance of ten or twelve miles. A gleaming peep of the river was caught in the foreground, with a sandy bank crowned with old trees; and above the trees again appeared the high slated roofs of a mansion, whose strong walls, formed of large flints cemented together, might also here and there be seen looking forth, grey and heavy, through the green, light foliage. Three or four easements, too, were apparent, but not enough of the house was visible to afford any sure indication of its extent, though the massiveness of the walls, the width of the spaces between the windows, the size of the roofs, and the multitude of the chimneys, instantly made one mentally call it the *Manor House*.

This mansion seemed to be at the distance of about a mile from the town; but upon a rising ground on the opposite side of the picture, seen above bridge and trees, and the first slopes of the offscape, appeared, at the distance of seven or eight miles, or more, a large irregular mass of building, apparently constructed of grey stone, and in some places covered with ivy—at least, if one might so interpret the dark stains apparent even at that distance upon various parts of its face. There was a deep wood behind it, from which it stood out conspicuously, as the morning sun poured clear upon it; and in front appeared what might either be a deer park filled with stunted hawthorn and low chestnut trees, or a wide common.

Such was the scene on which the traveller gazed, as, standing in front of the deep double-seated porch of the little inn, he looked down the road to the country beyond. There was no moving object before his eyes but the herd passing over the bridge; there was no sound but the lowing of the cattle, the whistling of their driver, and a bright lark singing far up in the blue sky.

It is time, however, to turn to the traveller himself, who may not be unworthy of some slight attention. Certain it is, that the good girl who was now sprinkling the passage and porch behind him with fine sand, thought that he was worthy of such; for though she had seen him before, and knew his person well, yet ever and anon she raised her eyes to gaze over his figure, and vowed, in her heart, that he was as good-looking a youth as ever she had set eyes on.

His age might be five or six and twenty, and his height, perhaps, five feet eleven inches. He was both broad and deep-chested, that combination which insures the greatest portion of strength, with length and ease of breadth; and though his arms were not such as would have called attention from their robustness, yet they were evidently muscular and finely proportioned. Thin in the flanks, and with the characteristic English hollow of the back, his lower limbs were remarkably powerful, ending, however, in a small well-shaped foot and ankle, set off to good advantage in a neat close-fitting shoe.

His countenance was as handsome as his figure, and remarkably prepossessing; the features, slightly aquiline; the colouring, a rich brown, though the eyes were found to be decidedly blue, when fully seen through the black lashes. His hair waving round his face, and curling upon his neck, was of a deep glossy brown, and the fine shaped lips, which, in their natural position were slightly open, showed beneath a row of even teeth as white as snow. The brow was broad, straight, and high, with the eye-brow, that most expressive of all the features, forming a wavy line of beauty, strongly marked upon the clear skin, and growing somewhat thicker and deeper above the inner canthus of the eye. Between the eyebrows, however, appeared the only thing that the most fastidious critic of beauty could have objected to. It was a deep scar, evidently the mark of a severe cut; whether received by accident in the jocund days of boyhood, or in the manly sports of the country, or in the field of battle, might be doubtful; but there it rested for ever, a clear, long scar, beginning halfway up the forehead, and growing deeper as it descended, till it formed a sort of indentation between the eyebrows, similar to that produced in some countenances by a heavy frown. Thus to look at the brow, one would have said the face was stern; to look at the eyes, one might have pronounced it thoughtful; but the bland, good-humoured, cheerful smile upon the lips contradicted both, and spoke of a heart which fain would have been at ease, whose own qualities were all bright, and warm, and gay, if the cares and strifes of the world would but let them have way.

We shall not pause long upon the stranger's dress. It was principally composed of what was then called brown kersey, a coarse sort of stuff used by the common people; but the buttons were of polished jet, the linen remarkably fine, the hat, with its single straight feather, set on with an air of smartness; while the fishing-basket under the arm, and the rod in the hand, and all the rest of an angler's paraphernalia conspicuous upon the person, reconciled the homely dress with the distinguished appearance. He was evidently bound for the banks of the clear stream; and yet, though it was the hour of all others which a fisherman should have cultivated, he lingered for some minutes at the door of the little inn; gazing, as we have depicted him, alternately up and down the street, with a slow, meditative look, as if enjoying the beauty of the morning, and the fair scene around him. It is true, that his eyes turned most frequently, and rested longest, upon the bridge and stream and old Manor House, with the wide country beyond; but still he occasionally looked to the other bend of the road, and once seemed to listen for some sound.

He had at length taken one step forward, as if to pursue his way, when the voice of the host of the Talbot, good Gregory Myrtle, was heard coming down the stairs, talking all the way for the benefit of any one who might hear, with a fat, jovial, ale-burdened sound, which at other times and seasons rejoiced the hearts of many a "gay companion of the bowl." The first indication of his coming was a peal of laughter, a loud "Haw, haw, haw!" at some conjugal joke uttered by his dame as he left his chamber.

"Well said, wife! well said!" he exclaimed; "it *is* good to be fat; for when I can no longer walk, I shall easily be rolled—Haw, haw, haw! Gads my life! I must have these stairs propped, or else choose me a chamber on the ground-floor. Sand the floor well, Molly—sand the floor well! Think were I to slip, what a squelch would be there. Ha, Master Harry! ha!" he continued, seeing the stranger turn towards him, "how was it I saw you not last night, when you arrived? You flinched the flagon, I fear me, Master Harry! Nay, good faith, that was not right to old Gregory Myrtle!"

"I was tired, good Gregory!" replied the stranger: "I had ridden more than fifty miles to be here to-day, and I wished to rise early, for the sake of my speckled friends in the stream."

"Ale keeps no man from rising," cried the host. "See how it has made me rise, like a pat of dough in a baker's oven! haw, haw, haw!" and he patted his own fat round paunch. "But whence come ye, Master Harry? from the court, or the city, or the wars?"

"From neither, Myrtle," replied the stranger; "I come from a far distance, to take my tithe of the stream as usual. But how goes on the country since I left it?"

"Well! mighty well!" answered the landlord, "all just as it was, I think. No! poor old Milson, the sexton, is dead: he had buried four generations of us, and the fifth has buried him. He caught cold at the justice room, giving evidence about that robbery, you remember, out upon the moor; and took to his bed and died."

"Which robbery do you mean?" demanded the other; "there were many going on about that time upon the moor and over the hill. Have there been any lately?"

"Not one since you left the country, Master Harry," replied the landlord.

"I hope you do not mean to hint that I had any hand in them," rejoined his companion, with a smile.

"God forbid!" exclaimed good Gregory Myrtle—"Haw, haw, haw! That was a funny slip of mine! No, no, Master Harry, we know you too well; you are more likely to give away all your own than take a bit of other people's, God bless you!"

"I think, indeed, I am," answered the young man, with a sigh; "but if I talk with you much longer, I shall be too late to rob the stream of its trout. Don't forget, Myrtle, to send up to the Manor for leave for me, as usual. I suppose his worship is awake by this time, or will be, by the time my tackle is all ready;" and so saying, he sauntered on down the street, took the pathway by the bridge, and turning along by the bank of the river, was soon lost to the sight.

CHAPTER II.

Sometimes in bright sunny expanse over a broad shallow bed of glittering stones and sand; sometimes in deep pools under high banks bending with shrubs and trees; sometimes winding through a green meadow; sometimes quick and fretful; sometimes slow and sullen; on flowed the little river on its course, like a moody and capricious man amidst all the various accidents of life.

Beginning his preparations close to the bridge, upon a low grassy bank which ran out from the buttress, and afforded a passage round beneath the arches, the stranger, whom the landlord had called Master Harry, had not yet completed all the arrangement of his fishing tackle, when one of those servants—who, in the great hall, were as famous for a good-humoured idleness in that day, as their successors are for an insolent idleness in the present times, and were known by the familiar name of *blue-bottles*—made his appearance, carrying his goodly personage with a quick step towards the fisherman. The infinite truth generally to be found in old sayings was never more happily displayed than in the proverb, "Like master like man!" and if so, a pleasant augury of the master's disposition was to be derived from the demeanour of his messenger. As he came near he raised his hand, touched his cap respectfully, though the fisherman was dressed in kersey; and, with a grave, complacent smile, wished him good morning.

"Sir Walter gives you good day, sir," he said, "and has told me to let you know that you are quite welcome to fish the stream from Abbot's Mill to Harland, which, God help us, is the whole length of the manor. He says he has heard of your being here these two years, and always asking leave and behaving consistent; and he is but too happy to give such a gentleman a day or two's pleasure. Let me help you with the rod, sir—it is somewhat stiffish."

The stranger expressed his thanks both to Sir Walter Herbert for his permission, and to the servant for his assistance; and the *blue-bottle*, who had also a well-exercised taste for angling, stood and looked on and aided till all was ready. By this time the day had somewhat advanced, and the steps passing to and fro over the bridge and along the road had become more frequent; but they did not disturb the fisherman in his avocations; and as he prepared to ascend the stream, whipping it as he went with the light fly, the old servant turned to depart with one more "Good morning, sir;" adding, however, as he looked at the birding-piece which the stranger carried across his shoulder, and then glanced his eye to some red coots which were floating about upon the stream as familiarly as if they had been small farmers of the water and held it under lease, "Perhaps, sir, you will be kind enough not to shoot the coots and divers; Sir Walter likes to see them on the river."

"I would as soon think of shooting myself, my good friend," replied the other; "I have heard that poor Lady Herbert was fond of them, and I would not repay Sir Walter's permission so ill."

The servant bowed and withdrew; and, as he passed on, took off his hat reverentially to an old gentleman and a young lady, who were leaning over a low parapet-wall flanking a terrace in the gardens just opposite the bridge. The last words of the servant and the angler had been overheard, and the result we may soon have occasion to show.

We will not write a chapter upon angling. It matters little to the reader whether the stranger caught few or many fish, or whether the fish were large or small. Suffice to say that he was an expert angler, that the river was one of the best trout streams in England, that the day was favourable; and if the stranger did not fill his basket with the speckled tenants of the stream, it proceeded from an evil habit of occasionally forgetting what he was about, and spending many minutes gazing alternately at the lordly mansion to be seen in the distance, and the old manor-house beyond the bridge. He came at length, however, to a spot where both were shut out by the deep banks overhead, and there he soon made up for lost time, though he still threw his line, in thoughtful mood, and seemed all too careless whether the fish were caught or not.

It was their will, however, to be caught; but at the end of four or five hours' fishing, he was interrupted again by the appearance of the same old servant, who now approached, bearing on his arm a basket evidently well laden.

"Sir Walter desired me to compliment you, sir," he said, "and to wish you good sport. He prays you, too, to honour him by supping with him, for he will not interrupt your fishing by asking you to dine. He has sent you, however, wherewithal to keep off hunger and thirst, and trusts you will find the viands good. Shall I spread them out for you?"

There is no sport in the world better calculated to promote the purposes of that pleasant enemy, hunger, than throwing the long light line over the clear brook; and the angler who, in the busy thoughts of other things, had left chance to provide him with a dinner, willingly availed himself of the good knight's hospitable supply, and did ample justice to all that the basket contained. But there was something more in his feelings on this occasion than the mere gratification of an appetite, though the satisfaction of our hunger has proved a magnificent theme in the hands of our greatest epic poets.

There were other feelings in the breast of the angler, as he sat down and partook of the viands provided for him, which rendered these viands grateful to the mind as well as to the body; and though the beauty of the scene around, the freshness and splendour of the bright spring day, the wooing of the soft air by the bank of the river, the music of the waters as they glided by him, and the carols of manifold birds in the neighbouring woods, were all accessories which might well render a meal, tasted in the midst of them, not only pleasant at the time, but memorable in after days, yet there was something more than all this which made the little basket of provisions thrice agreeable to him; something that made him believe he had been understood, as it were intuitively, by the only persons he would have stooped to seek in the neighbourhood, if he could have stooped to seek any one; something, perhaps, beyond that which may or may not be rendered clear hereafter, as the reader's eye is obscure or penetrating into the secrets of the human heart and character. He received, then, the gift with gladness, and sat down, to partake of it with something more than hunger. He accepted willingly also the invitation to sup at the Manor House; and bestowing a piece of money on the serving man, which amply repaid the pains he had taken, he suffered him to depart, though not till he had lured him down the stream to see several trout brought out of the bright waters with as skilful a hand as ever held a rod.

The fisherman was still going on after the old servant had left him, when he was suddenly roused by a rustling in the high-wooded bank above; and the moment after, he saw descending by a path, apparently not frequently used, a personage upon whose appearance we must dwell for a moment.

The gentleman on whose person the fisherman's eyes were immediately fixed, was somewhere within the ill-defined limits of that vague period of human life called the middle age. None of his strength was gone, perhaps none of his activity; but yet the traces of time's wearing hand might be seen in the grey that was plentifully mingled with his black hair, and in the furrows which lay along his broad, strongly marked brow. He was well dressed, according to the fashion of that day; and any one who has looked into the pictures of Sir Peter Lely must have seen many such a dress as he then wore without our taking the trouble of describing it.

That was a period of heavy swords and many weapons; but the gentleman who now approached bore nothing offensive upon his person but a light blade, which looked better calculated for show than use, and a small valuable cane hanging at his wrist. There was a certain degree of foppery, indeed, about his whole appearance which accorded not very well with either his form or his features. He was about the same height as the angler whom we have before described, but much more broadly made, with a chest like a mountain bull, and long sinewy arms and legs, whose swelling muscles might be discerned, clear and defined, through the white stocking that appeared above his riding boots. His face was quite in harmony with his person, square cut, with good, but somewhat stern features, large bright eyes flashing out from beneath a pair of heavy overhanging eyebrows, a well shaped mouth, though somewhat too wide, and a straight nose, rather short, but not remarkably so.

The complexion was of a deep tanned brown; and there were many lines and furrows over the face, which indicated that the countenance there presented was a tablet on which passion often wrote with a fierce and fiery hand, leaving deep, uneffacable traces behind. That countenance, indeed, was one calculated to bear strong expressions; and which, though changing rapidly under the influence of varied feelings, still became worn and channelled by each—by the storm and the tempest, the sunshine and the shower.

On the present occasion the expression of his face was gay, smiling, and good humoured; and he approached the angler he exclaimed, with a laugh, "You have dined well, Master Harry; and methinks, had you been generous, you might have saved me a nook of the pie, or a draught out of the bottle."

"I did not know you were so near, Franklin," answered the angler, somewhat gravely: "I thought you would have met me at the Talbot this morning; and, not finding you, I fancied that you had forgotten your promise."

"I never forget a promise." replied the other, sharply, and with his brow beginning to lower; "I never forget a promise, Master Harry, be it for good or evil. Had I promised to blow your brains out, I would have done it; and having promised to meet you here this morning, here I am."

"Do not talk such nonsense to me, Franklin, about blowing men's brains out," replied the angler, calmly; "such things will not do with me; I know you better, my good friend. But what prevented you from coming?"

"You do not know me better!" replied the other, sharply. "If I ever said I would blow your brains out—the which God forbid—by the rood I would do it! and as to what has kept me, I have been here since yesterday morning, seeing what is to be done. I tell you, Master Harry, that the time is come; and that if we lay our plans well, we may strike our great stroke within the next three days. I had my reasons, too, for not coming up to the Talbot; but you go back there and hang about the country, as if you had no thought but of fishing or fowling. Have your horses ready for action at a moment's notice, and I will find means to give you timely warning. You know my boy Jocelyn? When you see him about, be sure that there is something to be done; find means to give him a private hearing instantly, and have your arms and horses, as I have said, all prepared."

While the other was speaking, the angler had laid down his rod on the bank, and crossing his arms upon his chest, had fixed his fine thoughtful eyes full, calmly, and steadfastly, upon his companion. "Franklin," he said, at length, "I trust you to a certain point in the conduct of this business, but no further! I trust you because I believe you to be faithful, bold, active, and shrewd. But remember, there is a point where we must stop. What is it you propose to do? I am not one to be led blindfold even by you, Gray; and I remember but too well, that when in other lands fortune cast our lots together, you were always bent upon some wild and violent enterprise, where the risk of your own life seemed to compensate in your eyes for the wrong you at times did to others. Forgive me, Gray; but I must speak plainly. You have promised—you have offered to do me a great service—the greatest, perhaps, that man could render me; but you have not told me how it is to be done, and there must be no violence."

"Not unless we are obliged to use it in our own defence," replied the other sharply. "As to the rest, Master Harry, the enterprise is mine as well as yours: so do not make me angry, or you may chance to fail altogether, and find Franklin Gray as bad an enemy as he can be a good friend."

"No threats, Franklin," replied the other: "you should know that threats avail not with me. I thank you deeply for all your kindness, Franklin; but neither gratitude nor menaces can lead me blindfold. Years have passed since, in the same high and noble cause, and under the same great good man, we fought together on the banks of the Rhine; and you seem to have forgotten that even then, boy as I was, neither threats nor persuasions would move me to do anything I judged—though, perhaps, falsely—to be really wrong. A change has come over you, Gray; but no change has come over me. I am the same, and will remain the same."

"Did you not promise to leave the conduct of this to me?" cried his companion. "Did you not promise to submit to my guidance therein? But never mind! I give you back your promise. Break it all off! Let us part. Go, and be a beggar. Lose all your hopes, and leave me to follow my own course. I care not! But I will not peril my neck for any dastard scruples of yours."

"Dastard!" exclaimed the other, taking a step towards him, and half drawing his sword out of the sheath with the first impulse of indignation, while his brow contracted, so as to cover entirely the deep scar between his eyes. "Dastard! such a word to me!"

"Ay, to you, or any one," replied Franklin Gray, laying his hand upon the hilt of his sword also, as if about to draw it instantly, while his dark eye flashed and his lip quivered under the effects of strong passion.

The next impulse, however, was to gaze for a moment in the countenance of his young opponent; the expression of anger passed away; and withdrawing his hand from the hilt, he threw his arms round the other, exclaiming, "No, no, Harry! We must not quarrel! We must not part! at least not till I have fulfilled all I promised. I have nursed you as a baby on my knee; I have stood beside you when the bullets were flying round our heads like hail; I have lain with you in the same prison; and for your own sake, as well as for those that are gone, I will serve you to the last; but you must not forget your promise either. Leave this matter to me, and, on my soul, I will use no violence, I will shed no blood, except in our own defence! Even then they shall drive me to the last before I pull a trigger."

"Well, well," replied the other, "I will trust you, Franklin, though I have had many a doubt and hesitation lately."

"Did you not promise your mother on her death-bed," demanded the other, straining both his companion's hands in his—"did you not solemnly swear to her to follow my suggestions, to put yourself under my guidance till the enterprise was achieved?"

"I did, I did!" replied the angler. "I did; but then you promised, freely and frankly, to accomplish the object that was at that moment dearest to her heart; and I had no doubt, I had no fear, as to the means. I certainly did so promise my poor mother; but when she exacted that promise, you and I were both differently situated; and I fear me, Franklin, I fear me, that you are over fond of strife, that you are following paths full of danger to yourself, and that you will not be contented till you have brought evil on your own head."

"Pshaw!" replied his companion, turning away. "That is my affair; I will leave the more maudlin part of the business to you: let me have the strife, if there should be any; but remember your promise, Harry; and let this be the last time that we have such fruitless words."

The other made no reply; and Franklin, after gazing on him moodily for a moment, cast himself down upon the bank, and asked, "How do you bestow yourself to-night?"

"I am invited to sup at the Manor House with Sir Walter Herbert," replied the angler; "and I shall go."

"Go, to be sure!" exclaimed his companion: "It may serve us more than anything. Have you ever seen Sir Walter?"

"At a distance," replied the other; "but I never spoke to him. I know him well, however, by repute. They tell me he has fallen into some difficulties."

"From which, perhaps, you may help him," said Franklin, thoughtfully.

"Perhaps I may," answered the angler, in the same tone; "perhaps I may, if I can discover how it may best be done; but at present I only know that difficulties exist, without knowing why or how; for the estates are princely. However, if within my reach, I will try to aid him, whether fortune ever turns round and smiles upon me or not; for I hear he is as noble a gentleman as ever lived."

"Ay, and has a fair daughter," answered his companion, with a smile. "You have seen her, I suppose?"

"Never," replied the angler: "I saw her mother once, who was still very lovely, though she was ill, and died ere the month was out."

"Go! go!" cried his companion, after a moment's thought; "go tonight, by all means; I feel as if good would come of it."

"I do not know how that can be," said the other, musing, "but still I will go; though you know that, in my situation, I think not of men's fair daughters."

"Why not?" asked Franklin Gray, quickly, "why not? What is the situation in which woman and woman's love may not be the jewel of our fate? What is the state or condition that she may not beautify, or soften, or inspirit? Oh! Harry, if you did but know all, you would see that my situation is, of all others, the one in which woman can have the least share; and yet, what were I—what should I become, were it not for the one—the single star that shines for me on earth? When the fierce excitement of some rash enterprise is over, when the brow aches, and the heart is sick and weary, you know not what it is to rest my head upon her bosom, and to hear the pulse within that beats for me alone. You know not what it is, in the hours of temporary idleness, to sit by her side, and see her eyes turn thoughtfully from our child to me, and from me to him, and seem busy with the strange mysterious link that unites us three together. Why, I say, should you not think of woman's love, when you, if not riches, have peace to offer—when, if not splendour, you have an honest name? I tell you, Henry Langford, that when she chose me I was an unknown stranger, in a foreign land; that there were strange tales of how and why I sought those shores; that I had nought to offer but poverty and a bold warm heart. She asked no question—she sought no explanation—she demanded not what was my trade, what were my prospects, whither I would lead her, what should be her afterfate. She loved, and was beloved—for her, that was enough; and she left friends and kindred, and her bright native land, comfort, soft tendance, luxury, and splendour, to be the wife of a houseless wanderer, with a doubtful name. He had but one thing to give her in return—his whole heart, and it is hers."

His companion gazed earnestly in his face, as he spoke, and then suddenly grasped his hand. "Franklin," he said, "you make me sad; your words scarcely leave me a doubt of what I have long suspected."

"Ask me no questions!" exclaimed the other—"you have promised to ask no questions."

"Neither do I," rejoined his companion. "What you have said

scarcely renders a question needful. Franklin, when several years ago we served with the French army on the Rhine, and when first you showed that interest in me, which was strange, till my poor mother's sad history explained it in some degree, you promised me solemnly that if ever you should need money you would share my purse, which, however scanty, has still been more than sufficient for my wants."

"But I have never needed it!" interrupted the other. "The time has not come! When it does, I will."

"You trifle with me Franklin," rejoined his companion; "if you betake yourself to rash acts and dangerous enterprises, as your words admit——"

"I may be moved," said Franklin Gray, again interrupting him. "by a thousand other causes than the need of money; the love of activity, the restlessness of my nature, habits of danger and enterprise—"

"And is not the love of such a being as you have spoken of," demanded his companion, "is it not sufficient to calm down such a nature, to restrain you from all that may hurt or injure her? Think Franklin, think, if you were to fail in some of these attempts—if—if—you are moved!—think what would be her fate—think what would be her feelings;—nay, listen to me—share what I have, Franklin. It is enough for us both, if we be but humble in our thoughts and——

But the other broke away from him with a sudden start, and something like a tear in his eye. "No, no!" he cried, "no, no!" but then again he turned, ere he had reached the top of the bank, and said, in a low, but distinct voice, "Harry, if I succeed in this enterprise for you, and in your favour, you shall have your way."

"But no violence!" replied the angler, "remember, I will have no violence."

"None," rejoined Franklin Gray, "none; for I will take means to overawe resistance; and we will, as we well and justly may, enforce your rights and laugh those to scorn who have so long opposed them: and all without violence, if possible!" But the latter words were uttered in a low tone, and were unheard by his companion.

CHAPTER III.

PERHAPS the sweetest hour of a sweet season is that which precedes the setting of the sun upon a May day. All the world is taking holiday, from the lowing herd that winds slowly o'er the lea to the shard-born beetle and the large white moth. The aspect of the sky and earth too—clear, calm, and tranquil—are full of repose. The mistiness of the mid-day sunshine is away; and the very absence of a portion of the full daylight, and the thin, colourless transparency of the evening air, afford that contemplative, but no way drowsy charm which well precedes, by thought tending to adoration, the hour when, in darkness and forgetfulness, we trust ourselves unconscious to the hands of God. The heart of man is but as an instrument from which the great musician, Nature, produces grand harmonies; and the most soothing anthem that rises within the breast is surely elicited by the soft touch of that evening hour.

It had shone calmly over the world in those scenes we have lately described, and the last moments of the sun's stay above the horizon were passing away, while, within one of the rooms of the old Manor House of Moorhurst Park, the father and the daughter were sitting tranquilly in the seat of a deep window, gazing over the beautiful view before their eyes, and marking all the wonderful changes of colouring which the gradual descent of the sun and the slow passing of a few light evening clouds brought each moment over the scene. There is in almost every heart some one deep memory, some one powerful feeling, which has its harmonious connexion with a particular hour, and with a particular scene; and as the father and the daughter gazed, and marked the sun sinking slowly in the far west, one remembrance, one image, one sensation, took possession of both their bosoms. The daughter thought of the mother, the father of the wife, that was lost to them for ever. Neither spoke—both tried to suppress the feeling, or rather to indulge the feeling, while they suppressed its expression. But such efforts are vain, at least with hearts untutored by the cold policies of a superficial world. A tear glistened in the daughter's eye, and she dared not wipe it away lest it should be remarked. The father's eye, indeed, was tearless, but his brow was sad; and as he withdrew his gaze from the scene before him, and turned his looks upon his daughter, it was with a sigh. He marked, too, the bright drop that still hung trembling on her eyelid, catching the last ray of the setting sun; and, knowing the spring whence that drop arose, he cast his arms around her, and pressed her in silence to his breast.

At that very moment, however—for it is still at the time when the deep shy feelings of the warmest hearts peep forth to enjoy some cool secluded hour, that the world is sure to burst upon them like the cry of the beagles upon the timid hare—at that very moment, one of the servants opened the door of the chamber, and announced Captain Henry Langford. Sir Walter Herbert withdrew his arms from his daughter, and took a step forward; and Alice Herbert, though she felt prepossessed in their visitor's favour, felt also almost vexed that he had come so soon to interrupt the sweet but melancholy feelings which were rising in her father's heart and in her own. She gazed with some interest towards the door, however, and the next instant, the angler, whose course through the day we have already traced, entered the apartment. Rod, and line, and fishing-basket had been, by this time, thrown aside, and he stood before them well, but not gaily, dressed; with scrupulous neatness observable in the every part of his apparel, and with his wavy brown hair arranged with some care and attention.

His air was distinguished, and not to be mistaken—his person was, as we have before said, eminently handsome; so that, although a stranger to both the father and daughter, he bore with him a letter of recommendation of a very prepossessing kind.

As he entered, Sir Walter Herbert advanced to meet him, with the calm dignity of one who, in former years, had mingled with courts and camps—who felt within his breast the ease-giving consciousness of a noble and an upright mind; and he was met by the stranger with the same bearing.

Sir Walter, though not usually familiar, offered him his hand, saying, "Captain Langford, I am very glad to see you; and must explain how it is that I took the liberty of sending you the invitation that has procured me this pleasure. Without intending to act the part of eavesdroppers, my daughter and myself overheard, this morning, the conclusion of a conversation between you and one of my servants, regarding some birds that float about upon the stream; and the few words that fell from you on that occasion breathed a spirit which gave me a temptation too strong to be resisted of seeking your acquaintance, even at the risk of intruding upon the calm and tranquil solitude which you, who are, doubtless, a denizen of cities and courts, seek, in all probability, when you venture into the country."

"It could be no intrusion, sir," replied his guest; "and let me assure you that, in forbidding me to shoot the wild fowl on the stream, your servant imposed upon me no hard condition. Those birds have been a sort of companions to me, during my sport, for these two or three years past, and I should never have thought of injuring them; but would still less have wished to do so, when I knew that you took a pleasure and an interest in them."

"They are associated with past happiness," said Sir Walter; "and, though I believe it is foolish to cling to things which only awaken regret, yet I confess I do take a pleasure, a sad pleasure, perhaps, in seeing them."

"I cannot but think," replied his guest, "that there are some regrets far sweeter than all our every-day enjoyments. The only real pleasures that I myself now possess are in memories; because my only attachments are with the past."

"You are very young to say so, sir," answered Sir Walter; "you must at an early age have broken many sweet ties."

"But one," replied Langford; "for, through life, I have had but one—that between mother and son; but of course it broke with the greater pain from being the only one."

"And your father?" demanded Sir Walter.

"I never knew him," replied the stranger; and, seeing that the conversation might grow painful, Sir Walter Herbert dropped it; and, turning to his daughter, presented the stranger to her, which he had neglected to do before.

It might be that, as the old knight did so, the remembrance of what had passed not long before, regarding the beautiful girl to whom he was now introduced, called the colour rather more brightly into Langford's face; and certainly it produced a slight degree of embarrassment in his manner, which he had never felt on such an occasion before. She was, certainly, very beautiful, and that beauty of a peculiar cast. It was the bright and sun-shiny, united with the deep and touching. Her skin was clear, and exquisitely fair: her lips full, but beautifully formed; the brow broad and white; and the eyes of that soft peculiar hazel, which, when fringed with long black lashes, perhaps is more expressive than any other colour. The hair, which was very full and luxuriant, was of a brown—several shades lighter than Langford's own—soft and glossy as silk, and catching a golden gleam in all the prominent lights. She was not tall, but her form was perfectly well proportioned, and every full and rounded limb was replete with grace and symmetry.

Langford's slight embarrassment wore off in a moment; and the conversation turned upon more general themes than those with which it begun. Sir Walter and his daughter, from the few words they had heard in the morning, undoubtedly expected to find in their guest high and kindly feelings, and that grace, too, which such feelings always afford to the demeanour and conversation of those who possess them. But they found much more than they had expected— a rich and cultivated mind, great powers of conversation, much sparkling variety of idea, an inexhaustible fund of experience, and information regarding many things whereof they themselves, if not ignorant, had but a slight knowledge, which he had gained apparently by travelling far and long in foreign countries, and by mingling with many classes and descriptions of men. There were few subjects on which he could not speak; and, on whatever he did speak, there was something more displayed than mere ordinary judgment. The heart had its part as well as the understanding, and a bright and playful imagination linked the two together.

Had Sir Walter Herbert and his daughter felt inclined to be distant and reserved towards the stranger, whom they had invited, they could not have maintained such a demeanour long; for he was one of those who applied for admittance to every door of the human heart, and was sure to find some entrance; but when, on the contrary, they were predisposed to like and esteem him, even the first slight chilliness of new acquaintance was speedily done away; and ere he had been an hour in the house the reciprocation of feeling and ideas had made them far more intimate with him than with many persons whom they had known for long and uninterrupted years.

Music was talked of, and painting, and sculpture; and in each, Langford, without affecting the tone of a connoisseur, displayed that knowledge which is gained rather by a deep feeling for all that is fine and beautiful than from an experimental acquaintance with the arts themselves. He had heard Lulli—had been present when some of his most celebrated compositions had been first performed; and, though he talked not of the scientific accuracy of this piece of music or of that, he spoke with enthusiasm of the effect which each produced upon the mind; of what feelings they called up; whether they soothed, or inspired, or touched, or saddened, or elevated.

Then, again, when the conversation turned to the sculpture or the painting of Florence or of Rome, he did not—perhaps he could not— use the jargon of connoisseurs: he did not speak of breath, and juice, and contour, but he told of how he had been affected by the sight, of what were the sensations produced in his bosom, and in the bosoms of others whom he had known, by the Venus, or the Apollo, or the Laocoon, or the works of Raphael, or Guido, or Titian, or Michael Angelo. In short, he dwelt upon that part of the subject which referred to the mind, the imagination, or the heart; and in regard to which all those who heard him could go along with him—feeling, comprehending, and enjoying all he spoke of or described.

Alice Herbert, though she was not learned in such things, yet had a natural taste, which was not uncultivated. In the seclusion in which she dwelt, the ordinary household duties of a young Englishwoman of that period had not been enough for her; and her mind had been occupied with much and various reading, with music, as it was then known and taught. and with drawing; though in the latter art she had received no instruction but from her mother, who had acquired it herself while in exile at the court of France. Her father, also, had some taste in, and much feeling for, the arts, and she joined eagerly in the conversation between him and Langford, often leading it, with the sportive eagerness of a young and enthusiastic mind, to a thousand collateral subjects, which constantly elicited from their new companion remarks full of freshness and of genius.

She listened, well pleased—something more than well pleased, struck and surprised: and from that night's interview she bore away matter for deep thought and meditation—the most favourable effect that man can produce when he wishes to make an impression on the heart of woman.

Did Langford seek to produce such an effect? Perhaps not, or most likely, he would not have succeeded so well, but he was pleased himself: he, too, was struck and surprised; and, carried away by his own feelings, he took, unconsciously, the best means of interesting hers.

But the interview ended not so soon; and they had scarcely sat down to the evening meal when a fourth person was added to the party. He came in unannounced, and seemed to be a familiar and a favoured guest. Young, handsome, and prepossessing, with a frank and noble countenance, an air full of ease and grace, and an expression, in some degree, thoughtful, rather than sad; his coming, and the hour and manner in which he came, seemed to Henry Langford a warning, that if there were a day-dream dawning in his bosom, in regard to the sweet girl by whom he sat, it would be better to extinguish it at once. But feelings such as he had never experienced before came across his bosom; an eager and irritable anxiety, an inclination to retire into himself, and to watch the conduct of those around him; a tendency, whether he would or not, to be ungracious, not alone towards the stranger, but towards all; such were the strange and new sensations which he experienced. There is no stronger indication of a new passion having begun to take a hold of our heart, than a change in our ordinary sensations, in regard to things apparently trifling. Langford was a great inquisitor of his own bosom, and by that inquisition had, through life, saved himself from much pain. The examination, in the present instance, was made in a minute; and before the stranger had come round, and had been introduced to himself, he had asked his own heart more than one keen question. He had demanded, why he felt displeased at any addition to their party? why he felt disposed to deny to the stranger those graces of person and manner which he certainly possessed, and which were at once discernible? why he watched so eagerly the manner in which Sir Walter received him? why he gazed so intently upon Alice Herbert's cheek, to see if the tell-tale blood would rise up in it, and betray any secret of the heart? He asked himself all these questions in a moment, and suddenly felt that he had been dreaming—ay, dreaming sweet dreams, without knowing it. He banished them in a moment.

Sir Walter received the stranger kindly and familiarly, though with a slight degree of stateliness, which was from time to time observable in his demeanour to all. It was a stateliness evidently not natural to him, for his character was frank and kindly, and this, perhaps, was the only little piece of affectation that shaded—for it did not stain—a mind all gentleness, and warmth, and affection. He shook hands warmly with the young man, called him Edward, and suffered him to go round to shake hands with his daughter before he introduced him to their guest. While he did speak with Alice Herbert we have said that Langford's eye was fixed upon her cheek. It betrayed nothing, however—the colour varied not by a shade; and, though the lips smiled and the eye sparkled as she welcomed him, there was no agitation to be remarked.

Langford was accustomed to read other hearts as well as his own, and the translation he put upon the indications he beheld was—not that there was no love between the stranger and Alice Herbert—but that the period of emotion was past. He was not usually an unskilful reader of hearts; but in interpreting that book it is necessary to take care that no passion in our own breast puts a false gloss upon the text. Whether such was the case in the present instance will be seen hereafter; but, at all events, the knowledge Langford speedily obtained of what his own feelings might become, taught him to regulate and restrain them. He resolved that the coming of the stranger should produce no change in his demeanour; that he would not forget the suavity of his manner, nor let any one around remark an alteration which, to them, would be unaccountable, and which he never could have an opportunity of explaining.

After having given his visitor an opportunity of speaking for a moment to his daughter, Sir Walter Herbert introduced him to Captain Langford, saying, "Captain Langford, Lord Harold, the son of our good neighbour on the hill. Edward, Captain Langford, one whom I know you will esteem."

Langford gazed upon the new guest earnestly; but, whatever were his first thoughts, his mind almost immediately reverted to Lord Harold's situation in regard to Alice Herbert. The words in which the young nobleman's introduction to himself was couched, even more than what he had seen before, made him say in his own heart, "The matter is settled. Idle dreams! idle dreams! I thought I had held imagination with a stronger rein."

Lord Harold unslung his sword, and, giving it to one of the servants to hang it up behind the door, he sat down to supper with the party, and the conversation was renewed. The new guest looked at Langford more than once with a keen and scrutinising expression, though his countenance was not of a cast with which that expression suited, the natural one being of a frank and open character, with somewhat of indecision about the mouth, but an air of sternness, perhaps of fierceness, upon the brow. There was nothing in it, however, either very shrewd or penetrating; but, nevertheless, such a look was not uncalled for, as, the moment that Langford resumed his seat, after bowing to Lord Harold on their introduction, he turned deadly pale, and remained so for several minutes.

It might be that there was a struggle going on within to overcome himself, which none of those present knew or understood; but the outward expression thereof was quite sufficient to call the attention of the whole party; and it was, as we have said, some time before he had sufficiently mastered himself to resume the conversation with spirit. Even when he did so, there was a tone of sadness mingled with it, which rendered it quite different from what it had been before. It was no longer the gay, the sparkling, the playful; it was no longer the mountain current, rushing over a clear and varied bed, now eddying round every larger object in its course, now rippling brightly over the pebbles, which it seemed to gild as it flowed amongst them; but it had become a deep stream, strong, powerful, and, though still clear and rapid, yet calm, shady, and dark, from its very depth.

Lord Harold took his part in the conversation well and gracefully. A high education, and an early acquaintance with the court, which had polished but not spoilt him, acting upon a heart originally good, feeling, and generous, had improved what powers of mind he possessed as far as possible. His talents were, however, evidently inferior to those of Langford; and though he himself, apparently, was as much struck with the charm of the other's conversation as either Sir Walter or his daughter had been, yet he felt he was far surpassed by the new guest at the Manor House; and besides that sensation, which is in itself a heavy burden to be borne by those who seek to please, there was an indescribable something in Langford's presence which put a restraint upon him, and even made him bend down his glance before that of the stranger. It was late before any one prepared to depart, and the first who did so was Langford. He took leave of Sir Walter with graceful thanks for his hospitality and kindness, and the old knight expressed a hope that they should see him several times again before he left the country; adding, "Of course you do not mean to limit your angling to one day?"

"I really do not know," replied Langford, with a somewhat melancholy smile; "I may be summoned to the capital at a moment's notice; but, at all events, I shall not fail to pay my respects here before I go. I will take your hint, Sir Walter, as a permission to continue my depredations on the trout."

"As often and as much as you please," rejoined the old knight. "The stream, as far as my manor extends, shall always contribute to your sport."

"I hope," said Lord Harold, taking a step forward with graceful courtesy, "that Captain Langford will not make Sir Walter's manor the boundary. Our lands march, and the stream which flows on beyond, my father will make as much at his service as that in Sir Walter's property is already."

Langford thanked him, though somewhat coldly; but after he had taken leave of Miss Herbert, he turned to Lord Harold, and advanced as if to shake hands with him, then suddenly seemed to recollect himself, and, wishing him good night in a more distant manner, quitted the apartment.

Lord Harold remained behind for nearly an hour; and the conversation naturally rested on him who had just left them. The young nobleman praised him with a sort of forced praise, which evidently sprang more from candour and the determination to do justice, than from really liking him. Sir Walter spoke of him warmly and enthusiastically, declaring he had seldom met any one at all equal to him. Alice Herbert said little, but what she did say was very nearly an echo of her father's opinion. After his character, his appearance, his manners, and his talents had been discussed, his state of fortune and history became the subjects of conjecture. Lord Harold was surprised when he heard that the Knight of Moorhurst had invited an unknown angler to his table, and had introduced him to his daughter; and, though he said nothing, yet Sir Walter marked the expression of his countenance, and was somewhat nettled that the young man, even in thought, should comment on his conduct.

Lord Harold, however, soon obliterated any evil impression from the mind of the kind-hearted old knight; and turning the conversation to other things, his spirits seemed to rise after Langford was gone, and he found opportunity of whispering a word or two in Alice Herbert's ear. Whatever words those were, they seemed to take her much by surprise, for she started, turned pale, then coloured highly; and, after a few minutes passed in what seemed uneasy silence, she rose and retired to rest. Lord Harold gazed for a moment or two upon the ground, then looked earnestly at Sir Walter, as if there had been something that he would fain have spoken; but in the end, apparently irresolute, he took down his sword, gave orders to a servant to have his horse brought round; and, taking leave of the good knight, mounted and galloped away, followed by two attendants.

The moon had just gone down, but the night was clear, and the heavens sparkling with a thousand stars. Lord Harold's way lay through some thick woods for about two miles, and then descended suddenly to the bank of the stream, where the trees fell away and left the bright waters wandering on through a soft meadow. As the young nobleman issued forth from among the plantations, he saw a tall dark figure standing by the river, with the arms crossed upon the chest, and the eyes apparently bent upon the waters. The sound of the horses' feet caused the stranger to turn; and although the darkness of the night prevented Lord Harold from distinguishing his features, the whole form and air at once showed him that it was Langford. He wished him good evening, as he passed, in a courteous tone, and was pulling up his horse to have added some common observation; but Langford did not seem to recognise him, and merely wishing him "Good night" in answer to his salutation, turned away and walked down the stream.

CHAPTER IV.

THERE has scarcely been a poet or a prose writer, in any country, or in any tongue, who has not first declared that there is nothing like love, and then attempted to liken it to something. The truth is, that fine essence is compounded of so many sweet things, that, though we may find some resemblance to this or that peculiar quality, which forms a part, we shall find nothing which can compare with the whole—nothing so bright, nothing so sweet, nothing so entrancing, nothing so ennobling—must we add, nothing so rare. Every fool and every villain impudently fancies that he can love, without knowing that his very nature renders it impossible to him. Every libertine and every debauchee talks of love, without knowing that he has destroyed, in his own bosom, the power of comprehending what love is—that he has shut down and battened the pure fountain that can never be opened again. Every one who can feel a part of love—and that, in general, the coarser part—believes that he has the high privilege of loving, as though a man were to drink the mere lees, and call it wine. Oh, no! How infinite are the qualities requisite—each giving strength, and vigour, and fire to the other! There must be a pure and noble heart, capable of every generous and every ardent feeling; there must be a grand and comprehensive mind, able to form and receive every elevated thought and fine idea; there must be a warm and vivid imagination, to sport with, and combine, and brighten every beautiful theme of fancy; there must be a high and unearthly soul, giving the spirit's intensity to the earthly passion. Even when all this is done, it is but a sweet melody: the harmony is incomplete, till there be another being tuned alike, and breathing, not similar, but responsive tones. Then, and not till then, there may be love. Man, lay thy hand upon thy heart, and ask thyself, "Is it not so with me?" If so, happy, thrice and fully happy, art thou. If not, strive that it may be so; for, rightly felt, the most ennobling of all earthly impulses is love.

The night that we have seen commence passed over not tranquilly to any of the party which had been assembled at the Manor House. Alice Herbert laid her sweet limbs down on the couch which had so often brought her calm soft slumbers, but it was long ere she closed her eyes; and before she did so, there dropped from them some tears. Sir Walter lay upon his bed and thought, and a single sentence will show the subject of his meditation. "Poor boy," he said, in a low tone, after thinking long; "he is doomed to disappointment."

Lord Harold tossed in feverish anxiety; and for many an hour Langford cooled his burning brow by the night air on the banks of the stream. Day was fast dawning when he prepared to return to the inn; but ere he had crossed the bridge, a boy of ten years of age, or thereabouts, with fair curling hair, and a sunny countenance, crossed his path, saying quickly, "My master waits to speak with you."

"Where is he, Jocelyn?" demanded Langford.

"In the thick wood in the manor park," replied the boy, "just above the stream: but I will show you."

"Go on!" said Langford; and they were both soon hidden by the trees.

The park of the old manor-house, in its laying out and arrangement, resembled the period of our tale—that is to say, it lay between two epochs. There was still, in the neighbourhood of the house, the old trim flower garden, with its rows of sombre yew trees; there was also that more magnificent kind of billiard table in which our robust ancestors used to take delight, the bowling-green; there were also several long alleys of pine and beech, carried as far as the inequality of the ground would permit; but then, beyond that again, came the park scenery, in which we now delight—the deep wood, the dewy lawns, the old unpruned trees, with every here and there a winding walk, cut neatly amongst the old roots and stems, and taking advantage of all the most beautiful points of view. But we will dwell on such matters no longer; it is with pictures of the human heart that we have to do.

The dew was still upon the turf in the bowling-green, and in the long grassy walks of the flower garden, when Alice Herbert came forth to take her morning ramble alone. She was fond of taking the fresh air of the early day; and enjoyed, as much as ever poet or painter did, the varied lights and shades cast by the rising sun over the world; lights and shades like the fitful visions of our boyhood, when the rising sun of life renders all the shadows longer and deeper, and the brightness doubly bright. In these morning expeditions, when she went forth to enrich one hour of her young life with treasures from the bosom of nature—treasures which she stored up, hardly knowing that she did so, to be employed long after they were gained, in decorating and embellishing all her being—there was scarcely anything that met her eye, or any sound that met her ear, that was not marked and thought of; examined and commented upon; played with, embellished, and illustrated by her rich and poetical imagination. The fluttering butterfly that passed before her was not remarked for the beauty of its colouring alone; fancy found in it an image of a thousand other things; the mind moralised upon it, and the heart took the lesson home. Even the clouds, the slow fanciful clouds, as, writhing themselves into strange shapes, they floated over the spring sky, sweeping lightly with their blue shadows the soft bosom of the earth, gave equal food for imagination, and induced manifold trains of thought; and in the lark's clear melody, the ear of Alice Herbert heard something more than merely sweet sounds; her heart joined in his anthem, her thoughts took the musical tone of his sweet song, and her spirit rose upon his wings towards the gates of heaven.

It often happened that, in these walks, her father bore her company, and it was always a joy and satisfaction to her when he did so; for between father and daughter there was that perfect reciprocity of feeling that made it delightful to her to be able to pour forth in his ear all the thoughts that sprang up from her heart; and to hear, as she leant clinging to his arm, all the sweet and gentle, the simple, but strong-minded and noble, ideas which the face of nature suggested to her father's fancy. To him she would listen well pleased, though many a creature of the great world might have scoffed at the simplicity of the words he uttered. To him she would tell all she herself felt; for never, from her childhood upwards, had her father checked the confidence of his child, even by a laugh at her young ignorance.

Thus, when she came down in the morning to go out, she would pause for a moment at her father's door, to hear if he were stirring. If there were sounds within, she would knock gently for admission; if there were no sounds, she would pass on her way. This morning her father was still sleeping when she came forth, for he had passed a somewhat restless night, and she went on alone, with perhaps a more grave and thoughtful air than usual. She lingered for some moments in the flower-garden; and then, with a slow step, took her way up the gravel walk which led into one of the park paths, running along through the woods that crowned the bank above the stream.

The path she followed was like a varied but a pleasant life, now emerging into full sunshine as it approached the edge of the bank, now dipping down into cool and contemplative shadow, as it wound in again amongst the trees, now softly rising, now gently descending, but never so rapidly as to hurry the breath or to hasten the footsteps. It was broad, too, and even; airy and free. Along this path, then, she wandered, casting off as she went the slight degree of melancholy that at first shaded her, and turning her mind to its usual subjects of contemplation. She thus proceeded for more than a mile, and had turned to go back again to the house, when, as she approached a spot where another path joined that which she was following, she suddenly heard quick footsteps coming towards her.

The mind has often, in such cases, rapid powers of combination, seeming almost to reach intuition; and though Alice Herbert had no apparent means of ascertaining who was the person that approached, yet she instantly turned pale, and became, for a moment, a good deal agitated. With woman's habitual mastery over her own emotions, however, she recovered herself almost immediately, and was walking on as calmly as before, when Lord Harold, as she had expected, joined her in her walk.

"Good morning, Alice," he said; "I have just seen your father, and have come out to meet you."

"Good morning, Edward," was her answer. "You must have been early up to have been over here so soon. But as my father has risen, let us go in to breakfast."

"Nay, stay with me a moment, Alice," said the young man; "it is but seldom that I have a few minutes alone with you."

Alice made no reply, but continued on the way towards the house, with her eyes cast down and her cheek a little pale. Lord Harold at length took her hand and detained her gently, saying, "Nay, Alice, you must stay; I have your father's permission for keeping you a little longer, though I fear, Alice, from what I see, that I shall keep you here in vain. Alice," he added, after making an attempt to command his feelings, "dear Alice, did you mark the few words I said to you last night?"

Alice Herbert paused for a moment, and one might have heard her heart beating, so greatly was she agitated; but at length, evidently exerting a strong effort of resolution, she looked up and replied, "I did mark them, Edward, and they gave me very great pain, and I have been grieved about them ever since."

"Why—why?" demanded Lord Harold, eagerly. "why should they give you pain, when it is in your own power to render them for me, at least, the happiest words that ever were spoken; and to give me an opportunity of devoting my whole life to make you happy in return?"

"It is not in my own power, Edward," replied Alice, firmly but gently, not attempting to withdraw the hand that Lord Harold still held, but leaving it in his cold, tranquil, ungiven though unresisting—"it is not in my own power"

"Then am I so very distasteful to you," he exclaimed, sorrowfully, "that no attention, no pains, no affection, no time can make you regard me with complaisance?"

Alice was pained. "Indeed, indeed, Edward, you do me wrong," she said. "You are not distasteful to me. I do regard you with complaisance. You know that your society is anything but disagreeable to me; but yet, I cannot love you as you ought to be loved, as you have a right to be loved; nor can any attention, nor any kindness which you could show me, nor any time, make a difference in this respect. We have known each other from our childhood. You have shown me every degree of kindness, every sort of attention that any one can show. You have gained my esteem and my regard; I have always felt towards you almost as a sister; and perhaps that very feeling may have prevented me from feeling more."

"Nay, but, Alice, still hear me!" replied Lord Harold, earnestly—"hear me, hear me patiently; for remember, I am pleading for something more than life—for the whole happiness of life! You say you have regarded me as a brother, that you esteem me, that you do not dislike my society; were I to become your husband, might not these feelings grow warmer—stronger?"

"They might, or they might not," answered Alice; "but, Edward, I must not, I cannot, I will not put them to the test. There is but one thing that will ever induce me to marry any man—loving him deeply, strongly, and entirely: loving him with my whole heart."

"And is there such a man?" demanded Lord Harold, suddenly, and at the same time fixing his eyes keenly upon her.

Alice lifted hers in return, full, but somewhat reproachfully to his countenance. "Edward," she said, "that is a question you have no right to put! However," she added, after a moment's pause, "because we have been companions from our childhood, because I do really esteem you, I will answer your question. There is no one who has such a hold of me; and till I meet with such, I will never marry any one."

"Then, dear Alice, there is yet hope!" he exclaimed.

"You construe what I have said very wrongly," she replied. "Do not! Oh! do not, Lord Harold, by taking words of kindness for words of encouragement, force me to speak that harshly which I would soften as much as may be."

"Nay, Alice," answered Lord Harold, "your lesson comes rather late to produce any benefit to me. I fear that I may have mistaken, before now, words and acts of mere kindness for words and acts of encouragement. I have—I acknowledge it—I have entertained hopes; I have thought that Alice sometimes smiled upon me."

"Now, Edward, for the first time since I have known you," replied Alice, "you are ungenerous, you are unkind. Brought up together from childhood, seeing each other constantly, looking upon you almost as a brother, esteeming, as I acknowledge I esteem you, I could but act as I have acted. Has there been any change in my conduct towards you from what that conduct was five, six, or seven years ago? Ought there to have been any change in my conduct towards you, till I knew that there was a change in your feelings towards me? Would you not have been the first to accuse me of caprice, of unkindness, of forgetfulness of old regard and early friendship? Oh! Edward, why should anything thus come to interrupt such friendship—to bring a coldness over such regard?"

"Pardon me, pardon me, Alice," said Lord Harold, "I was wrong to refer to my hopes; but I meant not to say that you had willingly given them encouragement; I meant rather to excuse myself for entertaining them, than otherwise. Blame you, I did not, I could not. All that you have done has been gentle and right. Do not then, Alice, do not let anything which has passed to-day interrupt our friendship, or bring, as you say, a coldness over your regard for me. Let me still see you as heretofore; let me still be to you as a friend, as a brother. There is no knowing what change may take place in the human heart, what sudden accidents may plant in it feelings which were not there before. Some good chance may thus befriend me—some happy circumstance may awaken new feelings in your heart."

"I cannot suffer you to deceive yourself," she said. "Such will never be the case. It would be cruel of me, it would be wrong both to myself and you, could I suffer you to think I should change. Oh, no! This cannot have taken so strong a hold of you as not to be governable by your reason. I shall ever esteem you, Edward, I shall ever be your friend, but I can be nothing more; and let me beseech you to use your powers of mind, which are great, to overcome feelings that can only make you unhappy, and grieve me to hear that you entertain them."

She spoke in a manner, in a tone, that left no hope; but though he had become deadly pale, he seemed now to have made up his mind to his fate. "Fear not, Alice," he said, "fear not! Whatever I suffer, you shall hear no more of it. Love you, Alice, I shall ever, to the last day of my life; but trouble you with that love, will I no more. There is only one thing I have to request; and that I do from no idle motive of selfish vanity, from no fear of being pointed at and pitied by our friends as Alice Herbert's rejected lover, but from motives of some importance to all. Do not let it be known that such words have passed between us as have been spoken this day."

"You cannot suppose me capable of speaking of such a thing," cried Alice, both mortified and surprised.

"Oh, no!" he said; "but I mean to ask that it may remain a secret even from my father."

"With your own father," said Alice, "you must of course deal as you please, but with mine——"

"Yours knows my object in coming to-day already," interrupted Lord Harold, "and must, of course, know the result. Mine has given his fullest consent, upon my honour, to my seeking your hand. All I ask is, that he may not know I have sought it and it has been refused. Let me visit here as usual, let me——"

"I had heard," said Alice, "that you are going up to London. Why not do so at once?"

"I will," he answered; "I will. But that will be only for a few days; and, at my return, there must be no difference, Alice. Promise me that; promise, if but for the sake of early friendship, for the sake of childish companionship."

"Well," she said, after a moment's pause; "well, but there must be no mistaking, Edward."

He looked pained. "Do not suppose, Alice," he replied, "that I have any ungenerous object. When I ask this favour, I ask it for your sake as well as my own. You must not ask me how or why, but trust me."

"I will," she said; "I will! I have always found you honourable and generous; but, indeed, let me say, without thinking me unkind, that for your own sake, with such feelings as you possess towards me, it were better to be here as little as may be till you have conquered them."

"That will never be, Alice," he answered. "It is enough that you shall never hear more of them. But here comes Silly John, as people call him," he added, bitterly. "It is fit that a fool should break off a conversation begun with such mad and silly hopes as mine! Let us go back to the Manor, Alice; we shall never get rid of him."

The person who thus interrupted the painful interview between Lord Harold and Alice Herbert, was one of a class now much more rarely seen than in those times. There were, it is true, even then, hospitals and asylums for the insane, but they were few; and Silly John, as he was called, was not one of those whom the men of that day would ever have dreamed of putting in confinement. He was perfectly harmless, though often very annoying; and the malady of the brain under which he suffered was rather an aberration of intellect than the complete loss of judgment. It went a deal further, indeed, than in the case of the *half saved*, in that most beautiful of biographies, that quintessence of rare learning and excellent thought, *The Doctor*. He was decidedly insane upon many points; and upon all, the intellect, if not weak, was wandering and unsettled. His real name was John Graves: he had been an usher in a small school, and consequently was not without a portion of learning, such as it was. But his great passion was for music and poetry: the one would call him into a state of sad though tranquil silence, the very name of the other would excite him to an alarming pitch of loquacity. Withal, he was not without a certain degree of shrewdness in some matters; and what was still more singular and apparently anomalous, his memory of events and dates was peculiarly strong, and his adherence to truth invariable.

He now approached Alice and her companion with a quick step, dressed in an old wide coat of philomot colour, with a steeple-crowned hat, which had seen the wars of the great rebellion, rusty and battered, but still whole, and decorated with two cock's feathers which he had torn himself from the tail of some luckless chanticleer. His grey worsted hose were darned with many a colour; and in his lean but muscular hand, he carried a strong cudgel, which steadied his steps, being slightly lame in the right leg. When he had come within a few feet of the lady and her suitor, he stopped directly in the path, so that they could not pass without going amongst the trees; and, for a moment or two, looked intently in both their faces, with his small grey eyes peering into theirs, and his large head leaning considerably to the side, so as to bring the heavy ashy features quite out of the natural line.

"Well, John, what do you want?" demanded Alice, who had been familiar with the sight of the poor man from her childhood. "Is there anything I can do for you?"

"No, Mistress Alice; no, my pretty maid!" replied the man. "Only take care of your sweet self, lady. I came up to be at the conference— wherever there is a conference, there am I; and I heard you and Harold talking when I was on the other side of the bushes; and now, lo! the conference seems over."

"It is so for to-day, at least, John," replied Lord Harold; "so now let us pass, my good man."

"Call me not good, Harold," he replied.

"' There yet was good but One,
   That trod this cold earth's breast,
And now to heaven he's gone
  For our eternal rest.'

But you see I was right, Harold. They call me silly; but I am not silly in matters of love. I told you how it would be this morning as you crossed the bridge."

"My good man, I heard you say something," replied the young nobleman; "but what, I did not know."

"You should have listened, then," replied the madman. "Always listen when any one speaks to you. Did you not learn that at school? Always listen, especially to the masters. Now, if you had listened, you would have heard. I told you she would not have you."

Lord Harold turned red, and Alice felt for him; but he replied, good-humouredly, as they walked on with the madman following them—"I rather imagine, John, you have been listening to some purpose."

"No, I have not been listening, but I heard," replied the madman "and two other pairs of ears did the same."

"Indeed!" exclaimed Lord Harold; "and who might they be?"

"Oh, the fox and the dog!" replied Silly John, in a rambling way; "The fox and the dog, to be sure. The dog wanted to go away when you came, but the fox would not let him, saying, that if they stirred they would be heard and seen, and then folks would wonder what they came there for so early of a morning—was not that a cunning fox? But I could have told him what they both came there for, if I had liked, but that would never do."

"And pray what is the dog's name?" demanded Lord Harold, in a quiet tone, well knowing that an appearance of curiosity would often set their half-witted companion rambling to different subjects from that which had before engaged him.

"Oh, every dog has a name," replied the madman; "but they change their names as well as men and women, Harold. This dog's name was once Lion, and it is now Trusty, and to-morrow it may be Lord. I have known dogs have twenty names in their lives. God help us! we are queer creatures! And talking of dogs, I had a dog when I was second master at Uppington School,"—and so he rambled on.

There was no stopping him, or recalling him to the subject; and he followed Alice and Lord Harold, keeping close to the side of the latter, and talking incessantly, but now so deeply engaged in the wild and disordered stream of his own thoughts, that taking no further notice of the conversation which the young nobleman renewed with his fair companion, and continued with a low voice till they reached the house, he went on volubly, touching upon a thousand subjects, and darting after every collateral idea that was suggested by a chance word spoken even by himself.

CHAPTER V.

The day which we have begun in the last chapter, passed over without any other event of importance. Lord Harold left Alice at the door of the house, mounted his horse, and departed. Alice communicated to her father all that had taken place, and found him more grieved than she had expected, but not at all surprised. The angler was again seen fishing in the stream as the first shadows of evening began to fall; but his efforts were not so successful as before, and he retired early to rest.

The following morning was again a bright one—too bright, indeed, for his sport; and in the course of the forenoon Langford made his appearance at the Manor House and paid a lengthened visit. At first he found only Sir Walter Herbert at home, but the visitor seemed to enjoy his conversation much; and the good old knight suffered it to be sufficiently evident that the society of his new acquaintance was anything but disagreeable to him. In the course of half an hour, however, Alice Herbert herself appeared; and not only did Langford's eye light up with pleasure, but the conversation, which had before been of somewhat a grave, if not of a sad cast, instantly, as if by magic, became bright and sparkling, like the dark woods in the fairy tale, which, by a stroke of the enchanter's wand, are changed to crystal palaces and illuminated gardens. Alice, without knowing what had passed before, felt that her presence had produced a change. She felt, too, that her society had an influence upon Langford; that it called forth and brought into activity the treasures and capabilities of his mind; and, if truth must be spoken, it was not unpleasant to her to feel that such was the case.

We may go further still, and look a little deeper into her heart. Her acquaintance with Langford, short as it had been, had proved most disadvantageous to the hopes and wishes of Lord Harold; but in saying this, we mean no more than we do say. She was not—hers was not a nature to become in so short a time—in love with Henry Langford; nor, indeed, so rapidly to become in love with any one on the face of the earth. She was capable of deep, and intense, and ardent feeling; and the depths of her heart were full of warm affections. But the waves of profound waters are not easily stirred up by light winds; a ripple may curl the surface, but the bosom of the deep is still. She was not in love with Langford; but had she not known him, it is possible—barely possible, that though she would not have accepted Lord Harold at once, she might, as many a woman does, have suffered him to pursue his suit till she felt herself bound in honour to give him her hand, without feeling any ardent attachment towards him even at last, and trusting for happiness to esteem and regard. Her acquaintance with Langford, however, had given her feelings a more decided character, had taught her that she could not marry any one whom she did not absolutely love. It went no further; but as far as that, the sort of surprise and pleasure which his conversation had given her certainly did go; and now, on their second meeting, there might be a kind of thrilling satisfaction at her heart in finding that her society had an influence over him, that his eye sparkled with irrepressible light, that his thoughts, and manner, and feelings seemed to take a deeper tone as soon as she appeared.

So went on the conversation for some time; both feeling, while it proceeded, that though they might be talking of indifferent subjects, they were thinking a good deal of each other; and thus they established between themselves, all unwittingly, a secret sympathy, which but too often throws wide the doors of the heart, to admit a strange guest, who soon takes possession of the place.

The course of the conversation speedily brought Sir Walter to remark, "You must have visited many foreign countries, Captain

Langford, and apparently not as our young men usually do, in a hurried and rapid expedition, to see without seeing, and to hear without understanding. I must confess it was the case with myself, in my young days; but the habit of travel was not then so much upon the nation as at present, and it was something for a country gentleman to have been abroad at all."

"I have been very differently situated, Sir Walter," replied his guest; "though not born upon the continent, being, thank God! an Englishman, yet the greater part of my early life was spent in other lands. My mother was not of this country, and she loved it not—nor, indeed, had occasion to love it. We resided much in France and much in Italy: some short time, too, was passed in Spain; but those visits were in early years; and I have since seen more of various countries while serving with our troops under Turenne. I was very young, indeed, a mere boy, when the British forces in which I served were recalled from the service of France; but I was one of those who judged, perhaps wrongly, that England had no right to leave her allies in the midst of a severe war, and who therefore remained with the French forces till the peace was concluded. I have since served for many years in several other countries; and I have always been of opinion, that while there is no life which affords more opportunity for idleness than a soldier's, if his natural disposition so lead him, there is no life which gives so much opportunity of improvement, if he be but inclined to improve."

Alice had listened eagerly and attentively, for Langford had approached a subject which had become of interest to her: his own fate and history. Sir Walter listened, too, with excited expectation; but their guest turned the conversation immediately to other things, and shortly after took his leave.

When he was gone, Sir Walter himself could not refrain from saying—"That is certainly an extraordinary young man. Poor fellow! I much fear, Alice, that he is one of those whom the faults of their parents—the weakness of a mother, and the vices of a father—have sent abroad upon the world without the legitimate ties of kindred."

"Oh! no, indeed, my dear father!" cried Alice, "I cannot believe that. He would never speak so boldly and so tenderly of his mother, if there were any stain upon her name. He has twice mentioned her, and each time I have seen a glow of mingled love and pride come up in his countenance."

"Well, I trust it is so," replied Sir Walter, "for otherwise no situation can be more lamentable; with no legitimate relations of his own, with no hope of uniting himself to any upright and ancient house; for that bar sinister must always be an insuperable objection to every family of pure and honourable blood."

Perhaps Alice might not see why it should be so; but she knew her father's prejudices upon that point well, and she dropped the subject.

In the meanwhile, the person who had thus afforded them matter for speculation, returned to the inn, sat, read, and wrote for some time in his own chamber, and then sauntered forth with a book in his hand, and his rod and line left behind, in order to meditate more at leisure by the side of the stream, wherein, during the whole of the preceding evening, he had lost his time in unsuccessful angling. He was not at all inclined to renew his sport; and if truth were to be spoken, he took his book more to cover his meditations than to prompt them.

Let us draw back the curtain, however, for a moment, and look through the window in his breast, in order to see what were the motives and causes which rendered even that sport which has been called "The contemplative man's recreation," too importunate an occupation for the body, to suffer the agitated mind to deliberate with ease. We have seen what had been the effect of Alice Herbert's society upon him, during the first evening of their acquaintance: he could not but admire her beauty, for it was not of that cold and abstracted kind which may be seen and commented on by the mind, without producing any other emotion. It was of what we may call the most taking sort of beauty; it was of that sort which goes at once to the heart, and thence appeals to the mind, which cannot but admit its excellence. But still, even had he fallen in love that night, it might have been called love at first sight, and yet have implied a very false position. During each of the preceding years he had spent nearly six weeks in the small country town we have described; and, in the neighbourhood of Alice Herbert, he had heard from every lip but one account of her character. He had spoken of her with many, and every one with whom he spoke loved her.

He might therefore be well pleased to love her too, when he found that to virtue and excellence were joined beauty, talents, and sweetness, such as he had never beheld united before. We know also what was the conclusion he had come to when he saw her in the society of Lord Harold; and we may add, that he was more mortified, disappointed, and angry with himself, than he was at all inclined to admit. When, however, on the following day—placed in a situation from which he could not retreat unperceived—he had been an unintentional, and even an unwilling witness to a part of her conversation with Lord Harold, and when from that part he learned undeniably that she rejected that young nobleman's suit, he felt grateful to her for reconciling him with himself, and for removing so speedily the mortification of the preceding evening. That which had been at first but a mere spark upon Hope's altar, and had dwindled away till it seemed extinct, blazed up into a far brighter flame than before: and in their second interview he felt as if an explanation had taken place between them, and that she had told him, "I am to be won, if you can find the right way and use sufficient diligence."

But still there was much to be thought of, there was much to be considered; there were peculiar points in his own situation, which rendered the chance of gaining her father's consent to his suit almost desperate. He felt—he knew, that if he lingered long near her, he should love her with all the intensity of a strong and energetic mind, of a generous and feeling heart; he felt, too, from indications which he did not pause to examine, but which were sufficient for him, that there was a chance of his winning her love in return. But then, if giving his heart and gaining hers were to produce misery to both, ought he—ought he to pause for a moment, ere he decided on flying for ever from a scene of such temptation? But then came in again the voice of hope, representing prospects the most improbable as the most likely, changing the relative bearings of all the circumstances around him, and whispering that, even for the bare chance of winning such happiness, he might well stake the tranquillity of his whole life. Such were the thoughts that agitated him, with many another, on which it is needless here to touch. Such was the theme for meditation on which he pored while wandering on beside the stream.

The afternoon had gone by, and the brightness of the day had become obscured, not only by the sinking of the sun, but by some large heavy clouds which had rolled up, and seemed to portend a thunderstorm. Langford had looked up twice to the sky, not with any purpose of returning home, for the rain he feared not; and, in witnessing the grand contention of the elements he had always felt an excitement and elevation from his boyhood. There seemed to him something in the bright light of the flame of heaven, and in the roaring voice of the thunder, which raised high thoughts, and incited to noble efforts and great and mighty aspirations. He looked up twice, however, to mark the progress of the clouds, as writhing themselves into strange shapes, they took possession of the sky, borne by the breath of a quiet sultry wind, which seemed scarcely powerful enough to move their heavy masses through the atmosphere.

When he looked up a third time, Langford's eye was attracted to the opposite bank by the form of the half-witted man, Silly John, making eager signs to him without speaking, although, from the point at which he stood upon this slope, Langford could have heard every word with ease.

As soon as he saw that he had caught the angler's eye, however, the half-witted man called to him vehemently to come over, pointing with his stick towards a path through the trees, and shouting, "You are wanted there!"

Langford paused, doubting whether he should cross or not; for though the stream was shallow, and the trouble but little, still the man who called him was, as he well knew, insane, and might be urged merely by some idle fancy.

While he hesitated, however, the other ran down the bank, exclaiming, when he had come close to the margin—"Quick, quick, Master Harry, or ill may happen to her you love best!"

Langford stayed not to ask himself who that was, but crossed the stream in a moment, demanding, "What do you mean, John?—what ill is likely to happen to——"

He was about to add the name of her who had so recently and busily occupied his thoughts; but suddenly remembering himself, he stopped short, and the half-witted man burst into a laugh, exclaiming, "What, you won't say it, Master Harry? Well, come along with me; you will find I am right. I settled it all for you long ago, when I was an usher at Uppington School; and I said you should marry her, whether the old lord liked it or not. But come on! come on quickly! There are two of the foxes down there waiting by the dingle, just beyond the park gates. You know what foxes are, Master Harry? Well, you never thought to go fox-hunting this evening; but I call them foxes, because the law won't let me call them by any other name; and she has gone down to the old goody Hardy, the blind woman, to talk with her. Then she will have to read a chapter in the Bible, I warrant; so that she will be just coming back about this time, and then she will meet with the foxes; though, after all, they are waiting for Master Nicholas, the collector's clerk, I dare say; but they will never let her pass without inquiry."

While he spoke these wild and rambling words, he walked on rapidly, followed by Langford, who was now seriously alarmed; for, although what his companion poured forth was vague and incoherent, yet there were indications in it of something being really wrong, and of some danger menacing Alice Herbert. He remarked, too, that the half-witted man, as he walked along, frequently grasped the cudgel that he carried, and lifted it up slightly, as if to strike: but it was in vain that Langford tried to gain any clearer notion of what was amiss, for his questions met with no direct reply, his companion answering them constantly by some vague and irrelevant matter, and only hurrying his pace.

Thus they proceeded through the wood that topped the bank over the stream, across a part of the manor-park, to a spot where a belt of planting flanked the enclosed ground on the side furthest from the house and the village. It was separated by a high paling from a lane which ran along to some cottages at the foot of an upland common, and the lane itself was every here and there broken by a little irregular green, ornamented by high trees.

The ground around, indeed, seemed to have been cut off from the park, and probably had been so in former times.

There was a small gate opened from the park into the lane, at the distance of about a quarter of a mile from the spot at which Langford and his companion approached the paling, and at that hour of the evening they could discern the gate with the path leading up to it; for though the sun was just down, it was yet clear twilight. Towards that gate Silly John rapidly bent his steps; but they had not yet reached it, when Langford suddenly heard a scream proceeding from the lane on his right hand, and apparently close to them. The memory of the ear is perhaps stronger and keener than that of the eye; and, though he had never heard that voice in any other pitch than that of calm and peaceful conversation, the distinctive tone was as discernible to the quick sense in the scream now heard, as it would have been had Alice Herbert simply called him by his name. He paused for no other indication in a moment he was through the belt of planting; and vaulting at a bound over the paling, he stood in one of the little greens we have mentioned, an unexpected intruder upon a party engaged in no very legitimate occupation.

On the sandy path which marked the passage of the lane across the green, stood Alice Herbert, with a tall powerful man grasping her tightly by the right shoulder, and keeping the muzzle of a pistol to her temple, in order, apparently, to prevent her from screaming, while another was busily engaged in rifling her person of anything valuable she bore about her. So prompt and rapid had been the approach of Langford, that the two gentlemen of the road were quite taken unawares, and the one who held her was in the very act of vowing that he would blow her brains out if she uttered a word, when the muzzle of the pistol he held to her head was suddenly knocked up in the air by a blow from the unexpected intruder. The first impulse of the robber was to pull the trigger, and the pistol went off, carrying the ball a foot or a foot and a half above the head of Alice Herbert.

Instantly letting go his grasp of the terrified girl, the man who had held her threw down the pistol and drew his sword upon his assailant. But Langford's blade was already in his hand; and his skill in the use of his weapon was remarkable, so that in less than three passes which took place with the speed of lightning, the robber's sword was wrenched from his grasp and flying amongst the boughs of the trees, while he himself, brought upon his knee, received a severe wound in his neck as he fell. At that moment, however, another terrified scream from the lips of Alice Herbert called her defender's attention, and turning eagerly towards her, Langford at once perceived that it was for him and not for herself that she was now alarmed. The robber whom he had seen engaged in rifling her of any little trinkets she bare about her, had instantly abandoned that occupation, on the sudden and unexpected attack upon his comrade, and was now advancing towards Langford, better prepared than the other had been, with his drawn sword in one hand and a pistol in the other. The moment which Langford had lost in turning towards Alice had been sufficient to enable the man whom he had disarmed to start upon his feet again, and to run to the spot where his sword had fallen, and the angler found that in another instant he should be opposed singlehanded, and with nothing but his sword, to two strong and well-armed men. He did not easily, however, lose his presence of mind; and seizing Alice Herbert's arm with his left hand, he gently drew her behind him, saying, "Crouch down low that you may not be hurt when they fire. I will defend you with my life."

Scarcely had he spoken, when the second ruffian deliberately presented the pistol at him, and fired. Langford felt that he was wounded in the left shoulder, and the blow of the bullet made him stagger; but, in the course of a soldier's life he had been wounded before, more than once, and as far as he could judge, he was not now severely hurt.

His two assailants, however, were rushing fiercely upon him, and the odds seemed strong against him; but at that moment another arm, and a strong one, came in aid of his own. His half-witted guide had by this time scrambled over the paling, as well as his lameness would permit; and, with the cunning of madness, had crept quietly behind the two plunderers. As soon as he was within arm's length, which was but a moment after the shot was fired that wounded Langford in the shoulder, he waved his cudgel in the air, and struck the man who had discharged the pistol a blow on the back of the head, which laid him prostrate and stunned upon the ground.

Langford's quick eye instantly perceived the advantage, and he rushed forward, sword in hand, upon the other man. Finding, however, that the day was against them, the ruffian fled amain, after making an ineffectual effort to raise his companion; and, in a moment after, the sound of a horse's feet, as it galloped rapidly away, was heard in the road above.

"It is right that every man should have his nag," said the half-witted man, turning over the prostrate robber with his foot; "but thou wilt ride no more, simpleton! I wonder if these clerks of Saint

Nicholas, have lightened the burden of Master Nicholas, the clerk?" he continued, turning as if to speak to him whom he had guided thither; but by this time Langford had returned to the spot where Alice Herbert stood; and, holding both her hands in his, was congratulating her upon her escape, with all those feelings sparkling forth from his eyes which might well arise from the situation in which he was placed, combined with all the thoughts and fancies that had lately been busy at his heart.

Alice looked up in his face with an expression that could not be mistaken. It was full of deep gratitude. Perhaps there might be something more in it too; and without listening much to vanity, he might have read it: "I would rather be thus protected by you than by any one I ever knew."

There are times and circumstances that draw two hearts together in a moment, which might otherwise have been long in finding each other out; and such were the times and circumstances in which they stood. She was very pale, however; and Langford was somewhat apprehensive, also, that the worthy personage who had galloped off might return with more of his fraternity; so that, after a few words of congratulation and assurance to Alice, he called to his half-witted companion—"Come, John, come! Leave the scoundrel where he is: we have not time to make sure of him, and we had better get into the park and towards the manor as fast as possible."

Thus saying, he drew Alice's arm within his own, and led her to the gate, speaking eagerly to her of all that had occurred. The madman followed more slowly; but they had scarcely gone a hundred yards within the paling when Langford perceived that his fair companion was turning more and more pale every moment. Her eyelids too drooped heavily, and she said at length, in a low voice, "I am very faint." Scarcely had she spoken the words when he felt that she was beginning to sink, and placing her upon a bank beneath one of the old trees of the park, he bade their crazy companion hasten as fast as possible to the house, and bring some of the servants to assist in carrying their fair mistress home.

The man seemed to comprehend at once, and set off to obey; but Langford did not wait for the return of his messenger ere he endeavoured to recall Alice to herself. From a little brook which ran towards the stream, he brought up some water in his hands, in order to sprinkle her face therewith; but as he did so, something struck his eye which he had not before perceived, and which made his heart sink with sensations that he had never yet felt, even in scenes of carnage and horror such as man seldom witnesses: the sleeve of Alice Herbert's white dress on the right arm was dripping with blood, and Langford, in agony lest she should have sustained some injury, after casting the water in her face, tore her sleeve open to seek for the wound. No hurt was to be found, however; no blood was flowing down that fair smooth skin; the stains were less in the inside of her garment than on the out, and the blood which he now saw trickling down his own arm—the arm on which she had been leaning—so as to dabble the back of his hand, showed him whence that had proceeded which had stained her dress.

The cool air, the recumbent position, and the water he had thrown in her face, had by this time begun to recall Alice to consciousness;

and the joy of seeing her recover, of finding that she was unhurt, and of having successfully defended her, threw Henry Langford off his guard, so far at least that he pressed a long kiss on the fair hand he held fondly in his own. Alice's languid eyes met his as he raised his head; but there was a slight smile upon her lip, and he saw that he had not offended.

Her first faint words, as soon as she had sufficiently recovered herself to speak, were—"You are hurt! Oh, Captain Langford, I am sure you are very much hurt; and my being weak enough to faint when I found the blood trickling down my arm has delayed you but the longer in getting assistance. For Heaven's sake leave me here, and seek some one to attend to your wound as soon as you can. I shall be quite safe here. I have no fear now, but am only afraid that I cannot walk very fast; and, indeed, you should not be without help any longer."

Langford assured her that his wound was a trifle, that it was a mere nothing, that the blood he had lost could do him no injury. But Alice would not be satisfied; and, finding that Langford would not go without her, she insisted upon proceeding immediately. She trembled very much, and could walk but slowly; but she persevered in her determination, and had half crossed the park when they were met by Sir Walter himself and four and five of the servants. The feelings of the father at that moment may be conceived, but cannot be described; he threw his arms round his daughter, exclaiming, "My child, my dear child! But are you not hurt, my Alice? Yes, yes, you are! You are covered with blood!" and his own cheek grew deadly pale.

"It is his, my father," replied Alice, leaning upon Sir Walter's bosom, and holding out her hand to Langford; "I am quite unhurt, but he is wounded, and I am afraid seriously. He gave me his arm to help me home, and, in a minute, my whole sleeve was wet with blood. I was foolish enough to faint when I saw it, and that has made us longer; so pray look to his wound immediately."

All eyes were now turned upon Langford; and as Sir Walter hurried him and his daughter on to the Manor House, he loaded him with both thanks and inquiries. Langford assured him the wound that he had received was a mere trifle, that the ball had lodged in the flesh, and that he could move his arm nearly as well as ever; and then, to change the subject, he recounted to Sir Walter and Alice as they went how he had been led to the spot where he had found her, by the unfortunate half-witted man, John Grave.

"He shall wander about the world no more, if I can provide him with a home," exclaimed Sir Walter, turning to look for the person of whom they spoke; but he was no longer with the party, and they could hear his voice in the woods at some distance singing one of the old melodies of those times.

When they reached that door of the Manor House which opened into the park, Langford was about to take his leave, and proceed to the village to seek for a surgeon. Alice cast down her eyes as he proposed to do so; but Sir Walter grasped him by the hand, and led him gently in, saying, "In no house but mine, Captain Langford! Do you think, after having received such an injury in defending my daughter, that we would trust you to the attendance of an inn?"

Langford made but slight opposition. If there had been hesitation in his mind, and doubt at his heart, when he had gone forth that afternoon to wander by the side of the stream, both doubt and hesitation were by this time over; and, after a few common-places about giving trouble, he accepted Sir Walter's invitation, and became an inmate of one house with Alice Herbert.

CHAPTER VI.

WE must now return for a short space of time to the spot beneath the park wall where we left one of the assailants of Alice Herbert stunned by a blow from the cudgel of John Graves. He lay there for some minutes perfectly motionless and perfectly alone. At length, however, the sound of a horse's feet, cantering lightly along the road was heard, and a goodly gentleman, dressed in a fair suit of black, and mounted on a dun fat-backed mare, made his appearance in the lane, and approached rapidly towards the spot where the discomfited wayfarer lay.

The good round face of the new comer was turned up towards the sky, calculating whether there was light enough left to admit of his reaching Uppington in safety, or whether he had not better pause, and sleep at the little neighbouring town; and the first thing that called his attention to the object in his path was his dun mare, who had never before shied at any object on earth, recoiling from the body of the robber so violently as to throw forward the good round stomach of the rider upon her neck and shoulders with a sonorous ejaculation of the breath.

"Ugh! Gad's my life! who have we here?" exclaimed Master Nicholas, the clerk of the collector at Uppington, whose saddle-bags were in truth the tempting object which had brought forth the gentlemen of the road, when they had been unseasonably diverted from their purpose by the appearance of Alice Herbert—"Gad's my life, who have we here?" and, dismounting from his mare, with charitable intent, he bent down over the stranger.

There were two or three particulars in the sight that now presented itself which made the heart of the collector's clerk beat rather more rapidly than was ordinary. In the first place the stranger had in his hand a drawn sword, in the next place a discharged pistol might be seen lying within a foot of his nose, the sand was stained with blood hard by, and in the countenance of the prostrate man, the collector's clerk, who was a great physiognomist, discovered at once all the lines and features of a robber. The good feelings of the Samaritan vanished from his bosom as soon as he had made this discovery, and, stealthily creeping away, as if afraid of waking a sleeping lion, the gentleman in black regained his mare's back, made her take a circuit round the little green, and, riding on as hard as he could to the country town we have described in the commencement of this book, sent out a posse of people to take charge of the body of the stunned or defunct robber.

Before this detachment reached the spot, however, the personage it sought was gone. Shortly after the clerk had passed, he had began to recover, and speedily regained his legs, looking about him with some degree of wonder and amazement at the situation in which he found himself. Whilst busy in recalling all that had passed, the sound of some one singing met his ear, and, in another minute the head and shoulders of John Graves appeared above the park paling. The half-witted man saw that the robber was upon his feet again, and without any hesitation, he proceed to clamber over the fence, and approach his former antagonist.

"I have come to apprehend thee!" cried the madman, laying his hand boldly upon the collar of the robber's vest. Strange to say, the freebooter not only suffered him so to take hold of him, but very probably might have even gone with him like a lamb to the slaughter, so much was he overpowered by surprise, and so little did he imagine that such an act would be performed without some power to support it, had not two or three horsemen at that moment come galloping down the lane as hard as they could ride. A single glance showed the captive of John Graves that there was an infinite accession of strength on his side. He accordingly twisted himself out of his mad antagonist's grasp in a moment, and prepared to lay violent hands upon him in return. Silly John, however, seemed by this time entirely to have forgotten his purpose of arresting the robber; and looking round him as the others came up, with an air of wonder, indeed, but not of alarm, he muttered, "More foxes! more foxes!"

The worthies by whom he was meantime held a sharp consultation, of which he seemed to be the object; but at length one of them exclaimed, "Come along, come along! Bring him with you, and do what you like with him afterwards. If you stay disputing here, you will have the whole country upon you."

After a moment's hesitation, the plan proposed was adopted, and two of the robbers, seizing upon John Graves, dragged him along between them, at a much quicker rate of progression than was at all agreeable to him. After the first ten or twelve steps he resisted strenuously, and showed a disposition to be vociferous, which instantly produced the application of a pistol to his head, with a threat of death if he did not keep silence. He was quite sufficiently sane to fear the fate that menaced him; and the sight of the pistol had an immediate effect both upon his tongue and his feet, which now moved rapidly onward. The paths pursued by his captors were as tortuous as might well be, and the lane which had been the scene of their exploits was quitted almost immediately. For nearly an hour they hastened on as fast as they could drag the half-witted man along; but at length, much to his relief, the whole party stopped before a small lonely house on the edge of a wide common. There was a tall pole, with a garland at the top, planted before the door; and a bush hung above the lintel, giving notice to all whom it may concern that entertainment for man, at least, was to be found within. The sound of the strangers' arrival, in a moment drew out the landlord of the place, who seemed not at all surprised to see the company which visited his house at that late hour; and his own pale-brown countenance bore, in its hawk-like features, an expression very harmonious with the calling of his guests.

"Quick! take the horses up to the pits," he said, speaking to the boy of all work, who appeared round the corner; and shading the candle which he carried in his hand from the wind. "Why, Master

Hardie, who have you got there? By my life, it is Silly John! What, in the devil's name, did you bring him here for?"

"Why, Master Guilford," replied one of the men, but not he to whom he spoke, "here's Hardy and Wiley have got themselves into a pretty mess. They would go out against the Captain's orders to try a bit of business on a private account, and they have got more than they bargained for, I take it. Here is Hardie with a cut in his neck, which has made him bleed like an old sow pig; and Wiley was left for dead by a blow of this same fellow's cudgel whom we have got here. Hardie came up for us two upon the downs, or else it is likely Wiley would have been in the pepper-pot at Uppington by this time; for we caught his horse half a mile up the green lane."

This conversation had taken place while the party was alighting; but no sooner was that operation concluded than the landlord pressed them to come in quickly, and Silly John was hurried by them into a large room behind, with a long deal table, and several settles and benches, for its sole furniture, if we except a polished sconce over the chimney, from which a single candle shed its dim and flickering rays. Underneath the light, with his two arms leaning on the table, and his head resting again upon them, the curls of the fair hair falling over the sleeves of his coat, and his face hidden entirely, sat the boy Jocelyn, whom we have before mentioned; and the gang of plunderers had been in the room several minutes before he was aware of their presence, so sound was the slumber in which he was buried.

"Hark ye, Master Doveton!" said the landlord, as soon as the door was shut, and addressing the man who had given him an account of his companions' adventure; "hark ye! I think it a very silly thing of you to bring this fellow up here."

"Why, we did not know what else to do with him, Guilford," answered the other. "Wiley wanted to shoot him as soon as he heard that it was his cudgel which had beaten about his head so foully."

"You shall do no harm to him in my house, Master Doveton," replied the other; "the man is a poor innocent, whom I have known this many a year, and I won't have him hurt."

"Thank you, Master Guilford, thank you!" exclaimed the poor fellow, as he heard this interposition in his favour. "These foxes have almost twisted my thumbs off. Do not let them hurt me, Master Guilford, and I'll give you the crooked sixpence out of my tobacco-box."

"You see, Guilford," replied Doveton, while one or two others crowded round to hear the consultation, "the thing is we risk this fellow betraying us. He has seen all our faces, and could, I dare say, swear to us any where."

"What signifies *his* swearing?" demanded the landlord; "he is as mad as a March hare; nobody will believe his swearing."

"Ay, but he may give such information as will lead them to ferret us out," replied another of the gang; "now we do not want to hurt the man, but he must be got out of the way somehow."

"He sha'n't be got out of the way by foul means, howsoever, Master Doveton," replied the landlord, whose new character of protector was pleasant to him. "Come: nonsense! make him sit down and drink with you, and he'll forget all about it. He'll sing you as good a song as any man in the country; and, if he promises not to tell anything he has seen, you may be quite sure of him."

"Truth—truth, Master Guilford," cried the object of their discourse. "If my godfathers and godmothers at my baptism had known what they were about they would have called me Truth. Why not Truth as well as Ruth? I had a sister they called Ruth, though she never found out a Boaz, poor girl! but died without being a widow—how could she, when she was never married? If I had been married to Margaret Johnson myself, I should not have gone mad, you know; but I always tell truth. Did anybody ever hear me tell a lie in my life?"

So he rambled on, while the friendly landlord busied himself in hastily setting out the table in the midst for the coming entertainment of his worthy guests; and, at the same time, lent a sharp ear to the consultation which they held together concerning the madman. That consultation was not of a nature to satisfy him entirely; for, though it seemed that the party were willing to follow his counsel so far as keeping poor Silly John to drink with them, a word or two was spoken of its being easy to do what they liked with him when he was drunk, which did not at all please Master Guilford.

As he went round and round the table, however, setting down a cup here, and a platter there, he gave the boy Jocelyn a sharp knock on the elbow, which roused him from his sleep; and, the next time he passed, the landlord whispered a word in his ear. The boy took no particular notice at the moment, but rubbed his eyes, yawned, spoke for a moment to Doveton and the rest, and then disappeared from the room.

Large joints of roast meat soon graced the board; and the hall assumed very much the appearance of the palace of Ulysses, in the days of the suitors; except that, in all probability, it was a little more cleanly, and that the beef was not killed at the end of the table. Silly John was made to sit down between the two men, Hardcastle and Wiley, who were certainly not his greatest friends; but they, nevertheless, loaded his platter with food, which he devoured with a wonderful appetite, and filled his cup with ale from a tankard called a black jack, which circulated freely till supper was over.

The gentlemen into whose society he was thrown, however, were not of a class to rest satisfied with even the best old humming ale; and while one body of them demanded the implements and materials for making punch, another called for a pitcher of Burgundy, which, notwithstanding the size, character, and appearance of the house, was produced as a matter of course. John Graves had his ladleful from the bowl, and his glassful from the pitcher; and Doveton, who was beginning to get merry, and eke good-humoured in his cups, insisted upon having one of the songs the landlord had so much vaunted. The madman required no pressing; the very name of music was enough for him; and with a full sonorous voice, and memory which failed not in the slightest particular, he began an old song, one of the many in praise of punch.

"Now I will sing you a song in return, Master John," cried the rough-featured fellow called Hardcastle, who had been one of the assailants of Alice Herbert.

"Why, Hardie, thou canst never sing to-night," replied Doveton. "Thou canst never sing to-night, with the slit in the weasand thou hast gotten there. It will let all the wind out, and thy song will be like the song of a broken bellows or bursten bagpipe."

"Never you mind that, Doveton," replied the other; "my song shall be sung, if the devil and you stood at the door together; a pretty pair of you!" and he accordingly proceeded to pour forth, in a voice of goodly power, but very inferior in melody to that of the madman, a song well suited to the taste of his auditors:—

THE WATERY MOON.

The wat'ry moon is in the sky,
Looking all dim and pale on high;
And the traveller gazes with anxious eye,
   And thinks it will rain full soon:
And he draws his cloak around him tight,
But if I be not mistaken quite,
He will open that cloak again to-night
   Beneath the wat'ry moon.

The wat'ry moon is sinking low,
The traveller's beast is dull and slow,
And neither word, nor spur, nor blow
   Will bring him sooner boon.
But the saddle-bags are heavy and full,
And all too much for a beast so dull,
Up this steep shady hill to pull,
   Beneath the wat'ry moon.

The wat'ry moon is gone to bed;
The traveller on his way has sped;
The horse seems lighter the road to tread,
   And he'll be home very soon;
But with a young man he met on the hill,
Who lightened his load with right good will,
Hoping often to show the same kindness still,
   Beneath the wat'ry moon.

Scarcely had Hardcastle done his song, amidst great applause on the part of his companions, when a step was heard in the neighbouring passage, which made the whole party start and look in each other's faces. The next moment, however, the door was opened, and the personage of whom we have already spoken more than once, under the title of Franklin Gray, stood amongst them. It was very clear that he was an unexpected and not a very welcome guest at that moment; but, at the same time, the whole of the fraternity who occupied the hall, immediately put on the most agreeable look in the world, and strove to appear delighted with his coming. His brow was somewhat cloudy, indeed, but his bearing was frank and straightforward; and sitting down in a chair which had been placed for him with busy haste by the others, he fixed his eyes sternly upon the man who had suffered from the cudgel of Silly John, demanding, "What is all this I hear, Wiley?"

The personage to whom he spoke hesitated to reply, bit his lip, tried to frown, and to toss his head; and, before he had made up his mind what to say upon the occasion, the one who had been called Doveton answered for him.

"I believe, Captain," he said, "the best way when one has been in the wrong is to own it, and to tell the truth. Now, we have all, more or less, been wrong, I believe. Wiley, there, heard that Master Nicholas, the clerk of the collector at Uppington, was coming along the green lane this evening with all the receipts, and he thought it would be a good sweep for us all if we could get the bags. He asked us all to go, but only Hardcastle would have a hand in it, though the rest of us promised to exercise our horses upon the hill above, and come down if they were likely to be caught. Well, they fell in with a young lady first, and they thought they might as well have her purse too—"

Franklin Gray set his teeth hard, but said nothing; and Doveton, who saw the expression on the other's face, went on—"It was very wrong. I know, Captain Gray—quite contrary to your orders, to do anything of the kind; and more especially to attack a woman, which you spoke of the other day. But, however, temptation, you know, Captain, temptation will get the better of us all, at times. As I was saying, however, some one came to help the lady, with this poor silly fellow; and Hardcastle got a cut in his neck that won't be well these ten days, and Wiley a broken head, which I hope will teach him better manners for the rest of his life."

The brow of Franklin Gray never relaxed its heavy frown, except at the moment when Doveton announced the corporeal evils which had befallen the two adventurers as a reward for their disobedience; and then a grim smile for a moment curled his lip. It passed away, however, instantly, and he demanded, looking at Wiley, "Do you know who it was that came to the lady's help?"

"Oh! I marked him well enough," replied Wiley; "I shall not forget him; and, if ever the time comes——" The rest of the sentence was lost between his teeth; but he went on in a louder tone immediately after, adding, "He is one of your good friends, Captain Gray. I have seen you walking with him twice; and I think he might have known better than interrupt a gentleman in his occupations. We should not have hurt the young woman. What business was it of his?"

"The only pity is," said Franklin Gray, coolly, "that he did not send a bullet through your head."

"He has got one in his own shoulder," said Wiley, doggedly; "for I saw the ball strike, and I hope it may do for him."

"If he chance to die of it," said Gray, in the same calm, stern tone, "I will blow your brains out! Remember what I say, Master Wiley: you know me! Nay, a word more. When we joined together, and came down here, it was for a particular purpose, and you all swore an oath to obey my directions, and submit to my laws for the next three months. You and Hardcastle have scarcely been a fortnight with me, but you break your oaths; and when I especially told you not to enter into any petty enterprise, because we had a greater in hand, which you would ruin if you did, you go and disgrace yourselves by attacking a girl. Now it seems that you have received some punishment in the very act, and therefore I shall inflict no other; but be warned, both of you! I am not a man to be trifled with; and if once more either of you disobey, be sure that I will then be as severe as I am now lenient. Can any one tell," he continued, "who the lady was that was attacked by them? I can only suppose that it was old Sir Walter's daughter."

"Just so! just so!" cried Silly John Graves, from the other end of the table; "it was pretty Mistress Alice Herbert, and good Mrs.

Alice Herbert, too, which is better than pretty; and you too, seem to be good, which is better than brave—very good, indeed, for a fox, and a leader of foxes. I vow and protest you have read them a homily as fair as any in the book; and now pray let me go, for I have sung them a song such as they won't hear again in a hurry."

"Why have you brought him hither?" continued Franklin Gray, in a sharp tone, without making any reply to John Graves's observation. "Was it to end folly by madness, and conclude your own disobedience by insuring its own punishment?"

It took some time to explain to the leader of the band the motives which had induced them to bring the half-witted fellow thither, and how he had been found busy in the laudable occupation of arresting Wiley when the rest of the party came to the rescue.

"And therefore," exclaimed Gray, interrupting the speaker. "because he was likely to recognise Wiley, and bring him to the gallows, Master Wiley persuaded you to drag him up here, that he may recognise us all, and bring us to Tyburn along with him. It was worthy of you, Master Wiley."

"You are wrong for once, Captain," said Wiley; "if I had had my wits, I would have taken care that he should recognise no one. Dead men tell no tales, I said then; and I say so still."

"They tell tales that are heard long years after!" replied Franklin Gray, with melancholy sternness. "Ay! and often, when time has flown, and the hot blood has become cool, and the black hair grey, and the strong limbs feeble, and easy competence has soothed regret, and either penitence or pleasure has stilled remorse; I tell ye, my masters, that often then, in the hour of security, and tranquillity, and luxury, the avenger of blood needlessly spilt—the avenger, who has slept so long—will awaken, and the merest accident bring forth proof fit to lead us to shame, and condemnation, and death. No, no! I will deal with this man, but I must first go forth, and ascertain what are likely to be the consequences of this act of folly. In the mean time, Harvey, I leave him under your charge! See that no evil befal him, and keep as quiet as may be. No roaring, no singing, mark me! and, if possible, abstain from drink."

Thus saying, he left them: but returned much sooner than they had expected, and when he appeared was evidently much moved. His dark brow was gathered into angry frowns, and his bright eye flashed in a manner which made those who knew him best augur some sudden violence. He sat down at the table, however, and remained for a moment in silence, with his brow leaning upon his hand.

"I am foolish enough," he said, at length, " to follow the weak custom of the world, and be more angry at the bad consequences of an evil act than I was at the act itself: but I will not yield to such folly. What think ye, sirs? I find that the whole county is already in a stir against us on this bad business. There have been large parties of men from Uppington, scouring the lanes in every direction. Messengers have been sent out from the Manor to call a general meeting of the magistrates for to-morrow. There is foolish Thomas Waller and silly Matthew Scrope, and all the men who are likely to be the most active and violent against us, called to consult at the Talbot; and nothing is to be done but for each one of us to take his own way out of the county till the storm has blown over. Let us all meet this day week at Ashby. That is seventy miles off; and we can there see how to pass the time till we can return here, and pursue our great enterprise in safety. But one word more. We are all men of honour; and, if any of us should chance to fall into the hands of the enemy, we can die in silence: that is enough."

"But what is to be done with him?" demanded one or two of the fraternity, pointing to the unhappy lunatic; while, at the same time, some of the others came forward and whispered to their captain, apparently on the same subject, with somewhat sinister looks. But Gray replied, sternly, "No! I say, no! Leave him to me: I know him well, and he may be trusted. I shall remain a day, or perhaps two, behind you. Now to horse, and depart, but one by one."

The tone in which he spoke courted no reply; and the band quitted the room, every man according to his own peculiar manner of doing such things; for there is as much art in quitting a room as in entering one, though the first is much more important as an evolution. However, one walked straight out, without saying a word to anybody; one spoke for a few minutes with a companion, and then, suddenly turning, passed through the door; one entered into a conspiracy with another to go out conversing with each other; one stayed a moment to empty the remains of the tankard into a large cup, and drink it off at a draught; and another (Doveton) went up to Gray, shook him by the hand, wished him well, and told him he was very sorry that he had even connived at Wiley's scheme. The last was the only one who, in fact, suffered to appear the feelings which affected all the others, and embarrassed them in their exits. They all felt they had been wrong, with the exception of him who emptied the tankard; they all felt that Gray had just cause to be angry and indignant; but one feeling or another—pride, vanity, shyness, and many others, keep nine hundred and ninety-nine men out of a thousand from opening their lips under such circumstances. It is only the thousandth who candidly and straightforwardly walks up to the truth, and says, "I am sorry I have done wrong."

At length the room was left untenanted by any but Franklin Gray and his half-witted companion, who sat twirling his thumbs at the table, apparently lost to the recollection of what was passing around him. He was roused, however, by the voice of Gray pronouncing his name, and found the keen dark eye of the Robber fixed intently upon him.

"John Graves," said Gray, "do you know what those men pray me to do with you? They say that if I let you go, you will betray what you have seen this night, lead people to the places where we meet, or give evidence against us if ever we are in trouble; and they say that the only way to avoid this is, to silence your tongue for ever."

"No, no, no!" cried the poor man, fully awakened to his situation by such words; "pray don't! pray don't! I will never tell anything about it, as I hope for God's mercy, and that he will restore my wits in another world. Wits? I have not got wits enough to tell anything; besides, I won't, indeed I won't."

"If you will swear," said Gray, "by all you hold dear, never to tell any one what you have seen to-night; never to point any one of us out, by word, or look, or gesture, as men you have seen do this or that; never to lead any one to this our place of meeting."

"I will! I do!" cried the madman, solemnly; "I will betray you in no respect—"

"So far, so good," answered Gray; "but that is not all. I give you your life, when every voice amongst us but my own was for taking it; and with it you must promise, if ever I call upon you, to do me a piece of service."

The other gazed earnestly in his face, seeming, by a painful effort, to gather together all his remaining fragments of mind, to cope with one, who he feared was trying to lead him astray by the bribe of life. "What is it," he demanded; "what is it I am to do? I will break none of the commandments. I will neither rob nor murder, nor help to rob, or murder. Ah, man! remember, though perhaps I am crazy, as people say, I have a soul to be saved as well as others. It it must be, I will die sooner than do these things."

"I require no such things at your hands," replied Gray, moved a good deal by his companion's earnestness. "I may only require you to guide me on my way in a moment of difficulty; to lead me by the paths which, I am told, no one knows so well as you do, and, perhaps, to guide me into a house—"

"Not to take other men's goods!" cried Graves. "No, never! Guide you I will, in moments of difficulty; lead you I will, when you want it, but not to commit a crime, for then I am a sharer."

"What I shall ask you," said Gray, solemnly, "is to commit no crime. My purpose shall be to take no man's goods, but rather to restore to him who is deprived of it that which is his own."

"Swear to that!" exclaimed the other, "and I will lead you anywhere."

"I swear it now!" answered Gray; "and remember that, having sworn it, I shall never ask you to do anything but that which you now agree to do, and in consideration of which I give you your life. No questions, therefore, hereafter, even were I to ask you to lead me into the heart of Danemore Castle."

The madman laughed loud. "There should be none!" he answered; "for I know why you go."

"Indeed!" said Gray, with a smile; "but it is enough that you are willing. I trust to your word in everything, and doubt not that you will keep it to the letter. Hast thou any money, poor fellow?"

"Nothing but my crooked sixpence in my tobacco-box," replied the man, looking ruefully in his interrogator's face. "Pray, do not take that from me: it and I are old friends."

"I would rather give than take from thee," replied his companion. "There is a guinea to keep thee warm; and now thou art at liberty to go, so fare thee well."

As he said this, he turned away, and left the room, and poor Silly John continued gazing upon the gold piece in his palm with evident delight, though he held some curious consultations with himself regarding the lawfulness of taking money from such hands as those which had bestowed it. In those consultations much shrewd casuistry was mingled with much simple folly; but, in the end, the counsel for the defence, as usual, got the better, and he slipped the gold piece into his pouch, chuckling. He then crept quietly out of the inn; and. although it may seem strange to attach ourselves so particularly to a personage of the class and character of Silly John, yet must we nevertheless follow him a little further in his wanderings.

By the time that all this had passed, it was near midnight; and, instead of taking his way back to the little town of Moorhurst, the half-witted man walked on, with his peculiar halting gait, towards the high dim moors that might be seen rising dark and wild against the moonlight sky, like the gloomy track of difficulties and dangers which we too often find in life lying between us and the brighter region, lighted up by hope, beyond. On the edge of the moor was a low shed and a stack of fern, which the poor fellow must have remarked in some of his previous peregrinations; for towards these he directed his steps at once, pulled down a large quantity of the dry leaves, dragged them into the shed, and, having piled them up in a corner, nestled down therein, though not without having addressed a prayer and a thanksgiving towards the God whom, in all his madness, he never forgot. We will not inquire whether that act of adoration was couched in wild and wandering terms, whether it was connected or broken, reasonable or distracted—it was from the heart, and we are sure it was accepted.

By daylight he was upon his way, and an hour's walk brought him into the deep woods that backed the splendid dwelling of Lord Harold and his father, which was known in the country by the name of "The Castle;" for very few of the good folks round had ever seen any other building of the kind, and it was therefore "their castle," *par excellence*, It was by the back way that Silly John now approached the mansion, seeming quite familiar with all the roads and paths about the place; but before he reached the spot where the wood, cut away, afforded an open space, in which were erected the principal offices, he was met by a person, at the sight of whom he bent down his head, and glanced furtively up with his eye, like a dog who does not very well know whether it will be kicked or caressed.

The figure that approached him in the long dim walk was that of a tall thin woman, of perhaps fifty years of age, dressed in dark-coloured garments, exceedingly full and ample, with a sort of shawl of fine white lace pinned across her shoulders; while over a broad white coif, which she wore upon her head, was a black veil drawn close, and crossing under the chin. Her features were high and sharp, her eyes fine, and fringed with long black eyelashes, her lips thin and pale, her teeth very white, and her complexion, which must have been originally dark and troubled, now sallow, without the slightest trace of red in any part of the cheek. She did not frown, but there was a cold calmness about her compressed lips and tight-set teeth, and a piercing sharpness about her clear black eye, which rendered the whole expression harsh and forbidding. Although past the usual period of grace, yet she walked gracefully and with dignity, and bore every trace of having been a very handsome woman, though it was impossible to conceive that she had ever been a very pleasing one.

From the moment she saw him, her eye remained fixed upon Silly John, steadfastly, but not sternly; and he advanced towards her, crouching, as we have said, and sidling with a degree of awe which he would not have shown to the highest monarch on the earth from any reverence for mere external rank. But the sharp and seemingly cold decision of her character was exactly that which most strongly affects people in his situation; and "Mistress Bertha, the housekeeper of Danemore Castle," the servants used to declare, "could always bring Silly John Graves to his senses when she pleased." Although no smile curled her lip, and her countenance underwent no change, the tone of her voice, while she spoke the first few words, at once showed the half-witted man that he was not out of favour.

"Why, how is it, John," she asked, speaking with a very slight foreign accent, "how is it that you have not been up at the Castle for these six weeks?"

"Because I got my fill at the town and the Manor, Mistress Bertha," replied the other.

"Ay, that is it!" she exclaimed; "that is it! if every one would but say it. Men go for what they can get; and when they can get their fill at one place, they seek not another. The only difference between madmen and the world is, that madmen tell the truth, and the world conceals it."

"I always tell the truth," cried the half-witted man, caught by the sound of a word connected with one of his rooted ideas; "I aways tell the truth; do not I, Mistress Bertha?"

"Yes; but you are only half mad," answered the housekeeper; "for you can sometimes conceal it too. But go in, John; go into the Castle; and, if you go through the long back corridor below, you will find my little maid in the room at the end. Bid her give you the cold meat that Lord Harold left after his breakfast."

"After his breakfast!" cried the half-witted man. "He has breakfasted mighty early! But now—oh, I guess it; he has gone to London. I heard her tell him to go."

"Heard who tell him?" demanded Mistress Bertha, with an air of some surprise.

"Why, pretty Mistress Alice Herbert, to be sure," replied the other. "Did not I hear all they said as they came down the walk and through the woods?"

"Nay, then," said the housekeeper, smiling, as far as she was ever known to smile, "I suppose he's gone to buy the wedding ring, and have the marriage settlements drawn up. Methinks he might have told me, too."

"Nay, Mistress Bertha," replied the other. "no wedding rings! no marriage settlements! Mistress Alice is not for him!"

A slight flush came over the pale cheek of her to whom he spoke. "Not for him!" she exclaimed! Does she refuse him, then!"

"Yes, to be sure," replied John Graves; "every man is refused once in his life. I was refused myself, for that matter; but I was wise, and resolved that I would never be refused again."

"Art thou lying, or art thou speaking truth?" demanded Mistress Bertha, fixing her eyes sternly upon him. "Did she refuse him?"

"Truth!" replied the man: "I always speak truth! She refused him, as sure as I am alive: nothing he could say would move her. I knew it very well, and I told him so before; but he would not believe me."

Bertha stood and gazed upon the ground for several minutes. "I do believe," she said, speaking to herself, "I do believe that things possessed without right have a doom upon them, which prevents them from bringing happiness even to those who hold them, unconscious of holding them wrongly. Now is this poor boy, notwithstanding all his great wealth and high expectations, destined to be crossed in this long-cherished love, which was to make both himself and his father so happy! Poor youth! how long and deeply he has loved her! How his heart must have ached when I talked about her this morning! and shall I help to take from him anything he possesses?"

"We ought always to do what is right, Mistress Bertha," exclaimed the half-witted man, whose presence she had totally forgotten. "And both you and I know that right has not always been done."

"Out upon the fool!" exclaimed the housekeeper. "Hold thy mad tongue! How darest thou prate of right and wrong, not having wit to keep thee from running thy head against a post! Get thee in before me! Thou shalt give the Earl an account of this refusal!"

John Graves slunk away before her flashing eye and angry words, like a cowed dog, looking ever and anon to the right and left, as if for some means to escape; but she kept him in view, following closely upon his steps till they both entered the large mansion before them.

CHAPTER VII.

The injury which Henry Langford had received was more severe than he had at first imagined. The extraction of the ball was very painful, and so much inflammation succeeded that he was confined to his room for several days. The delay and restraint, in truth, annoyed him as much as the pain and restlessness which he suffered, for at that time there were various important objects before him, which he was prevented from pursuing with the calm but rapid energy of his character. He had one great consolation, however: that the injury he had sustained was received in defence of Alice Herbert; he had one great pleasure in the midst of his sufferings: to feel sure that she was thinking of him, and thinking of him with interest. Alice Herbert did not attend him as a lady of romance; she neither dressed his wounds nor sung to lull him to repose. She did not even show him that care and attention, visiting his sick chamber often in the day, making cooling drinks with her own hand, and pressing him to take care of himself, and to follow exactly the surgeon's directions, which many a lady of that very age would have done. Nay more, strange as it may seem, she did not display half so much interest towards him as she might have done towards any person in whom she was not so deeply interested. She took care, indeed, that everything should be done for his comfort and convenience; but she did so seeming to do it as little as possible. She did give up ever thought to him, and to how he might be best brought back to health especially during the three first days, while the surgeon shook his grave and not very sapient head, and declared that the result was doubtful; but she took great care that nobody should know that her thoughts were so employed.

When at length he was permitted to leave his room, she received him with a degree of timidity that was not without its share of tenderness. It seemed as if she felt that towards him she was placed in a different relationship to that in which she stood towards any other human being, and the feeling was strange and new to her, but it was not without its pleasure. Langford's manner, too, soon dispelled everything that was in the least embarrassing in such feelings, and left them all their delight.

With fever and loss of blood he had been greatly weakened, and there was a degree of languor in his conversation during the first two or three days which rendered it perhaps more interesting to Alice Herbert even that it had been before. It was still bright and sparkling; it was still rich and deep; but there was a softness and a gentleness in it which were the more winning from the contrast between the power of the thought and the mildness of the manner. The mind of Alice, too, had undergone some change, from what reason she scarcely knew. She was becoming fonder of grave thoughts; she was more pensive; and once or twice, even when she was alone, she blushed deeply at finding herself guilty of some little act of absence of mind—a thing she never had accused herself of before. She blushed, because she was conscious that on these occasions she was thinking of Henry Langford; her meditations, indeed, were such as she needed not to have blushed for; they were all pure, and upright, and good; but it was for their intensity that she blushed, not for the matter of them.

There was in Langford's manner towards her, however, a tenderness, a gentleness, an appealingness, if we may use the term, which, without words, very soon told her that if she thought deeply of him, he thought no less deeply of her. Her father was about this time a good deal absent from home; for the attack upon his daughter, at the very gates of his own park, had raised his indignation to a high pitch; and he declared that he would not rest, night nor day, till he had rooted out of the country the band of villains who deprived it of its ancient peace and security. Meetings of the justices in the neighbourhood were accordingly held for the purpose of causing the apprehension of the offenders; and at all these Sir Walter, who was himself an active though kindly magistrate, was present, taking a prominent part; so that, as we have said, he was much from home, and Alice Herbert was left, not alone, but in company with Henry Langford.

Such circumstances seldom lead but to one result, and must have done so now, had not that result been long before reached by the heart of each. Langford, however, was extremely careful; he could not, indeed, so far govern his manner as to prevent it from betraying the growing tenderness, the daily-increasing love that he felt for Alice Herbert; but not a word ever escaped his lips to confirm what his manner told unwittingly. They spoke of all the various matters, on all the multitude of themes, which are to be found in the treasury of rich and well-cultivated minds; there was not one fine subject in all the mighty universe, there was not an object in all the tide of bright and beautiful things which the God of nature has poured through every channel of the immense creation, that might not become for them a topic of discourse, for in all they could find sources for enjoyment and admiration.

And thus they went on conversing upon different things, deriving amusement, and instruction, and employment for imagination from all. Yes! conversing of indifferent things, but conversing as people who were not indifferent to each other; speaking of matters which had no reference to themselves, yet each learning as they spoke but the more to admire, to esteem, to love the other.

There were looks, too—unintentional looks—that betrayed the secrets of the heart more than words. When Alice Herbert's eyes were turned away, Langford would look at her with long and tender earnestness till she turned towards him, and then he would immediately withdraw his gaze. But still, more than once, she caught his eyes fixed upon her, and felt sure that they had been so long. She, too, while working or drawing, and conversing at the same time on any passing subject that was before them, would occasionally, when his rich eloquence poured forth in a current of more than ordinary brightness, raise her eyes to his face with a look of deep eagerness which made his very heart thrill.

Thus it went on, as might be naturally expected, and before three weeks were over, Alice Herbert found that there was but one happiness for her on earth; and Henry Langford knew that his fate was decided, as far as intense, and true, and ardent love decides, for weal or woe, the fate of every man capable of feeling it.

For the last two or three days, however, Alice had remarked that he was more thoughtful, perhaps more grave, than usual. The magisterial labours of her father were now nearly at an end. Though none of the offenders had been taken, he had satisfied himself that their bad neighbours had been driven from the vicinity; and two or three daring robberies, which were committed about this time in the next county but one, confirmed him in the belief. He was therefore much more at home with Alice, and with him whom we may now call her lover, and the delight which he took in Langford's society was every day more and more apparent, and every day more sweet and reassuring to his daughter's heart. The regard of the old man and the young man was evidently reciprocal, for Langford was one of those who could feel and estimate to the full the beautiful and natural simplicity, the straight-forward singlemindedness of the old Knight of Moorhurst.

However, during the two or three days which we have just mentioned, as having displayed an unusual degree of gravity in Langford's manner, his eyes would often rest with a sort of doubtful and inquiring look upon the face of Sir Walter; and Alice also fancied that her father was pale, thoughtful, and uneasy. Langford, too, though scarcely fully recovered, had been out several times alone, pleading urgent business; and, in short it was clear that, in the bosoms of many of the party tenanting the Manor-House, there were busy thoughts, which from some reason they concealed from each other.

Such was the state of things just three weeks after the affray with the robbers; when one evening Alice had walked out alone, in order to think over all that she felt, and all that she had remarked, without having her thoughts interrupted even by the conversation of those who were the objects of her meditation. She had now learned not to go very far from the house when alone, and she sat down for a moment in a seat at the end of the bowling-green, which was a small oblong piece of ground, hollowed out between high banks on every side, which banks, like the flat little lawn that they surrounded, were covered with smooth green turf, and were surmounted on three sides by a range of fine yew trees, cut with exact precision into the form of a high wall. Her father, before she left the house, had seated himself in his arm-chair in the library, to take the afternoon nap in which he sometimes indulged; and Langford, whom she had not seen for nearly an hour, she believed to have gone to the village.

It was not so, however; and ere she remained long in that spot, thinking over her situation, and somewhat schooling herself for feelings which she could not suppress, she heard a rapid footfall coming from the direction of the house, and the thrill that went through her heart, the agitation that took possession of her whole frame, showed the quick memory of love. Had she yielded to her first impulse, though there was no one upon earth in whose society she felt so happy as in that of the person who now sought her, she would have risen and made her escape through the trees behind her. She restrained herself, however, and sat still, with a beating heart, indeed, and with her breath almost suppressed, while Langford with a quick step crossed the bowling-green, and approached her. Although she strove to do so, although she would have given worlds to appear unconcerned, she could not raise her eyes to welcome the visitor with her usual smile, and she suffered him to traverse the whole open space as if she had not seen him, only looking up with a glance of consciousness, and a deep blush when he came close to her.

Langford was agitated too: but the agitation showed itself merely in a great degree of paleness. His step was firm, his manner calm and decided.

"I have sought you," he said, as he came up; "I saw you go away from the house, and thought you had gone to the flower garden."

Alice strove hard to reply as usual, but all that she could say was, "I thought it would be cooler here;" and there she stopped: she could go no further.

"We shall be less likely to be interrupted, too," replied Langford, "and that, with me, is a great object at the present moment, for I wish much to speak with you—to detain you for half an hour—nay, perhaps, for a whole hour with me alone."

Alice could now reply nothing indeed; but with eyes bent down, and the tears ready to rise up in them, she suffered Langford to take her hand and to proceed.

He seldom did anything like other men, acting upon principles which we may hereafter pause upon for a moment; and he did not now come at once to the declaration which Alice felt was hanging upon his lips, but went on to speak of things apparently of far less interest. "You will give me this half hour, or this hour, I know, sweet lady; and afterwards you shall give me more or not as you please. I had some idea of detaining you before you went out; but I am glad I did not, because I think when one has anything of great importance to say—anything, I mean, which deeply interests and moves us, in which the whole feelings of our hearts are engaged—I think that there is no place we can so well choose as in the face of nature, under the free canopy of heaven. One's spirit feels confined and crushed in chambers built by hands; one's heart has not room to expand; one's soul has not space to breathe forth at liberty."

He saw that by this time Alice's emotion had a little subsided; she had even ventured, at the last words, to look up in his face; and he now went on, coming nearer to the matter of his thoughts. "Alice," he said, "dear Alice, I would beseech you not to agitate yourself, and yet I must speak to you on subjects which will create much emotion."

Did Alice think, even for a moment, that he was too confident—that he was too sure of possessing such great influence over her mind? She did not; but even if such an idea had presented itself for a moment, it would have vanished immediately, for he went on: "I know that I must greatly agitate and move you; for if my brightest and dearest hopes are true, that heart is too deep and too intense in all its feelings not to be agitated by the words you must hear, and the words you must speak; and if those hopes are not true, if, like so many other of life's illusions, they have given me a moment of brightness but to plunge me in the deeper night, that heart is too gentle and too kind to tell me that the whole of the rest of my life is misery, without feeling wrung and pained. Alice, I have sought you, not to tell you that I love you; for that you must have known long——"

"Oh no!" she cried, suddenly looking up through a flood of bright and happy tears, "Oh no! I might think so, but I could not be sure of it!"

Langford smiled, and pressed her hand to his lips. "Do not think me presumptuous," he answered; "do not think me presumptuous when I say, that those words and that look have already given a reply, and made me most happy. Oh no! I am not presumptuous, for I know Alice Herbert too well not to feel that such words, and such a look, may well spare my agitating her further, on one subject at least. Yet tell me, Alice, am I as happy as I dream myself to be?"

For a moment she made him no answer, and he added, "Oh speak!"

"What can I say, Langford?" she murmured, in a low voice; "you, who know the human heart so well, must have read mine perhaps too deeply."

He gave up a few moments to thanks and to expressions of his joy: but after that, a graver shade came upon his countenance, and he said, "There is much, much, my beloved, to be spoken of between us. With that bright confidence which you shall never find misplaced, you have yielded your heart and your happiness to one of whose rank and station, fortune and family, you know nothing."

"I know himself," replied Alice, gazing up in her lover's face, "and I know that he is everything that is noble and good."

"May I ever justify such feelings, Alice," replied Langford; "but still, my beloved, it is necessary that you should know something of me, especially as I may have to draw still more deeply upon your confidence, to call for trust and reliance such as are seldom justified. During the last three or four days, Alice, my mind has been in a state of hesitation and doubt as to what course I should pursue. I felt that under some points of view I ought, in propriety, to communicate my feelings to your father, in the very first place; and yet, Alice, as I was sure that you knew that I loved you, as I had determined to bind you by no promise till your father's full consent was obtained, and as I had to confide in you, to consult with you, to ask your advice even upon a matter that must affect the whole course of my life, my fortune, my station, and everything—a matter which, for many reasons, I do not wish to communicate to your father at present, I have judged it best, and determined, to open my whole heart to you at once."

Alice listened with a slight look of anxiety, for she had entertained some hopes that Langford had communicated his purpose to her father before he came to seek her; but still her apprehensions of opposition from one who loved her so much, and esteemed him so highly, were not great, and she only replied, "But, of course, you do not wish our engagements to be concealed from my father?"

"Not *our* engagements, sweet Alice," replied Langford; "for while I hold myself bound for ever to you, I ask you to make no engagement, I suffer you to make none, till you have your father's full consent, and my love for you shall be told to him immediately. But let me first inform you how I am situated. The property which I actually possess is but small; sufficient, indeed, to maintain me in comfort and independence as a gentleman, but no more. My name and reputation, with my companions in the field, and with those under whom I have served, is, I have every cause to believe, fair—may I say it without vanity?—high. This small fortune, and this good reputation, are all that I absolutely have to offer; but, at the same time, I tell you that a much larger fortune, one that would at once place me on a level, in those respects, with yourself, is withheld from me unjustly, and cannot, I fear, be recovered by law."

"What matters it?" demanded Alice. "What matters it, Langford? My father's consent once given, will not his house, his fortune, be our own? What need of more?"

"To you, perhaps not, Alice," replied her lover. "But to me it would be painful—it would be the only painful part of my fate to know that a great disparity existed between your fortune and mine—to have any one insinuate that my Alice had married a mere adventurer. In regard, too, to your father's fortune, Alice, I have much, hereafter to say to you; I have something even to say to him. But of that we will not speak now. Suffice it that I could bear no great disparity. But, besides," he added, seeing her about to speak, "I have made a solemn promise, Alice, to pursue, without pause or hesitation, the recovery of this property."

"But you said," exclaimed Alice, "that it could not be recovered by law."

"It cannot," replied Langford, "for the papers by which it could be recovered are withheld from me by one who is both powerful and daring, and I cannot obtain them by any act which the law would justify."

"Then, give it up altogether," exclaimed Alice. "Do not, do not, Langford, attempt anything that is not justified by the law."

"But sometimes," replied her lover, "the law is in itself unjust, or else, as in the present instance, is impotent to work redress, and would justify the act if it proved successful. The papers are withheld from me by one, as I have said, who is both powerful and daring. What mandate of the law can make him give them up? While I, by force, if

I chose to exert it, might take them for myself; and the possession of them would at once justify the deed by which they were acquired."

"Oh, no, no! do not attempt it, Langford," cried Alice. "Suppose you were to fail in obtaining them, what terrible consequences might ensue! He might resist force by force; blood might be spilt, and the man I love become a murderer."

Langford paused for a moment upon the words, "The man I love;" and, casting his eyes towards the ground, he fell into a sweet but short reverie. A moment after, however, he returned to the subject, saying, "But my promise, Alice, my promise to the dead?"

"Langford," said Alice gravely, and somewhat sadly, laying her right hand at the same time upon his, in which he had continued to hold her left, and gazing up in his face with a look of tenderness and regard: "Langford, I am no great casuist in such matters; but I have always heard that no promise to do what is unlawful can be binding upon any man. God forbid that I should hold that it is right to do any evil, even to the breaking of the slightest promise; but here, Langford, you are between two evils: the breaking of a promise, and the committing of an unlawful act. The breaking of that promise can do wrong to no one; the keeping it may bring misery on yourself, on me, on all who know you; may be followed by bloodshed, ay! and the loss of your good name."

"You are eloquent, my Alice," replied Langford, "and I believe that you are right; but still the temptation is so strong, the matter involved is so great and so important, the means of obtaining those papers without force so very doubtful——"

"Oh, if there be means," exclaimed Alice, "if there be *any* means employ them. Speak with my father upon it: take counsel with him."

"Alice," replied her lover, "it is impossible. I must not speak with him, I ought not to speak with him, upon this subject. For his sake, Alice, for yours, I ought not. Alice, forgive me if I am obliged to use some mystery for the present. That mystery shall soon pass away, and you shall know all."

"I seek not to know it, Langford!" she replied, gazing up in his face; I am quite satisfied: I am quite sure! Now and for ever my trust is entirely in you. Tell me what you like: conceal from me what you like. I know that I shall never hear of your doing what is wrong; and as for all the rest, I care not."

Langford could not resist such words. He threw his arms round her, and pressed her to his heart. His lips met hers in the first kiss of love, and he set her heart at ease by promising to use none but lawful means to obtain even his right. He still held her gently with one arm thrown lightly round her, and her left hand locked in his, when the sound of a footstep met his ear, and he looked up. Alice's eyes were raised too, and her cheek turned very red and then very pale, for, at the aperture at the other end of the bowling-green, appeared no other than Lord Harold, advancing rapidly towards them.

The reader may have remarked that whenever we are interrupted in those seasons when the shy heart comes forth from the depths in which it lies concealed, and suns itself for a moment in the open daylight, the person who breaks in upon us is sure to be the one of all the world before whom we should least like to display the inmost feelings of our bosom. Had it been her father who now approached, Alice would have run up to him, placed her hand in his, hid her face upon his bosom, and told him all at once. But, both on her own account and on his, Alice would rather have beheld any other person on the earth than Lord Harold at that moment. He could not but have seen the half embrace in which Langford had held her; he could not but know and divine the whole; and Alice felt grieved that such knowledge must come upon him in so painful a manner; while —though not ashamed—she felt abashed and confused that any one should have been a witness to the first endearment of acknowledged love. Langford's proud nostril expanded and his head rose high; and drawing the arm of Alice through his own, he advanced with her direct towards Lord Harold, as if about to return to the house. The young nobleman's countenance was deadly pale, and he was evidently much moved, but he behaved well and calmly.

"Your father wishes to speak to you, Alice," he said; "I left him but now, just awake."

Langford saw that Alice could not reply, and he answered, "We are even now about to seek Sir Walter, my lord."

"I rather imagine that he has business which may require Mistress Alice's private attention," replied Lord Harold, in the same cold tone which both had used; "I have also to request a few moments' conversation with Captain Langford. I will not detain him long."

Alice suddenly raised her eyes, and looked from one to the other. "Langford," she said, aloud, "before I leave you, I have one word more to say."

"I will rejoin you here in a moment, my lord," said Langford, calmly. Lord Harold bowed; and Langford, with Alice's arm still resting in his, walked on towards the house. Alice spoke to him, as they went, eagerly, and in a low voice. His reply, as he left her at the door of the Manor was, "On my honour!—Be quite at ease!—Nothing shall induce me."

As soon as he had left her, he returned at once to Lord Harold, whom he found standing, with his arms crossed upon his breast, in an attitude of deep thought.

"Your commands, sir?" said Langford, as soon as they met.

"By your leave, Captain Langford," replied Lord Harold, "we will walk a little further, where we are not likely to be interrupted."

Langford signified his assent, and they proceeded in silence for some way till they reached a small glade in the park, where Langford paused, saying, "This is surely far enough, Lord Harold, to prevent our being interrupted in anything you can have to say to me, or I to you."

"Perhaps it may be," replied Lord Harold. "I have a question to ask you, which may perhaps lead to other questions, and I beg you to give me a sincere and open answer, as it may prevent unpleasant consequences to us both."

"If I think fit to give you any answer at all, Lord Harold," replied Langford, "I will give you a sincere one; but I must first know what your question is before I even consider whether I shall answer it or not."

"The question is simply this," rejoined Lord Harold, in a somewhat bitter tone: "Who and what the gentleman is who visits this part of the country, introduces himself into our families, and calls himself Captain Langford?"

Langford smiled: "Had I, my lord," he said, "either visited your property, even as a sportsman, in answer to your lordship's own invitation, or had I introduced myself into your family, I might have thought myself bound to give some answer to your question; but, as I have done neither the one nor the other, I will beg you to excuse me from replying to it, and I will pardon you for putting it."

"This is all very good, sir," said Lord Harold; "but you do not escape me by an affectation of dignity. In the first place, sir, you cannot suppose that I shall conceal from Sir Walter Herbert what I remarked to-day between yourself and his daughter."

Langford turned very red, but he still replied calmly: "In regard to that, my lord, you may do as you please. To be a spy upon other people's actions, or a tale-bearer, in regard to a matter accidentally discovered, and not intended for his eye, is certainly a pleasant employment for a gentleman. But all these things depend upon taste; and if Lord Harold's taste lead him in such a way, Heaven forbid that I should stop him!"

Lord Harold bit his lip: "I shall not be put out of temper, sir," he replied, "by your sarcasm; and were Captain Langford known to me as a gentleman of honour and character, I should—whatever might be my own personal feelings in this matter—I should be far from betraying a secret which came accidentally to my knowledge; but when Captain Langford is totally unknown in this part of the country, when I have reason to believe that he is not always called by the same name, or seen in the same character—when, in short, Captain Langford is a very doubtful personage, and I find him introducing himself into the house of my oldest and best friend, and, apparently unknown to that friend, engaging the affections of his daughter—I feel myself bound in honour to be no party to such a transaction, but to bring the whole matter to light as soon as possible."

Langford had remained standing while the other spoke, in an attitude of attention, and with his eyes bent down upon the ground. The moment that Lord Harold had done, he raised them, and, with a degree of tranquillity which the young nobleman did not expect, replied, "Perhaps, my lord, you are in the right. I rather believe, in your situation, I should act in the same manner."

Lord Harold looked both surprised and confused. "This is very extraordinary," he said, "and I cannot but believe that there is some design under it. I must insist, sir, upon having an explanation on the spot, as to who and what you are; as to what is your title to be in the society in which I find you, and what are your claims to the hand of one of the first heiresses in this country."

"Your pardon, my lord," replied Langford; "you are now going too far. I shall give every explanation that I think fitting to the father of the lady in question; to you I shall give none, till you show me some right which you may have to interfere in the affairs of Mistress Alice Herbert, which, I rather suspect, you cannot do."

Lord Harold again bit his lip; but he replied, almost immediately: "The right I have, sir, is twofold; that of one of her oldest friends, and that of an applicant for her hand."

For a moment Langford was about to demand, in reply, whether

Lord Harold meant an accepted or a rejected suitor; but he was generous, and refrained. "In neither quality," he said, "can I recognise in you any right to interfere; and you will pardon me if I say, that I will not only give you no explanation whatever on the subject, but will not condescend to hear you speak any further on a matter with which you have no title to meddle."

"Then, sir," replied Lord Harold, sharply, "nothing remains but to draw your sword. I do you honour in taking it for granted that you are worthy of mine;" and as he spoke he drew his weapon from the sheath, and with the point dropped, stood as if in expectation that Langford would follow his example.

Langford remained, however, with his arms crossed upon his chest, and a somewhat melancholy smile upon his countenance. "Once more," he said, "you must pardon me, Lord Harold: neither in this matter can I gratify you; not alone because it is a stupid and contemptible habit, only worthy of cowards, or of boys who have no other way of showing their courage, but—"

"Well said, Master Harry," cried a voice close beside them: "Well said, well said! I think, my little lordling, you had better put up your cold iron, and go your way home to your father. To think of a man wishing to bore a hole in his neighbour, like Smith, the house-carpenter, with his long gimlet! Let us look at your skewer in a handle, my lord;" and as he spoke, Silly John, the half-witted man of the village, whom we have before described, advanced, extending his hand to take hold of the blade of Lord Harold's sword.

The young nobleman pushed him sharply aside, however, bidding him begone, with an angry frown.

"Well, I'll begone," replied the half-witted man; "but I'll be back again in a minute, with more hands to help me;" and away he ran in the direction of the stream and the village.

"Now, sir! quick!" exclaimed Lord Harold. "If you would not have me suppose you both a coward and an impostor, draw your sword, and give me satisfaction at once."

"Your lordship may suppose anything that you please," replied Langford; "having done nothing that can reasonably dissatisfy you, I shall certainly do nothing to give you any other sort of satisfaction."

"Then, sir, I shall treat you as you deserve," replied Lord Harold, "and chastise you as a cowardly knave;" and putting up his sword, he advanced to strike his opponent.

But Langford caught his hand in his own powerful grasp, and stopped him, saying, "Hold, Lord Harold, hold, I *will* give you one word of explanation! If, after having heard that, you choose to draw your sword and seek my life, you shall do so; but remember, as you are a man of honour, to none—no, not to the nearest and dearest, must you reveal the import of these words;" and, drawing him closer to him, he whispered what seemed to be a single word in the young nobleman's ear. Langford then let go his hold; and, pale as ashes, with a quivering lip and a straining eye, Lord Harold staggered back. His companion turned upon his heel, and walked away; either not hearing, or not choosing to attend to the young nobleman's entreaty to speak with him one word more.

Langford took his way direct to the Manor House; but upon entering the door which stood open to the park, he perceived a good deal of bustle and confusion amongst the servants; and on asking if Sir Herbert were in the library, the reply was, "Yes," but it was added, that he and Mistress Alice were both busy with a gentleman, on matters of deep importance. While he was speaking with the servant, Langford, through a door which stood open at the end of a long passage, and afforded a view into the court, perceived Lord Harold come in, with a quick step and a somewhat disordered air, and mounting his horse, which was held by one of Sir Walter's grooms, ride slowly away, without even attempting to enter the house.

"I am about to walk to the village," continued Langford, speaking to the servant. "Will you tell Sir Walter so, when he is visible; for I expect a messenger from London, and may not be back to supper, if I find letters which require an answer."

He then proceeded through the house, gained the road which led over the bridge, and was proceeding towards the village, in the twilight, which was now beginning to fall, when he thought he recognised a form that was advancing towards him, though still at some distance. It proved to be that of the same fair-haired boy, named Jocelyn, whom we have more than once had occasion to mention. He spoke not a word when he came near, but placed a letter in Langford's hands, which the other tore open, and read, though with some difficulty, from the obscurity of the light.

"There is scarcely time," he said, after he had made out the contents of the epistle, which was very short. "There is scarcely time. Nevertheless, tell him I will be there: but say also, good Jocelyn, that my resolution is the same as when we last met. I will not try it!"

"I will tell him," was the boy's only reply; and leaving Langford, he ran down the road by the stream, with a rapid pace.

CHAPTER VIII.

THE moon had not risen; the sun had gone down; the sky, which for near a month had been as calm and serene as a good mind, was covered over with long lines of dark grey cloud, heavy, and near the earth; when a solitary horseman took his station under a broad old tree upon the wide waste, called Uppington Moor, and gazed forth as well as the growing darkness would let him. It was a dim and sombre scene, unsatisfactory to the eye, but exciting to the imagination. Everything was vague and undefined in the shadows of that hour, and the long streaks of deeper and fainter brown which varied the surface of the moor, spoke merely of undulations in the ground, marking the great extent of the plain towards the horizon. A tall solitary mournful tree might be seen here and there, adding to the feeling of vastness and solitude; and about the middle of the moor, as one looked towards the west, was a small detached grove, or rather clump of large beeches, presenting a black irregular mass, at the side of which the lingering gleam of the north-western sky was reflected in some silvery lines upon what seemed a considerable piece of water. That was the only light which the landscape contained, and it would have cut harsh with the gloomy and ominous view around, had not a thin mist, rising over the whole, softened the features of the scene, and left them still more indistinct and melancholy.

It was an hour and a place fit for sad thoughts and dark forebodings, and the horseman sat upon his tall powerful gelding in the attitude of one full of meditation. He had suffered the bridle to drop, his head was slightly bent forward, and his eye strained upon the scene before him; while his mind seemed to drink in, from its solemn and cheerless aspect, feelings as dark and dismal as itself. He sat there about a quarter of an hour, and not a sound had been heard upon the moor but the deep sort of sobbing creaking of a neighbouring marsh, or the shrill cry of some bird of night, as it skimmed by with downy and noiseless wings. There was not a breath of air stirring; no change took place in the aspect of the sky or the earth; it was as if nature were dead, and the feeling seemed to become oppressive, for the horseman at length gently touched his beast with his heel, and made him move slowly out from under the branches of the tree.

Scarcely had he done so, however, when the distant sound of a horse's feet was heard, as if coming at a very tardy and heavy pace from the west. The sound, indeed, would not have been perceptible at that distance, but for the excessive stillness of all around, and the eagerness with which the traveller listened. His eye was now bent anxiously, too, upon the western gleam in the water, and in a few minutes the dark figure of another man on horseback was seen against the brighter background thus afforded, riding slowly on, as the road he followed wound round the mere.

It was like a scene in a phantasmagoria, and in a moment after, two more figures were added, and all three suddenly stopped. None of the minute part of their proceedings were visible, and it was impossible, at that distance, to discern how they were occupied; but a moment after, there seemed a sudden degree of agitation in the group, then came a bright flash, followed at a considerable interval by the report of a pistol, and immediately after all three horsemen disappeared.

"What may this mean?" said the stranger, aloud. "I fear there is mischief." The sound of his voice seemed strange in the midst of this solitude, but he had scarcely spoken when the stillness was again broken by the noise of a horse's feet; but this time it came from another direction, not exactly opposite, but much to the right hand of the spot whence the former sounds had proceeded, and the beast was evidently galloping as fast as he could, over turf. It came nearer and nearer, and the watcher went back under the tree.

At length, another powerful cavalier became visible, approaching at full speed; and as he drew nigh he looked round more than once, and pulled up his horse suddenly by the tree. "Are you there?" he asked, in a low voice: and the next moment the other came forth and joined him.

"Quick! quick! master Harry," continued the one who had joined him: "Put your horse into a gallop, and come on with all speed."

"But I told you, Franklin," replied the other, holding back, "I told you that I would have nothing to do with it! What I saw a month ago under the park wall was quite sufficient: and I would have no hand in such a business, were it to put a crown upon my head."

"Foolish boy! the business is done without you to a certain point," replied his companion. "I have served you whether you would or not; and I suppose, of course, you will be ungrateful. Come on with me, and you shall have the key of the chest, which I have ventured my neck to get for you. You have nothing to do but to walk in and take what is your own. But come on quickly! You would not have me taken, I suppose; and I have reason to think I am followed."

Thus saying, he put his horse again into a gallop, and Langford followed at the same pace. Two or three times, as they rode on, Franklin Gray looked back over the moor; but no moving object of any kind was to be seen, except one of those creeping phosphoric lights which linger on the edges of an old marsh; no sound of any kind was to be heard. but the measured beating of their horses' feet upon the hollow-sounding turf.

At length, when they had gone about two miles further, Franklin Gray checked his horse's speed, saying, "There is no one following now—yet they made the signal from the hill! Did you not hear a pistol shot just before you came up?"

"Yes," replied Langford; "I heard it distinctly, and saw the flash. Was that a signal that some one was following you?"

"It was," answered Gray. "But how you could see the flash I don't understand, for they were down below the brow of the hill, where one can see both roads to the castle."

"Oh no!" said Langford. "The men who fired that shot were upon the moor close by Upwater Mere; and I very much fear, Gray, that some of these accursed evil companions of yours have been again committing an act that you neither knew of nor desired."

"If they have," exclaimed Gray, with a horrid imprecation, "I will shoot the first of them, were he my own brother."

"How many were there of them on the watch?" demanded Langford.

"Two," replied his companion.

"Then I will tell you what I saw," answered Langford. "As I sat on my horse and looked out over the mere, which just caught a gleam from the sky, the figure of a horseman crossed the light, as if he were going to the castle. Just at that minute two more came out upon him—from amongst the beeches, it seemed to me; then came the pistol shot; and a minute after they all disappeared."

Gray gave utterance to another terrible oath; and then, after thinking a few minutes, he added, "But it can't be any of my people! They dared not, after the warning I gave them about that bad business under the park fence."

"At all events," cried Langford, reining up his horse entirely, "had we not better go back and see? I fear very much, Franklin, that they have shot the man, whoever he is."

"No, no," replied Franklin; "if they have shot him, he is shot, and there is no need of our meddling with the matter."

"But he may be merely wounded," replied Langford; "we had better go back."

"No!" thundered Franklin Gray—"I tell you no! It is mere madness! We are but half a mile from the house; when I have got there, we shall learn who has done this, and I will send out and see if there is any one hurt. Come on, come on!"

Langford followed his bidding; and renewing their quick pace, they rode on for about half a mile further, till, amid a clump of tall trees, at the very edge of the moor, where some poor thin unproductive fields connected it with the cultivated country, they perceived a light shining from a small window in a tall building before them.

At that period there still remained scattered over the face of England a number of those edifices which, fortified to a certain degree, combined the modern house with the ancient feudal hold, and had been rendered very serviceable to both parties in the progress of the great rebellion. These fortified houses were of every size, from that which really well merited the name of castle, to that which was no more than a mere tower; and many of them, either from being injured by the chances of war, or from having lost a great part of their utility when the scourge of civil contention was removed from the country, had gone to decay, or had been applied to the calmer and more homely uses of the barn, the grange, or the farmhouse.

Such was the house which Langford and his companion now approached; and, as far as the darkness of the hour suffered its outline to appear, it seemed to the former to be a tall heavy tower of stonework, with four small windows on the side next to them. Beneath its protection, and attached to it on one side, with the gable end turned towards the road, was a lower building with a high peaked roof of slates; and close by, another mass of masonry, apparently the ruins of a church or chapel. The light that the horsemen had seen came from one of the upper windows of the tower; but there were lights also in the less elevated building by its side. A low wall stood before the whole, enclosing a little neglected garden; and through a gate which stood open in this wall, Franklin Gray led his companion in, and up to the door of the tower. There, beside the door, stood the ancient steps which many a burly cavalier in the Hudibrastic days, and in days long before that, had employed to mount his horse's back; and there, too, on either side of the entrance, was many a ring, staple, and hook, for the purpose of fastening up the troopers' horses, while their masters rested or caroused in the hall hard by.

Having attached their bridles to two of these hooks, Franklin Gray and his companion proceeded to seek admission into the tower. To gain this, Gray first struck the door three or four times distinctly with his heavy hand. The moment he had done so, a light step was heard running along within, and after manifold bolts and bars had been withdrawn, the boy Jocelyn threw open the door; and Langford followed his companion into a low narrow entrance hall, on the right of which was another door, and at the end a dim flight of stone steps leading apparently to the upper apartments.

Scarcely, however, had the foot of Franklin Gray fallen three times on that stone passage, when a light came gleaming down the stairs, and the next instant the flutter of a woman's garments was seen, as she descended with a step of joy. She was as lovely a creature as the eye of man ever rested upon, though the first years of youthful grace were passed, and though the sun of a warmer land than this had dyed her skin with a rich brown. Her eyes—her large full liquid eyes—were as black as jet, and the long dark fringe that edged both the upper and the under lid left but little of the white visible. The glossy black hair, divided on the forehead, was tied in a large massy knot behind, without any ornament whatsoever; but along the whole line might be traced a strong undulation, which told that, if free, it would have fallen in ringlets round her face; and even as it was, two or three thick curls escaped from the knot behind, and hung in glossy masses on her neck. Her age might be three or four and twenty, and her form had the fulness of that age, but without having lost any of the symmetry of youth.

She carried a lamp in her hand, and the light of it showed her dark eyes sparkling with joy as they rested upon Franklin Gray. Setting down the light upon the stairs, she darted forward at once, and cast herself upon his bosom, exclaiming, with a strong foreign accent, "You have come back! You have come back! Oh, I have been so uneasy about you!"

"But why, my Mona?" demanded Franklin Gray, with his whole tone and manner changed to one of the utmost gentleness, as soon as he addressed her. "Why more to-night than at other times, when I am obliged to leave you?"

"Oh, I do not well know," she replied; "but you kissed me twice before you went, and then you came back to kiss me once more, and bid me remember you; and I felt sure you were going on some dangerous expedition. I felt sad at heart myself, too, as if some evil would come of this night."

"Evil has come of it, I fear," replied Franklin Gray; but he then added quickly, seeing her turn pale at his words, "Evil not upon me, or of my doing, Mona. But go up again, beloved! and I will come to you directly. You see I have some one with me."

She turned her eyes upon Langford, whom she appeared not to have noticed before; and then bowing her head gracefully and slowly, she raised the lamp again, and disappeared up the steps.

When she was gone, Franklin Gray turned round and gazed upon Langford for a moment, with a proud yet melancholy smile. There was a world of meaning in his look, and Langford could only reply to it by exclaiming, with a glance still more sorrowful, "Oh, Gray, this is very sad!"

"Come, come," cried his companion; "it shall be amended some day, Harry. Come, Jocelyn," he continued, turning to the boy, "tell me, master page, who are in the hall, and how many?"

The boy's brow became grave at the question. "There are but three, sir," he replied; "there is James of Coventry, and there is Doveton and little Harvey."

"Indeed!" said Gray, shutting his teeth close, as if to keep down angry feelings that were rising fast—"indeed!" and with his right hand he threw open the door which led into a small dark room. That again he strode across, giving Langford a sign to follow, and then opened another door, which admitted them into a much larger chamber, well lighted, in the midst of which was a large table furnished with a flagon and some drinking cups. At the further end sat two men playing with dice, while a third, a short smart-looking personage, was standing behind, observing their game. They ceased when Gray and his companion appeared; and the merriment which they evidently had been enjoying, was over in a moment.

"But you three left!" said Gray, as he entered, "but you three left! Where are Hardcastle and Wiley?"

"They went out shortly after you, Captain Gray," replied one of the men who were playing; "I can't tell where they are."

"Doveton," replied Gray, in a calm grave tone, "you are a gentleman and a soldier; so are you, James; and Master Harvey, too, though he did not serve with us either in Germany or in the New World, has had the honour of serving in Ireland, and is a man of honour. Now, I ask you all, straightforwardly, where are these two men gone to? Marcham and Henry of the Hill I took with me; all the others I know about also; but where are Wiley and Hardcastle, and what are they about?"

"Why, really, sir," replied the man called Doveton, "we can only tell by guess; for since that business down in the green lane they have kept very much by themselves, and don't seem to deal fairly with us, especially Wiley."

"I'll tell you what, captain," said the man who was standing behind, and whom they called amongst themselves Little Harvey, "I wish Wiley was out from amongst us; he will get us all into mischief some day. He does not do things in a gentlemanlike way. I guess what he has gone after, but he has not succeeded, I see." And as he spoke, he gave a significant glance towards Langford, as if he were in some degree connected with the matter in question.

"Indeed!" said Gray; "I suspect your meaning, Harvey; but let us hear more plainly what you think. Though I direct and guide, and am always willing to take the greatest dangers on myself, still we are comrades, and should treat each other as such. What is it you think, Harvey?"

"I won't say what I think," replied the man; "but I'll say what I saw. When you sent the boy Jocelyn down to the Manor, Wiley cross-questioned him both before he went and when he came back; and when he heard him give you a message about a gentleman meeting you on the moor, he whispered a good deal to Hardcastle, who came up and asked me if I would go along with them upon an enterprise which must be quite secret, and which must be done without your knowing it. I refused; and told him, I thought that after the business down in the lane, he had better not let Wiley lead him; but to that he answered, that this was a matter which could not fail as the other had done, and that it would be over in five minutes. I said I would not go, however, and they went without me."

"Hark, they are coming!" said Gray, as the sound of horses' feet was heard stopping opposite the house. "Let them in the back way, Jocelyn, and bring in supper. Here! Come with me, Master Harry." And he led the way back into the hall by which they had at first entered, and in which there still remained the lamp that the boy Jocelyn had carried when he gave them admittance. Gray carefully shut the doors behind him; and when he stood alone in the passage with Langford, he unbuttoned his vest, and took from an inner pocket a key of a very peculiar and extraordinary form.

"There is the key, Master Harry," he said, speaking quickly, and with strong passions of some kind evidently struggling in his breast. "Your own fate is now in your power! Manage it as you will!"

"But tell me how this has been obtained," said Langford.

"I have no time for long stories," replied his companion sharply. "There it is! that is sufficient. But I will tell you so far, I—I alone —though directed by one who knew the house well, walked through it this night, from one end to the other; and within six yards of the old man himself, with nothing but a door between us, took this key from the hiding place where he thought it so safe, and brought it away undiscovered. Now, Harry, leave me! I am not in a humour to speak much. I have matters before me that may well make me silent. Mount your horse, and be gone with all speed. Why do you linger? Oh! I will send out ere ten minutes be over, and if there be a possibility of undoing what has been done amiss, it shall be undone, on my honour. Take the back road, he added, as he opened the door for Langford; "and for worlds go no more upon the moor to-night! I ask you for my own sake," he added, seeing his companion hesitate; "not for yours, but for mine!"

Langford made no reply, but mounting his horse, rode away with feelings of a nature the most mingled and the most painful.

Those of the man he left behind were of a different character, but still terrible. With Langford there were feelings which he seldom experienced, doubt and hesitation as to his own course of action, mingling with vague apprehension of evil, and deep regret to see a man possessed of many noble qualities, who had been his friend, his companion, and even his protector in the early days of youth, now plunged into a current, terrible in itself, and terrible in its consequences—following a course which he had long suspected that Gray did really follow, but without having conviction forced upon him till that night.

With Franklin Gray it was very different; his whole feelings, for the time, were swallowed up in one stern and gloomy resolution.

There was anger, indeed, at the bottom of that resolution; wrath of the most bitter and deadly kind; but even that was almost lost in the effort to exclude from his thoughts everything that might shake, even in the least degree, the dark and terrible determination he had formed.

As soon as Langford had quitted him he returned to the hall in which he had left his comrades, and there, as he expected, he found the party increased by the presence of the two men, Wiley and Hardcastle, whose names we have mentioned more than once, and whom we have seen busy in the attack upon Alice Herbert.

It was evident that some conversation had passed between them and the others regarding the indignation which they had excited in their leader, and while, in the rough countenance of Hardcastle, might be traced a great deal of shame and apprehension, in the more cunning face of Wiley appeared a degree of hesitating uncertainty, mingling strangely with dogged defiance, and making him look like an ill-tempered hound about to receive the lash, but not very sure whether to lie down and howl, or fly at the throat of the huntsman. The boy Jocelyn was busily bringing in some dishes, and setting them on the table; but he glanced at Franklin Gray from time to time, seeming to know better than any one present the character of the man with whom they had to deal, and to divine what was likely to be the issue.

Franklin Gray said not a word in regard to the matter which was in all their thoughts; but sitting down at the head of the table, he made some observation upon the bread, which was not good; and then added, speaking to the others—"Begin, begin! Marcham and Henry of the Hill won't be long."

"I heard them coming over the hill but now," said the boy Jocelyn.

Gray made no reply, and the rest began their meal in silence; but he ate nothing, looking curiously at the knife in his hand, as if there was something very interesting in the blade. He made the boy give him a silver cup, indeed, full of wine from the tankard; and as he was drinking it, the two others, whom he had mentioned, came in laughing, and seemed surprised to see the grave and stern manner in which the supper was passing.

The matter was soon explained, however; for no sooner had they sat down in the places left for them, than Franklin Gray fixed his eyes upon Wiley, and said, "Now, my masters Wiley and Hardcastle, we are all present but two: be so good as to tell me where you have been to-night?"

The time which had elapsed, the indifference, and even carelessness, which had hitherto appeared in Gray's manner, and a cup or two of wine which he himself had drunk, had removed the degree of apprehension which at first mingled with the sullen determination of Wiley; and he replied at once, with a look of effrontery, "I don't think that at all necessary, Captain! I rather believe that I have as much right to ride my horse over any common in the kingdom as you have, without giving you any account of it either."

"You hear!" said Franklin Gray, looking round calmly to the rest, "you hear!"

"Come, come, Master Wiley," cried the man, called Doveton, "that won't do, after what we all swore, when we came down here. Come, Hardcastle, you are the best of the two; come, you tell Captain Gray at once what you have been about. We must know, if it be but for our own safety."

"Oh! I'll tell at once," said Hardcastle. "Devilish sorry am I that I ever went; and I certainly would not have gone had I known how it would turn out. I'll never go again with Wiley as long as I live: I told him so, as we came over the common."

Wiley muttered something not very laudatory of his companion; but it was drowned in the stern voice of Franklin Gray, who exclaimed, "Go on, Hardcastle!"

"Why, we went out to the beeches by Upwater Mere," replied Hardcastle; "and we had not been there long, when up came some one on horseback, going along slowly towards the castle. It was not the person we were looking for, however——"

"Pray, who were you looking for?" interrupted Franklin Gray.

"Why, I think that is scarcely fair, Captain," said Hardcastle.

"It matters not," replied Gray; "I know without your telling me. Go on!"

"Well, as the young man came up," continued the other, "Wiley said we might as well have what he had upon him. So we rode up, and asked him to stop, quite civilly; but, instead of doing so, he drew his sword, and spurred on his horse upon Wiley, and——"

"Well," exclaimed Gray, impatiently; "what then? I heard the pistol fired," he said, seeing the man hesitate; "so tell the truth."

"Well," said Hardcastle, "well; and as he spoke he turned somewhat pale: "well, then Wiley fired, you know, and brought him down; and we pulled him under the beeches, and took what we could get. We have not divided it yet, but it seems a good sum."

As his companion had been detailing the particulars of their crime, the changes which had come over Wiley's countenance were strange and fearful. He had watched with eager anxiety the countenance of Franklin Gray, who sat nearly opposite to him at the other end of the table; but, being able to gather nothing from those stern dark features, he ran his eye rapidly round the faces of the rest, and after several changes of expression, resumed, as well as he could, the look of cunning and daring impudence which he had at first put on. The entrance of the boy Jocelyn with some plates, just behind him, however, made him give a sharp start and look round. Franklin Gray fixed his eyes upon the boy, and waved his hand; and Jocelyn immediately went round to the other side of the table.

"Hardcastle," said their leader, "I shall find some means of punishing you. As for you, Wiley——"

"You shall not punish me, Captain Gray!" interrupted Wiley, knitting his brows and speaking through his teeth; "for by ——, if you don't mind what you're about, I'll hang you all."

Franklin Gray sat and heard him calmly, keeping his eyes fixed upon him with stern unchanging gaze till he had done speaking. He then looked round once more, saying, "You hear!" and, at the same moment, he drew a pistol from under his coat. Every face around turned pale but his own; and Wiley started up from the table. But before he could take a single step, and while yet, with agony of approaching fate upon him, he gazed irresolute in the face of his leader, the unerring hand of Franklin Gray had levelled the pistol and fired.

The ball went right through his head; the unhappy man bounded up two or three feet from the ground, and then fell dead at the end of the table. Franklin Gray sat perfectly still, gazing through the smoke for about a minute; and through the whole hall reigned an awful silence. He then laid the pistol calmly down on the table before him, and drew forth a second.

Hardcastle crossed his arms upon his breast, and looked him full in the face, saying, "Well, Captain, I'm ready."

"You mistake me," said Gray, laying down the pistol on the table, with the muzzle towards himself. "My friends, if I have done wrong by the shot I have fired, any of you that so pleases, has but to take up that pistol and use it as boldly as I have done its fellow. What say you; am I right or wrong?"

"Right, right!" replied every voice.

"Well, then," said Gray, putting up the weapons again, "some of you take him down; and you. Doveton and Marcham, hark ye;" and he spoke a few words to them apart. "Take Hardcastle with you," he added; "that shall be his punishment!" so saying, he turned, took up a lamp that stood near, and quitted the hall.

Franklin Gray mounted the steps in the tower that we have mentioned, slowly and sadly; paused half-way up, and fell into deep thought. His reverie lasted but a minute: he then proceeded, and reached the room where the fair being whom he called Mona was watching anxiously for his coming. Her eyes questioned him; but he made no reply in words. He threw his right arm round her, however, and rested his face upon her bosom for several minutes, with his eyes shut; then pressed her to his heart, kissed her cheek, and said, "Come my Mona, come and see our babe sleeping."

CHAPTER IX.

For nearly three miles Langford rode rapidly on. His mind was in that state of confusion and uncertainty which admitted not of any slow movement of the body; but as he thought again and again of all that had occurred, he the more deeply regretted that he had ever gone to the rendezvous with Franklin Gray, although his purpose in there going was to separate his own proceedings for ever from those of one whose present pursuits could be no longer doubtful. When Langford had known him in former years he was a wild and reckless soldier of fortune, whose bold rash spirit had prevented rather than aided him in rising to those high grades in the service which his talents might otherwise have obtained. His heart had ever, as far as Langford had seen it, been kind, noble, and generous; there were many circumstances which had connected them closely in our hero's early life; and in himself and his fate, Franklin Gray had ever taken a deep and affectionate interest.

His hatred of inactivity, his love of enterprise, his daring courage, his strong and determined resolution, his rapid powers of combination, and that peculiar talent for command which is a gift rather than an acquirement, had made him loved and admired by the soldiery under him, and might have gone far to constitute one of the greatest generals of the age. But by his fellow officers he had never been loved, and by those above him he had constantly been used, but had never been trusted nor liked. In truth, there was a fierce and overbearing spirit in his bosom, a contempt for other men's opinions, and an abhorrence of the ordinary littleness of human nature, which prevented him from seeking or winning the regard of any one, towards whom some peculiar circumstance, or some extraordinary powers, had not excited in his bosom feelings either of tenderness or of respect; and for this reason he had never been loved. Why he had never been trusted was another matter. He had set out in life depending more upon feeling than upon principle as his guide; and though, as he went on, he had framed for his own bosom a sort of code of laws by which he was strictly bound, those laws did not always very well accord with the ordinary code of mankind, and if generally acted upon must have been disastrous to society. Those who disliked him—very often for his superiority to themselves—were glad to find in his failings a specious excuse for undervaluing his better qualities, and thus he had been always thwarted and bitterly disappointed in his progress through life.

Brought up as a soldier from his earliest years, he had ever looked upon strife as his profession, life as one great campaign, the world as a battle-field, mankind as either enemies or fellow soldiers. The great law that he had laid down for himself was, never to measure himself against any but those who were equal to the strife; and he would just as soon have thought of injuring the weak, the innocent, or the defenceless, as he would of murdering the wounded in an hospital. The proud, the haughty, and the strong he took a pleasure in humbling or overthrowing, even when bound to the same cause with himself;

and the constant single combats in which he was engaged had raised him up a bad name in the service.

In other respects, though no one could ever accuse Gray of injuring the peasant, or taking away a part of the honest earnings of the farmer—though, even under the orders of his general, he would take no part in raising contributions from the hard-working and industrious, and it was in vain to send him upon such expeditions, yet there had been many a tale current in the camp, of Gray and his troopers sacking and burning the castles in the Palatinate, driving the cattle from under the very guns of the enemy's fortresses, and sweeping the wealth from the palace of the Prince or the Bishop. Thus he had established in some degree the character of a daring, but somewhat marauding officer, and any soldier of more than ordinary enterprise and rashness ever sought to be enrolled in his troop. He had quitted the service of France in disgust some time before Langford, and they had not met again till Langford, called suddenly to the death-bed of a parent, found Gray, who had known her and hers in happier days, tending her with the care and kindness of a son.

Of what had taken place in the interim Langford was ignorant. From time to time Gray talked of other lands which he had visited, and more burning climates which he had known; but he did so in a vague and obscure manner, which excited curiosity without inviting inquiry. Langford had made none; and though they had met frequently since, and dark suspicions and apprehensions—springing from a comparison of Gray's former poverty and his known prodigality with the wealth he seemed now to have at command—had from time to time crossed his friend's mind in regard to the pursuits to which he had dedicated himself, it was only on the occasion of the present visit to Moorhurst that Langford had obtained a positive certainty of the painful truth. As soon as he had obtained that certainty, he determined to warn, to exhort, to beseech his former friend to quit the dangerous pursuits in which he was engaged; to offer once more to share with him all his little wealth, in gratitude for many an act of kindness gone before, and for a service that Gray was even then anxious to do him, at the risk of life itself; but on no account to participate in any scheme conducted by the other, however great and important the object to be gained for himself.

His own wound, and the temporary disappearance of Gray and his companions from that part of the country, had prevented Langford from notifying to him this intention fully, after the night of the attack upon Alice Herbert, though he had done so in general terms twice before, and he had gone to the rendezvous appointed by Gray, on the night of which we have just been speaking, supposing that it was to have preceded, not to have followed, the enterprise proposed. All that he had seen had been terribly painful to him; and in what had occurred upon the moor he had too good reason to believe that an act had been committed which he should not be justified in concealing. Yet, how was he to reveal it, without the basest breach of confidence, and the grossest ingratitude towards a man who had been risking all to serve him? How was he to denounce the crime that had been committed, and bring to justice the perpetrators thereof, without involving Gray in the same destruction?

Such were the matters in his thoughts, as he rode rapidly on towards the Manor House; but by the time he had gone about three miles his mind had been naturally led to inquire, who was the unfortunate person that had been attacked; and for the first time an apprehension crossed his mind that it might be Lord Harold.

"And yet," thought Langford, as he rode along, "he would never go over the moor at that time of night, and alone. He must have been home long before, too: nevertheless he set out very slowly; and he seemed to turn to the right, as if he were going by the moor. He may have loitered by the way, or visited some cottage, or called at some house. Good God! this uncertainty is not to be borne. I must, and will go back to the moor."

As he thus thought, he turned his horse short round, and galloped back as fast as possible, following the road which led to the piece of water called Upwater Mere. By the time he reached it, the moon was just rising, and spreading through the hazy sky, near the horizon, a red and ominous glare. It served to cast some light upon the road, however; and Langford, calculating with the keen accuracy of a soldier, had fixed exactly upon the spot before he reached it, where he had seen the unfortunate traveller encountered.

When he did reach that spot, the deep gory stains in the sandy road but too plainly showed him he was right; and he traced the course of the murderers along by the thick drops of gore, till the track was lost in the grass beneath the beech trees. The darkness which reigned under their branches rendered all further search fruitless; and, after having given up nearly half an hour to the painful, but unsuccessful task, he once more mounted his horse, and, with feelings of deep gloom and despondency, took his way back towards the Manor House.

It was nearly eleven o'clock at night ere Langford reached the gates; and the family generally retired to rest before that hour.

Certain doubts and apprehensions, however, in regard to the affairs of Sir Walter Herbert—doubts and apprehensions springing from a thousand minute incidents, which he had noticed while staying as a visitor in the house—had induced him to inquire farther, from sources whence he might derive certain information; and the information he had thus acquired made him now determine to return to the Manor that night, rather than go to the inn, though the hour was somewhat unseasonable.

He found all the servants up: and there was a look of anxiety and apprehension in the countenances of all, which led him to believe that his fears were not unfounded, and that the business in which Sir Walter had been engaged during the evening was both painful in itself, and such as could no longer be concealed from his household.

In those days, when difficulties and embarrassments overtook a country gentleman, the case was much more painful than it is at present. Habits of luxury and dissipation, ostentatious rivalry with one another, and many of the other vices which, in the present times, have rendered the transfer of property from the old gentry of the land but too common, and burthens upon that which does remain, very general, had then scarcely reached the country; and though the dissipated inhabitants of towns, the gay debauched peer, the fopling of the court, and the speculating merchant, might know, from time to time, every reverse of fortune, it seldom occurred in those days that the old proprietor of lands in the country experienced **any great and detrimental change**, unless tempted to quit the calm enjoyments of rural life for the more dangerous pleasures of the town.

Civil wars, indeed, and political strife had brought about, or laid the foundation for, the ruin of a great number of the country gentry; and such, in some degree, had been the case with Sir Walter Herbert. His father had served king Charles both with sword and purse, and had never received either payment or recompence. The matter had gone on slowly since, drop by drop, till the cup was nearly full.

Sir Walter had shut his eyes to the fact, and had carefully concealed from the eyes of those around him difficulties, the whole extent of which he did not himself know, and which he always hoped to remedy. It could not be, however, but that reports of embarrassment should get abroad, and it was well known in the country that, some five or six years before, he had become security to the amount of ten thousand pounds for a neighbouring gentleman, who failed to pay the debt, fled, and left the country. But every one knew, also, that the bond was in the hands of Lord Danemore, Sir Walter's acquaintance and neighbour: and every one, when the subject was mentioned, smiled, and declared that Lord Harold, the son of the peer, and Mistress Alice Herbert, would find means of cancelling the debt.

We have already had occasion to show that such expectations were vain: and the reports of embarrassments which had reached Langford's ears, from sources which he could not doubt, had rendered his suit to Alice Herbert as disinterested as it could be, but had prepared his mind for what he was about to hear.

"I am afraid something is the matter, Haliday," he said, addressing the servant who gave him admittance. "What has happened, do you know?"

"I am afraid something has gone wrong too, Captain," replied the servant, with a sorrowful expression of countenance; "but Mistress Alice, I dare say, will tell you all about it. She is sitting up in the library to see you; and begged you would come to her whenever you came in."

Langford waited for no one to usher him to her presence: but by two or three rapid steps passed the servant, and opened the library door.

Alice was sitting at a table with a book before her. It were vain to say that she was reading; for though her eyes had more than once fixed upon the pages, and had scanned several sentences, so as to make out the words, of the meaning of those words her mind was very little conscious. Her eyes were now tearless; but it was clear to Langford that she had been weeping not long before. The noise of his foot made her instantly rise, and the colour became a good deal deeper in her cheek; betraying a part, but a very small part, of the varied emotions that were going on within.

The heart of her lover was throbbing at that moment with many an anxiety, it is true; but, strange as it may seem, love and noble pride, ay, and even joy, engrossed by far the greater part. He guessed —no, he divined all that she felt, however; the pain, the care, the apprehensiveness, that burdened her breast, as she rose after waiting there alone to receive him in order to tell him the tale of her father's embarrassments; a tale which he well knew she had never herself heard before that night.

Langford would not have paused a moment under such circumstances for worlds; and, with a step as quick as lightning, he was by her side: he took her hand in his; he made her sit down again, and drew a chair near her; gazing upon her with a look so full of tenderness and affection, that—though sweet, most sweet to all her feelings—it made the tears again rise into her eyes. It matters not whether what we drop into a full cup be earth or a jewel; in either case the cup overflows. Langford was anxious to speak first himself, and was not sorry that any emotion not painful in itself should prevent her from commencing the conversation.

"Alice," he said, "dear Alice, something painful has happened, I know, and I guess the nature of it; but do not let it affect you too deeply. If you did but know how common these events are in the gay world of the metropolis, it would become lighter in your eyes than it is now, breaking upon you suddenly, and ignorant as you are of all such transactions."

"Then you have heard?" said Alice, gazing mournfully in his face.

"No, I have not," replied Langford; "but I have divined what is the matter: I divined long ago."

"Then you were indeed generous," she said, "to wish to link your fate with mine; for it seems to me an evil one."

"Not so, dearest," replied Langford; "not so! I would say, that all I ask is to share it, if I had not the vain hope, my beloved, of doing more, and rendering it a happy one."

"Oh! but Langford, I fear you do not know all," replied Alice; "and though I waited here on purpose to tell you, I do not know whether I shall be able to do so distinctly; for I am unacquainted with even the terms of these things. But I will tell you what happened when I came home. I found my poor father sitting here, in a terrible state of agitation, and Lord Danemore's lawyer with him, looking cold and stiff, and taking snuff, and a very different man, indeed, from what I have seen him in former days, bowing down to the ground, and scarcely venturing to sit down in the same room with my father. He it was who told me, for my father could not, that there was what he called a bond and judgment for ten thousand pounds and interest, which my father owed Lord Danemore; and that my father had offered to give him a mortgage on his estate for it; but that Lord Danemore would not take one, both because he wanted the money, and because he said that the estate was mortgaged already up to its value."

"That must be a mistake, I think," said Langford. "You will forgive me, Alice, for having made some inquiries lately; and will not, I know, attribute my having done so to any motive but the true one. I have, however, made such inquiries; and I feel sure that this lawyer of Lord Danemore's has greatly exaggerated, and has done so for the purpose of embarrassing your father."

"Oh! I cannot think he could be so cruel," exclaimed Alice, "when he saw the dreadful state of agitation in which my father was. However, he made it out, in short, that we had nothing on earth left but the pictures and the plate, and my poor mother's jewels; and he said, that all he wanted to know was, first, whether I would be willing to give up the little fortune that was left me by my aunt, to pay one half of the debt; and next, when my father would pay the remainder. He said, too, he had no objection to give him a week to do so."

"A week!" exclaimed Langford, "a week! The pitiful scoundrel! Is that the way he treats his master's friend? However, Alice, he shall find himself mistaken! Listen to me, my beloved," and clasping her hand in his, he glided his arm round her waist, and gazed fondly and tenderly in her face: "I have some means of knowing, Alice, what is taking place in this neighbourhood, which it is needless to explain: and certain circumstances induced me to believe that this claim would be made by Lord Danemore on your father immediately. Alice," he added, with a meaning look, "you know that there may be motives sufficient to induce Lord Danemore to entertain some slight feelings of anger towards you and your father at this moment."

Alice blushed very deeply, and looked up with surprise, saying, "What motives do you mean, Langford?"

"I mean on account of his son," replied Langford.

"I did not know," replied Alice, ingenuously, "that either you or anybody else, but my father, knew aught of that business, till to-night."

"Several persons knew it," replied Langford; "and though I do not mean to excuse Lord Danemore, yet we must allow something for anger—and I think that such was his motive."

"Oh, that it certainly was," replied Alice, "for the attorney did not scruple to acknowledge it; but I did not think myself justified in mentioning it even to you, Langford."

"I do not mean to excuse Lord Danemore's conduct," said Langford. "It was unjust and unkind; but, perhaps, it was consistent with human nature, and certainly was consistent with all I know of his nature, which is quick, vehement, and passionate, if we may believe one-half of what is said. But, after all, very likely this lawyer has outdone his instructions. However, Alice, as I said, he shall be disappointed. Learning that something of the kind was in agitation, I wrote several days ago to London, in order to be prepared to meet this matter. By this time my messenger is at the village, and brings with him a sufficient sum to discharge your father's obligation to Lord Danemore. For the last two or three days, Alice, I will acknowledge to you that my mind has been in a great state of doubt and agitation: the sum for which I have sent is more than one-half of what I actually possess; but it was no fear in regard to that which made me at all hesitate. I only doubted whether I should tell you all I feel towards you before I offered this little assistance to your father or not. I thought that if hope had deceived me, and Alice rejected my love, her father would then refuse to receive any aid from me, however needful it might be to him; and, therefore, on the one hand, I fancied it might be better to mention the subject of the money first. But then again, on the other hand, I thought if I did so it might place my Alice in embarrassing circumstances, should she find herself obliged to refuse a man who had come to her father's assistance in a moment of difficulty. I judged it would seem ungenerous of me even to ask her very soon after. In short, Alice, I gave way to hope and impatience, trusting that my Alice, by accepting me, would give me a right both to protect her and to assist her father."

"In short, Langford," replied Alice, placing her other hand upon his, "in short, you thought of everything that was generous, and kind, and noble, and acted accordingly."

"Nay, nay, not so, Alice," replied Langford; "but, of course, you have told your father what has passed between us."

"Immediately that man was gone," replied Alice, "I felt myself bound to do so, Langford; the more bound, from all the distressing and agitating events which had occurred."

"You did quite right, my beloved," he replied. "What did he say?"

"He said everything that was kind and affectionate," replied Alice. "He said everything that I should like to hear said of one I love; but he said that he feared you would be disappointed when you heard all this bad news, and that I was bound in honour to set you free from all promises, as much as if no proposal had ever been made. On his own part, he said that he should never raise any objections in regard to fortune; that he would never have done so even in his most prosperous days; but there was one question which he wished to ask regarding birth." Alice blushed, and cast down her eyes as she spoke. Then raising them suddenly and frankly to Langford's face, she added, "It is one of his prejudices, you know, Henry. But even if there should be any difficulty, his love for me and his esteem for you will make it but the matter of a moment."

Langford gazed in her face for an instant with a melancholy smile, which almost made her believe that her father's suspicions with regard to his history were correct. The next instant, however—whether he understood her meaning clearly or not—he answered, "Set your mind at rest, dear Alice; my birth is as good as your own! Is your father gone to bed?"

"He went up stairs about half an hour before you came," said Alice; "but he is not asleep yet, I am sure. I sat up both to tell you all this and to put my mind at ease about you and Lord Harold. You were so long absent that I was uneasy. If you had not given me your solemn promise not to quarrel with him, and if my father's grief and agitation had not occupied so much of my thoughts, I am afraid I should have been very foolish, and both terrified and unhappy at your not returning."

"I have been very busy about other things," replied Langford, the chilly recollection of all that had passed in the interval, coming back upon him like a sudden gust of cold wind; "but my conversation with Lord Harold only lasted ten minutes. I do not mean to say that he would not willingly have quarrelled with me, but I would not quarrel with him; and I trust that my reputation for courage does not require to be sustained by any such silly contests. However, dear Alice," he continued, suddenly turning the conversation back again to its former subject—"however, if your father be not asleep, it may put his mind more at ease to hear that means are provided for meeting Lord Danemore's claim upon him; and you may also tell him, my Alice, in order to remove every shade of doubt, that although my fortune be but scanty, as it at present stands, yet **there is** good hope of its being greatly increased, and that my birth is certainly not inferior to that of her whose hand is already too valuable a gift to need the enhancement of superior station."

As he spoke, he raised the hand he held, tenderly, but reverentially, to his lips; for he felt that he was bound to double every outward token of respect at a moment when Alice announced to him that her own expectations of high fortune were disappointed, and that the rich heiress, who had thought a few hours before she had great wealth and broad lands to give, was now dowerless, except in her beauty, her virtues, and her gentleness.

So he felt, and so he acted; and Alice saw his feelings and appreciated them to the full.

She rose then to go, but hesitated a moment as she wished him good-night, not knowing well how to express all the sensations that his conduct had produced. "Langford," she said, at length, "how shall I thank you? I will not attempt to do it now, the time is too short; but I shall find time, if endeavouring through life to make you happy be enough."

Langford could not resist it, and for a moment he pressed her to his bosom, adding—"Good-night, my Alice; good-night, my beloved. Hasten to your father before he is asleep, and I will remain for a few minutes here, to write a note to the landlord of the Talbot, bidding him send up to-morrow morning early the packet, which must have arrived to-night. I will tell him to address it to you; so that, before your father is awake to-morrow, you will have in your own hands the means of freeing him from all apprehension regarding this claim. I trust, too, dear Alice, that the time will come, when he will so much regard me in the light of a son, as to permit me to examine into the matter of these mortgages, and I think I can show him, and others too, that his estates are far from being as much involved as they have been represented to be."

They parted; and after Langford had written the note he spoke of, and had given it to a servant to take to the little town early in the morning, he retired to rest. He found in his chamber, busily engaged in laying out his toilet for the night, the old servant Halliday, who, during the whole time he had been confined in consequence of his wound, had attended him with the utmost care and attention, springing from a feeling that he was in some degree paying off a debt of his young mistress, in whose service that wound had been received. There was now in his countenance, though his nature was too respectful to suffer him to put any questions, an anxious sort of inquiringness, which Langford could not resist. "It is not so bad, Halliday," he said. "Your excellent master has alarmed himself too much. All will go quite well, depend upon it."

The man made him a low bow with an air full of gratitude. "I am very much obliged to you, Captain," he said. "I was frightened, I confess; for the steward, you see, told me, at least three months ago. But, however, we servants have no right to be talking about such matters; and though it is all out of love and regard to Sir Walter and Mistress Alice, perhaps we had better hold our tongues."

"Perhaps so, Halliday," replied Langford. "And now, good-night; all will go well, depend upon it."

The man again bowed low and respectfully, and left the room, and Langford proceeded calmly to undress himself; for—though his mind was oppressed, and the moment his thoughts were turned from the immediate subject of Sir Walter Herbert's affairs, they reverted naturally to the more painful topics with which they had before been engaged—he was not a man to suffer his feelings to overpower him, or to interrupt him in his ordinary habits and occupations. He felt deeply and strongly; but he was too much accustomed to such feelings to suffer the emotions of his mind greatly to affect his corporeal demeanour. It is those who feel by fits and starts alone that give full way to sudden emotions. Langford could feel as poignantly as any one. He did feel so at that moment; and yet he proceeded with his ordinary preparations for repose as if nothing had occurred to affect his feelings or to shake his heart. He ended by kneeling and commending himself and those he loved to the care of the Great Protector, and then lay down to rest, but not to sleep. That he could not command; and for many an hour he remained with his right arm bent under his head, his eyes cast upwards through the darkness, peopling vacancy with strange shapes, and suffering imagination to suggest to him many a melancholy and many a painful image, which, after all, were not so dark and gloomy as the reality soon proved to be. The sky was beginning to turn grey with the morning light, when he first closed his eyes. He started up again, however, in another moment, and then lay awake till it was broad daylight. Perceiving that such was the case, he was about to rise, but a degree of drowsiness came over him; and yielding to it for a moment, it took possession of him quite, and he fell into a deep sleep.

CHAPTER X.

Day had long dawned, as we have said, ere Langford woke; and even then he woke not of himself, nor till the servant, Halliday, had twice called him by name, standing close by his bedside, and looking upon him with an expression of much interest, indeed, but with a face from which all colour was banished, apparently by fear and agitation.

"Master Langford!" he said; "Master Langford! No guilty man ever slept so sound as that. Poo, nonsense! Captain Langford, I say!"

Langford woke, and looked up, demanding what was the matter.

"Why, sir," replied the servant, "here is good old Gregory Myrtle, the landlord of the Talbot, wants to speak with you immediately. I met him as I was going up to the village, coming down here as fast as he could roll."

"Then you have not got the packet I sent for?" said Langford, coolly.

"He has got it, sir, safe," replied Halliday; "but he would not give it up, for he was coming on to you himself."

"He should have given it, as he was directed," said Langford. "Tell him to wait; I will see him when I am dressed."

"But he says, sir, that he must see you directly; that his business is of the greatest importance; that there is not a moment to lose."

"Oh, then, send him up," said Langford, "if the matter be so pressing as that."

Halliday instantly disappeared, as if he thought that too much time had been wasted already; and while Langford proceeded to rise, good Gregory Myrtle was heard creaking and panting up the stairs, as fast as his vast rotundity would let him. His face, too, was pale, if pale it ever could be called; and he was evidently in a great state of agitation, though the jolly habitual laugh still remained, and was heard before he was well within the door of Langford's room.

"Haw, haw, haw!" he cried, as he laid down the expected packet before Langford. "Lord a' mercy, Master Harry, this is a terrible business," he continued. "Well, I never did think—however, it's all nonsense, I know," and he again burst into a loud laugh, ending abruptly in the midst, and staring in Langford's face, as if for a reply.

"Well, good Gregory," replied Langford, who, in the meantime, had broken open the seals of the packet, and seen that various bills of exchange which it contained, together with other equivalents for money, were all right—"well, good Master Myrtle, what is it that is very terrible? What is it you did never think? What is it that is all nonsense? I am in the dark, Master Myrtle."

"Gad's my life, sir, they won't let you be in the dark long," cried the landlord of the Talbot; "and I came down to enlighten you first, that you might not be taken by surprise."

"As to what?" said Langford, somewhat impatiently.

"Lord, sir! I thought that Halliday must have told you something, at least," replied Gregory Myrtle, "or that his face must if not his tongue, for it's all black and white, like the broadside of the 'Hue and Cry.' But the matter is this," he added, after pausing a moment to laugh at his own joke: "it seems that poor Lord Harold, who was a good youth in his way, though he was somewhat sharp upon poachers and deer-stealers, and the like, was murdered last night upon the moor."

"Good God!" cried Langford, clasping his hands. "Good God!"

"It's but too true, sir," continued Myrtle, throwing as much solemnity as he could into his jocund countenance, "it's but too true; and there's poor Lord Danemore, his father, distracted. And for the matter of that, I think Sir Thomas Waller and Sir Matthew Scrope are as much distracted too; for after having been with my lord since five o'clock this morning, they come down to my house, and begin examining witnesses and taking evidence, and sending here and there, and the end of it all is—for I heard them consulting over it through a chink in the door—they judge that you are the person who murdered him, only because that mad fellow, silly John Graves, came running down to the village last night for help, swearing he had seen you and Lord Harold with your swords drawn upon each other. So, while they were busy swearing in constables, and all that, I thought it but friendly-like to come down here and tell you, in case you might think it right to get upon your horse's back, and gallop away till the business is over."

"Swearing in constables!" said Langford, without seeming to take notice of the worthy host's suggestion. "Why, they don't suppose my name is 'Legion,' do they? One constable, I should suppose, would be quite as useful as twenty."

"Ay, Master Harry," replied Gregory Myrtle; "but they vow that you are connected with the gentlemen of the road, who have been sporting round here lately, and they are afraid of a rescue."

"Indeed!" said Langford; "the sapient men! However, Master Myrtle, ring that little bell at the top of the stairs."

The silver hand-bell to which he pointed was immediately rung, and Halliday, who had remained halfway down the stairs, was in the room in a moment. No sooner did he appear, than Gregory Myrtle, who put his own construction upon Langford's coolness, exclaimed, "Quick, Master Halliday, quick! Saddle the Captain's horse for him!"

"No, no, Halliday," said Langford. "You are making a mistake, my good Master Myrtle. Take this packet, Halliday, and give it into Mistress Alice's own hands as soon as ever you can. I am going out with Master Myrtle here upon this business, which I see you have heard of. What may be the result of these foolish people's silly suspicions, I cannot tell; but do what you can, Halliday, to keep the matter from the ears of Sir Walter and Mistress Alice as long as you can. Warn the other servants too; for there is no use of adding fresh vexation to that which your master and mistress are already suffering. You must all know very well that I have nothing to do with this business, and can make that clear very soon. Say, therefore, that I have gone out for a few hours, but left that packet for Mistress Alice, with my best wishes. Now, good Gregory Myrtle, go back to your inn, and tell Sir Thomas Waller and Sir Matthew Scrope that I will be with them in five minutes, as soon as I have dressed myself."

Our host of the Talbot pursued the direction he had received, rolled down the stairs, and laboured along the road towards the village, with his surprise and admiration both excited by the extraordinary coolness and self-possession displayed by Langford under such circumstances. By the time he had reached the middle of the bridge, he perceived a great number of people issuing from the door of his own house; and, ere he was halfway up the street of the little town, he encountered ten or twelve constables and special constables, headed by the two magistrates in person. No sooner did he approach than the stentorian voice of Sir Thomas Waller—all unlike the dulcet notes of Sacharissa's lover—was heard to exclaim, "Take him into custody, Jonathan Brown!"

"Where hast thou been, Gregory Myrtle, Gregory Myrtle?" exclaimed, in softer tones, almost in the same moment, the voice of Sir Matthew Scrope.

"You have been aiding and abetting felony!" cried Sir Thomas.

"You have been warning the guilty to escape!" said Sir Matthew.

"You have been helping the lion to fly from his pursuers!" said Sir Thomas.

"You have been proditoriously giving information of our secret councils!" said Sir Matthew.

"It is being an accessary after the fact!" said his companion.

"It is misprision of treason!" said the other.

"It is levying war against the king!" shouted Sir Thomas.

"It is a gaol delivery!" cried the head constable, determined not to be outdone by his betters.

6

"Haw, haw, haw!" exclaimed Gregory Myrtle, laying his two hands upon his fat stomach, "What is the matter with your worships?"

"Hast thou not gone down on purpose," said Sir Matthew Scrope, "to warn Harry Langford, alias Captain Langford, alias Master Harry, to evade and escape the pursuit of justice, by flying out of the back door while we are approaching the front? Hast thou not done this, Gregory Myrtle? and woe be unto thee if he have so escaped! Take him into custody, I say!"

"Well, your worships," said Myrtle, beginning to look a little rueful under the hands of the constables. "I have been down to Master Harry, I own it; but I went upon other business that I had to do with him. Does not everybody know that I had a packet down for him by a special messenger yesterday night, with orders to deliver it into his own hands? and if I did talk with him this morning of what was going on, did he not send his compliments to your worships, and bid me say that he would be up with you in five minutes, as soon as he had got his clothes on!"

"Poo, nonsense, man!" exclaimed Sir Thomas Waller, growing red in the face. "Do you think we are fools, to be taken in with such a story as that? Are you fool enough yourself to think that he will come."

"I say, as sure as I am a living man, he will come!" said Gregory Myrtle. "Ay, more, my masters," he continued, after giving a glance towards the Manor House, "I say, there he is coming."

All eyes were instantly turned in the direction in which his own had been bent the moment before, and the figure of a man, which seemed to have just issued out of the gates of the park, was seen walking with a slow calm step along the road towards the village. The magistrates, the constables, and the multitudinous crowd which followed them, all stood in silence and what we may call *thunderstruckness*, so little credence had they given to the assurances of Gregory Myrtle; for let it be remembered, that the first effect produced by an accusation against any one, upon vulgar minds, is to lead them at once to condemn him. I am afraid there is something in the human heart that loves the act of condemnation—an act which either gratifies malignity or vanity.

However that may be, the party assembled in the streets of the little town could not believe their eyes, and, indeed, would not believe their eyes long after the form of Henry Langford, a form with which many of them were perfectly acquainted, had become distinctly visible, approaching with slow calm steps towards the spot where they were gathered together. The matter, however, could no longer be doubted; and the magistrates stood still, not knowing very well how to act in such unusual circumstances.

Henry Langford, in the mean time, approached without the slightest appearance of hesitation or dismay at the sight of the formidable phalanx which they presented. Walking up to the magistrates with the calm and graceful dignity which characterised all his actions, he bowed slightly, saying, "I am told, gentlemen, that a most distressing occurence has taken place, and that you imagine there is some cause for supposing that I am implicated in this matter. Now, with your leave, gentlemen, we will go to the inn, as this is no place for discussing such subjects, and we will there investigate the matter accurately. Doubtless, you have had good reason for attributing to me the commission of a crime; but some person or another must have gone out of the way, to insinuate or to urge such a charge against me; and who it is that has been kind enough and liberal enough to do so, I shall make it my business to discover, in order to punish him as he deserves."

Langford concluded somewhat sternly; and the magistrates, entirely taken by surprise, looked rather foolish, and began to imagine that they might have been too hasty in their conclusions. There was a tone and an air, too, in the person whom they had suspected, which forbade all high words or violent measures. He spoke to them as certainly their equal, if not their superior, and there was so much of the consciousness of innocence in his whole demeanour that it was very difficult to conceive their suspicions were justified.

Not knowing well what to reply, they followed his suggestion in silence, the one walking on one side of him, and the other on the other. By the time they reached the Talbot, however, they began to recover from the effect of his presence, and Sir Thomas Waller, with what he conceived to be wise foresight and presence of mind, gave the chief constable a hint in a whisper to guard the doors well, and to take care that the prisoner did not escape. They did not, however, venture to treat him as a prisoner in any other respect; and walking up into the room where they had held their investigation, he sat down with them at the table, and begged in a grave but not sarcastic tone, that they would have the goodness to let him know on what grounds they for a moment conceived that he had had any share in the unfortunate death of Lord Harold.

The magistrates looked to their clerk, who had remained behind, putting the evidence in order while they had proceeded with the constables for the purpose of arresting Langford. The clerk, who, upon the whole, seemed a sensible little man, proceeded, as it was very common in those days, to take the whole business into his hands, and recapitulated coolly, but civilly, to Langford the heads of all the evidence that had been taken.

Langford now discovered that the charge against him was much more serious than he had at first imagined. He found that, in the first place, several persons had deposed that silly John Graves, whose adherence to truth was well known, had come down to the town in great agitation, begging for help to stop Lord Harold and Master Harry Langford from killing each other. It was proved, also, by the horse boys from the Manor House, that Lord Harold, after having been in the park with Master Langford, had returned for his horse about the same time that the other had returned; that the young nobleman had ridden away very slowly, and that Langford, after proceeding part of the way towards the village, had suddenly come back, mounted his horse, and ridden away very rapidly; that he had been absent till between ten and eleven o'clock at night, and that his horse was evidently fatigued, and had been hard ridden. Several people, too, had seen him pass at different times, and on several parts of the road leading to the moor; and, in short, there was quite sufficient evidence to prove that a quarrel had taken place between Lord Harold and himself; that they had both gone towards the same spot at the same time, and that he had been absent a sufficient number of hours to commit the deed with which he was charged, and to return.

As the evidence was recapitulated, the worthy magistrates gained greater and greater confidence every moment; and at length Sir Matthew Scope exclaimed, "If this is not sufficient to justify us in committing the prisoner, I do not know what is."

"Not, perhaps, in committing him, your worship," said the clerk, whose philology was choice without being very accurate; "but certainly in remanding him."

"Why, I did not exactly mean to say committing," rejoined the subservient magistrate; "remanding was the word I meant to use; but where can we remand him to? If we remand him to the county jail, Justice Holdhim will take the matter out of our hands, and we shall lose all credit with the good Earl for arresting the murderer of his son."

"Would it not be as well," said the clerk, "to take him up at once to the castle? It is not improbable that the noble Earl might like to examine him himself; and you can keep him confined there till you have obtained further evidence to justify his committal."

"A very good thought, a very good thought!" cried Sir Thomas Waller, rubbing his hands. "He shall be placed in my carriage with a constable on each side, and we will follow in yours, Sir Matthew, with the other constables on horseback."

Langford had listened in silence to the conversation between the magistrates and their clerk, and though he evidently began to perceive that the affair would be more serious and disagreeable than he had anticipated, he could not refrain from smiling at the arrangement of the stately procession that was to carry him to Danemore Castle. He resolved, however, to make one effort to prevent the execution of a purpose which would, of course, on many accounts, be disagreeable to him; and he therefore interposed, as the clerk was about to leave the room, saying, "You are rather too hasty, gentlemen, in your conclusions, and I think you had better be warned, before you commit an act which you may be made to repent of——"

"Do you mean to threaten us, sir?" exclaimed Sir Thomas Waller. "Take those words down, clerk! Take those words down!"

"I mean to threaten you with nothing," replied Langford, "but the legal punishment to which bad or ignorant magistrates may be subjected for the use, or rather misuse, of their authority. You will remark—and I beg that the clerk may take these words down—that one half of the matter urged against me rests upon the reported words of a madman, who has not been brought forward even himself."

"You would not have us take the deposition of an innocent, a born natural!" demanded Sir Matthew Scope.

"His evidence is either worth something or worth nothing," replied Langford. "You rest mainly upon his testimony reported by others, which is, of course, worth nothing; and yet you will not take his testimony from his own mouth, when I inform you, that if it were so taken, he would prove that, though Lord Harold chose to quarrel with me, which I do not deny, that I positively refused to draw my sword upon him, even when he drew his upon me."

"That might be," said the clerk, "to take more sure vengeance in a private way. Their worships have on the contrary to remark, that you have not in any way attempted to account for the space of time you were absent from the Manor House last night. Neither have you stated where you were, or what was your occupation; and, without meaning to say anything uncivil, sir, let me say, that there have been a great many nights, while you remained at the inn, which might require accounting for also. Their worships have not judged harshly of you, nor even given attention to suspicious circumstances, till they found that the whole of your conduct was suspicious." This was spoken while standing beside the chair of Sir Matthew Scrope; and, after whispering a few words in his ear, the clerk left the room.

Langford remained, with his eyes gloomily bent upon the table, without speaking to either of his companions, busy with varied thoughts and feelings, which began to come upon him, thick and many—to weigh him down, and to oppress him. During the early part of the disagreeable business in which he had been engaged, he had thought solely of his own innocence, and of the absurdity, as it seemed to him, of the charge against him; but as the matter went on, other considerations forced themselves upon his attention. He was conscious he could give no account of where he had been on the preceding night, when the murder was committed; and yet he felt that he was called upon strongly to do so, not for the purpose of freeing himself from suspicion, but with a view to bring the real murderer to justice. Yet how could he reveal any part of what he knew, without bringing down destruction on the head of Franklin Gray, who had no share in the deed; who, at the very time it was committed, was engaged in serving him, even at the risk of life; to whom he was bound by so many ties of gratitude, and whose good qualities, though they did certainly not serve to counterbalance his crimes, yet rendered him a very different object in the eyes of Langford from such men as Wiley and Hardcastle? At all events, he felt that it was not for him to bring a man to the scaffold who had saved his life on more than one occasion, and who had shown himself always willing to peril his own in order to procure a comparatively trifling benefit to him.

Mingled with all these feelings, was deep and bitter sorrow for Lord Harold; and thus many conflicting emotions, all more or less painful, together with the most painful of all, the knowledge that he could not do his duty with that straightforward candour and decision which in all other situations of life he had been accustomed to show, kept him in stern and somewhat gloomy silence.

The magistrates, in the meanwhile, conversed apart in a low voice, Sir Thomas Waller delighted with the plan they were about to pursue, and anticipating great credit with Lord Danemore for the arrest of his son's murderer; while Sir Matthew Scrope, who seemed to stand in considerable awe of the old nobleman, declared, that he never half liked to come across the Earl, who was so fierce, and fiery, and imperious. In about a quarter of an hour the clerk returned, and announced that all was ready, and Langford, surrounded by a complete mob of constables, was placed in the rumbling carriage of Sir Thomas Waller, and borne away towards Danemore Castle.

The two magistrates followed in the carriage of Sir Matthew, and the train of constables, mounted on all sorts of beasts, came after swelling the procession; while good Gregory Myrtle stood at his door declaring, that he never saw such a piece of folly in his life: and the poor chambermaid, dissolved in tears, wiped her eyes and vowed it was impossible so handsome a young man could murder any body.

CHAPTER XI.

AFTER a slow progress of between two or three hours, along roads, which in those days frequently tossed the heavy carriage wheels high in air over some large unbroken stone, and still more frequently suffered them to repose in deep beds of sand or mud, till the efforts of four strong Flanders horses had dragged them forth—the vehicle which contained Henry Langford gained the brow of Danemore Hill, and came within sight of the building, which in that part of the country was known under the name of the Castle.

This view was obtained from the side of the park which lay in front, and which was separated from the road merely by a low park paling crowned with open palisading at the top. A part of the park itself lay between the mansion and the road, which were at the distance of about three quarters of a mile from each other, the ground sloping with a thousand fanciful undulations, and covered with short turf of a rich bright green in all the dells and hollows, though becoming slightly brown upon the tops of the knolls, where the fierce summer sun, like the withering glare of the great world, had already taken off the freshness of the vegetation.

Scattered here and there were groups of old hawthorns, contorted into many a strange and rugged form; while on either hand appeared clumps of fine old trees, the chestnut, the beech, and the oak. The latter were seen gradually deepening and clustering together to the right and left of the house till they joined a thick wood, through which every here and there stood forth, dark and defined amidst the tender green of the other plants, the sombre masses of the pine and fir; like some of those stern memories of sorrow, of sin, or of privation, which are to be found in almost every human heart, and which still make themselves known in gloomy distinctness, amidst the freshest scenes and brightest occupations of life.

In the midst, backed by that thick wood, stood the house, or Castle, as it was called, and the name was not ill deserved. It was an irregular pile of building, erected in different ages by its different lords, and showing the taste of the various individuals who had possessed it, as well as of the various ages in which it had been constructed. On the left was an old unornamented tower, in the simplest style of the old Norman architecture. It was like one of the plain towers of some of the Kentish churches, with square cut windows, or rather loop-holes, under a semicircular arch, which denoted the original form. It was crowned by a plain parapet with a high conical roof.

Then came a long range of buildings in a much later style of architecture, with oriel windows, and a good deal of rich stone carving and ornamental work; then two massive towers, projecting considerably before the rest of the façade, and joined to it by two corridors, through each of which was pierced a gateway, under a pointed arch; and then again, as the building sunk into the wood, upon the right, were more towers and masses of heavy masonry, united in general by long lines of building of a lighter and more graceful character. On the older parts the ivy had been suffered to grow, though not very luxuriantly. The space in front, too, was kept clear of trees; and even as the carriage passed along, at the distance of nearly a mile, the wide esplanade on which the Castle stood, with a part of the barbican, which had been suffered to remain, was distinctly visible.

The constables who sat with Langford in the carriage of Sir Thomas Waller, gazed up, with feelings of awe and reverence, towards an edifice, which the people of the country but seldom approached. The eyes of Langford, too, were fixed upon it, but with sensations which they little understood. All that they remarked was, that he kept his eyes fixed upon the Castle steadfastly during the whole time that it was visible as they passed along in front; that he looked at it calmly, though gravely; and that, when he had done, he raised his head as if waking from a reverie, and then suddenly turned and gazed from the other window, where a wide and beautiful view was seen, spread out below, reaching to the old Manor House, and the wooded banks and hills beyond.

The carriage then rolled on, and, winding round under the park, entered by a castellated lodge, and drove slowly up to the mansion, the vehicles passing under the arches of the two large towers, which projected from the centre of the building. A loud-tongued bell gave notice of their coming, and three or four servants, fat, pampered, and saucy, made their appearance to answer its noisy summons.

Sir Thomas Waller was the first to speak, and, with an air of importance, he demanded immediately to see the Earl. One servant looked at another, and he, who seemed to be the chief porter, replied shortly that that was impossible, for the Earl had gone out.

"Gone out!" cried Sir Thomas, in surprise. "How? where?"

"He is gone out on horseback," replied the man, "that is how, sir; and as to where, I fancy he is gone to the moor, where my young lord was killed."

"But we must, at least we ought, to see my lord the Earl," said Sir Matthew Scrope, "for we have brought up a prisoner for him to examine."

"I can't say anything about that," replied the man, with a sort of sullen incivility; "my lord is out, but I will go and ask Mistress Bertha, if you like."

"I do not know what Mistress Bertha can do in the matter," said Sir Thomas Waller.

"Oh! she can do anything she likes," replied the man with a sneer, to which he did not dare to give full expression.

"Well, ask her—ask her, then," said Sir Matthew; "you know who I am; you know I was with the Earl three or four hours this morning. You know I am a justice of the peace, and one of the quorum."

Sir Matthew did not seem by this announcement to raise his dignity greatly in the eyes of the servant, who walked away, with slow and measured steps, to make the proposed application. He returned in about five minutes, saying, that Mistress Bertha's reply was, that, as it might be a long time before the Earl returned, the magistrates had better leave the prisoner locked up there, and come back in the evening about the hour of his lordship's supper.

Sir Matthew Scrope and Sir Thomas Waller looked at each other.

There were some points in this suggestion which they did not much like; but then, again, the magical words, "His lordship's supper," which were coupled in their imagination with fine and exquisite wines from foreign lands, fat haunches, rich sauces, and many another delicacy and luxury, which rumour declared to be prevalent in Danemore Castle, rapidly removed all objections from their minds; and after a few minutes' consultation they determined to obey to the letter.

The next object of consideration was, how to secure their prisoner, and in what room to place him; but their conference on that point was soon cut short by the porter, who interrupted them by saying, "You had better leave all that to Mistress Bertha; for, depend upon it she will put him where she likes herself, and most likely has settled it already. The best way will be to bring him in, and go to her. She is in the long gallery."

Although the two magistrates did not at all approve of the whole business being taken out of their hands by a woman, they nevertheless yielded with some symptoms of displeasure; and Langford, being made to descend from the carriage, was escorted by the two constables through a long dim entrance passage, which led into a handsome vestibule beyond. He offered no resistance to their will; he made no observation; he asked no question; but with a calm and thoughtful dignity, which had its effect even upon the pampered servants of the castle, he walked on, looking casually at the different objects he passed, as if almost indifferent to the part he was himself acting in the scene.

From the vestibule a handsome flight of stone stairs, lighted by a tall painted window, led up to a gallery extending on either side for about seventy yards; and up these stairs Langford was led, following the two magistrates, who went on with slow steps, preparing to give Mistress Bertha, the housekeeper, a just notion of their dignity and importance. At the top of the stairs they were met by that personage herself, dressed as we have before described her, except that her broad white coif was no longer surmounted by the black veil with which she covered her head when she went abroad. Her thin aquiline features might have gained an additional degree of sharpness; her sallow skin was, if anything, more sallow; and the cold severe expression, which always reigned in her countenance, was now increased to a degree of stern bitterness which somewhat humbled the tone of the two magistrates.

They approached her, however, with a very tolerable degree of pomposity; and Sir Thomas Waller introduced himself and then presented Sir Matthew Scrope, announcing to her that they were magistrates of the county, and two of the quorum. As he spoke, the attention of the housekeeper wandered beyond the two worshipful gentlemen altogether, and was attracted to the prisoner, who followed them. There was something in his good looks, his calm and dignified demeanour, his apparel, or his expression of countenance, which made the thin eyelids of Mistress Bertha's eyes expand from the bright dark orbs they covered at the first moment they lighted on him, and she demanded, "Is that the prisoner?"

Sir Thomas Waller replied that it was; and then recapitulated what he had been saying in regard to the dignity of himself and Sir Matthew Scrope.

"Yes, yes," replied Mistress Bertha, with her slight foreign accent, "I know who you are, both of you; and now you have nothing to do but to leave the prisoner here till the Earl comes home. You can return at his supper hour. I do not know that he will eat with you himself, but if he do not, meat shall be provided for you."

"There can be no reason, madam," said Sir Matthew Scrope, "why the Earl should not sup with us; we have supped with men of as high rank, I trow."

"When a man has lost his only son," said the housekeeper, sharply, "is that no reason why he should not sup with two fat country knights, to whom his sorrow and his presence would only bring gloom and stiffness? Better sup by yourselves, and eat, and drink, and make merry, as you are accustomed to do."

"Gadzooks!" said Sir Thomas Waller, in a low voice to his companion, "I think the old lady is right; but madam," he added in a louder tone, "we must be made sure of the safety of our prisoner."

"Leave that to me, leave that to me," replied the housekeeper, shortly. "Follow me, Williams and Hanbury, to guard the prisoner; and you, John Porter, come on too. Come with me, young gentleman," she added, speaking to Langford in a more benign tone. "You do not look as if you would commit a murder; but, God knows, looks are deceitful things. Come with me."

"But, madam, we have no authority," interrupted Sir Matthew Scrope.

"Authority!" exclaimed the housekeeper, fiercely raising up her tall thin person to its utmost height, "who talks of authority in this house? You may well say you have no authority, for you lost it all the moment you crossed that threshold. No one has authority here but the Earl; and, when he is absent, myself—now that that poor boy is gone," she added, while a bright drop rose into her eyes, sparkled upon the black lashes that fringed them, and then fell upon the sallow skin beneath. "I trust in God you did not kill him, young gentleman; for if you did, you committed a great crime."

"Indeed I did not, madam," replied Langford; "I should sooner have thought of killing myself."

"I believe you, I believe you," replied the housekeeper; "but yet I must have you as safely guarded as if you had. If you want to see where I put him," she continued, speaking to the magistrates in a somewhat gentler tone than she had hitherto used, "you may come with me: there is a room which no one even enters but my lord and myself: it is high up in the oldest tower; and even if he could get through the windows—which he cannot—there is a fall of sixty feet below, clear down. But come and see it if you will, and you shall have some refreshment after."

Carrying a large key which she had held in her hand from the beginning of the conversation, she led the way to the end of the gallery in which they stood. Then, passing through another handsome corridor, she ascended a staircase in the older part of the building, which brought them to an ante-room, opening into a large bed-chamber, with windows on each side; whilst through the western window, and close to it, might be seen projecting the heavy mass of the large square tower that we have mentioned in describing the building. A small low door was exactly opposite to them as they entered, and to the lock of this Mistress Bertha applied the key. It turned heavily, and with difficulty, as if not often used; and the door moving back, gave entrance into a lofty and cheerful chamber, lighted by four small windows.

The strength of the door and the height of the windows showed at once that escape from that chamber was impossible; and the magistrates, holding in remembrance the refreshments which their somewhat ungracious companion had promised them, expressed themselves perfectly satisfied with the security of their prisoner. Langford was accordingly desired to enter the place of his confinement, and did so at once, merely turning to address the housekeeper as he passed. "Madam," he said, "I am sure you will be good enough to give my compliments to Lord Danemore whenever he returns, and to inform him, first that I assert my perfect innocence of the charge which these two worthy persons have somewhat too hastily brought against me; and, secondly, that I beg he will take the most prompt and immediate means for investigating the whole affair, as it will be unpleasant for me to submit to this treatment long; and there are plenty of persons in the neighbourhood who will see that justice is done me."

The housekeeper made no other reply than bowing her head; but when Langford had entered, and she had shut and locked the door, she turned sharply and contemptuously upon the magistrates, saying, "He did not do it! he never did it! you will make yourselves a laughing-stock in the country."

Sir Thomas Waller was about to reply, but she silenced him at once by ordering one of the servants who followed her to have the cold meats laid out in the little hall, and find the butler for a stoup of Burgundy. A proposal made by Sir Matthew Scrope to leave two of the constables behind in the ante-room, she cut short, less pleasantly, telling him that she would have no constables in her master's house except such as were intended to be thrown out of the window.

By this time both magistrates began to find out that it was to no purpose to contest matters in Danemore Castle with this imperious dame; and they accordingly followed her in silence back to the head of the great stairs. There she made them over to the care of one of the men servants, who in turn led them to the lesser hall, where a collation was set before them, which well repaid them for all their patient endurance.

In the meanwhile, Langford had remained in the solitary chamber which had been assigned to him. As soon as the door was closed, he took nine or ten turns up and down the room, in a state of much agitation, then gazed out for a moment from each of the windows by which it was lighted, and then sat down at the table, and placed his hands for several minutes before his eyes. It is not needful to enter into any detailed account of his feelings; his situation was particularly painful in every respect; and though he was not one of those who give way to each transient emotion, something might well be allowed for discomfort, anxiety, and indignation. When he had thus paused for a few minutes, thinking over his fate, he lifted his eyes and gazed round the chamber which served as his place of confinement, seeming to take accurate note of all it contained.

The room itself was a cheerful and a pleasant room, with a vaulted ceiling richly ornamented; while the thick walls of the tower were lined with oak, very deep in hue, and finely carved with Gothic tracery. The form of the chamber was perfectly square, and its extent might be four-and-twenty feet each way. The furniture, too, was good though ancient, and of the same carved oak as the panelling. It consisted of a large table, and a smaller one, eight or nine large high-backed chairs, and several curious carved cabinets. But the objects which most attracted the attention of Langford were two small panels, distinct from the rest of the wainscotting, and ornamented in such a way as to show that they were not all intended to be concealed, with a small pointed ogee canopy above each, similar to that which surmounted the door by which he had entered, but only smaller in size. In each of these panels was a key-hole surrounded by an intricate steel guard; and it was evident that each covered the entrance of one of those cupboards in the wall, in which our remote ancestors took so much delight.

Besides the door by which he had entered, there was a smaller one on the opposite side of the room, leading, as Langford conceived, to a staircase in one of the large buttresses; and as he had been a prisoner before, and had found it useful to know all the outlets of his temporary abode, his first action, after gazing round the room, was to approach that second door and try whether it was or was not locked. It was firmly closed, however; and he took his way back towards his seat, pausing by the way to examine the two small closets, and murmuring to himself, as he did so, "This is very strange!"

As he spoke, he drew forth from his breast the key which had been given him on the preceding night by Franklin Gray, and put it in the lock, but did not turn it, though it fitted exactly. He withdrew it again almost instantly, and replaced it in his bosom, then folded his arms upon his chest, and took one or two turns up and down the room, pausing at every second step, and gazing thoughtfully upon the floor.

By the time he had been half-an-hour in this state of confinement, he heard a key placed in the lock of the door by which he had entered. In another moment it opened, and the tall, stately figure of Mistress Bertha appeared. In one hand she carried several books, and in the other some writing paper, with a small inkhorn suspended on her finger. She shut the door after her, but did not attempt to lock it; and then laying down the books and implements for writing on the table, she turned round and gazed fixedly in Langford's face.

"Have we ever met before?" she said at length. "Your face is familiar to me. It comes back like something seen in a dream. Have we ever met before?"

"If we have," replied Langford, "it must have been many years ago, when the face of the child was very different from the face of the man."

She still gazed at him, and after a considerable pause said, "I have brought you some books that you may read, and wherewithal to write if you like it. In return for this write me down your name."

Langford smiled, and, taking up the pen, wrote down his name in a bold free hand. The woman gazed at him as he did so, then carried her eye rapidly to the writing. A bright and intelligent smile shone for a moment upon her thin pale lip; and she said, "Enough! enough!

that is quite enough. You have been taught to believe that I have wronged you more than I really have; and although I have given you much good counsel and much true information, you have doubted and have not fully trusted me. I tell you now, and I tell you truly, that I have not wronged you, at least as far as my knowledge of right and wrong goes, and therefore I am still willing to do all that I can to serve you. The history of the past I may tell you at some future time, and I will show you that I wronged others less than they thought I did. But there is one whom I will not name, who has wronged you and yours deeply; and I know his nature—I know human nature too well not to be sure that implacable hatred and constant persecution is the offspring of such acts, rather than sorrow, remorse, and atonement. It was on that account that I bade you never come here. It was on that account that I bade you fly his presence. Fate, however, has brought you here at a moment when the mortal agony at losing the only creature he really loved may yet tame his fierce heart and bend his iron will. I can do but little for you, for I am bound by an oath—an oath which has bound me for many years; but fate, which has brought you here, and has wrought an extraordinary thing in your behalf, may yet do much. I will leave it to its course. But with regard to your own conduct, beware! I warn you to beware. Choose well your moment, and of all things be not hasty. But hark, what is that I hear below? There are his horses' feet, and I must leave you. Thank God, those idiot justices are gone."

"Yet one moment," said Langford, as she turned to depart: "I may have thought that you wronged me and mine, but I have not doubted—I have not suspected you, as you suppose. On the contrary, in many things, as you may have seen, I have followed your advice—in others, that of one whom I was more strictly bound to confide in."

"Ay, and it was she who taught you to believe—it was she who was weak enough to believe herself, that I had been guilty of that which I would scorn."

"No!" exclaimed Langford—"No! You mistake: she never did believe you guilty. She owned, that once, in a moment of anger, she implied so; but she did you justice in that respect through the whole of her life. She told me more than once, too, that she had herself seen you, and assured you, that she did not doubt you, as you imagined—that anger, having passed away, justice and right judgment had returned."

"But all her words were cold," said Bertha, "and all her letters had something of restraint in them."

"Consider her situation," said Langford in return; "and remember that she had some cause to blame, as yourself acknowledged; though, in regard to other things, she might have done you injustice."

"She did bitter injustice to herself," replied the woman, "and drove me to attach myself to others, though I would fain have attached myself to her; and, having done so, would have served her with my heart's blood;—but I must not linger; I will see you again, ere long—farewell!" and thus saying, she left him, locking the door behind her.

CHAPTER XII.

Langford had not been left five minutes alone ere the sound of voices of persons rapidly approaching caught his ear. At first he imagined that they proceeded from the side by which he himself had entered; but the moment after he became convinced that they came from the direction of the other door, which, as he justly supposed, communicated with a staircase in one of the large buttresses. At first, of course, the sounds were indistinct, but, a moment after, a key was placed in the lock, and a loud, deep voice was heard exclaiming, "I will stop for nothing till I have seen him face to face! Where is this murderer of my son?"

The door was thrown violently open before these words were fully spoken, and the Earl of Danemore himself stood before the prisoner.

He was a tall, handsome, powerful man, wide-chested, broad-shouldered, and still very muscular, without being at all corpulent. He might be sixty-three or sixty-four years of age, and his hair was snowy white. His eyebrows, however, and his eye-lashes, both of which were long and full, were as black as night. There was many a long, deep furrow on his brow, and a sort of scornful, but habitual wrinkle between the nostril of the strong aquiline nose and the corner of his mouth. On his right cheek appeared a deep scar, round, and of about the size of a pistol-ball; and on the chin, was a longer scar, cutting nearly from the lip down into the throat and neck. He was dressed in a suit of plain black velvet, with the large riding boots and heavy sword, which were common about fifteen or sixteen years before the period of which we now speak, but which were beginning by this time to go out of fashion.

On entering the room, his teeth were hard set together, his brow contracted till the large thick eyebrows almost met, and his whole air fierce and agitated. His quick eyes darted round the room in a moment, and alighted upon Langford, who turned and faced him at once.

The moment, however, that their looks met, a strange and sudden change came over the whole appearance of Lord Danemore. He paused abruptly, and stood still in the middle of the room, gazing in Langford's face, while the frown departed from his brow, and he raised his hand towards his head, passing it twice before his eyes, as if he fancied that some delusion had affected his sight. His lips opened as if he would have spoken, but for a moment or two no sounds issued forth; and the calm, quiet, steady gaze with which Langford regarded him seemed to trouble and agitate him.

"What is your name? what is your name?" he exclaimed rapidly, when he could speak. "Who brought you here?"

"My name is Henry Langford," replied the prisoner—"an officer, in the service of his majesty; and if you seriously ask, my lord—for I suppose, I have the honour of speaking to the Earl of Danemore—if you seriously ask who brought me hither, I have only to reply two very silly persons calling themselves magistrates, who have entertained or rather manufactured, amongst themselves a charge against me for which there is not the slightest foundation."

"Henry Langford! Henry Langford!" repeated the Earl, casting his eyes on the ground, and then raising them again to Langford's face, every line and feature of which he seemed to scan with anxious care. "Pray of what family are you?"

"My father," replied Langford, "was a gentleman of some property in England, of which property, however, I have been unjustly deprived;" and as he spoke, he fixed his eyes steadfastly upon the Earl; but that nobleman's countenance underwent no change, and he proceeded— "My mother was also a lady of some property——"

"Where were you born?" demanded the Earl, quickly.

"Though your questions are rather unceremonious, my lord, for a perfect stranger," Langford replied, "I will not scruple to answer them. I was born in a small town in this country."

"Not in France?" demanded the Earl, quickly. "I do not ask without a motive—not in France? Are you certain it was not in France?"

"Perfectly certain," replied Langford. "My mother's family, however, were French—related to the illustrious family of Beaulieu."

"So," said the Earl, "so! How nearly are you related to that family?—are you sure not in France?"

"Quite certain," replied Langford. "I have lived much in France, which may have given me some slight foreign accent; and as to my relationship to the Beaulieus, I can really hardly tell how near. I have only heard my mother say that she was nearly related to them."

"It cannot be! It cannot be!" said the Earl, drooping his head, and looking down upon the ground. "Is your mother living?"

A cloud came over Langford's brow: "She is not," he said.

The Earl again seemed interested. "How long has she been dead?" he asked.

"About two years," Langford replied, and thereupon the Earl once more shook his head, saying, "It cannot be. You are very like the late Marquis of Beaulieu," he added—"extremely like; and though circumstances have compelled me to discontinue my acquaintance with that family, I knew the Marquis once, and loved him well. I could have almost fancied that you were his son, and for his sake I cannot regard you with any other eyes than those of kindness. But yet what do I say?" he continued, while his brow again grew dark. "They tell me you have murdered my son, my only son. How strange, if the son of the man who had so nearly killed the father, should, five-and-twenty years after, have slain the son!"

"You forget, my lord, and you mistake altogether," replied Langford. "In the first place, I am not the son of the Marquis of Beaulieu; and, in the next place, I assure you most solemnly by all I hold dear—I pledge you my honour as a gentleman and a soldier, and my oath as a Christian and a man—that I have had no more share in this unfortunate event than you have."

"I would willingly believe you," answered the Earl, "most willingly, for yours is a countenance from which I have been accustomed to expect nothing but truth and honour. Yet why do these men accuse you? Why, if there be not proof as strong as truth itself why do they dare to bring an accusation against one of your high house? Oh, young man! young man! if you have slain him by fraud or villany, I will take vengeance of you by making you the public spectacle, and giving you up to the rope and scaffold: chains shall hang about you even in your death, and your bones shall whiten in the wind. But, if you have slain him foot to foot and hand to hand, you shall meet a father's vengeance in another way. Ay! old as I am, I will take your heart's blood, and you shall find that this arm has lost nothing of its skill and but little of its strength. You shall learn what a father's arm can do when heavy with the sword of the avenger!"

"Once more, my lord," replied Langford, calmly, "I assure you that I am perfectly innocent. I assure you that, neither fairly and openly. nor covertly and treacherously, have I had aught to do with your son's death. The sole ground for suspicion against me has been what I will not conceal from you, my lord, that, upon a slight quarrel between us, he drew his sword upon me, in the park of Sir Walter Herbert."

"Ay, Sir Walter Herbert!" exclaimed the peer, with a bitter sneer; "the pitiful old fool! He and his fair dainty daughter, Mistress Alice, they would none of my son, would they not? He shall pay for it in prison, and she shall see him rot before her eyes. Ay, now I guess how it all is. She has found a lover in fair Master Henry Langford, has she? and he has murdered a rival who might have proved troublesome. They shall answer for it, they shall answer for it! Ho! below there!" he continued, approaching the door. "Bring me up the papers which those two knights left!"

Langford suffered him to proceed with the wild and rapid starts to which the vehemence of his passions led him; but when he paused, the prisoner took up the conversation, saying, "I was about to tell you, my lord, that your son did seek a quarrel with me; did draw his sword upon me; did try to induce me to follow his example, but in vain."

"What!" interrupted the peer, "did you refuse to fight him? How was that? a soldier, and a man of your race?"

"I did refuse to fight him, my lord," replied Langford, "for particular reasons of my own. I have had many opportunities of showing that fear forms no part of my nature, and I am not at all apprehensive of ever being mistaken for a coward."

He spoke with a calm and easy dignity, slightly throwing back his head, while the fine formed nostril expanded with a sense of honourable pride. The Earl gazed upon him attentively, the angry fire that had been in his eyes gradually subsiding as he did so, and he repeated more than once, in a low voice, "So like! So strangely like!"

At that moment, with the rapidity of one accustomed to obey the orders of a quick and imperious master, a servant appeared bringing in the bundle of papers which contained the evidence collected against Langford at Moorhurst. The Earl cast himself into a chair, spread the papers out upon the table, and ran his eye rapidly over them, one after another. Langford had also seated himself, and watched the proceedings of the Earl attentively, though neither of them spoke for some minutes.

When the Earl had done, he looked up in the prisoner's face, and, after pausing with a thoughtful air for several moments, he said, "This is a case of suspicion against you, but nothing more. I, myself, the person most interested, cannot make more of it; and from what I see of you, from your face and from your family, I will add that I do not believe you guilty."

"My lord, you do me justice," replied Langford, "and it makes me right glad to see you so inclined. There was an old custom which was not without its value, for human nature cannot be wholly mastered even by the most consummate art; and I am now willing to recur to that old custom, to give you further proof that you judge rightly of me. Let me be taken to the room where your poor son lies. I will place my hand upon his heart, and swear to my innocence. I do not suppose, my lord, that the blood would flow again, if I were culpable; but I do believe, that no man conscious of such a crime as murder, could perform that act without betraying by his countenance the guilty secret within him. I am ready to perform it before any persons that you choose to appoint."

"Are you not aware," demanded the Earl, sternly, "that the body has not been found?"

"Good God!" exclaimed Langford, his whole face brightening in a moment, "then, perhaps he is living yet. This is the most extraordinary tale that ever yet was told—a man arrested—accused—well nigh condemned for the murder of another who is probably alive. A thousand to one he is still alive! Oh, my lord be comforted, be comforted!"

"You deceive yourself, young man," replied the Earl, with a melancholy shake of the head, "you deceive yourself. His death is but too clearly proved. His white horse returned last night alone, with his own neck and the saddle stained with blood. The road by Upwater Mere was found drenched with gore—with my child's gore! and his cloak was found amongst the beeches hard by, pierced on the left side with a pistol shot, which must have been fired close to his bosom, for the wadding had burnt the silk. It, too, was stiff with blood. There were traces of several horses' feet about, but no trace of where the body had been carried, though I myself—I, his father—have spent several hours in seeking the slightest vestige that might direct me. Doubtless it is thrown into the mere," and as he spoke he covered his eyes with his hands, and remained for several minutes evidently overpowered with deep emotion, against which he struggled strongly but in vain.

Langford, too, was moved, and after having waited in silence for several minutes, in the hope that the agitation which his companion suffered would pass away, he ventured to address some words of comfort to Lord Danemore; saying "I am deeply grieved, my lord, that you have such cause for apprehension, but still I cannot help hoping that all these causes for believing the worst may prove fallacious, and that your son may yet be restored to you."

"No, no, sir, no!" replied the Earl, "I will not deceive myself, nor do I wish to be deceived. Such evidence is too clear. I am not a child or a woman, that I cannot bear any lot assigned to me. I can look my fate in the face, however dark and frowning its brow may be, and say to it, 'Thou hast but power to a certain degree, over my mind thou canst not triumph, and even whilst thou wringest my heart and leavest my old age desolate, I can defy thee still!'"

Langford bent down his eyes upon the ground, and did not reply for several minutes. He did not approve the spirit in which those words were spoken, but yet it was not his task to rebuke or to admonish, and when he did reply, he again sought to instil hope.

"Your lordship says," he observed at length, "that the evidence is too clear. It is certainly clear enough to justify great and serious apprehensions, but not to take away hope, or to impede exertion. I remember having heard of an instance which occurred in far distant climates, where the causes for supposing a person dead were much more conclusive than in the present instance. A sailor had left the ship to which he belonged, and wandered on shore in a place infested with pirates. He did not return. Boats were sent after him, and in tracing the course of one of the rivers up which he was supposed to have taken his way, his clothes were found bloody, torn, and cut with the blows of a sword: a leathern purse, which he was known to have carried full of money, was found further on, devoid of its contents; and further still, a mangled and mutilated body, in which almost all his comrades declared they recognised his corpse; and yet, three years after that, he rejoined the ship to which he belonged, having made his escape from the party of robbers by whom he had been taken. The body which had been found was that of another man, though the clothes and the purse undoubtedly were his own."

While he spoke, the Earl turned deadly pale, gazed upon him for a moment or two with a straining eye, then suddenly started up, and without a word of reply quitted the room.

Langford at first seemed surprised, but smiled slightly as he saw him go: then calmly sat down at the table, took up the papers which the Earl had left behind him, read over the evidence against himself, and wrote in the margin a number of observations, wherever any strained or unjust conclusion seemed to have been drawn by the magistrates. He had been occupied in this manner about an hour, when the Earl again made his appearance. His manner was very different from what it had been on the previous occasion. There was a want of that fierce energy which had before characterised it; there was a doubtfulness, a hesitation, and a vagueness, quite opposed to the keen, sharp decision of his former demeanour. He treated Langford more as an acquaintance, more even as a friend, than as a prisoner. Two or three times he spoke of the chances of his son being still alive, and referred vaguely to the story which Langford had told him, but then darted off suddenly to something else.

At length, however, he took up the papers on which the other had commented, and, without noticing the observations that he had written, said it was unjust, upon a case where there was nothing made out against him but suspicion, that he should be detained as a close prisoner. "If, therefore," he said, "you will give me your word not to attempt to make your escape, the doors shall be thrown open to you; this chamber and the next shall be your abode for the time, though they should have put you somewhere else, for this room is appropriated to me. Here," he continued, in a thoughtful and abstracted tone, "when I wish to think over all the crowded acts of a long, eventful, and constantly changing life, I come and sit, where no sound interrupts me but the twittering of the swallow, as it skims past my windows. Here I can people the air with the things, and beings, and deeds of the past, without the empty crowd of the insignificant living breaking in upon my solitude, and sweeping away the thinner but more thrilling creations called up by memory. I know not how it is, young gentleman, that there is scarcely any one but you whom I could have borne patiently to see in this chamber; but your countenance seems connected with those days to which this room is dedicated. There is a resemblance, a strong and touching resemblance, to several persons long dead; and that likeness calls up again to my mind many a vision of my youthful days—days, between which and the dark present, lies a gulf of fiery passions, sorrows, and regrets. I know not wherefore they put you here, or who dared to do it, but it is strange that, being here, you seem to my eyes the only fit tenant of this chamber except myself. Here I sit and read the letters of dead friends—here I sit and ponder over the affections and the hatreds, the hopes, the fears, the wrath, the enjoyment, the sorrow, the remorse of the past; here often do I sit and gaze upon the pictures of those I loved in former times—of the dead, and the changed, and the alienated; of persons who, when those pictures were painted, never thought that there could come a change upon them, or upon me, either in the bodily or the mental frame; never dreamed of the mattock, and the grave, and the coffin, and the slow curling worm that has long since revelled in their hearts; no, nor of fierce and fiery contention, envy, jealousy, rivalry, hatred, the death of bright affection, and the burial of every warm and once living hope. Here am I still wont to gaze upon their pictures, and I know not how it is, but it seems to me as if your face were amongst them."

"I fear me, my lord," said Langford, "that those endowed with strong feelings and strong passions are most frequently like children with a box of jewels, squandering precious things without knowing their value, and gaining in exchange but gauds and baubles, the paint and tinsel of which is soon brushed off, leaving us nothing but regret. There is no time of life, however, I believe, at which we may not recover some of the jewels which we have cast away, if we but seek for them rightly; and I know no means likely to be more successful than that which you take in tracing back your steps through the past."

"It is a painful contemplation," said Lord Danemore, "and I fear that in the dim twilight of age, let me trace back my steps as closely as I will, I am not likely to find again many of the jewels that I scattered from me in the full daylight of youth."

"Perhaps, my lord," replied Langford, "you might, if you were to take a light. However," he added, seeing a look of impatience coming upon the Earl, "I am much obliged to you for your offer of a partial kind of freedom. I never loved to have a door locked between me and the rest of the world; and I willingly promise you to make no attempt to escape during the whole of this day, for of course my promise must have a limit. In the course of that day, you will most likely be able to procure further information in regard to this sad affair; and I do trust and hope that it may be such as may relieve your bosom from the apprehensions which now oppress you."

"I must exact your promise for two days," said the Earl; "for I have sent to tell those two foolish men who brought you here, that I cannot deal with them to-day, and have bidden them, in consequence of what you have said, though with but little hope, to cause search of every kind to be made through the country round. There are one or two questions, also, which I would fain ask you, but I will not do it now ; yet I know not why I should not; but no, not now ! Have I your promise?"

"You have," replied Langford.

And the Earl, after pausing and hesitating a moment or two longer, quitted him by the chief entrance, leaving the doors open behind him. "There is but one thing I ask of you," added the Earl, as he turned to depart; "should you leave these two rooms, lock the door of the one in which you now are till you return, for I do not suffer the feet of ordinary servants to profane it."

When Langford was alone, he paused for a moment or two to think over his situation; and then, with a natural desire to use the freedom that had been given him, opened the door of the chamber in which he had been placed, and proceeded through the bedroom beyond, to the head of the staircase. Remembering the Earl's request to lock the door, he turned back to do so, and when he again approached the stairs, the voice of some one singing below rose to his ear. The tone in which the singer poured forth his ditty was low, but after listening for a moment, Langford recognised the voice of the poor half-witted man, John Graves, and a sudden hope of finding means of clearing himself by the aid of that very person struck him. He descended the stairs slowly, and at the bottom of the first flight found the wanderer sitting on the lower step, with his head hanging down in an attitude of dejection ; laying his hand upon his shoulder, Langford caused him to start up suddenly and turn round.

"Ah, Master Harry!" cried the man, in one of his saner moods, "is that you? It is you I came to see. I heard they had taken you up, and locked you up here, and I came to see if I could help you, for you have always been kind and generous to me ; and then, if I could not help you, I could sing you a song, and that would do you good, you know ; I always said you ought to have your rights, you know ; but I must not say so here, or they will scold me, as they did before."

"Come up hither with me, John," said Langford; "I believe that you can help me, if you will. But how came you here ? Do they suffer you knowingly to wander about the house in this manner?"

"Not as far as this," replied the man, laughing ; "not as far as this. They would soon drive me down if they saw me above the grand stairs. But about the passages below they never mind me. Only I sometimes creep up, and find my way about all the rooms, and if I hear a step, hide behind a window-curtain. It is no later than last night that I and another—but I must not speak of that. Never you mind, Master Harry, you will have your rights still."

"Perhaps so, John," answered Langford, "though I do not think you well know what my rights are. However, now follow me up here." Thus saying, he led the way to the apartments which had been assigned to him, followed quickly by the madman, whose step was as noiseless and stealthy as if he had been going to murder the sleeping. When he saw Langford approach the door of the inner room, he cast an anxious and furtive glance towards the top of the stairs, and listened, and as soon as the lock was turned and the entrance free, he ran in and closed it after him, looking straight towards one of the small cupboards in the wall, saying, "There! there! Be quick, for fear some one should come!"

Langford gazed on him with some surprise, and then replied, "You know more of these matters than I thought you did. However, you mistake. I want you merely to bear a letter and a message for me."

"But the papers! the papers!" exclaimed the other. "Are you not going to take the papers?"

"No!" exclaimed Langford. "Certainly not by stealth, John."

"Then it is you that are mad," replied his companion; "and they have mistaken me for you. I will go and make affidavit of it."

"I should not hold myself justified in taking them stealthily," replied Langford. "Perhaps ere I quit this house I may claim them boldly; and some time or another I must make you tell me how you know so much of matters I thought secret; but time is wanting now, and we may be interrupted. I have some reason to think that, if you will, you can find out for me a person called Franklin Gray."

"Can I find him out?" said the madman. "Ay, that I can; in two hours I can be with him."

"Will you bear a message from me to him?" demanded Langford, "without forgetting a word of it, and without telling a word to any one else?"

"That I will joyfully," replied the other; "I never forget—I wish I could—it is that turns me mad—I remember too well; and I will tell nothing though they should put me to the torture. I always tell truth if I tell anything; but I can hold my tongue."

"Well then," said Langford, "tell Franklin Gray for me, that I am kept a prisoner here on a charge of shooting poor Lord Harold. If he be shot, I entertain but few doubts in regard to who it was that did it; and I ask Franklin Gray, in honour and in memory of our old companionship, to give me the means of clearing and delivering myself."

"Franklin Gray shot him not." replied the madman; "that I know full well. Franklin and I are friends; don't you know that, Master Harry? For a fox, he is the best of foxes! But I'll do as you tell me, however."

"I know he did not shoot him," answered Langford: "I am as sure of that as you are. Nevertheless, carry him my message. But hold," he said, seeing the man turning abruptly to depart, "I will write a few lines to good Sir Walter Herbert, which I shall be glad if you will give into his hands, or into the hands of his daughter."

The half-witted man signified his willingness to do anything that Langford told him; and sitting down at the table, that gentleman wrote a few lines to Sir Walter Herbert, briefly explaining to him his situation, and begging him, in case of his being detained beyond the close of the subsequent day, to take measures to ensure that justice was done him. This epistle he had no means of sealing, and merely folding it up in the form of a letter, he put it into the hands of his hair-brained messenger, and suffered him to depart.

CHAPTER XIII.

THE man who, as we have said, received in that part of the country the name of Silly John, stole quietly down the stairs, and finding nobody to impede his proceedings, had no sooner entered the corridor below than he was seized with a determination of descending to great staircase, thinking, as he expressed it in his commune with himself, that it would make him feel like a lord for once in his life.

We all see and know that every step which we take in our onward path through existence, whether directed by reason or prompted by caprice, whether apparently of the most trifling nature or seemingly of the utmost consequence, not only affects ourselves and the course of our own fate, but more or less influences the state, the fortunes, and the future of others, even to the most remote bounds of that vast space in which cause and effect are constantly weaving the widespread web of events. So philosophers teach us; and such was certainly the case in the present instance; for the whim which led Silly John down the grand staircase of Danemore Castle, was by no means without its effect upon Henry Langford; and might, under many circumstances, have produced consequences of very great importance. The whole house was silent, for the servants of all classes and denominations were busy at their afternoon meal; and the half-witted man, after looking round to see that no one was near, put on an air of mock dignity, stuck the cock's feather more smartly in his hat, threw out one leg and then the other with a wide stride, and saying to himself in a low tone, "Now I'm a lord!" began to descend the staircase. At that moment his eye fell upon a sword, with its belt and sword-knot, hanging up in the corridor, and in order to make his figure complete, he turned back and decorated his person therewith.

When he had got to the bottom of the stairs, however, he looked at the sword with a somewhat wistful eye, as if he would fain have retained it to ornament his person; but then muttering to himself, "No, no, I must not steal! Remember the eighth commandment, John Graves!" he unslung the sword, and looked it all over. When he had done, he burst into a laugh, exclaiming, "It is Master Harry's sword; the very sword with which he slit that fox's neck when they attacked Mistress Alice. They have taken it away from him, but I'll take it back again; and so saying he ran hastily up to the door of the chamber in which he had left Langford, and after tapping loudly with his knuckles, laid the weapon down upon the threshold, and tripped rapidly away.

While Langford opened the door, and with some surprise took up his own sword, of which he had been deprived by the magistrates when he had been brought to the Castle, Silly John made the best of his way down the stairs, out of the front gates, across the esplanade, and into the park. The feat that he had performed seemed to have given him a sort of impetus which he could not resist; and he ran on across the park as fast as his lameness would let him, scrambled over the park paling, and never stopped till he had arrived at that point of the road where it branched into two divisions. There, however, he paused, and entered into one of those consultations with himself which were not unfrequent with him, and which formed a peculiar feature in his madness.

He suddenly remembered that he had two commissions to perform, and that he had no directions as to which was to be first executed. On all such occasions of difficulty, Silly John argued with himself on both sides of the question with the nicety of a special pleader, weighing every motive on either part, starting difficulties and solving them, seeing differences and shades of difference where none existed; and, in fact, acting the part of Hudibras and Ralpho both in one.

On the present occasion he stood discussing the question of whether he should first deliver the letter to Sir Walter Herbert, or the message to Franklin Gray, for nearly an hour; and was seen by many persons who passed, laying down to himself the reasons, *pro* and *con*, with the forefinger of his right hand tapping the forefinger of his left, at every new argument on either side. As he found it utterly impossible to settle the matter by dint of reasoning, he fell at length upon an expedient which decided it as rationally as any other means he could have brought to bear upon it. Fixing himself firmly upon the heel of his uninjured foot, he extended the other leg and arm, and whirled himself round as if on a pivot, determining to follow that road to which his face was turned when he stopped.

It happened that the direction in which he at length found his face was towards the Manor House; and he accordingly bent his steps thither with all speed. The quantity of time which he had lost in his consultation with himself, however, and that occupied in going, rendered it very late in the day before he arrived; so that, although the servant to whom he delivered the note asked him in a kindly tone to come in and take some beer, he looked wistfully at the sky, from which the sun had just gone down; and shaking his head, walked away, turning his steps towards the moor. The distance, as we have before shown, was considerable; and as he went, the long twilight of a summer's evening grew dimmer and more dim, faded away entirely, and night succeeded. Still, however, the poor fellow toiled on up the hill, followed the road that led across the moor, and passed the very spot where Langford had seen the pistol fired on the preceding night.

As he went by the beeches, he thought he heard a rustling sound beneath them; and though accustomed to go at all hours through the wildest and least frequented paths, either fatigue and want of food, or some other cause, had unnerved him, and the sound made him start. He ran on upon the road as fast as he could, and then turned to look behind him. There was no moon—the night was sultry and dark, and it was difficult to distinguish any object distinctly; but he saw, or believed he saw, two men come out from the beeches as if to follow him, and he again ran on with all speed, taking his way across the moor. After he had gone about half a mile, he cast himself flat down amongst some fern and heath, and lay there for ten minutes or a quarter of an hour; after which he arose again, and hurried on towards the dwelling of Franklin Gray. Twice he thought he heard steps behind him; and his heart rejoiced when he saw the gate in the wall that surrounded the court. The gate was locked, however; the whole house looked dark and untenanted; not a window in the tower, or in the large building by the side, showed the slightest ray of light; and as he stood and shook the gate, he distinctly heard quick steps coming on the very path he had pursued.

A degree of terror which he had seldom before felt now took possession of him; and he ran round the wall as fast as he could, seeking for some entrance at the back. The first gate that he met with resisted like the other; but a second, fifty or sixty yards further on, opened at once, and he hurried on towards the part of the building before him. He still seemed to hear the steps behind him; and with fear that amounted almost to agony, he felt along the wall for a bell or some other means of making himself heard. As he did so, his hand came against a door, which gave way beneath his touch, and he had almost fallen headlong down some steps. He caught, however, by the lintel in time, and glad of any entrance, went down slowly, feeling his way with his foot and hands till he reached a level pavement. The air was cooler than it had been above; and a small square aperture at a considerable distance before him, while it gave admission to the wind, also showed the sort of faint dim light which yet lingered in the sky. Towards it he took his way, after having listened for a moment with a beating heart, to ascertain whether he was pursued, and made himself sure that he was not.

For a few paces, nothing interrupted his progress; but the next moment, he stumbled over some object on the ground; and as he attempted to raise himself, his hand came in contact with something that felt like cloth. He instantly drew it back, but, after pausing a moment and hesitating, he stretched it out slowly again, and it lighted upon the cold clammy features of a dead man's face. Starting back, he again fell over the object which had thrown him down before, and which he now found to be a coffin.

Although all these circumstances were in themselves horrible, they served in some degree to relieve the mind of poor John Graves, who now remembered the ruins of the old church, which stood near, and naturally concluded that he had got into the vaults. The confusion of his brain prevented him from remembering that the place had been long unused for its original and legitimate purposes, and he was not one of those who feel any horror at the mere presence of the dead. On the contrary, the sight of the clay after the spirit had departed, seemed to offer to his madness a curious matter of speculation, and he was fond of visiting the chamber of death amongst all the cottages in the neighbourhood.

After he had a little recovered himself, then, he muttered, "It's a corpse! I wonder if it's a man or a woman;" and he put out his hand again towards the face, and ran it over the jaw and lips, to feel for the beard.

"It must be a gentleman, to be put in the vault," he continued; "his hand will tell that! Poor men's hands are hard; and the rich keep their palms soft. I wonder if it is gold makes men's palms soft? Yes, it is a gentleman," he continued, as he slid his hand down the arm to the cold palm of the dead man.

But at that moment a light began to stream through the door by which he had entered, and his terror was once more renewed. "If they catch me here," he muttered, "they will think I am come to steal the coffin plates;" and as the increasing light showed him some of the objects around, he perceived a broken part of the wall which separated that vault from the next, and which lay in ruin amidst the remains of former generations, with many a coffin, stripped of all its idle finery by the hand of time, piled up against it, together with dust and rubbish, and the crumbling vestiges of mortality.

Behind the screen thus formed the half-witted man crept, and lay trembling with a vague dread of he did not well know what; while the light, which by this time had approached close to the door, remained stationary for a moment; and two or three voices were heard speaking in a low tone. The next moment three men descended into the vault, one of whom bore a flambeau in his hand; but for the first two or three minutes after they entered, Silly John could only hear without seeing, as his terror prevented him from making the slightest movement.

"You may as well wipe the blood from off his face before you put him into the box," said one, as he and his companions seemed to stand by the corpse and gaze upon it with curious and speculating eyes.

"That was a deadly shot," said the other. "Poor devil! he never spoke a word after."

"He well deserved it," said a third voice, "that's my opinion; and when that's the case, the deadlier the shot the better. But let us make haste, Master Hardie; though I do not see why he should be buried with that smart belt on. Come, let us toss up for it. Here is a crown-piece. You toss, Hardie."

While this conversation had been going on, the poor half-witted man had remained ensconced behind the coffins and broken wall, trembling in every limb. This tremor assuredly proceeded from fear, and not from cold, for the air, which had been sultry all day, had now grown oppressively hot; and the heavy clouds, which had been rolling up during the evening, like a vast curtain between earth and the free breath of heaven, had by this time covered the whole sky; while a few large drops of rain, pattering amongst the ruins of the church and the broken stones and long grass without, formed no unmusical prelude to the storm that was about soon to descend.

Scarcely had Doveton spoken (for he it was who took the lead upon the present occasion) when a faint blue gleam suddenly lighted up the inside of the vault, proceeding from the small square window, and flashing round upon all the grim and sombre features of the place, coffins, and sculls, and bones, and broken and disjointed stones, and high piles of mouldy earth, consisting chiefly of the dust of the dead. It came like the clear and searching glance of eternal truth, making dark secrets bright, and bringing forth from their obscurity all the dim hidden things of earth. That gleam flashed upon the countenances of the three robbers, as they stood around the corpse, unmoved, unshaken by the solemn aspect of death, by the awful picture of their own mortality. The sudden glance of the lightning, however, made them each start involuntarily. He who held the crown-piece in his hand let it drop. No thunder followed the first flash, but another far more bright and vivid succeeded, playing round the buckles and clasps of the very sword-belt that one of them was in the act of removing from the corpse. A crash, which could not have been louder had the fragments of a mountain been poured upon their heads, came instantly after, shaking the whole building as if it would have cast down the last stone of the ruin.

"By ——," cried one of the robbers, uttering a horrid imprecation, "what a peal!"

"Ay, and what a flash!" said another, "but come, take off the belt, for fear he gets up off the trestles and stops us!"

"Ay, if we let him," said Doveton; "but may I never speak again, if I did not think I saw his lips move! There! there!" he continued, as another flash of lightning shone again upon the features of the dead man, reversing all the lights which the flambeau had cast upon it, and making the whole features, without any real change, assume an expression entirely different. "There! there! I told you so! Look, he is grinning at us!"

"Pooh, nonsense!" cried another; "the man's dead! he'll never grin again. Yet, by my life, there is the blood running!" And so far he spoke truth; for the jerk which had been given to the body in order to detach the sword-belt, had caused a stream of dark gore to well slowly down and drop upon the ground.

"Let the belt be! let the belt be!" cried Hardcastle. "Hold the torch to his face and see if he does move! No, no; he is still enough! But, after all, one does not like dragging him out in such a night as this, to bury him upon the cold moor. It would not matter if he were alive; but let us stay here till the storm is over, and you, Harvey, run and get us some drink. It's neither a nice night, nor a nice place, nor a nice business; so we may as well have something to cheer us."

"I have no objection to the flagon," said Doveton, as Harvey left them to obtain the peculiar sort of liquid cheerfulness to which men engaged in not the most legitimate callings generally have recourse; "I have no objection to the flagon; but you know we must have done the job before morning, Hardie, and the grave is not dug yet."

"Oh, we'll soon dig the grave," replied Hardcastle; "the ground is soft upon the moor, and it need not be very deep. Do you think, Doveton, that when folks are dead they can see us? I have often thought that very likely they can see and hear just as well as ever, but can't move or speak."

"I hope not! I hope not!" cried his companion; and at that moment came another flash of lightning, gleaming round and round the vault, followed by the tremendous roar of the thunder, and the rushing and the pattering of the big rain.

The whole scene was so awful; the corpse, the robbers, the vault, the thunder-storm, their speculations upon the dead, the mixture of superstition and impious daring which they displayed, the revel that they were preparing to hold by the side of a murdered body, and the images of the flagon and the grave, formed altogether a whole so terrible and so extraordinary, that the poor man who lay concealed and witnessed the strange and dreadful proceeding, could endure it no longer; but starting up in a fit of desperation, he darted forward, overthrowing the pile of coffins before him, and rushing with the countenance of a risen corpse towards the stone steps which led into the vault. Surprised and terrified, the two robbers started back, the flambeau fell and nearly extinguished itself upon the ground; the body of the dead man was overthrown at their feet; and rushing on without pause, John Graves had gained the stairs and effected his exit, before they knew who or what it was that had so suddenly broken in upon their conference.

Running as if a whole legion of fiends had been behind him, heeding not the deluge of rain that was now falling from the sky, but staggering and putting his hand to his eyes when the bright gleam of the lightning flashed across his path, the half-witted man hurried back again with all speed towards the moor, nor ceased for a moment the rapid steps which carried him forward, till he had reached the beeches by Upwater-mere. There sitting down and clasping his hands over his knees, he remained with his whole thoughts cast into a state of greater confusion than ever, watching the liquid fire as it glanced over the water, and talking to himself whenever the thunder would let him hear his own voice.

It seemed, however, as if the same ghastly objects were destined to pursue him through that night; for the storm had scarcely in a slight degree abated, and a faint grey streak just made its appearance through the clouds, marking where the dim moon lay veiled behind them, when he heard coming steps; and, as his only resource, he clambered into one of the beech-trees, and sat watching what took place below. The only objects that he could distinguish were the forms of three men carrying a burthen between them. They laid it down under the trees; and for the space of about half an hour there was the busy sound of the pickaxe and the spade, the shovelfuls of earth cast forth, and the slow delving noise when the heavy foot pressed the edge into the ground. At the end of that time the burden was lifted up, deposited in the pit, and the earth piled in again. It was done with haste, for the grey dawn was beginning to appear; and John Graves could clearly distinguish the forms of Doveton, Hardcastle, and Harvey, as, each taking up a part of the tools they had employed, they hurried away to escape the clear eye of day.

When they were gone, the half-witted man came down from the tree, and stood gazing upon the spot where the fresh grey earth of the moor, mingling with the thin green grass under the beech-trees, showed the place where they had concealed the body.

"And liest thou there, Harold?" he said, speaking aloud, though there was nobody to hear, as was very much his custom; "and liest thou there, poor boy? with nothing around thee but the cold damp earth, and the grey morning of a storm shining upon thy last bed? And did they nurse thee so tenderly for this? Did thy father spend wealth, and care, and thought—did he wrong others, and endanger his chance of Heaven, and squander hope and fear, and passion and cunning, all for this? that thou shouldest lie here, without his knowing where thou restest—that thou shouldest lie here, like the daisy which his proud horse's feet cut off as he galloped along, without his knowing that it was broken? Alack and a-well-a-day! Alack and a-well-a-day! Poor boy, though thou hadst something of thy father's fire, and something of thy mother's weakness, thou wert good and generous, and tender and compassionate. I know not how it is, Harold, but I am more sorry for thee than for people that I have loved better, and I cannot bear to think that thou shouldest lie here, on this gloomy moor. Nor shalt thou, if I should dig thee out with my own hands! But then they'll say I killed thee," he added, after a moment's thought, "as they have said already of one who would as soon have killed himself. So I'll go and tell thy father, my poor boy; but no, I forgot, I must first go back to that man, for I promised, and I always keep my promise. It could not be Gray that killed thee. No, no, I do not think that; he's not fond of blood. He spared my life, so why should he take thine? I do not half like to go to him; yet I must, because I promised."

Poor Silly John lingered for some time beside the grave after he had finished this soliloquy, and then turned his steps back again with some degree of confidence gained from the open daylight, towards the abode of Franklin Gray. He still hesitated, however, and apprehensions of some kind made him wander at a distance from the house for several hours before he could make up his mind to approach it. He even went to a small alehouse, and strengthened his resolution with beer, and bread and cheese; but what, perhaps, afforded him more courage than anything, was the act of paying for his morning's meal with part of the money which Franklin Gray himself had given him.

As we have before seen, the conclusions at which the poor man arrived were very often just, and his madness consisted rather in a kind of wandering, an occasional want of the power of seizing and holding anything firmly, than in folly. In the present instance, then, he inferred from the sight of the money given him by Franklin Gray, that a person who had treated him so kindly would not ill-use him or suffer him to be ill-used; and, accordingly, he gained courage from the contemplation, and set out for the tower. Although he had been twice there before, since Franklin Gray had been the tenant thereof, yet, on both those occasions his visits had been after dark; but, as he approached at present the scenes of all the horrors of the preceding night, he could scarcely believe his eyes, so different was the whole when displayed in the broad sunshine from that which it appeared under the shadow. In this instance, however, the face that it wore in the open day was the deceptive one, and is but too common through the world, and in life, and in the human heart. The tower, and the large building by its side, and the court within its walls, were converted into a farm-house, with its barns and its yard full of straw, and ploughshares, and farming implements, while carts stood around bearing the name of "Franklin Gray, Farmer," though the name of the place which followed was that of a distant part of the country, where probably he had exercised the same kind of farming which he now carried on. There were two or three stout men in farming habiliments about the yard too, whose faces were not unfamiliar to the eye of John Graves, and an honest watch-dog stood chained near the stable-door, as if the good farmer was in fear of nightly depredators. A flaxen-headed ploughboy whistled gaily in the court; and at the moment that Silly John approached, a very lovely creature, habited in plain white garments, and carrying a beautiful child of little more than a year old in her arms, was crossing on tiptoe the dirty yard, wet and muddy with the storm of the preceding night.

"A dainty farmer's dame, indeed!" said the half-witted man to himself; "but I'll speak to her rather than to any of the foxes. Women are always kindest."

His singular appearance had already attracted the attention of the person who was the subject of his contemplation, and she seemed at once to comprehend his character, and the nature of the affliction under which he laboured.

"He is one of the happy," she said, speaking low, and to herself. "What would you, poor man?" she added, with her sweet-toned voice and foreign accent. "Do you seek money or food?"

The half-witted man did not reply directly to her question, but, caught by her appearance and by her accent, his mind seemed to wander far away to other things, and he answered, "Ay, pretty lady, there have been others such as you. Many a one quits her own land and marries a stranger, and is soon taught to repent, as women always will repent, when they have trusted those they knew not, and forgotten their own friends, and cast their country behind them."

She whom he addressed answered first by a smile, and then said, "Not always! My husband will never make me repent: he never has made me repent, though long ago I did all you said, trusted a stranger, forgot my own friends, and cast my country behind me. But what would you, poor man? Can I help you?"

"Only tell Franklin Gray," replied the other, "that Henry Langford has been taken up on the charge of killing Lord Harold, and that they keep him a prisoner in Danemore Castle; so that now's the time to help him. I want nothing more, lady, but God's blessing upon your beautiful face;" and so saying, he hurried away and left her, while a slight degree of colour came up into the cheek of Mona Gray, as much at the earnestness of the look which he gave her, as at the allusion to her beauty.

CHAPTER XIV

THE world we live in is full of beautiful sights and sweet sounds; it is a treasure-house of loveliness and of melody. Whether the eye ranges over the face of nature at large, and marks all the varied, the magnificent, the sweet, the bright, the gentle, in wood, and mountain, and valley, and stream; or rests, wondering and admiring, on the bright delicate fabric of a flower, the rich hues of the butterfly, or the lustrous plumage of the birds, beauty and brightness are everywhere. The air we breathe, too, is full of sweet sounds; whether in the singing of the birds, the murmuring music of the stream, or the hum of all the insect world upon the wing, everything is replete with harmony. But of all the lovely sights, and of all the touching sounds whereof nature is full, there is nothing so beautiful, there is nothing so sweet, as the sight and the words of natural affection.

Alice Herbert—for to her we must now turn—sat by the bedside of her father on the morning of that day, the eventful passing of which we have already commemorated in the chapter just concluded, as far as it affects the greater part of the characters connected with this tale. Joy and brightness were upon her countenance; and in the small and beautiful hand that rested on her lap she held open the packet of papers which had been left her by Langford. She gazed in the countenance of her father with a look of eager and gratified affection, which gave to her features a look of additional loveliness, and added the crowning beauty to the whole. Her voice, too, sweet and melodious as it always was, seemed, at least to her father's ears, to have a more musical tone than ever, as she told him, with a heart thrilling with joy and satisfaction at having such news to tell, that she held in her hand the means of freeing him from the painful situation into which he had been plunged by the events of the night before; and that those means had been furnished to her by him whom she so deeply loved.

The feelings of Sir Walter himself were also very sweet; they were sweet to receive such assistance from a daughter's hand; they were sweet from perceiving the happiness which to give that assistance afforded her; they were sweet from the very act of appreciating all her sensations; from the power of understanding and estimating the ideas and feelings of her whom he loved best on earth. They were sweet, but not wholly sweet. There was a sensation mingled with them, as there must almost always be with every enjoyment and delight of our mortal being, which tempered, if it did not sadden—which took some little part off the brightness of the joy. It may be, that such slight deteriorations, that such partial alloys thrown into the gold of happiness, do, like the real alloys which render the precious metals more fitted for the hand of the workman, render our pleasures more adapted to our state of being. At all events, the slight shade of something less than happiness which mingled with Sir Walter Herbert's feelings, was not sufficient to do more than give them a deeper interest. It was the thrill of a fine mind on receiving a benefit. Pride had nothing to do with it; and, yet, when Alice Herbert showed him the various notes and bills of exchange which she held in her hand, a slight flush appeared upon his cheek, a momentary feeling of embarrassment came over him. He would not, however, have let Alice perceive for the world that he felt the least embarrassment; he struggled against it, and conquered it in a moment.

"This is indeed generous and noble of Langford," he said. "This is like what I always supposed him; this is what I could desire and hope in him who is to possess my Alice. But I must rise, Alice, my beloved. I must rise and see him; and thank him myself. I long to tell him how I appreciate his good and noble character, and to show him that I do so by seeking his advice, assistance, and counsel in a situation to which some carelessness and some want of wisdom, perhaps, have brought my affairs; though I feel assured and am confident Alice, as you tell me he himself said last night, that matters are by no means so bad as that lawyer would unkindly have us believe. Go down, my love, and have the breakfast prepared; I will join you speedily."

Alice did as he bade her, leaving the papers with him; but although her heart was very happy, she could have much wished that Langford himself had not been absent. She knew that a thousand causes, of the simplest and most natural kind, might have taken him out at that early hour of the morning; but yet there was a feeling of apprehensiveness in her bosom that she did not attempt to account for, but which in reality proceeded from the events of the preceding evening; agitation which had taken from her heart that feeling of security in its own happiness which seldom if ever returns when once scared away. The first great misfortune is the breaking of a spell, the dissolving of that bright and beautiful illusion in which our youth is enshrined, the confidence of happiness; and there is no magic power in after-life sufficient to give us back the charm. It may come in another world, but there it shall be a reality, and not a dream.

Alice Herbert, then, felt apprehensive she knew not of what; but in the silence of the old servants, and the solemn gloom that seemed to hang over them as they laid out the morning meal, there was something which increased her uneasiness. She asked herself, why Wilson walked so slowly, why Halliday no longer bustled about as usual, forgetting for a moment his reverence for the ears of his master, in directing and scolding the other servants if they went wrong: and though she ultimately concluded that they had all heard some report of the difficulties into which her father had fallen, and that such a report had rendered their affectionate hearts sad, yet the conclusion did not altogether satisfy her; and she longed both for Langford's return, and for her father's appearance at the breakfast-table.

Sir Walter did at length appear, but his first question was for Langford, to which the servant Halliday answered as he had been directed. The good knight seemed perfectly satisfied, and, sitting down to table, commenced his breakfast, talking to his daughter with an air that showed that the slight embarrassment under which he at first laboured was gone; that the despondency which had been produced by the imperfect insight into his affairs, given by the events of the preceding night, was passing away, and that hope and expectation were beginning to brighten up and smile upon him once more.

Ere breakfast was over, however, the servant Halliday entered the room, and approaching the end of the table where his master sat, informed him that Gregory Myrtle, the landlord of the Talbot, desired instantly to speak with him.

"What does he want, Halliday?" demanded the knight; "will not the good man's business wait?"

"I believe not, your worship," replied Halliday; "he says it is a matter of much importance."

"Well then, send him in," said Sir Walter; "he is a good man and a merry one, and I will discuss the matter with him while I finish my breakfast."

Halliday looked at Alice, but he did not venture to say anything, and retiring from the room, he soon after re-appeared, ushering in the portly form of Gregory Myrtle.

The worthy host of the Talbot, however, for once in his life, had lost that radiant jocundity of expression which his countenance usually bore; and the first question of Sir Walter was, "Why, how now, Master Gregory Myrtle, what is the matter with thee, mine host? Thou lookest as solemn and as much surprised as if thou hadst seen a ghost on thy way hither. I hope nothing has gone wrong with thee, good Gregory?"

"I have seen a sight your worship," replied the landlord, laying his hand upon the white apron which covered his stomach, "I have seen a sight which I never thought to see, and which has made me as sad as anything can make Gregory Myrtle. I have seen Master Harry Langford taken away from mine house by two magistrates on charge of murder!"

Sir Walter gazed on him for a single instant with astonishment, but then immediately turned towards his daughter, forgetting all his own feelings in hers. Alice, as pale as death, had sunk back in her chair, and was covering her eyes with her hands, while she seemed to gasp for breath under the agitation of the moment. Sir Walter started up, and approached her tenderly, while Halliday ran from the other side of the room with water. She put it away with her hand, however, saying, "I shall be better in a moment! It was but the shock! Go on, Master Myrtle!"

Sir Walter gazed tenderly on his child, but the colour soon came back into Alice's cheek, and she begged her father not to attend to her, but to go on with the sad business which had been so suddenly brought before him. Sir Walter again sat down to the table, and as his mind turned from his daughter to the charge against one whom she loved and whom he esteemed, surprise and indignation superseded all other feelings, and the blood mounted up into his cheek, while he demanded, "Of whose murder, pray, have they had the folly to accuse him?"

"Folly, indeed, your worship," replied Gregory Myrtle; "but they accuse him of having murdered Lord Harold last night upon the moor."

The blood again rushed rapidly through every vein back to Alice Herbert's heart, and her fair hand clasped almost convulsively the arm of the chair in which she sat. Her father's heart had instantly directed his eye towards her, and, rising from his seat, he went gently up to her, and took her by the hand, saying, "Let me help you to your own room, dear child. I must make inquiries into this matter; but it is not a subject for your ears, my Alice."

"Yes, indeed," she replied, making an effort for calmness. "I have now heard the worst, my dear father, and shall be anxious to know all the rest. If I were away, I should be still more uneasy than I am here; pray go on."

"The charge is perfectly absurd!" replied Sir Walter, returning to his chair. "No one that knows Langford can for a moment suspect him of committing any crime. I will investigate the affair to the bottom, and of course take care that he is not subject to the annoyance of confinement any longer, my Alice. But go on. Master Myrtle!"

Alice listened eagerly to all the details which Gregory Myrtle now gave, for her mind was not at all at ease in regard to the real state of the case. Not that she ever suspected Langford of having murdered the unhappy Lord Harold: of course such an idea never entered her mind; but she remembered that Langford had been absent the greater part of the preceding evening, and even a portion of the night. She knew that he had left her for the purpose of returning to Lord Harold, whose feelings, she doubted not, were irritated and excited by what he had seen take place between her and his rival; and she did fear that Langford, notwithstanding the promise he had given her, might have been driven or tempted to draw his sword under some strong provocation. She knew that he had great powers of commanding himself; and she believed that, even had such an occurrence taken place, he would have been perfectly capable of conversing with her over her father's affairs, as he had done. At the same time she recollected that, although absorbed by the situation of her father, and occupied by her own feelings and sensations, she had remarked that Langford was pale, thoughtful, and seemingly agitated by emotions different from those which might be naturally called forth by the subjects on which they spoke.

On the other hand, he had assured her that no encounter had taken place between him and Lord Harold, and she did not think that, even to spare her feelings, Langford would say anything that was not true; but yet she thought that their meeting might have taken place even after Langford had left her. She accounted for his previous absence by supposing that he had gone to seek some friend to act as his second upon the occasion, and, in short, imagination found many a way of justifying the apprehensions that love was prompt to force. Under any ordinary circumstances, though she might bitterly have regretted that one whom she loved had stained his hand with the blood of a fellow-creature, yet she would have entertained no apprehensions for his safety in a mere affair of honour. But Alice had known from her infancy the Earl of Danemore, and had formed, almost without knowing it herself, an estimate of his character, which was but too near the reality. There was in it a remorselessness, a vehemence, a determination, an unscrupulous pursuit of his own purposes, which had been apparent to her, even as a child. She knew well, she felt perfectly convinced, that he would halt at no step, that he would hesitate at no means, in order to obtain vengeance upon any one who had lifted a hand against his son; and she was well aware, too, that Lord Danemore united to his unscrupulous determination of character, talents and skill which gave him but too often the means of accomplishing his purpose, however unjust.

Such knowledge and such feelings added deep apprehensions for Langford's safety to the pain that she would at any time have felt at the idea of one she loved taking the life of another human being; and the whole was mingled with sincere grief to think that one who had been her playmate in childhood, and had loved her truly in her more mature years—one whom she esteemed and felt for deeply, though she could not return his love, had been cut off in the spring of life, before many blossoming virtues had yet borne fruit.

She listened eagerly, therefore, and anxiously to the words of the good landlord of the Talbot, while he detailed all those facts connected with the arrest of Langford which we have already dwelt upon. Her father, indeed, felt and showed much more indignation and surprise that the charge should be brought at all, than apprehension lest it should prove just; and when, from some part of the conduct of the magistrates, as detailed by the worthy landlord, it appeared that they accused Langford of having slain Lord Harold in an unfair and secret manner, Alice shared in the indignant feelings of her father, and raised high her head at the very thought of her noble, her generous her gallant lover, being suspected of an unworthy act for a moment.

By the showing of Gregory Myrtle, it very speedily appeared to Sir Walter and his daughter, that the magistrates had not dealt quite impartially in taking or seeking for evidence; and that they had shown a strong inclination to find out that Langford was really guilty. From what Sir Walter knew of the character of one, if not of both of those worthy gentlemen, he easily conceived it to be possible that they should be somewhat desirous of recommending themselves to Lord Danemore by an overstrained and excessive zeal in discovering the murderer of his son. But when he heard that the body of Lord Harold had not even been found, his indignation grew still greater, and he sent back Gregory Myrtle to the village, with directions to collect together every one who could give any information on the subject, promising to come over to the Talbot as soon as his horses could be saddled, and investigate the matter to the bottom.

"As soon as this is done, Alice," he said, "I will ride over to the castle, notwithstanding the painful event that has occurred, discharge this long-standing debt to my good Lord Danemore, who has thought fit to make so unhandsome a use of it; and then insist upon even justice being shown towards our noble friend Langford, who, I doubt not, can prove his innocence in five minutes."

The worthy Knight hastened all his proceedings; for when the cause of a friend was in his hands, none of that easy and somewhat apathetic indifference displayed itself with which he was but too apt to regard his own affairs. His riding boots were drawn on with speed, and he twice asked for his horses before the grooms could have had time to saddle them; nor had he for many years before been known to ride so fast as he did in going from the gates of his own park to the door of the Talbot. Almost the whole population of the little town was gathered about the inn, enjoying the satisfaction of a legitimate subject of marvel and gossip: and the glad and reverential smiles, the bows of unfeigned respect, and the homely but affectionate greeting with which they received the good knight as he rode up, showed pleasingly how much beloved the virtues and good qualities of all its members had rendered the family of the Manor.

Sir Walter, however, was detained at Moorhurst much longer than he expected, for everybody was anxious to give testimony before him, and many more crowded forward than could afford any satisfactory information, or throw the most trifling light upon the case; and yet, as each and all of them had something to say in favour of Langford, Sir Walter could not find it in his heart to refuse to listen to any. The clerk of the parish was called upon to take down their depositions; and certainly, if the fact of having established a good character in a country town could have assisted any man in a similar predicament, it might have done so with Langford in the present instance.

Sir Walter Herbert, however, did not lose sight of the great object, though he suffered himself to be deluged by much irrelevant matter; and he soon found that the only legitimate cause for supposing Langford at all connected with the death or disappearance of Lord Harold was the fact of the half-witted man, John Graves, having run down, during the preceding evening, and besought several persons to come up and prevent Langford and the young nobleman from killing each other. As he was known to adhere invariably to the truth, two or three of the town's-people had gone up with him into the park in order to keep the peace, but on finding all quiet, and nobody there, had returned without further search.

Sir Walter discovered also that the two magistrates who had preceded him in the investigation had not even demanded to see John Graves himself, though his testimony, taken second-hand, was that in fact on which the whole case rested. This he determined immediately to remedy; but the half-witted man was by that time nowhere to be found, and though Sir Walter waited for many hours while persons were despatched to seek for him in all directions, the good knight was at length obliged to give the matter up for the day, and return to the Manor House.

During his absence, Alice was left for several hours with no companion but her own painful thoughts. She felt, as she might well feel, quite sure that Langford was innocent of any base, or cowardly, or treacherous action; she felt sure of his honour, his integrity, his uprightness. But that certainty, that confidence, though it gave her support, could not deliver her from apprehension. All her thoughts were gloomy. The bright joy which Langford's acknowledgment of his love on the preceding evening had afforded her, had been like one of those sweet warm summer-like days in the unconfirmed infancy of the year, which are succeeded immediately by storms and tempests. Her mind had rested for a moment in a vision of perfect happiness;

but now, whichever way she turned her waking eyes, there was something painful in the prospect. Although she was very willing to believe that her father's pecuniary affairs were not in near so bad a state as Lord Danemore's lawyer had made them appear, yet there could be no doubt that they were greatly embarrassed, and that his income and resources were so much smaller than those of his ancestors, that it would be a duty to curtail his expenses, to diminish his establishment, and, in an age when luxury and splendour were daily increasing, to forego many of the conveniences and comforts which he had hitherto enjoyed, and all that dignified but unostentatious state which his family had kept up for many generations.

She knew, too, that to do so would be a bitter pang, well nigh to the breaking of the heart that felt it; and although, for her own part, there was scarcely a pretty cottage in the neighbourhood in which she could not have made her home with cheerfulness and happiness, she looked forward with painful apprehension to the time when her father might have to quit the Manor House, and discharge the old servants who had served him so long, and be no more what he had been amongst the many who looked up to and reverenced him.

Such was one dark subject of contemplation; the death of Lord Harold was another. She thought of him as she had seen him the evening before, full of youth, and health, and energy; she thought of him as she had seen him in other days, full of joy and gaiety, and that bright exuberant life which it is difficult to imagine can ever be extinguished, when we gaze upon it in all its activity and brightness; and yet a single moment had ended it for ever.

Her mind then turned to the father of him who was gone; and she pictured him sitting in his lonely halls, childless, solitary, desolate, left without hope and without consolation to pass through the chill winter of his age, till he reached the dark and cheerless resting-place of the tomb. She pitied him from her very heart; she could have wept for him; but then her thoughts turned to Langford, and she asked herself, if it were possible that a man who had just suffered so severely as Lord Danemore himself, could seek to bring misery and sorrow upon others? Abstractedly, she would have thought such a thing impossible; but when she reflected upon the character of the man, she felt but too deeply convinced that his own misery would but make him seek to render others as miserable; that his despair would be bitter and turbulent, not calm and mild; and that to see the hearths of others desolate, the hearts of others broken, would in all probability be the consolation he would choose.

She was pondering sadly upon these gloomy subjects of contemplation, as well upon that chief and still more absorbing one, the situation of him whom she so dearly loved, when the servant Halliday appeared to announce to her that Master Kinsight, Lord Danemore's attorney, was at the gate, and would not go away. He had told him, the servant said, that his worship was out, and that she herself was busy, and not to be disturbed; "but he still hangs there, Mistress Alice," continued the man, "and he is no way civil; so much so, indeed, that if I did not know his worship is averse to having anybody cudgelled, I would drub him for his pains."

"Do no such thing, Halliday," replied Alice, "but bring him in here; I will speak to him myself."

In a few minutes the lawyer entered the room, and threw himself down into a chair with very little ceremony. "So, Mistress Alice," he said, in a tone, the natural insolence of which was increased by the unconcealed hatred of Sir Walter's servants, "I find your father's out; gone out, I suppose to avoid me, for he knew I was coming about this time for his answer and yours, as to what we were speaking of last night."

"My father has gone out, Master Kinsight," replied Alice, calmly, "upon business of importance; but I can give you the answer that you require, as well as if he were present. He is going over to Danemore Castle as soon as possible, to pay the money and interest which you came to claim, having found the means of doing so, without any further delay."

"Ay, indeed, madam!" exclaimed the lawyer, with evident surprise; "indeed! Pray how?"

"That, I should conceive, sir," replied Alice, in the same tone in which she had before spoken, "is no business of yours."

"Your pardon, madam, your pardon," cried the lawyer, "it is business of mine. Your father must have borrowed the money, and to have borrowed the money he must have given security, and we hold mortgages over his whole property to its full value, and therefore—"

As he paused and hesitated, Alice replied, "I do not yet see, sir, how that would make it any business of yours. However, to satisfy you, the money was lent by my father's friend, Captain Langford, without any security whatever."

"Do you mean to say that the money was lent," he exclaimed, rudely, "actually lent, paid down? Come, come; I shall not go out of the house till I hear more of the matter, for I do not want to be trifled with, or to tell my lord that the money is ready when it is not."

"Sir," said Alice Herbert, raising her head with a look of indignation, "you are insolent. The money is, as I have told you, now in the house, ready to be paid to your master—as I suppose I must call Lord Danemore—whenever my father is at leisure to do so. I expect him ere long; and if you choose to remain till he returns, you may wait in the servants' hall. At present I myself am busy, and wish to be alone."

The lawyer looked somewhat disconcerted; but he paused thoughtfully for a moment, biting his lip, twirling his hat, and laying his finger on his brow, as if uncertain what to do. At length, he exclaimed, "No, no, I'll not wait; I'll go over to the Earl directly, and take instructions."

So saying, he bade Alice a short and saucy adieu, and quitted her presence and the house, not finding a servant who would even show him the attention of holding his horse while he mounted.

CHAPTER XV.

For several weeks Henry Langford had enjoyed a degree of happiness which he had never before known. From the night in which he was wounded in defence of Alice Herbert, till the evening preceding the day on which we last left him, had been a period full of sweet hopes and new sensations, ending with the crowning joy of all, the knowledge of loving and being beloved. That period of bright light, however, had now been suddenly contrasted with as deep a shadow as had ever fallen on any part of his existence, and yet in the course of that existence he had known some sorrows and some cares. None, however, had touched him so deeply as this; for now he was imprisoned, not in consequence of having fallen into the power of a foreign enemy, taken in battle, and esteemed even while restrained—but accused of a base and cowardly crime, separated from those he loved best, placed in a situation from which it might be difficult to extricate himself, and feeling more deeply and painfully for the unhappy youth of whose murder he was accused than any one knew.

Sitting in solitude and in silence, the remainder of Henry Langford's day, after the half-witted man had left him, passed over in gloom and anxious thought. It was not that he yielded to despondency; it was not that he suffered hope to extinguish her torch, or even to shade its light for a moment. Knowing himself innocent of the crime with which he was charged, knowing that he possessed the love of Alice Herbert, and feeling sure that that love would never alter, there was always a balm for grief and anxiety. But still, even when he thought of Alice Herbert herself, when he remembered the situation of her father, and knew that any false steps might plunge the worthy knight into irretrievable ruin, he could not be without anxiety on that score either; and, whichever way he turned his eyes, there were clouds upon the horizon that threatened to gather into a storm.

The treatment which he received from the Earl of Danemore, indeed, was in all respects consolatory. That nobleman, it was clear, hardly entertained any suspicion of his having had a share in the murder of his son. Several times in the course of the evening, servants were sent to ascertain if he wanted anything. The ordinary meals of the day were regularly set before him; and when night fell, lights were brought, and various kinds of fine wine were left in the room, sufficient to satisfy him if by chance he had addicted himself to the evil habit of deep drinking, but too common in those days.

Some short time after the lights had been brought, he heard a step approaching his room by the smaller staircase, and the Earl again appeared. The expression of his countenance was agitated and anxious; but he apologised courteously for intruding, and then added, "I thought you might be pleased to learn that the whole of Upwater Mere has been dragged with the greatest care, without anything having been found to confirm my apprehensions in regard to its having been made the receptacle of my poor son's body. It is very foolish, under such circumstances, and with such proofs of his death as we have, to give way to hope; but yet I cannot help yielding a little to your reasoning of this morning."

"I hope and trust, my lord," replied Langford, "that reasoning may not prove fallacious. Far be it from me to wish to instil false hopes, but I would certainly, were I you, not give myself up to despair till the truth of the calamity is better ascertained."

"I know," replied the Earl, "that coincidences very often happen, giving much unnecessary alarm. Indeed, the story which you told this morning is an extraordinary proof of the fact. I remember having heard it before," he added, in a careless tone, "though I forget where it was. Pray, where did the incident happen?"

Langford mused for a single moment, and then looked up with something of a meaning smile. "It occurred, my lord," he replied, "in the Gulf of Florida, many years ago. I therefore do not know it from my own personal knowledge; but I have heard it from one who was present, and who told me the whole particulars of that and many another adventure in those seas."

It was now Lord Danemore's turn to muse, and he did so with a cloudy brow, gnawing his nether lip, as if struggling with some powerful emotions. "Pray, do you know the name of the captain of the ship?" he asked, at length, affecting the same careless tone with which he had before spoken.

"Yes, my lord," replied Langford; "I know his name and his whole history from that time to the present hour."

Lord Danemore turned very pale, and then mused for several minutes in silence. Nor was it unworthy of remark that he did not demand the name of the captain of the vessel, though the moment before he had seemed so much interested in the subject. He remained gloomy and silent, however, as we have said, knitting his brow thoughtfully, and his first words were—though in so low a tone that Langford did not hear them—"People may know too much."

Perceiving his lips move, and seeing that he was evidently much affected by what had passed, Langford, who had spoken with some degree of emphasis, added, with apparent indifference, "Yes, oh yes; I know his whole history well. He was an English gentleman of a brave, daring, and enterprising disposition, who, having been driven from his own country, and deprived for the time of his own possessions, pursued a wild and fitful course of life; now serving with gallant distinction in the armies of foreign countries, now becoming a rover on the high seas, and acquiring for himself a fearful and redoubtable fame, till the restoration of the king suddenly recalled him to fortunes and honours in his own land."

Lord Danemore made no direct reply; but putting his hand to his head, he said, "It is very hot; I have seldom known a more oppressive night."

As he spoke, the storm, which had been long coming up, burst forth with a bright flash, which blazed with a blue and ghastly light round the dark wainscotted chamber in which they sat, lighting up every cornice and ornament in the carved oak, and seeming absolutely to play amidst the papers on the table. At that very instant both Lord Danemore and Langford raised their eyes each to the countenance of his companion, and gazed upon each other with a firm and questioning glance.

"That was a bright flash," said the Earl, with a lip that curled slightly as he spoke; "I do not know that I ever saw a brighter—except in the Gulf of Florida!"

He added nothing more, nor waited for any reply, but rose as he spoke, and abruptly quitted the room. He trod the stairs down to his own private apartments with a heavy but irregular step, and paused at the bottom for several moments ere he opened the door which gave entrance to his own dressing-room, thinking, with a gloomy brow and eyes bent steadfast, sightless, upon the ground. At length, he entered and cast himself into a chair, clasping his strong bony hands firmly over each other; and oh! what a wild chaos of mingled feelings, and strong passions, and memories, and regrets, and dreads, and expectations. did his bosom at that moment contain.

All those passions were now called up in his bosom; and the struggle between them was the more tremendous, inasmuch as they were, in many points, arrayed nearly equally against each other. Henry Langford had in a few words laid before him the picture of his life, and had shown a deep and intimate knowledge of that darker part of his history which he had believed to be buried in profound oblivion. For more than twenty years he had heard no allusion to those days of wild and roving adventure, when, driven forth, as he fancied, for ever from his native land, stripped of his rank and his possessions, he had given way to the impulses of a rash, daring, and fierce spirit, had piled upon his own head many a heavy remorse, and seared his own heart with many a deed of evil. He had believed that all the companions of those days were either gone or scattered far from the high and lordly path in which he now trod; he had imagined that he had removed every trace of that bond of fate which united the proud, cold, wealthy Earl of Danemore, the domineering spirit of the country round, to the wild rover of the western seas, whose deeds of daring and of blood were still remembered with awe and fear in a land fertile of strong passions and great crimes.

There were many who remembered him in exile, indeed, but in that part of his exile when his daring courage and great powers had been employed in noble warfare and in an honourable cause; but he thought that the very fact of being so remembered would be an additional safeguard against all suspicion in regard to another period. There was, indeed, a lapse of several years in which his history was unknown to all such companions of his brighter days; and he had more than once been asked where he was when some great event had happened on which the conversation at the moment turned. But Lord Danemore was not a man to be interrogated closely by any one; and, as we have said, he firmly believed that all those who could have answered such questions by pointing to the dark and evil events which had been crowded into a few short years of his life, were far removed, plunged beneath the rolling waves of the ocean, buried upon the sandy beach of distant lands, or with their bones whitening—a public spectacle—in the sun.

Now, however, suddenly, after a long and sunshiny lapse of peaceful years, the memories of former acts were recalled when he least expected them—recalled by one who seemed to have a perfect knowledge of every fact he could have desired to hide; and the dark train of images conjured up from the past: the regret, the remorse, the shame, which he had banished long and carefully, were now linked hand in hand with apprehensions for the future, with the fear of exposure, if not the dread of punishment. His mind, however, was in no unfit state for receiving gloomy impressions, his heart was already excited for the entertainment of fierce and angry passions. Through the whole of that day, from a very early hour in the morning, he had been torn with grief and anger, now mourning over the loss of his son with the deep anguish of wounded affection, now vowing vengeance against that son's murderer, while his heart felt scorched and seared by the burning thirst for revenge.

Disappointment, too, deep and bitter disappointment, had had its share—the disappointment of a proud and ambitious heart. On the son now lost he had fixed all his hopes and all his aspirations, in him had he trusted to see his life prolonged, through him had he expected that future generations would carry on his name with increasing wealth and greatness. Now all was over; the son on whom he had relied was gone; he was childless, lonely, cut off from hope and expectations, to live in darkness and solitude through the chill autumnal twilight of his age, and then to die, leaving all the vast possessions which he had obtained to a distant kinsman, whom he hated and despised.

Such had been, in some degree, the state of his feelings, so shaken, so agitated, when he suddenly found that shame was likely to be added to the other burdens cast upon him, and that the vice and crimes of other years were rising up in judgment against him even at the latest hour. The drop thus cast in was sufficient to make the cup overflow. Never through life had he been accustomed to put any restraint upon the fierce passions of his heart, and now what was there that could act as any check upon them? what was there to prevent him from seeking their gratification? what was there to oppose the desire which instantly sprang up within his heart, of silencing for ever the voice which might tell the dark secrets of other years?

Nevertheless, there was a check, there was something that opposed him in the fiery course he might otherwise have pursued: ay, and opposed him strongly, though it was but a feeling connected with other years, though it was but one of those strange associations between the present and the past which often have a firmer hold upon us than more immediate interests or affections. There was something in Langford's face, there was something in his manner and whole appearance, there was something in the very tone of his voice, rich, and musical, and harmonious, which called up as forcibly to his mind a period of sweet, and early, and happy days, as the tale he had told brought over the glass of memory the dark and awful features of another epoch.

At the sound of that voice, at the glance of that eye, the forms of many bright, and dear, and beloved, many who had been known and esteemed in times of innocence and of happiness, rose up as clearly before him, as if some magic wand had waved over the dark past, and brought out of the dim masses of things irrecoverably gone the images of the dead clothed in all the semblance of life and reality. The associations thus raised were all sweet; and in regard to him who called them up, there was a strange feeling of tenderness, of affection, and of interest, which at the very first sight had made him feel confident that he could never have been the murderer of his son, that he who seemed connected with the brightest portion of his early life could never be one to render the latter part of his existence all dark and desolate.

Then again, when he remembered that the same man held in his possession the great, the terrible secret of his former deeds, all his feelings and his thoughts were changed, and sensations almost approaching to despair came over him—a stern, dark, eager resolution, akin to those fierce determinations and sensations which had filled up that portion of his being to which his thoughts were so suddenly directed.

He sat, then, and gazed upon the ground, with his hands clasped over each other; and twice he murmured to himself, "People may know too much." He pondered upon every word that had been spoken, and for nearly half an hour his thoughts wandered, with a vague uncertain rambling, over the various epochs of the past, connecting them with the present, and then turning again and again towards the past, while anguish and pleasure were still strangely mingled in the retrospect. Still, however, when he remembered the words of Langford, and felt himself to a certain degree in his power, the same dark but ill-defined purpose returned of removing for ever from his path one who held so dangerous a tie upon him. He felt, indeed, a reluctance, a hesitation, a doubt, which he somewhat scorned himself for feeling; and he nerved his mind more and more every moment to execute his determination calmly and deliberately. "I will never live in the fear of any mortal man," he thought. "Were he ten times as like, he should not bear my fate about with him! How! shall he be my only consideration? Surely I am not become either a child or a woman, to waver in such a case as this!"

As he thus thought, he rose from his seat, and strode up and down the room with his arms folded on his chest. Over the large and massy mantelpiece of many-coloured marbles, hung a number of weapons of different kinds; pistols, and swords, and firelocks, and daggers, some of foreign, and some of British, manufacture. There appeared the long Toledo blade, the broad Turkish dagger, the Italian stiletto, the no longer used matchlock, and many another weapon, arranged in fanciful devices; and each time, as the Earl turned up and down the room, he paused and gazed upon them, then bit his lips, and recommenced his course across the chamber. When this had proceeded for about a quarter of an hour, some one knocked at the door, and he started sharply, as if caught in some evil act. The next moment, however, he called to the person without to come in, speaking in an angry tone; and a servant, who, from his dress and appearance, seemed to be his own particular valet, appeared, announcing that Mr. Kinsight, the lawyer, had just arrived on important business.

"I am glad of it," said the Earl; "take him to the library: I will come directly." And as soon as the servant was gone, he added, "This man may be of some use."

He then carefully locked the door which led from his dressing-room to the room which had been assigned to Langford, and descended to the library, to confer with an agent worthy of his purposes.

CHAPTER XVI.

THE prisoner, in the meantime, was not left in solitude; for scarcely had Lord Danemore quitted his chamber, bearing with him a world of dark thoughts and excited passions, when Langford was visited by the person who, more than any one in that house or neighbourhood, seemed to know his history and understand his situation. Mistress Bertha, as she was called, came, ostensibly in her character of housekeeper, to ask if there were anything to be done for the promotion of his comfort: saying, that she had been so commanded in the morning by the Earl. She lingered, however, after she had received his answer, though for some minutes she scarcely spoke; and when she did, she merely uttered a comment on the storm that was raging without. Langford seemed to understand her character well, and he too kept silence, leaving her to say anything that she might desire to say, in her own manner and at her own time.

"It is an awful night," she said; "an awful night, indeed. It is such a night as the spirits of bad men should depart in. I never pass such a night without thinking that there is a likeness between it and the dark stormy heart of the wicked. But it matters not," she added, after a long thoughtful pause. "I have linked myself to his fate, and I must not sever the bond. He is my master, and has been good to me, though he may have wronged others. I will remain by his side."

She paused again, and Langford merely replied, "It were too late now to think of it."

"I understand your meaning," she said, "and it is too late. You would say that in former times I ought to have adhered to the wronged and the oppressed, and so I would, but I was driven from them. It is needless now, however," she continued—"it is needless to say one word more on that score; let us talk of other things. Has he been with you again?"

"He has scarcely left me a moment," replied Langford; "and I fear with less friendly feelings towards me than when we met before. I showed him that I knew much of his former life; for, in truth, good Bertha, the blow must be struck now or never."

"It must, it must!" she replied; "but not too rapidly. Be cautious, be careful. After he left you this morning, I was with him long, and his feelings were all such as you could have hoped for. What had passed between you I know not; but there was a softness, a tenderness had come over him: a light as from other days seemed to shine into his heart, and to flash upon affections and feelings long buried in darkness. He spoke to me of things he has not spoken of for many a year; he used words and he named names that I never thought to hear him utter again. The sight of you seemed to form an eddy in the current of time which carried him back to a happier and brighter part of its course. Be careful, however. Be careful how you deal with him. If you act well and wisely, ere the drops are dried up which are now falling from the clouds, you may tell him all; you may ask him all. But I know him well; and one rash word, one hasty act, may undo your fortunes at the very moment they are well nigh built up."

"I will be careful," replied Langford; "I will be careful, because I am bound by every tie to use all gentle means, rather than harsh ones. But still it is hard completely to restrain one's self, and to seek with softness and concession that which is wrongly withheld, and which I have every right to demand with the loud voice of justice."

"To demand, and not obtain," replied Bertha; "for there is no means by which you can gain your purpose except by gentleness."

Langford smiled. "Be not quite sure of that," he said. "I have at this moment my fate in my own power."

"Indeed!" she exclaimed; "indeed! how so?"

have said, I am bound by every consideration to use gentle means. If I find that they will succeed, I will employ none other; but should they fail, I will boldly and openly assert my own rights, and both claim and take that which is my own."

Bertha's eye, while he spoke, fixed upon one of those small doors in the wainscotting, which we have more than once mentioned, and she shook her head with an incredulous smile. "Because," she said, answering his thoughts more than his words, "because I have placed you here, and because there is between you and what you desire but one small partition. That partition is of iron, which, had you a thousandfold the strength you possess, you could never break through."

"I know it," replied Langford. "I know it well; but yet I tell you, that in those respects my fate is in my own power. However, I will use all gentle means, though no subtlety; but in the end I will do myself right."

"Be it as you say," she answered; "but of one thing beware. It seems that you have rekindled in his bosom a hope of his son Harold being still living. Avoid that; the boy is dead, beyond all doubt: struck down, poor fellow! in his pride of life—broken off in his dearest dream of happiness and love. But let it be so; it is well it should. He would have lived but to deeper grief; he would have remained but for greater anguish. Give the father no hope! For your own sake, give him no hope that the boy is still alive!"

"But I entertained hope myself," replied Langford; "and it was not in my nature, Bertha, to see a father grieving for the death of his son, and not try to afford him what consolation I could."

She shook her head mournfully, adding—"He is dead. I feel that his fate is accomplished. He could not live. He had no right to live. The date is out. He is taken away. But I must stay with you no longer; yet in leaving you, remember my words: use none but gentle means. Urge him alone by the kinder feelings of his nature, for if ever there was a man in whom there dwelt at once two strong spirits, powerful for good and powerful for evil, it is he."

"I will remember your advice," replied Langford, "and thank you for it. I will use gentle means; but by one means or another right shall be done."

She lingered for another moment or two, as if desirous of saying more, but then turned and left him; and proceeding down the staircase into the hall, she encountered the lawyer, just alighted from his horse.

The man of law bowed low and reverentially to one whom he knew to possess great influence over his patron; and, more for something to say than on any other account, added to the usual salutation of good evening, "It is a terrible night, Mistress Bertha; a good soaked posset now were not amiss to warm one."

She looked upon him, however, with cold and motionless features, merely replying in an under voice, as he passed on, "The time will come, I rather think, when you will be glad of something to cool instead of to warm you."

The lawyer must have caught the meaning of what she said, as well as the servant who was conducting him; for a well satisfied smile came upon the face of the latter, while the attorney shrugged his shoulders, and said aloud, "She is a rare virago."

He was conducted by the servant into the library of the castle, where, against the wide and lofty walls, and round the massive pillars that supported the roof, were ranged in due order a vast number of dusty volumes, containing the wisdom and the learning, and the folly and the dulness, of many preceding ages. Lights were placed upon the table; and after waiting for a few minutes, gazing upon the ponderous tomes around him, without, however, venturing to disturb any of them by taking them from their places of long repose, he was joined by the Earl, on whose strongly-marked countenance the keen and practised eye of the lawyer recognised at once the traces of strong emotion.

Deep and reverential was the bow with which the Earl was greeted by the same man who had so lately treated Alice Herbert and her father with contempt and indignity. He remained standing though the Earl had seated himself, and even then did not sit down till he had been twice told to do so. The Earl at the same time would gladly have had the lawyer abate so much of his respect as to commence the conversation himself, for the nobleman's mind was full of dark purposes and stormy passions, and he wished them to be led forth by degrees, lest the fierce crowd, in rushing out too hastily, should throw open the innermost secrets of his heart to a stranger. The lawyer, however, did not venture to do so, being rather overawed than otherwise by the state of agitation in which he beheld his noble client; and the Earl, putting a restraint upon his words, to prevent himself from hurrying forward to the subject of his thoughts at once, began the conversation by saying, "This is a stormy night, sir. What business, may I ask, has brought you hither at such an hour and in this weather?"

The lawyer, though he had gained no small knowledge of the world by long dealings with every different class of men, and by seeing them under every different circumstance and affection, was, nevertheless, embarrassed in regard to his demeanour towards Lord Danemore, situated as he knew him to be at that moment. He had expected to find him, as he did find him, deeply agitated; but the agitation which he had imagined he should behold was bitter grief for the death of his son. Now there was something in the aspect of the peer which made him see at once that many other feelings were mingled with his sorrow, and as he did not know what those feelings were, and desired solely so to shape his whole conduct as to make it agreeable to his patron, he was excessively anxious to discover, by some means, what was going on in the Earl's breast, in order to direct his course accordingly.

Finding, however, that he was not able to make such discoveries, he judged it the best plan to throw before the Earl the subject furthest removed from the death of his son; and to counterbalance grief by exciting anger. He replied, therefore, after a moment's thought—"Nothing but important business, my lord, would have induced me to intrude upon you at such a moment. Your lordship, however, will recollect that you gave me your commands how to proceed in regard to the old Knight at Moorhurst, in which, I am sorry to say, I have been frustrated by a most unexpected incident."

"Frustrated, sir!" exclaimed the Earl, the whole of whose passions were in too excited a state not to take fire at every new obstacle cast in his way. "Frustrated. By all the powers of Heaven, I will not be frustrated! What? do you mean to tell me there is any flaw in the bond, any error in the transaction, which will debar me of my right? If so, look to yourself, sir, for you drew up the whole. Or would you have me believe that he has money to discharge the debt? I tell you, sir, he is a beggar; he is ruined—undone—as you well know. What is the meaning of all this? Frustated! Shall he frustrate me?" and he ended with a scoff of angry derision.

"It is for the purpose of preventing it, my lord," replied the lawyer, meekly, "that I came hither to-night. I wish to lay the case before you, and take your lordship's commands."

"Well, sir, well," rejoined the Earl, recovering from the first burst of passion, "tell me the facts, that I may judge."

From not knowing the new matter which had been cast into the fiery furnace of the Earl's bosom, the lawyer was more and more puzzled at his demeanour every moment. He saw that there was an under-current of feelings running more rapidly than the natural course of those excited by the matter on which they spoke. And in order to fathom his mind, and ascertain of what feelings that undercurrent was really composed, he resolved to throw in, even unnecessarily, the name of Lord Harold, and he answered—"The facts are these, my lord. After seeing you yesterday, and taking precise instructions from you as to the course I was to pursue, I went over to Moorhurst, where I found your lordship's lamented son."

As he spoke a dark cloud came over the countenance of the Earl, but it was of a different kind and character from that which had hung upon his brow before; and the lawyer, at once perceiving that he had not found the right road, instantly turned to the straight-forward path, finding that he must take his chance of going right or wrong in a country where there was no finger-post to direct him. "I was apprehensive," he continued, "lest his generosity might step in to interfere with your lordship's just views and purposes."

"Speak not of my son, sir," said the Earl, sternly; "speak not of my son; for although now that the first anguish is past, I have conquered the quivering of my wounded heart, and the flesh is still, yet I love not that any one should lay his finger on the spot, unless it be a surgeon to heal the injury. Go on with the matter in hand. What said Sir Walter Herbert?"

"Why, he said, my lord, that he could not pay the money," replied the lawyer; "and he fell into a great state of agitation, and would not believe that his affairs were so bad, till I showed him that they could hardly be worse; and then Mistress Alice was sent for, and I must say, never were such airs as the young woman gave herself."

"The young lady, sir!" said the Earl, sternly; "you forget yourself. The person whom I considered meet to be the bride of my son, may well merit her proper name from a low person like yourself."

The attorney was not without the natural feelings of humanity, and he did not fail to experience all those sensations which, under different circumstances induce one man to knock another down. But the effect of our feelings when they are prevented from operating in their natural direction, is often, by their recoil, to drive us in a way directly contrary. Though the lawyer then would have given a great deal to have repelled the insulting language of Lord Danemore, yet he would not have given for that purpose the hundredth part of the advantage which he derived from his patronage and employment; and this being the case, it always happened that the more rude and overbearing the peer showed himself in his demeanour towards the lawyer, the more servile and humble became the lawyer towards the peer.

In the present instance. he begged his lordship's pardon a thousand times, but excused himself on the plea that the conduct of Mistress Alice—her expressions regarding his lordship himself—had been so bold and haughty, that his indignation got the better of his manners.

"However, my lord," he continued, "she agreed at once to give up the pittance that she possesses, for the relief of her father; but still the plate and the jewels, and all the rest, would have to be sold to make up the sum required. I doubt if even that would do, and he would certainly be obliged to go out of the house, and be reduced nearly to a state of beggary."

There was a degree of satisfaction apparent in the countenance of the Earl which made the lawyer stop to let it work, and he watched every shade of expression that passed over the face of Lord Danemore, as he gazed with a curling lip upon the ground. With a sudden start, however, the peer raised his eyes to the countenance of the lawyer, and beheld there—reading it in a moment as a familiar book—all that was passing within his agent's mind.

"You are right, sir," he said, going boldly and at once to the subject of the lawyer's thoughts; "I do hate that man, and if you think that you have made a discovery, you deceive yourself, for there is nothing to conceal. Other men hate their neighbours as well as I, and I see not wherefore I should not have my own private enmities, and gratify them like others. He is one of those good honest people whom the world delights to praise, and the vulgar love and honour. He sets himself up for modest simplicity, and yet affects a state and station which he has not the means to maintain. He is one of your positive lovers of right, too, yielding but formal respect to his superiors, but denying them all authority in matters of importance. In times long gone, when first I returned after the Restoration, I met with more difficulty and opposition in establishing my just rights and influence over the tenantry and people in the neighbourhood, from that mild justice-fancying, learning-loving Sir Walter Herbert, than from all the other petty squires and magistrates in the county. If it had not been for the love my poor boy entertained for him and for his daughter, I would have swept him from my path long ago; but go on, go on with your tale. What obstacle has since arisen?"

"Why, last night, my lord," replied the lawyer, "I left all matters in as fair a train as well might be. The old man had become as pale as ashes, and the young lady, notwithstanding all her pride, had more than once wept bitterly. I gave them till this morning to make up their minds as to how they would act; but when I went thither about two or three hours ago, I found the old knight from home, and my young mistress with her pride and haughtiness all in fresh bloom again. The end of the matter is, my lord, that it seems a friend has been found foolish enough to advance the money without any security whatsoever—a Captain Langford, whom I never before heard of."

"Who? who?" demanded the Earl.

The lawyer repeated the name; and his noble companion, starting up, struck the table a blow with his clenched hand which made the lights dance and flicker as they stood. "This is too much!" he said; "This is too much! I know now where I must aim."

The lawyer had risen at the same time as the peer, and Lord Danemore, striding across towards him, grasped him firmly by the arm, saying, in a low voice. "That very man—that very Langford, is now in this house, having been brought hither by those two foolish justices, Sir Thomas Waller and Sir Matthew Scrope, on charge of being the murderer of my son."

The lawyer, forgetting one half of the awful circumstances of the moment, rubbed his hands with a look of satisfaction. "That will just do, my lord! That will just do!" he exclaimed. "If we can get any proof whatsoever that the money is furnished by this Langford, we will, when it is tendered, which will doubtless be the case to-morrow, seize upon it as the property of a felon, and then proceed against Sir Walter as if he had never had it. Long ere this Langford comes to be tried, by one means or another we can lay the old man by the heels in gaol, and then, by one process or another, mount up such an expense at law as will leave him scarcely a coat to his back."

The Earl smiled, partly with satisfaction at the ready means of gratification which had been found for him in one instance, and partly with contemptuous insight into the workings of the lawyer's mind, feeling that degree of pleasant scorn with which the more powerful but not less evil minds regard the minor operations of the tools they work with in the accomplishment of wicked purposes. The lawyer remarked the expression, and fancied that it was well-pleased admiration of his skill and readiness; and again he rubbed his hands, and chuckled with conceit and pleasure.

The Earl, however, waved his hand somewhat sternly. "Cease, cease," he said; "I can have no laughter here! This house is a house of mourning and of vengeance. We will have no laughter! Your idea is a good one, and you shall be rewarded if the execution answers to the conception. But there is more to be done; there are still greater things to be accomplished—things that are painful to me, but which yet I must do; things I shall remember and regret but which yet I will not shrink from."

As he spoke there came over the strong stern features of the old man's face a dark and awful expression which made even the lawyer shrink and draw back, accustomed as he was to see human passions in all their direst forms. It was the expression, the irrepressible expression of a powerful mind deliberately summoning all its energies to the commission of a crime known, appreciated, and abhorred. The evident effect produced upon the lawyer seemed in some degree to affect his patron, who, ere he spoke further, took two or three gloomy turns up and down the room, and then again drawing near him, said, "But this Langford; what is to be done with Langford? He remains to be dealt with."

The lawyer gazed in the Earl's countenance, doubting in his own mind what he meant; and imagining that the very fact of having aided Sir Walter Herbert was so great a crime in the eyes of the Earl as to call down his vengeance as remorselessly upon the one as upon the other. It was a pitch of vindictiveness at which even his mind was staggered, and he said with some embarrassment, "But, my lord, from what your lordship said just now of those two justices, I fancied you thought the gentleman not guilty."

The Earl gazed upon him steadfastly for so long that the lawyer shrunk beneath his eyes. He then answered deliberately, "I do not think him guilty, but yet I would prove him so."

"But, my lord," stammered the lawyer, "my lord, if the man be innocent! I dare say he did not know he would offend your lordship by helping Sir Walter, otherwise——"

"Hush!" exclaimed the Earl. "It is no such pitiful motive as that which moves me. I have other reasons for my actions, other causes for my determination. Whether the man murdered my son or not is of little import in this question. Hearken to me, my good friend; he must be swept from my path. I have strong and sufficient causes for wishing him hence. He must be removed. He and I cannot live long in the same world together!"

"Good God! my lord," replied the lawyer, this is very terrible. I really know not how to act, or what to think."

"Think," said the peer, "that if by your means I succeed in this business—if, by your zeal for myself and my family you convict this man of the murder of my son, wealth and distinction shall be yours for the rest of your life, but if you do not——"

"But, my lord," said the lawyer, presuming upon the situation in which they were placed so far as to interrupt the Earl, "these are great and terrible things; and if I undertake to accomplish that which your lordship wishes, I must have my reward made sure to me. We do not do such things without reward, nor with any uncertainty."

Lord Danemore now felt, by the bold tone assumed by his subservient tool, a part of the bitterness of wrong action; but he was prepared for that also, and he replied at once, "You are bold, sir, to speak to me in such a manner; but I understand your meaning, and I have a hold upon you yet. We are here alone, with no one to witness our conversation; you therefore judge that I may promise and not perform. But that same exclusion of all witnesses is my security, if not yours; and I now tell you, that if you do not accomplish that which I command, I will withdraw from your hands all those sources of emolument you now enjoy from me; and I will keep this promise in the one case, as surely as I will keep the other in the other case. Make me no reply now: I give you half an hour to determine, and will return to you at the end of that time."

The Earl turned, and walked towards the door; but before he had reached it, the lawyer raised his voice, saying, "My lord, my lord! Do not go! I have determined! What you wish shall be done at all risks, and I will trust to your lordship's promise fully. Only name what is to be my reward!"

The Earl smiled with a dark and bitter smile while he replied, deliberately, "The sum which shall be tendered me to-morrow by Sir Walter Herbert."

"Enough, enough, my lord," said the lawyer; "it shall be done."

The Earl turned and came back to the table. "You understand," he said, "the money shall be yours—when he is dead."

The lawyer was very pale, as well as his patron, but he answered, distinctly, "I do understand, my lord!"

As he spoke, a sudden flash of the lightning glared upon the countenance of each. That of the peer was stern, calm, and determined; that of the lawyer was quivering under a fearful degree of emotion: but what is singular, though the storm had been proceeding during the whole time they were together, so fierce had been the struggle in the bosom of each that neither had noticed the strife of the elements without. The moment, however, that the fearful words had passed, that the dark determination was taken, both remarked the flash and heard the peal of thunder that followed. They were neither of them men to shrink at portents; and though the thunder made the lawyer start, it seemed to both but a confirmation of their compact.

"It is a tremendous night," said the Earl; "you must sleep here, my good friend."

The lawyer muttered forth some few words of thanks, and withdrew; but sleep visited not that night the soft pillow on which he laid his head.

CHAPTER XVII.

The storm of the preceding night had ceased, and left the earth all glittering with golden drops, when the sun rose up and poured the full tide of his glorious light upon that world where, during his absence, so many dark and fearful scenes had been enacted. About nine o'clock, and along a tortuous and unscientific road, which seemed to have been cut solely with a view of mingling the bright sunshine and the cool green shades amidst the pleasant woods through which it wandered, rode along Alice Herbert and her father. Their thoughts were full of matter of deep moment: cares, fears, anxieties, were busy in their bosoms; but yet it were false to say that the sweet scenes through which their way was laid, the cheerful aspect of the summer world, the voice of the blackbird and the lark, the soft calm air of the bright morning, did not soften and soothe all their feelings. It is not alone that in the breast of almost every one there goes on a sort of silent superstition, drawing auguries almost unknown to ourselves from every varying feature of the scenes through which we are led, finding the frowning look of boding fate upon the sky, when the dark clouds roll over it, or the bright smile of hope when it spreads out clear and bright above us; but it is that there are mysterious links of harmony between all our feelings and the universal creations of our God; and that the fine electric chain along which so many strange and thrilling vibrations run, is carried from the heart of man to the uttermost verge of heaven.

The brightness of the morning sunk into Alice's soul, and soothed the painful memories within her; the easy motion, too, of her light jennet, as he cantered untiringly forward through the fresh early air, had something in it inspiring and gladsome. He went along with her as if there were no such things as obstacles or barriers in all life's road, as if all things were smooth and easy as his own soft pace. Sir Walter, too, felt the same; he was peculiarly susceptible to the impressions of external nature, and readily yielded his whole heart to the bright influence of everything fine and beautiful throughout the range of creation. Though in early life he had mingled in many scenes of active strife and endeavour, his heart was all unused and fresh, and retained all the capabilities of enjoyment which bless our early years. He too, therefore, felt his heart lighter, and the fountain of hope welling up anew within him from the gladsome aspect of the morning; and as he rode on with his daughter, followed by two or three servants on horseback, he conversed cheerfully and happily over coming events, and spoke of Langford being immediately set free, of his own affairs restored to order and abundance, and of the happiness of all parties being secured, as if he had held in his hands the keys of fate, and could open the storehouse of fortune, to bring forth what pleasure he pleased for after years.

He spoke, too, without any animosity, of the Earl of Danemore and of his proceedings towards him; and Alice, on her part, was enchanted to hear him do so; for she had feared, from the tone of her father's feelings on the day before, that, either in regard to his own affairs or to those of Henry Langford, some sharp collision would take place between him and the Earl on the first occasion of their meeting. It was partly on that account, when Sir Walter had announced his intention of going over in person to the Castle, both to discharge the debt to Lord Danemore, to lay before him the evidence which he had procured concerning Langford, and to request him to set the latter at liberty, that she had besought him, in terms which her father could not resist, to take her with him.

"The proceeding will seem strange," she said; "but I do not think Lord Danemore is a man who will think it so. He has shown me much kindness, and I should wish to see him, and condole with him under his present grief, both because I do sincerely feel for him, and because I wish him to know that any grief or disappointment I may have occasioned his poor son was not mingled with any unkindness of feeling on my part, any lightness of conduct, or any wish to inflict a wound. He has no one near him to console him or to comfort him; we are the only people he has at all associated with, and I used to think that he was fond of my society, and would hear things from me which he would listen to from no one else."

His daughter's arguments were almost always good to the mind of Sir Walter Herbert; and even if he did understand that she was afraid he might become somewhat over-vehement with the proud and passionate man he was about to see, his was one of those kindly natures free from that irritable vanity which is jealous of all interference; and he suffered his daughter to have her way, because he knew that her motive was good, and felt that he as well as another might fall into error.

Thus they rode on: and, as they went, Sir Walter himself found a thousand excuses for the conduct of the Earl; showed Alice how, in that nobleman's seeming want of liberality towards himself, fatherly pride, wounded by the rejection of his son, might have the greatest share; and how, in the detention of Langford, the magistrates who had arrested him were most to blame; while it was natural that a father's heart, torn and wrung as his must be, should make him regard mere suspicion as direct proof, and suffer his eager desire for vengeance to blind his eyes to the real object.

Judging from such expressions, Alice now felt little doubt that her father's first interview with the Earl would pass over tranquilly; and having no longer the strong motive which had, at first, induced her to cast off a certain feeling of timid shyness which she experienced in regard to seeing Lord Danemore for the first time after all that had taken place between herself and his son, she proposed to remain for a time with Mistress Bertha, the housekeeper, and not to see the Earl till after the business on which Sir Walter went was concluded.

"Perhaps it may be better, my love," replied Sir Walter; "although I never liked that woman, who is as stern and harsh a being, I think, as ever was created. Yet she was always fond of you, Alice: and in regard to my conversation with the Earl, put your mind at rest; I feel too much sorrow for him, at the present moment, to let any degree of anger rest in my bosom, or to suffer anything that he can say, knowing as I do the violence of his nature, to make me forget for one moment that he is a father, mourning for the unexpected loss of his only son."

Their plans being thus arranged, Sir Walter announced to the porter of Danemore Castle that his daughter would remain with Mistress Bertha, while he craved audience with the Earl, on important business.

There was something in the demeanour of Sir Walter Herbert which even the insolent servants of Lord Danemore could not resist; there was the mingling of courtesy and dignity, the conscious right to command, but that right waved for kindness' sake, which is sure to win respect even from those the most unwilling to pay it. The worthy Knight and his daughter, then, were shown, with some degree of ceremony, into one of the large, cold, stately saloons of the Castle, while the servant proceeded to announce their coming to his master. He returned in a few minutes, saying, that the Earl would join Sir Walter there ere long, and that, in the meantime, he would conduct the young lady to Mistress Bertha's room.

She had not been long gone when Sir Walter was joined by the Earl, who was followed into the room by the lawyer, hanging his head and bending his back, like a sulky dog trudging at its master's heels. Lord Danemore received Sir Walter with stately coldness, begged him to be seated, and, as if totally unconscious of anything that had passed before, requested to know what was the cause of his being honoured with Sir Walter Herbert's presence.

"I should not have intruded upon you, my lord, especially at such a moment," said Sir Walter, "but that I am desirous both of offering you any assistance and co-operation in my power in the very painful inquiries which must fall to your lot to make; of laying before you a considerable mass of information which I have already obtained, and at the same time of discharging an obligation which I only deeply regret that it has not been in my power to liquidate long ago."

"Thanking you for your offers of assistance, sir," said the Earl, "we will, if you please, turn to the latter point you have mentioned, first. Although I ordered my views upon the subject to be notified to you before the loss I have sustained, yet I shall not suffer that loss to interfere with the progress of a business which it must be as agreeable to Sir Walter Herbert as to myself to bring to a conclusion."

The Earl spoke in a cold and cutting tone, which brought the warm blood into Sir Walter's cheek. He replied, calmly, however, saying, "Of course, my lord, it is as agreeable to me as to you to conclude a business of this nature, which has produced, I am sorry to say, feelings between us which I hoped would never have existed."

"It seems to me, sir," said the Earl, "that we are entering upon irrelevant matter. I can accuse myself of having done nothing that I was not justified in doing; nor do I perceive that any persons have a right to accuse me of being wanting in feelings of friendship, when they were themselves the first to reject advances by which, considering all things, I believe they might think themselves both honoured and favoured."

"We might view that fact in a different light, my lord," replied Sir Walter, who was becoming somewhat irritated; "however, not to touch any further upon subjects of an unpleasant nature, I am here to tender you payment of the bond which you hold of mine, although, as you are well aware, my lord, the debt was in reality none of mine, but incurred through the villany of another."

"With that, sir, I have nothing to do," said the Earl; "but what are these papers that you offer me?"

"They are, my lord," replied Sir Walter, "as you may see, bills of exchange from houses of undoubted respectability in the capital; of course it is hardly possible to carry in safety such a sum in gold. Should your lordship, however, as by your countenance I am led to suppose, object to receive the amount in this manner, I will, of course, cause the bills to be immediately turned into money."

"I am far from objecting to receive the amount in this manner," replied the Earl; "indeed, it might be, in many respects, more convenient; but there is something peculiar here; more than one of these bills is endorsed with the name of Henry Langford."

"Such is the case, my lord." replied Sir Walter. "Of that gentleman I shall have to speak to you in a few moments; but it was your lordship's wish that we should adhere in the first instance to this business, and, such being the case, we will conclude it, if you please. Are you willing to receive those bills in payment? or shall I cause them to be turned into money, as may be done immediately?"

A dark and fiend-like smile of satisfaction had been gradually coming over the countenance of the Earl; and there was a struggle in his mind between the natural quickness and impatience of his disposition, and the desire which he felt to protract the actual execution of his purpose, in order to enjoy every step he took therein. Impatience, however, at length predominated; and he replied, taking the whole packet of bills of exchange from the table—

"There will be no occasion, I am afraid, to cause these bills to be turned into money, for some time at least; although, Sir Walter Herbert, I cannot receive them as payment of your debt. They are, as I am informed—and the name upon the back of some of them bears out that information—they are the property of a person now under charge of felony; and I therefore find myself called upon, in my capacity of magistrate, to take possession of them, till the accusation against him is proved or disproved."

Sir Walter, for a moment, sat before him thunderstruck, without making any reply, while the Earl continued to fix upon him the full gaze of his stern dark eyes, enjoying the surprise and pain he had occasioned. The instant after, however, Sir Walter recovered himself, and replying to the look of the Earl with one as stern and resolute, he said, "I conclude that your lordship is jesting, though the moment for so doing is strangely chosen; but I cannot believe that the Earl of Danemore wishes to prove himself a villain more detestable than the needy sharper who fleeces a confiding dupe. Concluding that there was something in noble blood which implied honour and integrity; trusting that a long line of generous ancestors afforded some tie to honesty and upright conduct, if nothing more—believing the person who calls himself the Earl of Danemore not to be the bastard of a noble house, but one who had some cause to hold its honour high—thus thinking and believing, I placed in his hands those papers, which he is bound either to receive as payment of his debt, or to restore to me in the same manner as he received them."

The Earl was too well satisfied to yield to anger; and he replied, with the same cold and bitter calmness which he had displayed throughout, "You are right, sir, in all your conclusions, except the last. Noble birth should be coupled with integrity; high ancestors are a tie to honour; the Earl of Danemore has every reason to believe himself the legitimate son of his father; but, nevertheless, he may take a different view of his duty from Sir Walter Herbert, in a matter where Sir Walter Herbert is an interested party—too much so, indeed, to judge with his usual clearness. These papers, which it is now my purpose to seal up and deliver into the hands of my worthy friend here present, Master Kinsight, are evidently the property of this same Henry Langford, who stands accused of the murder of my son."

"My lord, my lord," interrupted Sir Walter, "if you have taken any pains to investigate this matter, you must be well aware that the case made out against that upright and honourable man, Captain Langford, is not even a case of suspicion, far less one which justifies his detention for a moment. It is not even proved that your son is dead; and I pray to God that it may not be so."

"Prove that, sir, prove that," exclaimed the Earl, "and none will be more glad than I shall be; but even then, I very much fear these papers would remain to be dealt with according to law, as there can be no doubt whatever that this same Henry Langford, if not a principal, is an accessary to all those acts of pillage and robbery which have lately disgraced this neighbourhood. You are not aware, Sir Walter, of all the facts; you are not aware of all that has been discovered this very morning, Master Kinsight here having, with all his own shrewdness, obtained proof, almost incontestible, that this same Henry Langford is one of a band of plunderers who have established themselves in this county, and whose acts speak for themselves."

Again Sir Walter Herbert was struck dumb. "My lord," he said, at length, after a considerable pause, "I am a magistrate of the county, and, consequently, may be permitted to demand the nature of the evidence against Captain Langford, especially as I have both taken a very active part in putting down the system of violence and outrage which has, as you observed, disgraced this neighbourhood, and have investigated the matter thoroughly since the attack upon my daughter, of which you most probably have heard, and from which she was delivered by the courage of Captain Langford alone. I, therefore, must beg to see the evidence against him, as I have with me the depositions of various witnesses which clear him of all suspicion in regard to the disappearance of your son."

"I do not feel myself called upon," replied the Earl, "nor, indeed, do I think it would be right and just, to make any one acquainted with the discoveries we have already made, before the whole train of evidence is mature. There are two learned, wise, and most respectable magistrates, Sir Thomas Waller and Sir Matthew Scrope, who are even now engaged in collecting information on the subject, and it would be not only an insult to them, but an effectual means of frustrating the ends of justice, were any other person permitted to interfere, especially when that person is avowedly a supporter of the culprit."

"All this is very specious, my lord," replied Sir Walter; "but it may be doubted—and I am one of those who do doubt—whether personal motives on your lordship's part may not mingle with the view you take of the case, and whether your known power and influence in this neighbourhood may not have more to do with the decision of the magistrates you mention than the considerations of right and justice."

"Your language, Sir Walter Herbert, is growing insulting," replied the Earl, "and, indeed, so has been your whole conduct. I have passed it over as yet, out of consideration for the foolish fondness which my poor son entertained towards a member of your family. It must go no further, however, or you shall find that I am not to be insulted with impunity. The imputations, too, which you cast upon two respectable men are altogether unworthy; and I beg to say that I shall hear no more upon this or any other subject from you. My lawyer shall have my directions to deal with you, in regard to your debt to me, with moderate determination; and any evidence that you may have collected in reference to the prisoner had better be communicated to the two magistrates who have the case before them. I must beg now to be excused any further conversation on the subject."

"Then I am to understand, my lord," said Sir Walter, "that you positively and distinctly refuse to return to me the bills of exchange which I have, with foolish confidence, placed in your hands."

The Earl bowed his head in token of assent, and Sir Walter proceeded, "You will permit me, if you please," he said, "to call in one of my own servants to witness my demand, and your refusal."

"That is unnecessary, sir," replied the Earl; "I will give you an acknowledgment under my own hand, that I have taken possession of certain bills of exchange belonging to Henry Langford, accused of felony. Draw it up, sir," he continued, turning to the lawyer.

The lawyer did as he was directed, employing all the most cautious expressions, and the Earl, after having read the paper over, signed it, and delivered it to Sir Walter Herbert.

"Your lordship's conduct is certainly most extraordinary," replied Sir Walter; "but this business shall soon be cleared up, for I have determined that I will not rest one moment till the best legal assistance has been procured for the noble gentleman you seem disposed to persecute, and who has been deprived of his liberty upon the accusation of having murdered a person who is by no means proved to be really dead."

He was turning to quit the apartment, and the Earl was in the act of directing his lawyer in a low voice to have him arrested at once for the debt, when two or three hard blows upon the door, as if struck with a heavy stick, called the attention of the whole party, and caused the good Knight to stop, expecting to see the door open, and some one enter. The door, indeed, did open, but it was only pushed forward a small space, just giving room sufficient to admit the head of the half-witted man John Graves.

As soon as he beheld him, Sir Walter exclaimed, "Here is one who probably can tell us more of the matter than any one else; for, if I am rightly informed, it was upon his testimony, received second-hand, that these magistrates acted."

"That I can, indeed," said the half-witted man, still standing in the doorway; "I can tell you more about it than any one else, for I saw him buried last night with my own eyes under the beech trees."

"Who? who?" demanded several voices at once; while the Earl, with the feelings of a father breaking forth, and overpowering all others, strode forward and gazed in the man's face.

"Why, the boy," replied the other; "the boy Harold; and I came to tell you where he lies."

The Earl covered his eyes with his hands, and for a few minutes an awful silence spread through the room. Sir Walter Herbert could not have found in his heart to break in upon the first moment of parental grief for any consideration; and he suffered the bitter agony to have its way without attempting by one word of consolation to soothe that deep wound which he himself believed to be incurable, and only likely to be aggravated by any earthly appliance. The lawyer, though feeling very differently, was yet afraid to speak; and Silly John, as he was called, stood gazing upon them, infected by the feelings expressed in the countenance of the Earl and Sir Walter, when he announced the sad confirmation of their worst fears.

It was the Earl himself who first broke silence. "Sir," he said, turning abruptly to Sir Walter, "I desire to be alone. This is no time for any other business than that either of mourning for my son, or punishing his murderers; with regard to other matters, you shall hear from me hereafter. Your fair scornful daughter, I understand, accompanied you hither, and now waits for you. Pray tell her that, though bound by courtesy to receive the visits of a lady at all seasons, yet at present the heart of the father is not very well attuned to hear consolatory speeches on the death of his only son, from the lips of one who first encouraged and then rejected that son's addresses, and who, it would appear, by such conduct brought about his death."

"My lord," replied Sir Walter, mildly, "so deeply am I sorry for you, that I will concede to your sorrow even the privilege of being unjust, and will not defend my child, though she be altogether innocent of that with which you charge her. She is now in Mistress Bertha's room, waiting my coming; and, taking leave of you with deep sympathy for your loss, I will seek her there and return with her to my own dwelling."

"Seek where you may find, Sir Walter," said Silly John, turning with a lacklustre smile upon the Knight; "seek where you may find: for you will not find Mistress Alice nor Mistress Bertha either where you think they are; for I saw them stepping quietly up stairs towards the old north tower; and the lady and her lover are by this time looking into each other's eyes."

"This is somewhat too much!" exclaimed the Earl, with an angry frown; "I did not know that the young lady was so great a proficient in policy: but by your leave, Sir Walter, I must interrupt their conference;" and striding towards the door with flashing eyes, he threw it open and advanced towards the great staircase.

Sir Walter followed quickly, and at the foot of the stairs touched the Earl's arm slightly, with a meaning look, saying at the same time, "I trust, my lord, that in your present excited state you will not forget who Alice Herbert is, and that her father is present."

The Earl turned, and gazed at him from head to foot. "I shall not forget *myself*, sir," he replied; "the Earl of Danemore is not accustomed to injure or insult a woman!" and thus saying, he strode up the stairs with the same quick pace.

CHAPTER XVIII.

There was a thrill in the heart of Alice Herbert as she followed the servant through the long passages of Danemore Castle, which sprang neither from old associations nor from the solemn silence which reigned through the whole building. Since she had last trod those long corridors new feelings had taken possession of her bosom; new thoughts, new hopes, new happiness, had arisen in her heart; and every pulse that throbbed in that heart had some reference to the earnest affection which now dwelt within her. As she passed along, then, following the servant, who with slow and solemn steps led the way, she could not but remember that she was probably in the same house with Henry Langford, and a vague fancy that by some means she might see him, if it were but for a moment, made her heart beat and her whole frame tremble.

The room to which she was led was vacant, and she sat down to meditate over the past and the future, both of which had a world of absorbing thoughts and feelings to engage her attention. But yet her eyes wandered round the small chamber, which she had not visited for many years, and she remarked that to the crucifix and missal which usually lay upon a table near the window, marking the faith of the occupier of that apartment, were now added the grinning skull and mouldy bones, which may well serve as mementos of our mortality.

She had not been there long, however, when the slow stately step of Mistress Bertha was heard near the door, and the next moment she entered the room, gazing upon Alice with a calm, but somewhat sad, expression of countenance, as she answered her salutation.

"Good morrow, Mistress Bertha," said the young lady; "I hope you have been well since we last met, which is now a long time ago."

"Well, quite well, lady," replied Mistress Bertha; "it is a long time ago; and many things have happened in the space between, which should not have happened. Fate, however, has had its way. We must all fulfil our destiny; and you and I, as well as others, are but working out what is to come to pass."

"If you mean, Mistress Bertha," said Alice, "that I have not been here of late so frequently as I used to be, I think, when you remember all that has happened, you will not judge that I acted wrongly in making my visits scarce at Danemore, where my father's reception has long been cold."

"I blame you not, Mistress Alice; I blame you not," replied the housekeeper. "What right have I to blame you? You liked him not; you loved him not. That was not your fault, nor the poor boy's either. You were fated for another, and that other fated to snatch from *him* that which he held dearest. We cannot control our likings and dislikings; they are the work of destiny. There have been those who loved me that I could never love, those who have treated me well and kindly, who through long years befriended me, and with tenderness and affection did all to win regard; and yet when they had done all, they failed; and, seizing gladly on some rash word, some hasty burst of passion, I have cast their benefits behind me, and left them, because I could not love them. What right, then, should I have to blame others for feeling as I have felt, and doing even less than I have done?"

"I am sure, Mistress Bertha," replied Alice, gently, "I am quite sure, from what I know of you, that, though you might act sharply, you would never act unjustly, and never be guilty of any degree of ingratitude, though you almost accuse yourself of being so."

"You do not know, you do not know," replied the other; "I have been guilty of ingratitude. I know, and acknowledge, and feel, that to her who was kind to me from her youth, whose fathers had protected my fathers, and whose generosity had raised me from low estate, I know and feel that I was ungrateful; that I could not, that I did not, return her love for love, and that I quitted her at the first rash and thoughtless word. So far I did wrong, and felt evil: but I did no more; my heart was not made, as many another is made, to hate because I knew that I had wronged. I went upon my way and she upon hers, but I sought for no opportunity of doing her ill. On the contrary, I would willingly have atoned for what I had done by serving her in those matters where she felt most deeply. I did serve her as far as I could; but there are things which I must not do—no, not even now."

"I know not to what your words allude," replied Alice, speaking to her gently and kindly, wishing to soothe rather than in any degree to irritate one towards whom she had always experienced feelings of great kindness, and even respect; for although Mistress Bertha, on many occasions, had given way in her presence to the sharp and unruly temper which evidently existed within her heart, yet the occasions on which it had been exercised, Alice had always remarked, were those where there was either an open and apparent, or a concealed but no less certain cause, for the contempt or anger to which she yielded such unbridled sway. "I know not to what your words allude, but I doubt not that you judge of yourself harshly—too harshly, Mistress Bertha, as I have often seen you do in regard to yourself before."

Bertha gave a melancholy smile, and shook her head, as she replied, "Young lady, clear your mind of that great error; the greatest, the most pernicious of the poisonous dainties with which human vanity feeds itself in all this world of vain things! We never judge of ourselves too harshly. The brightest and the best, the noblest and the most generous, if they could but look into their own bosoms with eyes as clear and righteous as those that gaze upon them from the sky, would find therein a thousand dark forms and hideous errors, of which their hearts accuse them now but little. Ay; and if in the whole course of human actions we could see the current of our various motives separated from each other, how much that is vile and impure should we find mingling with all that we fancy bright and clear! No, no! man never judges himself too harshly, let him judge as harshly as he will. God sees and judges, not harshly, we hope, but in mercy; and yet, what sins does not his eye discover, what punishments will he not have to inflict!"

Alice was silent; but after a momentary pause Bertha resumed the conversation nearly where she had first begun it. "I blame not you," she said, "young lady, for not loving one who loved you. It was not destined so to be, though there may have been a feeling of pride, too, in your dealings with him. The poor boy who is gone had not the eagle eye and ruling look of this one—an eagle eye and ruling look gained from a noble race in other lands; and well do I know how, with young happy things like you, the eyes lead captive the imagination; ay, and fix chains of iron upon the heart. Yet you judged well and nobly, too, if I see aright. That face and form are but an image of a mind as bright, and he has every right to have such a mind now that all that was dark, and fierce, and harsh in the proud streams that mingle in his veins has been purified, and tempered, and softened by long adversity."

"Of whom do you speak, Mistress Bertha?" demanded Alice, with a conscious blush mantling in her cheek as she asked the question.

"Of whom do I speak!" echoed Bertha, gazing on her; "would you have me think that you do not know of whom I speak?"

"No," answered Alice, blushing still more deeply; "no, Mistress Bertha, I do not wish to deceive you. I know, at least I guess, you speak of Captain Langford; but—but—"

Bertha gazed thoughtfully down upon the ground for a few moments; "I had forgot," she said at length, "yet he did wisely—he always does wisely! But I had not believed that there was a man who, in the unchained moments of the heart's openness, would act so wisely and so well! I understand you, sweet lady. You were not aware that I knew rightly the story of your heart; and I knew it only by having divined it. Yet to show you how well I have divined it, I will tell you the motive that brought you hither with your father. You came with the view of seeing him you love!"

The ingenuous colour once more rose warm in Alice's cheek; but she replied, with that sparkling of truth and sincerity in her pure eyes that there was no doubting one single word, "No, Mistress Bertha," she said, "you are wrong. I come hither with no such motive, with no such view. My father had business with the Earl, so painful, so irritating, that I sought to accompany him, solely with the wish to soothe and calm both; but I found as we rode along that Sir Walter's mind was already prepared to treat all things gently and kindly, in consideration of Lord Danemore's sad loss; and, therefore, I thought it better to come to this room than to intrude upon the Earl's grief till I was quite sure he would be well pleased to see me. But, on my word, the thought of seeing Captain Langford never entered my mind till I was crossing the hall to come hither. Then, indeed, remembering that he had been brought hither, and having learned that he had been most wrongly detained—at least all yesterday—I thought he might still be here, and that, perhaps, I might see him. Nor will I deny, Mistress Bertha," she added, "that I much wish to do so, if it be possible."

"I believe your whole tale, Alice Herbert," replied Bertha, "I believe it all and every word; for I have seen and watched you from your childhood, and I know that you are truth itself. You shall see your lover, Alice. You shall taste those few bright moments of stolen happiness which are dear, all too dear, to every young heart like thine."

"Nay, nay, Bertha," said Alice, in reply, "though I will not deny that his society is happiness to me, I have a greater object in view; I have to learn how I—I, his promised wife, may aid him at the present painful moment. Nor, Bertha," she added, while at the very repetition of the words her cheeks again grew red, "nor do I wish that the moments spent with him should be stolen moments. I ask you openly, if it be possible to let me see him and speak with him. I wish no concealment. I seek not to hide either my regard for him, nor my interview with him. Sure I am that my father would approve it, and I have none but him to consider, in framing my actions."

Bertha gazed upon her glowing countenance and sparkling eyes, as she raised them, full of timid eagerness, to her face, with a look of pleasure not unmixed with surprise. "You are, indeed, a noble creature and a lovely one," she said; "yours may well be called generous blood. But it shall be as you wish; and yet be under no fear for your lover. They cannot injure him! It is not his destiny. He is born for a very different fate, and the fools who took him were only tools in Fortune's hands, to cut a pathway for him to the point where he is now arrived. Fear not, Alice, but come with me, and you shall see and speak with him; alone, if you will."

"No, not alone!" said Alice, again colouring; "not alone! That were needless—useless."

"Come with me, then," said Bertha, "come with me, then; though it is little needful that you should see him, to take council with him for his liberation. Ere to-morrow morning he will be free. They cannot hold him there long. To think of holding him there at all is idle and empty; and there is one of them, at least, that feels it to be so, though he knows not well why."

As she spoke, she led the way out of the room in which they were, and along the corridor towards the great hall. Alice made no reply, for her heart beat so fast, and her limbs trembled so much, that she was glad to take refuge in silence in order to hide her agitation. She knew that she was going to do nothing but what was right. She felt that every sensation of her heart, every purpose of her mind, was pure, and noble, and good; and yet—why or wherefore she could not tell—there was something in the act of thus going privately to see her lover in the house of another, which made her tremble like a guilty creature, though conscious of innocence in thought and deed. She looked anxiously at each door as she passed, lest it should be opened, and some one issue forth to interrupt her. She hurried her pace up the great staircase, gazing round with feelings of apprehension she could not comprehend; and when at length they reach the extremity of the building, and stood before the last door upon that side, she was obliged to lay her hand on Bertha's arm, and beg her to stop for a moment, in order to recover breath, and gain some degree of command over herself.

At length she said, "Now, now I am ready," and Bertha opened the door of the outer chamber. It was tenanted by a single servant, apparently busy in the ordinary occupations of the day, putting this article of furniture in one place, and that article in another, with that sort of tardy diligence remarkable in houses where there are many servants and but little to do.

He started, however, and turned round when he heard the door open; and then advancing towards Bertha, he said, "My lord ordered me, Mistress Bertha, not to give any one admission here;" he then added, in a low sort of confidential tone, "The orders came early this morning for me to hang about here, and when I had done with the rooms, to remain upon the staircase, so as to make sure that the prisoner does not escape, without locking the doors, however—though I don't see why my lord should take such a round-about way, when by doing nothing but just turning the key he could keep the young man in as long as he liked."

"The Earl has his reasons for all that he does," replied Bertha, walking on. "You will do very right to stop every one; but of course your lord's orders do not apply to me. Come with me, young lady; you may be admitted, as I told you."

The man looked surprised and bewildered; for Mistress Bertha, as he well knew, was not a person to be contradicted with impunity, and yet he feared that he would be doing wrong in letting the two visitors pass.

Half the advantages, however, which are gained in this world, either over our adversaries or rivals, are obtained by taking advantage of their astonishment; and before the man had time to make up his mind as to what he ought rightly to do, Mistress Bertha and Alice had passed him, and the door of the inner chamber was open.

Langford was sitting at the table, writing, and the sound of the opening door made him raise his eyes. For a moment it seemed as if he could scarcely believe that what he saw was real; but then a look of joy and satisfaction, which would have repaid Alice well, had she had to encounter a thousand dangers and difficulties in making her way to visit him, spread over his countenance, and, rising up, he advanced to meet her.

Without doubt or hesitation, he cast his arm around her, and pressed his lip upon her cheek. "Thank you, dearest Alice, thank you," he said, "this is, indeed, most kind and most good; how can I ever show myself grateful enough for such a token of affection?"

Alice burst into tears. To see him sitting there—him whom she loved, and honoured, and esteemed—a prisoner, and accused of dark crimes, had wrung her heart almost to agony; but his words and his look, and the tone of his voice, and the touch of his hand, and the pressure of his lips, seemed to sever the bonds which held the varied emotions struggling together in her breast, and they all burst forth together in that profuse flood of tears.

"It is we that must be grateful to you," she said, as soon as she could speak; "it is we that must be grateful to you. I cannot help suspecting, nay believing, that you are suffering in some degree on our account; but for fear we should not have time to speak fully, let me tell you, Langford, the principal object of my coming here. I was afraid that you might not have means allowed you of communicating with any of your friends, and, therefore, I was anxious to see you, to ask what can be done for you, what lawyer can be sent for to you, or what means can be taken to prove your innocence?"

"My Alice has never doubted my innocence, then?" said Langford, gazing tenderly upon her. "I knew, I felt sure, she would not."

"Of anything like crime, Langford," she said, "I knew you were innocent, perfectly innocent! I might imagine, indeed—for we women can hardly judge or tell to what lengths you men may think the point of honour should carry them—I might imagine, indeed, that you had taken this unhappy young man's life in honourable quarrel; but even that I did not believe."

"Oh, no!" replied Langford; "I should never have dreamt of such a thing. Nothing could have provoked me to do so. Besides, Alice, did I not give you my word? and believe me, dear Alice, believe me, now and ever, that I look upon my word given to a woman as binding as my word given to a man. Nay, if it were possible, I should say more binding, because she has fewer means of enforcing its execution. No, no! dear Alice, I parted with him in the park, within ten minutes after I left you. It is true, he did try to provoke me to a quarrel, but I was not to be provoked."

"I am ashamed of having doubted you, even in that, and for a moment," replied Alice; "but that doubt sprang solely from a belief that men often think it a point of honour to conceal their intentions from women in such matters as these, and believe themselves justified in using any means to do so. But now, Langford, tell me quickly, what can be done to prove you innocent? What is there that my father or myself can do to free you from a situation so painful?"

"I know little," replied Langford, "that can be done under present circumstances. It is their task to prove that I am guilty, more than mine to show that I am innocent: but I hear steps upon the stairs. Who have we here, I wonder?"

As he spoke, he opened the door into the other room, which Bertha had closed behind her; and nearly at the same moment, as the reader may have anticipated, the outer door at the top of the stairs was thrown open, and the Earl of Danemore, with a countenance on which hung the thunder-cloud of deep but suppressed wrath, strode in, followed closely by Sir Walter Herbert.

The colour came and went rapidly in Alice's cheek, and her heart beat very quick. The servant in the outer room looked tremblingly towards Mistress Bertha; but Bertha herself remained totally unmoved, with her long sinewy hands, clad in their white mittens, resting calmly upon each other, and her dark eyes raised full upon the Earl, while not a quiver of the lip nor a movement of the eyelids betrayed that she was affected by any emotion whatsoever. Langford drew a little closer to the side of Alice, while the Earl turned his first wrath upon the servant.

His words were few and low, but they were fully indicative of what was passing in his heart. "I commanded," he said, "that no one should be admitted here! You have disobeyed my commands. Answer me not a word. You have disobeyed my commands, and you shall have cause to remember it to the last day of your life. Silence,

I say! Get you gone, and send hither Wilton and the other groom of the chambers. Madam." he continued, advancing towards Alice, with a bitter and sarcastic sneer curling his lip, " Madam, long as I have had the honour of your acquaintance, I did not know that you were so skilful a tactician till to-day. To engage me with your serviceable and convenient father, while you came hither to lay your plans with a personage accused of the murder of my son, is a stroke, indeed, worthy of a great politician——"

Alice had turned pale when he first approached her; but at the words, "your serviceable and convenient father," the blood rushed up into her cheek; and though, while turning to look at Sir Walter, whose eyes were beginning to flash with indignation, she suffered the Earl to finish his sentence, she stopped him at the word " politician," by raising her hand suddenly, and then replied at once, with her sweet musical voice sounding strangely melodious after the harsh tone in which Lord Danemore had been speaking—

"Forbear, my lord," she said, " forbear! Let me prevent you from using any more words that you will be ashamed of and grieve for hereafter. My motive in coming to this house to-day was anything but that which you imply. I came, my lord, because I feared that my father, justly irritated at some unworthy treatment, might act towards Lord Danemore as Lord Danemore is now acting towards me: that is to say, might speak angry words which he would soon be sorry for. I found, however, my lord, that the kind gentleness of that father's heart was already sufficient to make him forget the injuries which Lord Danemore sought to inflict, in the sorrow which Lord Danemore now experiences; and, though there was a time, my lord, when I believed that the voice of Alice Herbert had some power to soothe, to tranquillize, and to console you, I did not flatter myself that such was the case now, and I remained in consequence without."

The Earl seemed somewhat moved. He had listened in silence, and drew himself up to his full height, with an air of attention and thought. When she paused, however, he demanded, but in a softer tone, " And your coming here, madam—here, into this room—was, doubtless, perfectly accidental; a singular coincidence brought you into the apartments of this worthy gentleman."

"No, my lord," replied Alice, with a degree of calm dignity that set his sneers at defiance, "quite on the contrary; as soon as I found that Captain Langford was still here, I asked Mistress Bertha to conduct me to see him, which, your lordship will perceive, was very natural," she added, with the colour becoming deeper and deeper in her cheek, " if you consider, first, that he was severely injured in my defence; next, that I have promised him my hand; and, lastly, that I knew him to be both unjustly charged with a great crime, and in the power of one who sometimes suffers a nature, originally most noble, to be influenced too much by strong passions; and a judgment, originally clear and right, to be darkened and obscured by his own desires and prejudices. My lord," she added, " the tone which you are pleased to assume towards me obliges me to speak candidly; I thought it very possible that, circumstanced as he is, and in your power, this gentleman might meet with obstacles in establishing his innocence, and in communicating with those who would defend and advise him. Under these circumstances, I acted as I have acted, in order to bear any communication from him, either to my father, or to any other person with whom he might think fit to take counsel."

"Madam," replied the Earl, with far less acerbity of manner than before, "I find that you can judge severely, too. This gentleman shall have every opportunity of proving his innocence."

"That, my lord, I will take care of," interrupted Sir Walter Herbert; "for I certainly will not trust, in the case of my friend, to the justice of those who, without a shadow of reason, first charged him with a crime of which he is innocent, and then acted towards him as if they had nearly proved him guilty."

"He shall have every opportunity of proving his innocence," reiterated the Earl, sternly; "but Sir Walter Herbert is the man who judges too hastily. But yesterday, I said to this same gentleman, this Captain Langford, as he is pleased to call himself, that his bare word not to quit these apartments was sufficient. To-day, I say that those bolts and bars, strong as they are, are not too strong to guard him withal: for I have not only received, as you well know, the confirmation of my poor son's death, but I have it proved, beyond all doubt, by the testimony of those who saw him, that the man who stands before us, after separating from that son in the park, was seen by four different people galloping up towards the very moor and at the very time at which the unhappy boy was murdered. He shall have the full opportunity of explaining or disproving this hereafter; at present he is a close prisoner here, till he can be removed to-morrow to the county gaol."

Alice's cheek grew very pale as the Earl spoke; not that she for a moment suffered her confidence in Langford's innocence to be shaken; not that one doubt or one suspicion ever crossed her mind; but that the words used by the Earl were such as to call up before the eye of imagination every dark and painful object which could by any chance connect itself with her lover's situation. The image of Langford, in the county gaol, immured in a close, noisome cell, as a common felon, together with all that she knew and all that she had heard of the prisons of England—then a disgrace to the land—presented itself to her mind, and made her heart sink within her.

The eyes of her lover, however, were upon her. He saw the colour fade away in her cheek; he saw the anxious quivering of that beautiful lip which had so lately spoken boldly in his defence; but Langford knew and understood the heart whose treasured affection he had obtained, and taking her hand in his, he pressed it to his lips, saying, "Fear not, dear Alice! Let them do their worst. So confident am I in my own innocence, and in the just laws of a free land, that not the slightest apprehension crosses my mind, though I may see a disposition to deny me justice. Strange, too, as it may seem to you, I am well contented to remain in this house for some time longer; and perhaps," he added, "I could, even by a single word, change entirely the feelings and views of its noble owner."

"I may understand you better than you think, sir," replied the Earl, gazing upon him with the same knitted brow; "I may know you better than you believe; but you would find it difficult to change my views and purposes. At present I have but to say, that I cannot suffer Mistress Alice Herbert to remain here any longer. Bertha," he continued, turning to the housekeeper, you have done bitterly wrong in bringing her hither. I am willing to believe that you knew not how wrong; but I will deal with you hereafter upon this matter."

"Earl of Danemore, I did right!" replied the woman, "and I tell you that it is you who know not what you are doing; but the time will come when you will repent."

The Earl's brow grew very dark, but he evidently made a great effort to command his passions, and he only replied, "You have served me too faithfully and too long for my anger to have way. But provoke me no further; I am not in a mood to bear with your bold temper. Now, madam," he continued, turning to Alice, "we wait your pleasure."

Langford pressed her hand in his, and grasped that which Sir Walter extended towards him; "Farewell," he said, "farewell, for the present. It is useless to stay longer now. All that you can do for me is to engage some person learned in the law to watch the proceedings against me, in case I should not be liberated before to-morrow evening. I fear nothing in the straight-forward course of justice; but there are circumstances in my situation and in my fate," and as he spoke he fixed his eyes upon the Earl, "which may bring persecution upon me, though they ought to have the most opposite effect."

The Earl returned his look stedfastly and sternly, then turned upon his heel, and waving his hand ceremoniously towards the door, followed Sir Walter and Alice out of the room. He found the servants that he had sent for at the head of the stairs, and gave them charge to guard the prisoner better than he had been previously guarded, to keep the door constantly locked, and to remain, the one at watch on the outside of the door, while the other kept guard at the foot of the stairs. He then walked slowly down into the vestibule, and, in cold silence on all parts, saw Sir Walter and his daughter mount their horses and depart.

CHAPTER XIX.

COULD we but have the heart of the wicked laid open before us; could we but see how it is torn and wrung by the evil passions that harbour within it; could we but mark how, even in the strongest and most determined breast, when bent upon evil purposes, or engaged in wicked acts, fear and apprehension go hand in hand with every deed of evil, while repentance, remorse, and punishment follow more slowly, though not less surely, in the distance; what an instructive, what an awful lesson it would be, and how fearfully we should shrink back from the commission of the first crime, as from the brink of a precipice which, once overleapt, dashes us down over a thousand pointed rocks, even into the gulf of hell itself!

When Sir Walter and Alice Herbert had left him, the Earl of Danemore pressed his hand upon his burning brow for a few moments, while wild and thrilling thoughts, all painful, all angry, all evil, crossed and re-crossed each other through his brain. He then turned with a rapid step, and entered the room where the lawyer had lingered, fearing to follow to a scene where the violent passions which he knew existed in his patron's breast were likely to be excited into fury. The Earl closed the door, and casting himself down into a chair, covered his eyes with his hands.

He was roused, however, in a moment, by a voice saying, "Do not grieve so, Danemore; do not grieve so. It's a sad thing, truly, to have one's fine boy killed, and never see him again; but we must all die once, and you'll die too, and very likely not long first, for you are an old man now. Then we shall be all comfortable again, when we get on the other side of the mole's habitation. Let me speak to him, Master Kinsight; why should I not comfort him? We should all comfort each other."

"I have been trying, my lord," said the lawyer, in an apologetic tone, as the Earl raised his eyes towards the half-witted man, "I have been trying to get out of this foolish fellow who were the people that he saw bury your lordship's noble son. He admits that he knows them all, but declares that he will never mention the names of any of them."

The Earl passed his hand once or twice before his eyes, as if to clear away other images from before his mental vision, ere he returned to the subject which was again suddenly presented to him.

"He shall be made to tell," he said, at length, in a stern tone, knitting his dark brows as he spoke; "he shall be made to tell, after he has pointed out the spot where the poor boy lies."

"Why, my lord," answered the lawyer, "we do not need his help for that, as he himself says that it was under the beech trees by the Mere; but I am sure I do not know how your lordship will make him speak, for I have been trying for this half hour, threatening him with your lordship's displeasure, and to have him put in the cage, and everything I could think of, but without effect."

"There are ways would make the dumb speak," replied the Earl. "I have seen,"—he continued; but then, suddenly breaking off, he changed his form of speech, and added, "I have heard, I mean to say, of old Spaniards in the new world, who loved their gold better than their life, and would have died sooner than reveal the spot where their treasures were hidden; and yet there have been found ways to make them speak; there have been found means to make them scream forth the name of every treasure-cave they had."

"But, my lord," replied the lawyer, with a somewhat apprehensive look, "but, my lord, you know in this country we dare not make use of any such means."

The Earl gazed at him sternly, and yet somewhat contemptuously. "We will do everything lawfully, Master Lawyer," he said; "we will do everything lawfully. First, we are justified, I think, in keeping this good man in strict confinement till he has declared the names of the murderers or their accomplices. Next, I believe there is no law which can compel us, till he is fully committed, to give him either meat or drink; neither are we told that light must be admitted to the place where he is held. Dost thou hear, Sir Fool? If thou tellest not immediately the names of all those who were engaged in this hellish act, thou shalt be shut up without a crust of bread, or a drop of water, or a ray of light; and hunger, and thirst, and darkness, shall be your companions till you do tell."

The unhappy man gazed in his face for a moment with a wandering and haggard look, as if he scarcely understood or believed the menaces held out to him. He replied, at length, however, in a low sad tone, "I have vowed a vow, and it can't be broken. They call me mad, but I never broke a promise nor told a falsehood. Let the wise ones say as much if they can. No! you may quench the light of these eyes for ever; you may deny me food, or make me perish of thirst; but you shall never make me tell one word more than I have told."

"We shall see," replied the Earl, "we shall see;" and he added a few indistinct words to the lawyer, who withdrew, and almost immediately returned, accompanied by two or three of the lower grade of serving men, who instantly laid hands upon the object of the Earl's indignation, and dragged him out of the room to fulfil the orders which they had previously received by the mouth of the attorney.

After they were gone, Lord Danemore paused for a moment thoughtfully, and the shadows of dark passions might be seen traversing his high and haughty brow. Ere he spoke he recovered his calmness, and there was even a degree of melancholy in his tone as he said, "Men drive me to things that I would not willingly do. It is not the fault of the lion that he is a beast of prey, nor would he, except when pressed by need, destroy or devour any being, if the hunters did not torment him by pursuit. There is a weakness in my heart towards this youth which must be conquered. I cannot view him as the murderer of my son, although the tidings we have this day received would in some degree prove this to be the case. Nevertheless, I will conquer such feelings. I will overcome such folly, for these very papers prove that it is necessary he should be removed from my path."

As he spoke, he laid his hand on the packet of bills of exchange, which had been sealed up, and remained upon the table.

The lawyer gazed in his face with a look of some wonder and inquiry; but the Earl proceeded without explanation.

"You will act as we before determined," he said; "the evidence that we have got is now strong, you will take means still further to strengthen it. There wants but one link in the chain. Amongst all those that you know in the country round, cannot some one be found, think you, to supply that link? Some poacher, some deer-stealer, who may have seen the shot fired or the blow struck, while lurking about on his unlawful avocations? Some one who might merit forgiveness for his other offences by bearing testimony in this matter?"

The lawyer looked down, and hesitated. Although his nature was no ways scrupulous, yet the bold, straightforward, uncompromising decision of his patron alarmed rather than encouraged him.

"I will do my best, my lord," he said, in a low tone; "nothing shall be wanting that I can do; but at the same time if we can let the matter prove itself, it would be much better than risking anything by manufacturing testimony."

"See that he escape me not," said the Earl, sternly; "see that he escape me not. Woe be unto you should he do so. Trifle not with petty means, sir. Timidity in such matters is ruin. Boldly, fearlessly, but skilfully and carefully, pursue your plan. You have already the strongest of all foundations to build upon. See that you build well, or you shall answer to me for it. And now to other matters, though connected, as you will see, with that of which we have spoken. This Sir Walter Herbert must be dealt with immediately. If we do not at once engage him so deeply in his own affairs that he shall have neither time, nor wish, nor opportunity to meddle with others, he will find means to mar our schemes, and disappoint all our expectations. Besides, you know my feelings on the subject; with him the matter must be brought to a speedy conclusion."

"That may well be done, my lord," replied the lawyer; "now that he has tendered you, in payment of his debt, that which you cannot accept, it is very natural that you should immediately take measures against him. I myself am not much skilled in such matters, and might make some mistake; but I saw yesterday at the town-house a person who is now down here upon some special business, whom I can well trust, and who will, I know, so manage the matter, that, once having fixed his hands upon this knight, no turn, no shift, no evasion, scarcely even the power of the law itself, will make him let go his hold."

"Indeed!" said the Earl; "indeed! Pray, who is this tenacious personage?"

"His name, my lord, is Bolland," replied the lawyer; "he is a man who, in the good city of London, has made himself a reputation little inferior to that of a great general. His origin, indeed, was somewhat low, having been a butcher in the city, a bankrupt, with some suspicion of fraud in his transactions, and for a certain period, we are told, a gambler, in a small way of trade."

"A goodly commencement for a future lawyer!" said the Earl, with a bitter sneer curling his lip. "Of course he has prospered in the world?"

"Your lordship's pardon," replied the other, somewhat sharply, "he is no lawyer, nor has aught to do with the law but in following its mandates. He is now a sheriff's officer of the county of Middlesex, but he is not one to scruple at where he exercises his calling. I have heard that he is amassing great wealth by the skill with which he deals with his poor victims; sometimes suffering them to go at large on payment of a weekly sum, sometimes even furnishing them with money when, by putting them in this or that calling, he can ensure to himself cent. per cent. repayment; but never does he suffer any one to slip through his fingers; and if your lordship will permit me, I will mount my horse directly, seek out Master Bolland, and charge him to execute a writ against this Sir Walter."

"Do, do," said the Earl; "but yet," he continued, "I fear that all we can do will hardly be in time to prevent this meddling old man—fool I will not call him, for fool he is not—from taking such steps as may embarrass our proceedings."

"I do not know, my lord," replied the lawyer; "I do not know; but one thing I can answer for, that if you but trust the matter to me and Bolland, and pay him well for his trouble, Sir Walter Herbert shall be in the county gaol ere the sun goes down to-night."

"Indeed!" exclaimed the Earl, "that were quick, indeed. Promise him this night a hundred pounds if he contrive to execute the writ as you mention. Now go; no time must be lost."

But as he saw the lawyer rise to obey his directions, a look of doubt and hesitation came over his countenance for a moment. "My poor boy loved the girl," he said, "and therein there is a tie between those Herberts and myself which I feel to be a weakness; and yet it comes upon me even now when I think I am destroying the father of one for whom he felt so tenderly. Stay, Master Attorney, stay. My poor boy loved the girl!"

Accursed be all those, doubly accursed, who, when better feelings are coming over our hearts—when the well of sweet waters is gushing up, which is found somewhere in almost every desert—when a touch of human affection is softening the harsh asperity of anger, blunting the sting of hatred, or relaxing the iron grasp of revenge!—accursed be all those, I say, who at such moments come in, and rouse up again within us the evil passions that have been lulled to sleep, and might, perchance, be strangled in their slumber, if some fiendish voice from without did not waken them into fresh activity!

The lawyer saw, with pain, the shade of unwonted gentleness that passed over his patron's countenance, for his own mind was made up altogether of the considerations of petty interest, and he foresaw loss in any relaxation of the other's harsh determinations.

With the skill of a demon, he instantly perceived how he might turn the rare drop of honey into gall and bitterness; and he replied, "Yes, my lord, he did love her dearly, but she did not love him as he deserved to be loved; and the last most painful feelings of all his life were brought about by her conduct to him."

"It is true!" said the Earl, frowning; "it is true! Go, and lose no time. I have a sad task before me in the meantime, and I would fain have intrusted you with it, Master Kinsight; but it cannot be. You would not have time and opportunity to accomplish both."

"Pray what may it be, my lord?" demanded the lawyer, eagerly, fearful of losing some other lucrative occupation. "My business with Bolland will be over in a minute. I give him but directions, and trust the rest to him. Pray what may it be?"

"Can you not divine, man?" demanded the Earl, fixing his large stern eyes upon him; "can you not divine, that it is to seek and bring home the dead body of my unhappy son from the spot where this idiot says they have laid him."

"Oh, my lord!" exclaimed the lawyer, with some touch of human feeling breaking even through his sordid nature, like a misty ray of sunshine streaming through a dark cloud; "Oh, my lord! such is no task for you. It would wring your heart sadly to be present yourself. Besides, the magistrates ought to be there. Now, after I have spoken with Bolland, and left the business in his hands, I shall have plenty of time to see Sir Matthew Scrope and Sir Thomas Waller, and go with them to the spot. Leave it to me, my lord, leave it to me; and if I bring those two worthy justices over here with me, we may, perhaps, find some means of making this half-witted man give us further information regarding the murderers."

"Bring them not! bring them not!" replied the Earl, vehemently. "Mark me, my good friend! In this matter I am moved by many very opposite feelings. You know—you must feel, for you are a father yourself, how I thirst to discover, and to drink the heart's blood of my son's murderer! and yet I doubt that this fool, if forced to speak to any other ear but my own, might reveal matter which might tend to exculpate him whom we have there shut up above, and who must be swept from my path, if I would have any peace during my remaining years. I am not a man to live in doubt or hesitation; and as soon as any man gives me cause to fear him, the matter between us must be brought to an issue at once, and he or I must fall! No," he added, "no! bring not those men hither! I am sick of them. We must use them as tools, but not let them use us. Take them, then, with you to search under the beech trees, but bring them not hither. When all is done, return yourself, and let me know. I shall have occupation enough in the meantime to busy my thoughts with things less sad, though not less painful, perhaps, than the task which I make over to you—and now go quickly."

"Shall I take these papers with me?" demanded the lawyer, laying his hand upon the packet of bills of exchange which had been sealed up before Sir Walter Herbert.

"No!" answered the Earl, sternly; "leave them where they are."

"I thought they were to be deposited with me?" rejoined the agent, with a lingering affection for the money which he could not restrain, even though he feared to offend his patron.

"I say, sir, leave them where they are, and go upon your errand," rejoined the Earl, in a tone not to be misunderstood; and without uttering another word, he pointed towards the door, and drove the lawyer out of the room by the fierce sternness of his gaze.

As soon as he was gone and the door closed, the Earl took up the packet and deliberately broke the seals; then examined each of the papers minutely, muttering as he did it, "I thought so—I thought so. They have watched all that I have done; they have tracked me from land to land, and they have gained that knowledge of my past deeds which they think will give them power over me, and force me to do that which they know I would never do without. But they shall find themselves mistaken. Yet when I think upon all the past, the memory of friendship and of love is stronger even than hatred and apprehension; and I find that the lines graven on the soft heart of youth in early days may be crossed and traversed by many others in after life, but can never wholly be erased. Would to God that they had not driven me to it; would to God that they did not thrust themselves in the path of one who is forced to go forward on his way; who cannot, who must not, go back; who must trample on all that oppose him! But I am weak again; I am weak, to think of such things. He has sought his fate, and he must find it. Yet I will see him once more; I will make myself sure of myself and of him before I do that which can never be recalled; but not now—not in the broad day. He is too like the dead; and the dark glimmer of the lamp, or the blue gleam of the lightning, gives the only light by which we should meet. I doubt that woman Bertha, too—I doubt her much, but yet I love not to question her about such things; for she will come harshly upon the bitter subject of the past, and will turn once more those memories, which time is softening and rendering more gentle, into all that is dark, and bitter, and fearful."

Such were some of the words that broke from the bosom of a man torn by contending passions. They were spoken also; they were words as well as thoughts; for he was one with whom the struggles of the impatient spirit within, especially in his solitary moments, often mastered the guard set habitually upon the lips, and gave voice to thoughts and feelings, when alone, which he most anxiously concealed when the watchful and oppressive world was around him.

Again and again he looked over these papers, and again and again some new comment sprang to his lips; but his thoughts evidently became more and more painful as his mind was drawn forcibly back to dwell upon the past; and at length, covering his eyes with his hands, he gave way to many a bitter and mingled feeling, and groaned aloud in agony of heart, as he recollected the deeds he had done—the flowers he had trampled on—the treasures he had scattered from his path, never to be found again.

CHAPTER XX.

ABOUT four hours after the period at which we closed the last chapter, a number of persons were to be seen collected between the grove of beech trees on the moor and the long sheet of shallow water called Upwater Mere. They were of a varied and a motley character; for there might be seen the worshipful and the honourable of the county on horseback; and thence downward, going in progression through the ownership of many a four-footed beast, appeared all classes of the community, till you came to the poorest of poor labourers, who had not even a cur to follow him.

At the head of the group, and leading its operations with pompous dignity, appeared the portly persons of Sir Matthew Scrope and Sir Thomas Waller; and behind them again, prompting their motions, though appearing to submit to their will, were four other personages on horseback; that is to say, their own joint clerk as justices of the peace; Master Nicolas, clerk of the receiver of the county, whose narrow escape from the hands of the Philistines we have recorded in another place; Master Kinsight, attorney-at-law, agent and lawyer to the Earl of Danemore; and a certain black-bearded, round-faced, keen-eyed gentleman, strong, though not long, in limb, mounted upon a spirited blood nag, with a certain knowing look both about master and beast which betokened in each great acquaintance with the ways of the world.

The lawyer Kinsight called him Master Bolland, and often commented to him in a whisper upon the proceedings of the party they accompanied. Bolland rarely made any verbal reply, but he looked volumes; and the wink of his black eye was made, by its different characters, to express almost as many things as Lord Burleigh's shake of the head.

The greater part of the body had come thither in procession from the neighbouring county town. Some had joined it on the way, and some had been found already waiting on the heath; but as soon as the whole party was assembled by the side of the beech trees, a perquisition was commenced in order to discover any ground which might seem to have been recently moved; and, ere any very long search had been made, a part of the thin green turf showed, amidst the rank blades of grass which covered the ground beneath the trees, a quantity of scattered mould, clearly indicating the spot they sought.

As soon as this discovery was made, a new difficulty presented itself. It was found that, with a degree of foresight common to county magistrates in those days, the worthy and worshipful knights who came to exhume the body reported to be interred there, had forgotten to order any spades, shovels, or pickaxes to be brought with them; and there they were, in the midst of a wide moor, where no implement of the kind was to be found within a mile or two. On the first mention of this want, one of the more active of the lads who had accompanied the party, set off as hard as his legs could carry him in the direction of the little town of Moorhurst; but as that town was at several miles distance, some of the other person present suggested that it would be better to send up to the farm which had lately been taken by Farmer Gray, just upon the edge of the moor; and while this suggestion was actually being followed, a discussion naturally arose in regard to Farmer Gray, his character, habits, appearance, station, fortune, and farm.

"Ay, he has got a bad bargain of it," said a sturdy farmer in a white smock frock, which concealed the greater part of a strong short-backed pony that he bestrode; "ay, he has got a bad bargain of it; and if he do not mind what he's about, he'll do for himself. I might have had the farm for an old song if I had liked, but I'd have nothing to do with such poor swampy stuff. Why, the place has been out of lease for two years!"

"He'll do very well," grunted another of the same class. "I'm sorry I did not take the place myself. He'll do very well; he comes from Lincolnshire, and knows that sort of land. At least, I saw 'Franklin Gray, Squash-lane, Lincolnshire,' upon one of his carts. He'll do very well. He has the finest horses in the country, too."

"I wonder you call those fine horses, Master Brown," said a respectable labourer, who overheard the conversation; "they are no more fitted for hard work than my sick wife Jane; and as for the matter of that, Farmer Gray will never be much liked hereabouts, for he's brought all his own labourers with him, and that's a hard case upon the people of the place. They say he has been a soldier, too; and I'm sure he don't look like a farmer, or anything half as honest. Why, he goes about in a laced jacket, like a gentleman; and I never saw him at market, not I."

"I'll tell you what," cried a sturdy drover who had joined the group, "he's as good a judge of cattle, for all that, as any man in this country. He knows a beast when he sees it, doesn't he! Why, he bought half a score of me the other day, and paid me down, drink-money and all, without a word."

Such were the comments that took place upon Franklin Gray, in one of the groups into which the party had divided itself. Something similar, with a very slight variation from the different class and character of the speakers, was taking place amongst the rest; and all the little investigating spirit which is excited by the arrival of a stranger in a country place, especially if that stranger be somewhat reserved in his habits, was exercising itself in regard to Franklin Gray, amongst the whole of the assembly on the moor.

Lawyer Kinsight ventured to hint that he suspected Farmer Gray had been a bankrupt in Lincolnshire before he came into their county; but this was instantly contradicted by several others who had had dealings with him, and who represented him as possessing all those excellent qualities which gold invariably bestows upon its owner. Two or three of the young men talked of Farmer Gray's beautiful wife, but declared she was as coy and backward as if she had been old and ugly. Some had only caught a sight of her; some had heard her speak; and some had never even seen her, but were in raptures with her beauty on the mere report of others. What between the rumours of the wife's beauty, the husband's wealth, and the report of his wearing a laced jacket like a gentleman, Sir Matthew Scrope and Sir Thomas Waller found the two organs of curiosity and reverence in their respective brains considerably excited regarding Franklin Gray, and they entered into slow and solemn discussion as to whether, under existing circumstances, they should or should not pay him a formal visit.

At the end of about half an hour, however, some one was seen coming slowly across the moor on horseback, accompanied by two or three others; and in due time appeared the person who had been sent for the spades and shovels, accompanied by Franklin Gray himself, with two or three men furnished with implements for digging. Gray was mounted on a fine powerful horse, full of fire and activity, which he sat in a very different manner from that in which the personages around him bestrode their beasts; and there was something in his whole appearance and demeanour which made the greater part of the men assembled take off their hats as he rode up.

There was only one person present, with the exception of the drover, who showed the slightest sign of recognition, and that was Master Bolland, who gave a sudden start, and then turned pale, as the stern fierce eye of Franklin Gray fixed, for a moment, full upon him, with a meaning, perhaps a menacing, look. He ventured upon no other token of acquaintanceship, however; and Gray, riding up at once to the magistrates, bowed to them somewhat haughtily, and said, "I am happy to hear, from this good man, that your worships have discovered the place where the poor young nobleman's body has been concealed; indeed, I expected no less from your known wisdom, as soon as I heard that you had taken the matter in hand. I have now come down at once to offer you every assistance in my power, and to say that I hope some means will be immediately taken for putting a stop to all these terrible things that are daily occurring in the county. Indeed, no one is so much interested as I am; for, having taken this lone farm here, I am obliged to cross the moor constantly, often with large sums about me, and it is but fit that we should have protection under such circumstances."

"That it is, indeed, Master Gray," said Master Nicolas, the clerk, "I am just in the same condition as yourself; and I hope at the very next meeting of the magistrates something will be done."

"Depend upon it, depend upon it!" said Sir Matthew Scrope, "something shall be done, Master Nicolas; something shall be done, Master Franklin Gray! I should be very glad to confer with you on the subject, sir," he added, addressing the latter, for whom his reverence was getting very high; "and we will taste together my last year's cider, which is now just in its prime. But now let us fall to work;" and he and the rest accordingly dismounted from their horses, and directed the labourers to dig up that part of the ground which bore marks of having been lately moved.

Shovelful after shovelful of earth was thrown out, and the work had proceeded some way, when, cantering quickly along the road, appeared two or three persons, who proved to be Sir Walter Herbert and his servants. The countenances of Sir Matthew Scrope and Sir Thomas Waller immediately fell; and the first impulse of the former was to bid the workmen suspend their proceedings; after which he turned to his comrade, beckoned up the clerk and the Earl of Danemore's lawyer, and held with them a quick whispering conference apart.

In the meanwhile, Sir Walter came up and dismounted from his horse, while every head was uncovered around, and every face beamed with a smile of pleasure and satisfaction to see him there.

"I have come," he said, "gentlemen, to be a witness of the execution of that painful task which you have undertaken, and to see, perhaps for the last time, the body of my poor young friend, Lord Harold, whose death has unfortunately been made the pretext for accusing another friend, not less noble and excellent, of a foul and horrible crime."

"Pretext, sir, pretext!" exclaimed Sir Thomas Waller; "I do not know what you mean by pretext. Do you mean to charge me, sir? Do you mean to insinuate, sir?—should such imputations as these go on, I shall certainly order the work to be suspended, for we are not going to proceed with this matter to be insulted."

"Sir Thomas," replied the other, "I have no intention of insulting you; and the only effect of your ordering the work to be suspended will be, that I shall order it to go on. You forget, sir, that I am not only a magistrate, as well as yourself, but Lord of the Manor on which you stand. Go on, my good fellows, and make good speed!"

The men required no other authority, but with redoubled activity plied their work, and in a few moments a long deal case was discovered, rudely put together. The labourers tried to take the top off at once, but they could not accomplish it, and after digging round it on all sides, they lifted the heavy burden carefully out and laid it upon the edge of the pit. The whole crowd gathered round, pressing somewhat roughly upon the principal personages, who occupied the front stations about the grave. Sir Matthew Scrope put on his spectacles, and rubbed his hands, as if arriving near some long-desired consummation. Sir Walter Herbert stood near the foot of the coffin, if it could be so called, and gazed upon it with a brow of sorrow and something bright glistening in his eye. Franklin Gray looked on sternly, with his arms crossed upon his broad bull-like chest, and his brow gathered into a heavy frown.

There was some difficulty in wrenching up the top. But at length one of the labourers, forcing the spade between it and the sides, tore it open, and exposed to view the ghastly spectacle of death within.

Those who were without saw nothing but the form of a dead man; but amongst those who immediately surrounded the chest, there were exclamations of surprise, which made the rest press forward to get a nearer view, and it was then perceived by all who had known Lord Harold that the body was that of a stranger. In the centre of the forehead was a small round wound, spreading from which on every side was a dark discoloured bruise, and a considerable quantity of blood had run down and disfigured the face, on which it had been suffered to remain. Still the features were sufficiently distinct to show every one that this was not the corpse that they expected to find; and though each countenance around was pale with agitation and awe, yet on the lip of Sir Walter Herbert and of many others there appeared a smile of hope renewed.

That smile was almost immediately done away, however, when they could look further, for across the breast of the dead man lay a paper, on which was written, in a large bold hand "The punishment of him who shot Edward Lord Harold."

The first who read the paper was the magistrate's clerk, and the words were circulated in a low murmur from one to another around. But at the same time Master Nicolas, the clerk to the receiver of the county, pressed forward, as if moved by some sudden impulse, and getting as near the head of the corpse as he could, he gazed eagerly in its face, exclaiming, "It is! yes, I declare it is! It is the very same man whom I saw lying on the road that night when the robbers laid hold of Mistress Alice Herbert, and he was one of them, too, beyond all doubt,"

"Doubtless it must be the same," said Franklin Gray, gravely. "I think I never saw a more rascally countenance in my life, or one that seemed more likely to deserve the fate that he has met with."

"His clothes are very good, however," said Sir Matthew Scrope; "they don't look like those of a robber. Why, I declare there is as much lace as would cost two or three marks any day."

"It's the same man, however," reiterated Master Nicolas; "that I will swear to; and that he was a robber, there can be little doubt, from what happened to Mistress Alice Herbert. "Is it not so, Sir Walter?"

"Undoubtedly," replied Sir Walter. "There is no doubt—there can be no doubt that robbery was their purpose. Nor is it improbable that this is one of them. One man was wounded and disarmed by my excellent friend, Captain Langford. The other was beaten down and stunned by the poor innocent John Graves, and he it was, Master Nicolas, whom you saw upon the road. Let all these matters be taken down," he continued, looking round him for some one who was capable of the task.

"Where is the coroner?" Sir Walter demanded, abruptly, when he could not discover that officer amidst those around. "He should have been here. Why was he not summoned? When a body supposed to be murdered is discovered buried in a lonely common like this, it is natural to ask, where is the coroner? and to deprecate excessively his not being on the spot. May I ask, Sir Matthew, whether, in all the informal and somewhat extraordinary steps which you have thought fit to take, you have remembered the simple one of calling to your aid the coroner of the county?"

"Why, sir," replied Sir Matthew Scrope, in some confusion, "we were so hurried to decide, we were so pressed onward for time, that I do not know how it was, the coroner was forgotten."

"In short, sir," replied Sir Walter Herbert, "you forgot all except that which might serve your own purpose: you forgot all except that which might condemn an innocent man; and the regular course of justice in the land was in no degree attended to! This must be remedied. I, as a magistrate, must demand that the coroner be instantly sent for. He should have witnessed the exhumation. He should have been present at every step through all this business; and you, my good friends, the yeomen of this county, will witness that in taking cognizance of all these transactions, the proper officer of the crown has not been upon the spot—has not received any summons to attend, and that, from the very beginning to the close, two magistrates alone have conducted the whole investigation, showing a great disinclination to any open inquiry into their conduct or purposes."

"That we will!—that we will!" cried several voices; and one or two persons from the little town of Moorhurst gave point to Sir Walter's charge, by mentioning the name of Langford, and declaring that he had won the love of all around him, instead of injuring anybody.

At the same time, however, the attorney was seen whispering eagerly to Master Bolland, who on his part seemed to show some slight degree of hesitation, listening silently to the promptings of the lawyer, eyeing from time to time Sir Walter Herbert, and then scanning the crowd around.

Sir Matthew Scrope by this time was at the end of his eloquence, and though he swelled and coloured like an offended turkey-cock, he made no reply to Sir Walter Herbert. The other magistrate, however, bristled up in his own defence, vowed that what they had done in regard to Langford was perfectly justifiable, and ended by striking his clenched fist upon his thigh, and swearing, with not a very worshipful oath, that the prisoner should be fully committed to the county gaol the very next day, in spite of all the Walter Herberts in the land.

The old knight was about to reply, and probably in the heat of the moment might have said things that he would afterwards have regretted; but, during Sir Thomas Waller's angry declaration, Master Bolland had walked round; and now, with a thin slip of parchment in his hand, he laid his finger on Sir Walter Herbert's shoulder, saying, "Sir Walter Herbert, knight, I arrest you in the name of the sheriff of the county of ——, at the suit of the Earl of Danemore."

The old man turned very pale, and put his hand to his head, saying, "This is most strange, and most unhandsome!"

The people who stood around were all taken by surprise, and all felt more or less a sensation of grief, compassion, and indignation, so that there came a profound silence for the space of about a minute over the whole multitude. Even Sir Matthew Scrope and Sir Thomas Waller gazed as well as the rest with painful emotions in the pale but noble countenance of the old Knight of Moorhurst, as, standing by the side of the dead body which they had so lately disinterred, he felt a momentary regret that he himself was not cold, and silent, and feelingless, like it.

The silence lasted for about a minute, but then it was suddenly broken by an unexpected event. One of the young farmers, who had been standing by Bolland and the lawyer while they conversed, glanced from the honoured countenance of Sir Walter Herbert to the shrewd, mean face of Master Kinsight. He seemed to struggle during that temporary silence with strong emotions; but then, giving way to a burst of unconquerable indignation, he struck the lawyer a violent blow in the face, with his clenched fist, exclaiming, "D—n thee! it is thou hast done all this mischief!"

The lawyer was stretched by that one blow at his feet, with the blood starting from his mouth and nostrils. A general commotion took place amongst the people; violent hands were laid instantly upon Bolland. They declared that "Sir Walter, good Sir Walter, should not be taken from among them." The magistrates in vain endeavoured to interpose; and the peasantry, trampling the lawyer under their feet, dragged the sheriff's officer forward to the side of the Mere, declaring they would half drown him for his pains, and do the same to Sir Matthew Scrope and Sir Thomas Waller, if they did not get upon their horses and ride away with all speed.

The warning was not lost upon them; but each, scrambling upon his beast, and followed by their clerk and Master Nicolas, got out of the affray as fast as they could, and made the best of their way back to the county town, where they arrived as the evening was just closing in.

In the meanwhile, Bolland was saved from the fate prepared for him by the voice of Sir Walter Herbert, who with much difficulty made himself heard, and induced the peasantry to release the bailiff.

"Master officer," he added, as soon as he saw that the people had taken their unwilling hands off Bolland, who, with his under-jaw stuck out and his hat knocked off his head, remained standing with an air of dogged determination by the side of the water, "Master officer, having been appointed to see the law executed, I am not one to resist it, and am ready to submit to your arrest this moment!"

"Hang me if thou shalt!" cried one of the farmers. "If that man put a finger on thee again, I'll beat the soul out of him; so look to it, bailiff! and with your leave, Sir Walter, we'll see you safe down to your own house; for go with him you shan't, whether you like it or not!"

Sir Walter looked with some degree of hesitation in the face of the officer, who nodded as if to signify that he understood him, and then replied aloud, "It's no use, sir, it's no use! The writ's gone to the devil amidst these mad people, so you had better do what they would have you."

"So be it then," replied Sir Walter Herbert; "and I doubt not ere to-morrow to be able to raise funds to discharge this claim of Lord Danemore's. But now let us look after that unworthy but unfortunate man, Kinsight, whom I saw knocked down and trampled upon. My good friends, you have been violent, much too violent, in this business. No one has a right to interrupt the course of the law; far less to injure those who, however ungenerously they may demean themselves, are not overstepping its authority."

While Bolland slunk away, and, joining a group of people from the county town who had held aloof from the affray, mounted his horse, and made his way across the moor, Sir Walter returned to the spot where the attorney had been knocked down, and beheld, with feelings of great pain and anxiety, that though he still breathed, he was quite insensible, and had evidently received various severe injuries. It was in vain that he endeavoured to impress upon the peasantry about him that a great wrong and a great crime had been committed.

The only answer he could obtain was, "It serves him right!" and with difficulty he prevailed upon some of the labourers to place the hurt man upon the cover of the large wooden case they had dug up, and to carry him down to the small town of Moorhurst, in order to obtain medical assistance. The body of the dead man which they had disinterred, and which has been already recognised by the reader as that of the robber, Wiley, was also carried down to Moorhurst; and, before he even returned to the Manor House, Sir Walter despatched a messenger to the coroner, briefly narrating the events that had occurred.

While the rescue of Sir Walter Herbert was taking place, Franklin Gray had remained looking on, with his arms folded on his chest, and an expression of no slight satisfaction curling his lip. As soon as Bolland, however, was set free and rode away, Gray threw himself upon his horse again, and galloped after him over the moor. He overtook him at the distance of about four miles from the county town, and called to him by his name. It was evident from the countenance of Bolland, as he turned round to see who it was that followed him, that he had no great taste for Franklin Gray's society. The other, however, pushed on his horse till he came upon a line with him; and then, just touching him with the cane he carried in his hand, he said, "Stop a moment, Master Bolland; I want a word with you."

"Do you mean really to say *stop?*" demanded Bolland, with a grim smile. "How am I to take you, Captain?"

"Why, not in the sense you're afraid of," answered Gray. "I only want to ask you a question. Are you fully aware, Master Bolland, that I could hang you to-morrow, if I liked it?"

Bolland hesitated, but then replied, "Why, perhaps I could do the same good turn for you, Captain."

"That would be difficult," answered Gray. "I know my own fate, Master Bolland: and though there is no fear of my ever dying in my bed, like a consumptive school-girl, there is as little chance of my dying on a scaffold. As to you, you are as sure of being hanged as if the rope were now round your neck;* but I, for my part, have no wish to put it there, and I want a plain answer to my simple question. Are you fully aware that I could hang you to-morrow, if I liked it?"

"To be candid with you, Master Gray," replied Bolland, "I believe you might, if you have still got a certain awkward piece of paper in your hands; but I think it would be a dangerous matter for you to undertake, for I might give the beaks a clue——"

"That has nothing to do with the question," rejoined Gray; "all I wanted to be sure of was that you knew how we stood towards each other. I like to have some hold upon gentlemen of your cloth, who think fit to look as if they had seen me before."

"Oh, I am a man of honour, Captain," replied Bolland; "you know I would not do an unhandsome thing by a gentleman for the world."

"I am now quite sure that you would not do so by me," replied Gray; "so good night, Master Bolland." And thus speaking, he turned his horse and galloped off over the moor, upon which the shades of night were now rapidly descending.

CHAPTER XXI.

WITH a sad heart, Sir Walter Herbert turned towards his own dwelling, after having taken all the proper steps to secure medical assistance for the lawyer of the Earl of Danemore, and to have a proper investigation instituted regarding the death of the man whose

---

* He was, indeed, tried some years afterwards for forgery and made a very brilliant defence on his trial, which however availed him nothing. He was hanged for the offence, which was one of the least crimes he had committed, and at his death were disclosed a thousand acts of infamy which had been perpetrated by him under the mantle of our dreadful law of imprisonment for debt.

body had been found buried in the moor. Every circumstance combined to sadden and pain him; the imprisonment of Langford and the uncertainty of his fate, the strange and somewhat fearful event attending the finding of the dead body, the scene of violence and outrage which had occurred on the attempt to arrest him, the dangerous condition of the lawyer, and the severe punishment likely to be inflicted, if he should die, upon the warm-hearted people who had taken part in the affray, might well have rendered the good knight melancholy and desponding, even if care had not pressed heavily upon him in regard to his own affairs.

He went home, however, under the full impression that the writ against him would be renewed on the morrow, and that twelve or fourteen hours was the whole space of time which would be allowed him to prepare for the payment of the debt. He had to tell his sweet daughter all these painful facts; he had to require of her to give up for the sake of his liberty the small fortune which she called her own; he had himself to take means as rapidly as possible to sell the old family plate, which he had seen standing on his sideboard for fifty years; and bitterer than all, he had to sell those jewels which had been worn by the wife he had always truly loved; many a sweet token of early affection; the gems that she had received on her wedding morning, and many a trinket and ornament which marked in the calendar of past time some bright days, some happy hours, that could return no more.

Even then, perhaps, all would not be sufficient, and he thought of what more could be sacrificed to satisfy the claim against him. His horses, his carriages, they could indeed be sold, but this would not go far; his library, if disposed of in haste, would not bring half its value; his pictures, though chosen with much knowledge and fine taste, would be thrown away in that remote part of the country; and he pondered, and calculated, and doubted till he reached his own doorway.

"Halliday," he said to the servant whom he met, "I wish you would mount Whitefoot as soon as possible, and ride over to the county town. There tell honest Master Antony Evelyn, attorney-at-law, to come over here without a moment's delay, bringing his clerk with him; and also if you can find Brooks the jeweller, make him come too."

The man bowed without reply, and Sir Walter went into the room where his daughter sat expecting him. Her arms were round his neck in a moment; and the expression of her countenance, which had become very pale under the grief and agitation of the last few days, told him, without her speaking, how anxiously she had watched for him, and how apprehensive she had been of some new evil.

"I have been detained very long from you, my sweet Alice," he said, trying to look as cheerful as he could; "but several extraordinary things have occurred to detain me. Nay, look not alarmed, dear Alice; some of those things are to a certain extent satisfactory. The body of poor Lord Harold has not been found, but in the place where it was supposed to be laid, was discovered another body, that of a man who had evidently met with a violent death; and on the breast was placed a paper, intimating that it was the corpse of him who had murdered Lord Harold, or something to that effect. This must tend, my dear girl," he continued, taking his child's hand between both of his, as he saw that the very mention of such circumstances affected her very much—"this must tend greatly to hasten our dear friend Langford's exculpation, as he could have no hand in the burial of this unknown person, having been at that very time in confinement on this false charge, when poor Silly John Graves saw the corpse interred. It must, therefore, I say, greatly tend to hasten his exculpation."

"Thank God for that, my dear father!—thank God for that!" replied Alice; not with the usual levity with which such an exclamation is often uttered, but with true thankfulness, deep and sincere. "If Langford were but free, I think—at least I hope—that you and he, by consulting together, might soon find means of removing all the other terrible things that now seem to be hanging over us."

"His liberation would at once remove one great difficulty," replied Sir Walter; "for the Earl would no longer have a pretext for detaining the money which I tendered him, as he most unhandsomely and ungenerously did this morning; but I see that it is the Earl's object to pain and injure me."

"But tell me what more has happened, my dear father," said Alice, seating herself beside him; "I see by your face that the rest of your tidings are not so agreeable as the first part. Indeed, I know that you always tell me the pleasant news first, and then would fain not let me hear the rest at all. But, indeed, dear father, I am prepared—I am fully prepared; and wherefore am I your child, if not to share and lighten your cares and anxieties?"

"Thou dost lighten them, my Alice," answered her father; "thou dost lighten them by thy very looks; but still, my dear child, I have much that is painful to tell, and if it were possible, would fain keep it to my own breast. But it must be told, Alice, for your father must at length come to his child for aid."

"Oh that his child's powers to grant it were as great as her will, my father. Do you know, I do not look upon a little adversity, my dear father, with so evil an eye as you do. I could almost wish for it, if it did not go too far, and make you unhappy; to show you how easily I could bear it, and to have the means of paying you back all the kindness, and tenderness, and care you have shown me."

She spoke with a smile, but there was nothing harsh to the feelings of Sir Walter in her playfulness even at that moment, for it was mixed with sadness, like the gleam of the blue sky through a stormy cloud. He pressed her to his bosom, and he told her all that had occurred; and she felt more bitterly than even he had, the insult and the degradation which had been offered to him. She thought of her father's years and of his character; she thought of him, not only as her own parent, but as the benevolent master, the kind friend, the liberal landlord, the benefactor of all that came near him; and when she heard that an attempt had been made, unannounced, to arrest him for debt, in the midst of the tenantry that reverenced him, in the face of the country where he had lived and done good through a long life, indignation was strong in her heart; and, as she would not give it words, it broke through the silken lashes of her eyes in tears.

"There are many painful points in this business, dear Alice," continued her father; "should this lawyer die, which seems to me but too likely, from his state, poor young Rapson, who struck him the first blow, is likely to fall under severe punishment."

"Oh, heaven forbid that he should die!" exclaimed Alice, eagerly; "though he is a bad man, and an unkind one, I trust that so severe a fate may not overtake him, especially under such circumstances as these."

"I trust not, also, my sweet Alice," replied her father; "the man doubtless acted but as he was told to act; and, indeed, the whole demeanour of Lord Danemore this morning shows that these ungenerous actions are his, not those of the mere tools that he employs. But I am grieved for the dangerous situation in which this rash young man has placed himself; for though the first blow is all that is to be attributed to him, and the more severe injuries the man has received proceeded from his being trodden under foot by the people——"

Alice covered her eyes with her hands, and gave a slight shudder at the image thus presented to her sight; and her father seeing the effect his words had produced, turned to the more immediate matter of which he had to speak. In fact he had but dwelt upon the collateral part of the business, from an unwillingness to approach things that he thought would be more personally painful to his daughter. Feeling that it must be done, however, he now went on.

"Well, well, Alice," he continued, "I will not speak of these horrible things any more, though what I have to say may be equally painful. I am afraid, my dear child, that in the course of to-morrow we shall have a new visit from this sheriff's officer. He knows, from all that has passed, that I will not resist the law, and that my doors will never be shut in order to avoid its execution. Under these circumstances he is sure to pursue his object, and consequently I must in some way be prepared to meet him. The sacrifice of the small fortune you possess independent of me, which that rascally lawyer proposed to you some nights ago, your father must now propose himself, however painful it may be to him."

"Thank you, thank you, my dear father," exclaimed Alice, throwing her arms around his neck, "you cannot think how happy you make me."

"But, alas, my dear child," continued Sir Walter, "this is not all. What you can supply will be but a part; I must instantly be prepared with a much larger sum; the house must be stripped of its paintings, all our old favourite horses must know other masters, the plate must be sold; even the carriages and the furniture, except merely that of those rooms which we inhabit, must fetch what they may. The shelves of my library must be emptied; ay, Alice, and even more, for even this will not be enough. Your mother's jewels, my sweet girl, those jewels which were always destined for yourself, which are, indeed, yours by right, they too must go to adorn strangers."

Alice's heart was very full, and the tears would fain have rushed up into her eyes; but the resolute determination of a woman's mind, when roused by noble motives to a great effort, will triumph over mental as well as over bodily pangs, and bear them as if they existed not. By a sharp struggle, Alice repressed the fountain of her tears, for she knew that the slightest sign of reluctance would add to the anguish of her father's heart: that to give way to her own sorrow would more than double his. Not a tear then stained her cheek, and she only replied, "What better use could they be put to, my father, than to avert such a painful event as that which you expect. As jewels, of course, I care not for them, and only think of them as my mother's; but I know how willingly that dear mother would have sacrificed them to buy one moment's comfort, and I will only ask for one ring as a remembrance, if it makes no difference—the ring which she always wore."

She spoke calmly, though not cheerfully; but Sir Walter knew all that was passing in his daughter's heart, as well as if he could have seen its movements, and the gentle restraint she put upon herself affected him, perhaps, more than her tears would have done. He pressed her hands in his, and then turned to the window to conceal his emotion.

The sun had just set, and the sky was still full of light, though, half-way between the horizon—where the deep blue distance cut upon the bright golden expanse of the heavens—and the zenith—where the orange hues melted into rich purple—there hung a dark heavy cloud.

Alice had followed her father to the window, and both, as they gazed upon the expanse before them, suffered imagination to find an image in the scene. Sir Walter thought that the warm golden space below resembled the past years of his existence, that the dark cloud looked like his present fate, and that the purple sky above was that far land beyond the grave to which his footsteps were rapidly hastening. His daughter's was a more hopeful vision, and with her, fancy reversed the objects. The calm purple sky over their heads was the sweet tranquil past; the dark cloud was, indeed, the present; but in the golden light beyond, she saw a future of warm happy days. There was an indistinct feeling, however, that her father read the sight less cheerfully, and she told him how she read the heavens before her.

Sir Walter sighed, but he would not check her by giving the more melancholy picture; and even as she spoke, the wind moved the heavy cloud slightly to the east, and in the midst of the bright and intense light below burst forth a clear brilliant star, outshining all the splendour that surrounded it.

"There, there!" cried Alice, with all the enthusiasm of a young and ardent heart, finding in that sight fresh auguries of hope. "There, there!"

Her father turned and pressed her to his heart, only replying, "May it be so, beloved; may it be so."

The rest of the evening passed, till about ten o'clock at night, in making various painful arrangements for effecting what Sir Walter had proposed. He had calculated that between ten and eleven o'clock his servant Halliday would return with the lawyer and the jeweller whom he had sent for, and when about half-past ten the bell at the great gates was rung, he doubted not that it gave notice of their arrival. One of the other servants, however, appeared a few minutes afterwards, and with a grave face, and a manner that seemed to court interrogation, he announced that two strange men demanded to see Sir Walter.

"I suppose Master Evelyn has not been able to come himself," said the knight, "and has sent some of his clerks. Show them in."

The man proceeded to obey, but when the door opened, with grief and astonishment Sir Walter beheld the face of John Bolland, who was followed by another person of the same stamp.

"How is this, sir," exclaimed the Knight, "how is this? you know very well that it is not legal to execute an arrest for debt after sunset, and I am even now making preparations for paying this sum to-morrow morning."

"Ay, you see, Sir Walter," replied Bolland, with an air of cool insolence, "that may suit your purpose very well, but it won't suit mine; for I'm to have a hundred guineas, you see, if I arrest you before twelve o'clock to-night."

Alice clung to her father with a pale cheek, and a heart through which the blood seemed to force itself with pain; but Sir Walter pressed her hand, saying, "Do not be alarmed, Alice; this act is illegal, and I shall certainly resist it. You are, sir," he continued, turning to Bolland with a frowning brow, "you are engaged at this moment, as you very well know, in an illegal attempt, and you may consider it as more owing to my respect for myself than to your situation, that I do not order the servants to throw you out of the window."

"Not quite so illegal as you may think, Sir Walter," replied Bolland, "the caption was made this morning, be so good as to recollect. I then had my right hand upon your shoulder and the writ in my left. That was at a legal hour, I take it, Sir Walter; and your being rescued by a mob has nothing to do with the matter. I am responsible for you to the sheriff; I came here not to arrest you, but to claim my prisoner, and if you resist, it is at your peril."

Sir Walter pressed his daughter to his bosom, and bent down his head. "I am afraid, my child," he said, "that what this man alleges is but too true."

Alice replied nothing for a moment or two; but then, gently disengaging herself from her father's arms, she took two or three steps towards the officer; and, gazing earnestly in his face, she demanded, "You are not surely going to take my father out of his own house at this time of night?"

"Why, I must do my duty, young mistress," replied the man; "and as I shan't get paid unless I have him in quod to-night, I'm afraid he must budge."

"Oh! my dear father, my dear father!" exclaimed Alice, turning to Sir Walter, "all this man wants is money. What is a hundred pounds to your comfort? We have more than that in the house, a good deal more, I know. Give him the hundred pounds he wants, and he will come back to-morrow for the rest, when you have settled everything and are ready to pay it."

"No, Alice, never," replied Sir Walter; "I will never so countenance extortion and villany. I should be unworthy of the respect and esteem of any one were I to do it; as unworthy as he who has already offered him that sum for worse purposes. No, my child, no; I will go, however bitter it may be. I will not sink myself in my own esteem. All I ask, sir, is time to write a letter to my lawyer, in case he does not arrive to-night before I go, and to put some papers of importance in order."

"Well," answered Bolland, "I've no objection to that. I suppose you'd like to travel in your own coach; so while the horses are putting to, you can give me and my friend here a bit of supper, and do what you like, provided you give us your word of honour that you'll come back here within the hour. I always like to deal gentlemanly with a gentleman, and am not so hard as many would make me out."

Sir Walter pledged himself as was required, and taking his daughter by the hand he left the room, up and down which Bolland continued to walk, whistling the air of an indecent song, and commenting with some taste upon the pictures, till two or three servants brought in the supper he had demanded, eyeing him while they laid it out as if they would much rather have beaten him to a mummy than provided him with food. He sat down, however, with perfect carelessness, helped himself liberally to beef and ale, and encouraged his companion to partake. Shortly after, the sound of a horse's feet was heard passing by, and Halliday ere long thrust his head into the room, gazing upon the two officers with a very menacing countenance. He said nothing, however, but retired and shut the door.

When about three quarters of an hour had passed, and Bolland was beginning to get somewhat impatient, the door again opened, and Alice glided in, clad in a travelling dress. "You have of course no objection, sir," she said, approaching the officer, "to my accompanying my father?"

"Why, I never object to anything in reason, my young mistress," replied the man. "You see, for all such things we have a regulation, which is, that when civility is shown, civility money should be given."

"Only tell me what you demand," she said; "and if it be in my power you shall have it."

The man gazed in her face for a moment, as if calculating how much he should ask, and then replied, "Why, five guineas is about the fee; but I should think a young lady like you would find a prison a poor place to be in."

"So will my father find it," replied Alice, sadly; "and I should find a palace a poor place if I were away from him at such a moment of care and anxiety; but I intend to take a woman servant with me, of course."

"Oh, that will be a guinea more, then," answered the hard-hearted man, with a shrewd wink to his follower; "if you will do it like gentlefolks, you must pay for it."

Alice made no reply, for she well knew that she was imposed upon, but was yet determined to submit to the imposition; and, drawing forth her purse, she paid the money demanded at once, to have it over before her father entered the room.

It was scarcely done when he appeared, but she had already obtained his unwilling consent to her going, and he only said, "I wish you could be dissuaded, my Alice; you do not know what you undertake."

Several of the servants had followed him into the room, as well as the maid who was to accompany her mistress; and Sir Walter placed a letter in the hand of Halliday, saying calmly, "Let that go to Master Evelyn by day-break to-morrow. He might perhaps have saved me much pain if he had come over to-night. My good friends," he added, addressing the servants with that calm fatherly suavity of manner which, though it had deserted him two or three days before, when the principal facts of his pecuniary situation were first brought to his notice, was now completely restored. "My good friends, keep all together in your master's absence, for I trust I shall soon return to you again. I think I need not bid you, who have been such good and faithful servants to me for many years, keep an orderly and economical household till I return. I believe there is not one of you who would feel at any time disposed to riot or intemperance, but certainly not during your master's absence, under such circumstances as those in which you now see me."

One or two of them murmured something in a low voice, but there were tears in the eyes of all, and, amidst kind but ineffectual wishes, Sir Walter and his daughter descended to the court-yard, and entered the carriage, which was already prepared. There was something in the old knight's demeanour which did not suffer the impudence even of a Bolland to go too far; and when Sir Walter and his daughter, and the maid-servant had entered the coach, the officer approached the side, saying, "I'll tell you what, Sir Walter, it's customary with us to go in the carriage with our prisoners, if they have a carriage; but as I dare say you'd like better to go by yourselves, we'll mount our horses and return as we came."

Sir Walter bowed his head without reply. The door was shut, and with slow and solemn pace, as if unwilling to perform their task, the four strong horses which had been harnessed to the ponderous vehicle dragged it forth from the court-yard, and taking the lower road through the park, bent their way towards the county town. When they had gone about half a mile, the clock of Moorhurst church, which they were leaving behind them, was heard clear and distinctly, striking twelve.

"Bear witness, John!" cried Bolland to the man who followed with him on horseback behind the carriage—"bear witness that I had him out of his own house before twelve o'clock: so that I've fairly won the money. Take care, master coachman, how you drive," he shouted, "for the night is as dark as pitch."

"I drove this road before your father was hanged," growled the coachman, "and I trust to drive it after you're hanged a foot higher than he was."

In the meanwhile, of all the party in the carriage, perhaps Sir Walter was the least sad. His spirits had rallied wonderfully now that the worst was over, and, sitting with his daughter's hand in his, he talked even cheerfully of the means of extricating himself from his present difficulties. All the little legal knowledge that he possessed was called up, and he said that he doubted not to be able easily to obtain good bail at the county town, which would give him plenty of time to effect the sale that he proposed without the great loss attendant upon more hurried proceedings, even if Langford should not be set at liberty before that time, and the money which the Earl had detained restored.

Of Langford's situation, too, he spoke cheerfully, in order to cheer his daughter; and as her hand lay in his, she also made a great effort to appear tranquil, though more than once, under cover of the darkness, she suffered the silent tears to stream down her cheeks, and found therein substantial relief.

Their journey was necessarily very slow, and though the distance from Moorhurst to the town was not more than fourteen miles, and a full hour had elapsed since their departure, they had not proceeded one-third of the way when a red light began to spread over the sky above them, increasing every moment in intensity till every part of the sandy lane through which they were dragged slowly along became plainly visible to the eyes.

In vain they wasted conjectures as to what this could mean; they had no means of discovering; and the strong light still continued for nearly an hour. It was beginning slightly to abate when they traversed the further end of the moor, about two miles beyond the spot where the affray had taken place in the morning. They then entered a road between high banks, where the blaze, though dimmed, suffered them to see their way very plainly, when suddenly the horses' heads were seized, and a loud voice cried, "Stop!"

Sir Walter smiled as he heard it, saying to two men who had presented themselves, pistol in hand, at the side of the vehicle, "You will get little here, my good friends, for I am now, alas! a prisoner for debt."

"We know that," replied one of the men, much to the Knight's surprise, "and we don't want your money, but we want the carriage. You must get out as fast as possible. Quick, master coachman, down from your box! If you don't get the horses off faster, we shall cut the traces! Take those two fellows behind," added the same voice, "and tie them where I told you."

According to the peremptory orders they had received, Sir Walter, his daughter, and the maid, issued forth, and found themselves surrounded by a number of men who were all well armed, while some horses stood near, in a field on the top of the bank, with a group of other persons beside them. The gentry who had stopped the carriage seemed to take very little heed of those it had contained, and to be in urgent haste. The only further words that were addressed to the group from Moorhurst were by the man who had first spoken, and who, like the rest, had something drawn over his face so as completely to conceal his features.

"Move further off," he said. "Take up your position under that bank, and do not stir from it till we are gone."

The same personage immediately aided with his own hands in unharnessing the horses which had brought them; this done, he turned the beasts loose, much to the dismay of the coachman. Four others were immediately attached to the carriage with the speed of lightning, and the same voice then exclaimed, "Now, come down."

Two women, one of whom bore a child in her arms, instantly descended by a path down the bank, and, without speaking, entered the carriage. "Now, two of you," said the voice again, "carry him down. Put your hands under his arms, to prevent hurting him."

No sooner were these words spoken, than another part of the group at the top of the bank began to move slowly down; but no sooner had it reached the bottom of the bank, than a new voice said, in a weak but somewhat haughty tone, "I can walk very well now; take away your hands: I can walk quite well." With a sudden movement, Alice took two steps forward, and saw a man advancing to the carriage between two others, who seemed to wish to give him assistance and support against his will. Without uttering a word, she grasped the arm of the maid, and drew her a step forward, pointing with her finger

"Good God!" exclaimed the woman. But a quick gesture from her mistress stopped her from saying more. Two or three other persons got into the carriage. All the rest mounted their horses, except one, who sprang upon the box. The vehicle drove rapidly off, and Sir Walter, his daughter, and the two servants, were left alone in the road, for on looking round for Bolland and his follower, they could see them nowhere.

CHAPTER XXII.

It was night again, nearly approaching to midnight, and the Earl of Danemore sat alone in the small dark wainscotted room immediately beneath the chamber which had been assigned to the prisoner. More than once he had called his attendants to ask impatiently if the lawyer had returned, and as the clock in the great hall struck eleven without his appearance, he ordered several of the servants to go out in different directions to seek him, forbidding them to return without bringing word of where he was, and what had been the result of his proceedings during the day.

Solitude, a quick imagination, violent passions, and dangerous designs, all combined to produce a state of anxiety and impatience bordering upon phrensy. Now he sat with his head leaning on his hand, gazing expectantly at the door; now he strode up and down with his arms crossed upon his chest, and his bosom full of deep but rapid thoughts; now he paused and listened either to the footsteps of the prisoner above, as with a calmer and less irregular stride, Langford paced up and down in the room above, or to the sighing of the strong wind as it whistled round and round the high tower in which both chambers were situated.

At length, after having listened to the steps for some time, and then gazed intently on the ground in deep meditation, he seemed to be seized by a sudden resolution, and advanced at once to the door which opened on the stairs leading to the apartments above.

"I will go up to him!" he said: "I will confront him boldly! I will speak over the whole theme! I will dare every painful subject! He shall not say that I feared to encounter anything, or to grapple with any enemy, amongst the living or the dead. He shall never say that I was a coward in thought, or word, or deed, or that I feared boldly to meet aught that could be urged against me. I will go, and brow to brow, tell him what he has brought upon his head."

His first steps up the stairs were rapid and vehement; those that followed were more slow; and at the door of Langford's room he paused once more and thought. As he did so pause, he could distinctly hear the prisoner cast himself somewhat heavily into a chair, hum a few words of an old ballad, and, as it were, seduced by the music, go on with the song in a louder tone, and with a clear, mellow, and not uncultivated voice. He sang one of the sweet and simple airs of Lulli, which had a touch of melancholy, mingling, one scarcely knew how or where, with the general cheerfulness of the strain; but the English words which were adapted to it were even more gay than the music.

Strange to say, however, Langford thought not at all of the words that he was singing; nay, nor of the music itself. While he did sing his thoughts were busy, deeply busy, upon other things; and the music was but a mechanical application of the animal part of his nature to the sweetest of all arts, in order to obtain some soothing and tranquillizing power to calm his spirit ere he lay down to rest.

SONG.

The dew is on each leaf and flower,
  The sky is full of light;
Beauty and brightness mark the hour
  That parts the day and night.
     Wake up! wake up! my own sweet love!
     Raise up those beaming eyes,
     To find an answering look above—
     An image in the skies.

The lark! the lark! thine own sweet lark,
  Pours forth his thrilling lay;
And all that's cold, and all that's dark,
  Fly from the porch of day.
     Wake up! wake up! my own sweet love;
     Raise up those beaming eyes,
     To find an answering look above—
     An image in the skies.

There's music ready for thine ear,
  There's perfume on the breeze;
Wake up and add to all that's dear,
  What's dearer than all these.
     Wake up! wake up! my own sweet love!
     Raise up those beaming eyes,
     To find an answering look above—
     An image in the skies.

According to the differences of our natures, there is for each man's heart a key, as it were, to be found in some one of the senses. With one man it is the grosser sense of the palate, and the things that he has tasted—the cup that he has drunk in particular lands and scenes, will, when again met with, carry back the mind to earlier days, and the feelings thereof, the affections, the hopes, the fears, will crowd upon him like phantoms from the grave, conjured up by objects that seem to have no apparent connexion with them.

To some, again, certain sweet odours, the perfume of a flower, or the mingled sweetness of the morning's breath, will have the same effect. While to a few, the sight of some peculiar effect of light and shade, and to others a strain of music, a tone of voice, the carol of a bird, or the living hum of morning, will call up scenes long past, re-awaken memories and affections that have slumbered for years, and give us back the gentleness of our youth. But when the chord of association is thus struck, let the sensations produced be joyful or melancholy, there is something in the first bursting forth of the past upon the present—there is something in the rapid drawing back of the dim curtain of years from between our actual feelings and the feelings long lost, too thrilling to be experienced without deep emotion; and our natural impulse is to melt in tears.

The Earl stood and listened while Langford sang; and the deep mellow tone of his voice, the well-remembered air of Lulli—the words which, though he heard them not distinctly, he knew by heart—all served to unchain the long-fettered feelings of his better days; the stern heart was bent, the proud, impetuous, revengeful spirit was softened for the moment, and the old man's eyes glistened with unwonted dew. It lasted but for a moment. Habit and circumstance re-assumed their sway; and, with a slight stamp of the foot, he drew up his head, which had been bent down under the influence of manifold emotions, and entered the room in which the prisoner sat.

Langford turned in some surprise to discover who it was that came to visit him at so late an hour, and his astonishment was not diminished on perceiving the Earl, who advanced into the room with a brow contracted even more than usual, by the angry effort he had made to conquer what he believed to be the weakness of his own heart. He paused for a moment on the side of the table opposite to Langford, gazing at him sternly but silently, as if scarcely prepared to begin the explanation he had sought.

Langford returned his glance calmly and gently, flinching not the least beneath his eye, but gazing in return with a look expressive rather of inquiry than of any other feeling. At length, as the Earl still continued silent, he spoke, saying, "Your lordship, I conclude, has something to communicate to me, and I fear from your countenance that it is not of a pleasant nature. I am very glad, however, that you have come, as there is one subject on which it is necessary that I should speak to you, and I am led to believe that the moments in which I can do so are drawing to a close."

"You do well to believe so, sir," replied the Earl; "the moments in which any communication can take place between us are, as you say, drawing to a close; they are few and short. You are right also in supposing that I have something to tell you, otherwise I should not have sought you. What I have to tell, however, requires but few words; it is, *that I know you.*"

"I am glad to hear it, my lord," replied Langford, with perfect calmness, "as, if you really do know me, you will know, as I believe you do know, that the charge brought against me is false, if not absurd. But in the first instance it will be better to show me that you really do know me."

The Earl gazed upon him with his keen large eyes full of meaning, and then demanded, "Before you ever entered these gates, have you not twice written to me?"

"I have," replied Langford.

"Twice," continued the Earl, "you have demanded that to which you have no right; and now the object of your coming hither is not less clearly known to me than all your former proceedings. But in a word, I ask you, is not your name of Langford a false one? Are you not he whom men call the Chevalier of Beaulieu?"

"I am," replied Langford; "but as your lordship has accused me of demanding that to which I have no right, let me reply at once that I have a right, the strongest and the greatest! Has not every member of a noble family a right to demand that any unjust stain cast thereon should be removed? Have not I, especially, charged as I was by the dying breath of my noble relation, the Marquis of Beaulieu, never to cease my exertions to recover the means of taking a stain from our honour—have not I, especially, a right, I say, to demand those papers at your hands, which afford the only possible method of doing so?"

"I say no!" replied the Earl, sternly: "I say, no! Even if the papers whereof you speak existed, I say—"

But Langford interrupted him more vehemently than he had ever before spoken, "My lord," he said, "those papers do exist, or you have not only broken your most solemn vow, but your plighted word of honour as a gentleman. Your vow, my lord, you perhaps might break, for in one instance at least you did break it, and a noble heart along with it; but I would not believe you to be the being who would forfeit your plighted honour—no, not to gain a kingdom! Unsay those words which cast so foul a doubt, if not an imputation upon you! and let me know, that though in the current of your fiery passions you may not have scrupled to wring the hearts and destroy the hopes of others, do not leave me to believe that you have deliberately pledged your word and then have broken it. No, no! my lord, I know that those papers are not destroyed!"

The traces of contending passions came over the countenance of Lord Danemore like the shadows of dark clouds carried over the landscape by a rapid wind; and while Langford spoke, it seemed sometimes as if he felt inclined to strike him to the earth—sometimes as if a strange and unwilling admiration took possession of him, and restrained his anger. "You are a bold and daring man," he said, in reply; "but you have spoken the truth. The papers are not destroyed, though I do not admit their contents to be such as you may imagine."

"Thank you, my lord; thank you," replied Langford, earnestly; "thank you for clearing yourself from the painful doubt in which you involved your character. Though you may have bitterly wronged my family, still I take a deeper interest than you know in seeing your honour pure, in this respect at least. In regard to the papers," he continued, with a slight change of tone, "if they were not such as I believe, you could have no reasonable objection to give them to me. If they are such as I believe, they are necessary to the honour of my family; and, deputed as I am by every member of that family to claim them at your hands, I demand them—not as a concession, but as a right. But, at the same time, I offer now, as I offered before, to pledge myself, in order to remove all evil and dangerous consequences to yourself, that those papers shall never be made public in England—shall only be so far recorded in France as to clear the honour of our race, and then utterly destroyed."

A scornful and bitter smile came upon the lip of the Earl, as he whom we shall still call Langford, uttered these words. "You are mistaken," he replied, sternly; "you are altogether mistaken. I trust myself in the power of no one; and even the very words that you uttered yesterday have put between you and me a barrier which can never be passed."

"I know not to what words your lordship alludes," replied Langford. "Nothing that I have said, nothing that I have done, ought to put any such barrier between us. Most careful have I been, in no respect, either in conversation with yourself or others, to cast an imputation upon you."

"It may be so," replied the Earl; "it may be so; but nevertheless, clearly and distinctly, I refuse you those papers. Now, sir," he continued, with the same bitter smile; "now, sir, use your threats. Now, sir, let me know what tale you will tell if I do not accede to your demands. Now, sir, let me know whether you and yours will travel to Florida to seek for matter against me!"

"Your lordship is altogether wrong," replied Langford. "That I know your history well in every particular and in every point is true, but that I will divulge any part of it that might do you injury, except that part which it is necessary to the honour of our race should be divulged, is not only far from my intention, but never should take place, even if your lordship should continue your refusal to give up those papers, and to do the act of justice that is demanded at your hands."

"Indeed!" exclaimed the Earl, pondering; "indeed! then why did you refer to matters which should be buried in the deep silence of long-gone years?"

"Accident had some share in my so doing," replied Langford, "and a wish to lead your mind back to the past had also a part therein. But at once to show you, my lord, that I am inclined to take no advantage, and to pursue my course as uprightly and honourably as possible, let me now tell you that I not only know of the existence of those papers, but know also well where they are preserved, and could while here have made myself master of them at once, had I been inclined to take that by private means which I demand openly!"

As he spoke he pointed to the small carved door in the oak panelling, and the Earl's eyes followed the direction of his hand, but with no expression of surprise.

His lip, at the same time, curled with a bitter sneer, and he replied at once: "I am not inclined to believe in the communication of miraculous knowledge to any of us poor mortals now-a-days, and therefore doubt not that your information has been derived from some source less than supernatural. There is in this house, sir, a woman called Bertha, brought up by the family of Beaulieu from her youth, and retaining for them still a deep veneration and regard, although a quarrel with one of that race induced her to quit them and enter into my service. The attachment that she showed to myself and my family through many years have taught me to trust her deeply; but when I found that she placed, on the idle pretext of greater security, a stranger accused of dark crimes in a chamber reserved entirely for myself, I began to doubt her;—when, added to that, I found that she held frequent private conferences with him, my doubts increased; and when I found that she brought others to communicate with him contrary to my expressed will, my doubts grew into certainties."

"Under such circumstances," replied Langford, fixing his eyes inquiringly upon the Earl's countenance—" under such circumstances you have of course discharged that woman from your service?"

"Not so, sir," replied the Earl; "not so. It may be my purpose to punish as well as to dismiss; but ere I do either, I shall take care to learn in what degree she has betrayed me. But to turn, sir, from your idle affectation of insight into my secrets to your equally empty boast of power, let me tell you, that though you may have been placed in a room reserved for years to myself, and though in that room all my most private papers may be preserved, you are as impotent to get possession of them as a blind man to tell the hour by the sun-dial."

"My lord, you are mistaken," replied Langford, calmly; "I am not so powerless in that respect as you imagine. I have had them now for two days at my will and pleasure to take or to leave. I have them now at my disposal; but I had determined to use all gentle and reasonable means first, to urge you by every persuasion to do justice, and only in the end to do myself right in your presence, and before your face. You have come now most opportunely, and I will not suffer the occasion to pass; but in the first instance let me once more entreat you to do a tardy act of justice, ere you force me to things most unpleasant to me."

The Earl had gazed upon him as he spoke with an expression of some surprise and doubt; so tranquilly confident was the tone and manner of one whom he had believed to be entirely in his power. At the last words, however, his brow gathered again into a frown; and he replied, "I am not to be menaced sir; I tell you, you shall never have them; and such menace puts them further from your reach than ever."

"My lord, I use no menaces," replied Langford; "my wish, my only wish, is to persuade. Oh, consider, sir! Here you now stand at the verge of age, touching upon that cold season when the only consolation for declining years, the wintry sunshine of our being's close, is a clear conscience and the memory of good deeds. If, alas! you are deprived of the power of looking back upon many such actions— nay, hear me out. If there be in the past much that is painful, much that you would fain forget, much that can never be repaired, remember, oh remember! that what cannot be repaired may often be atoned. Thus, in one instance at least, the means of atonement are in your own power, and to seize upon them in every instance is the only way to bring back even a portion of that calm serenity of heart which once you knew in days of innocence, but which I feel too sure has long departed from your bosom."

"Sir, I never knew it," burst forth the Earl; "my life has been made up of passions and regrets; and as it began, so shall it close."

"Oh no, my lord! oh no!" cried Langford; "let it not be so! I must wring your heart, but I trust it may be in some degree to heal it. You lately had a son whom you loved deeply; for his sake, I believe you have persisted for years in a course of injustice which the nobler part of your nature, I am sure, disavowed. My lord, he has been taken from you. The inducement to remain in wrong has been removed by the will of God, who therein has at once punished and opened the way to atonement. Let me beseech you, let me entreat of you, not to suffer this opportunity to pass by unnoticed. Do tardy justice, and instead of hardening yourself to crush and to injure one who could love you well, and against whom you can never succeed, think of what a satisfaction it will be to you, when from your own death-bed you look back and see that you have done all to repair a great wrong that you committed."

"And do you make the assassination of my son," demanded the Earl, "a plea for my gratifying one who is accused of murdering him?"

"My lord, I have taken it for granted throughout," replied Langford, "that you know me to be perfectly innocent of that deed. What I demand of you also, I have a right to demand. I ask you not to gratify me, but to do an act of justice; I ask of you to do honour to yourself, by taking away a stain from an honourable house that you have wronged."

"Right!" exclaimed the Earl, with one of his dark sneers, as if the recollection of something he had before intended to say came suddenly back upon him; "in what consists your right? and how have you any connexion with the honour of the family of Beaulieu? Do you suppose that I am blind or stupid? Answer me! If you are so near and honourably akin to the dead Marquis of Beaulieu, how are you not the heir of his title and estates? What right has his bastard to prate of the honour of his family?"

The blood rushed rapidly into Langford's cheek; his eye flashed, and his brow contracted; but it was only for a moment. With what was evidently a great effort, he mastered his own passions immediately, and replied, "The coarse term you have used is inapplicable to me, Lord Danemore. Your other question, as to why I have not succeeded, I could answer by a single word if I so pleased; and, did I feel as much assured of your son's death as you do, I would so answer it."

"Doubtless, doubtless!" exclaimed the Earl, impatiently; "everything can doubtless be explained if certain *ifs* and *buts* be removed. But I tell you, sir, till they are removed, I shall listen to you no further, nor shall I detain you long, for I came to tell you what may be told in but few words. Mark me, young man! There are certain memories called up by your looks and by your voice which might have moved me to the weakness of sparing you, had you not been foolish enough to show me, that, like a winged insect which we are forced to crush, you can sting as well as buzz. You have yet to learn that I live in the fear of no man, and that when once any one has shown me that he may be dangerous to me, the struggle commences between us, which ends but with the life of the one or the other. There is already sufficient proof against you to bring you to the gibbet; more will not be wanting, or I am mistaken; but I would have you know that your fate is of your own seeking, and that when you and yours spied out and investigated the actions of my early life, you raised up the scaffold for yourself. To-morrow you will be taken hence; a gaol will then receive you. A public trial and public execution will be the end which you have obtained by measuring yourself against one who never yet failed in the accomplishment of that for which he strove."

As the Earl spoke he turned, as if to quit the apartment, but Langford, who had listened calmly and attentively, exclaimed, ere he laid his hand upon the door. "Stay yet one moment, my lord; our conference is not finished yet. With regard to your urging against me an accusation which you know to be false, either from motives of hatred, revenge, or fear, you will reconcile that to your own conscience as you can. You will fail in your attempt: but if you did succeed, you would pile upon your head coals of fire which would consume your very heart to ashes! The matter on which I now detain you is *these papers!* I am not accustomed to say I will do what I cannot do; therefore when I told you that if you did not do justice I would with my own band right myself and my family, I made no vain boast."

The Earl turned and gazed upon him, both in surprise and anger, but his rage and his astonishment were doubled when the prisoner took from his pocket the key, the easily-recognised key, which had been given to him by Franklin Gray upon the moor. Prompt, however, and decided in all his determinations, the Earl instantly raised his voice, and shouted in a tone of thunder to the servants whom he had that morning ordered to remain without.

"My lord," said Langford, "you raise your voice in vain. I have every reason to believe that the persons you placed there have been gone for more than an hour; and even if they were there still, those bolts and that lock would prevent them from entering. Of that I have taken care."

Even while he spoke, the Earl had strode across the room towards the outer door, muttering, "They will soon return;" but the key of the door between the two rooms, which had been left in the inside, was now gone, and after gazing upon lock and bolt with impotent rage for a moment, he turned fiercely towards the other door which led by the stairs in the turret down to his apartments below. Langford, however, had seized the moment, and casting himself in the way, was in the act of locking that door also, when the Earl turned towards it.

Lord Danemore instantly drew his sword; but Langford was not unarmed, as he had supposed. His own blade, which had been restored to him by the half-witted man, John Graves, was in his hand in a moment; but it was only to show himself prepared that he used it, for, waving the Earl back with his hand, he exclaimed, "My lord, do nothing rashly! Remember, you have to deal with a younger, stronger, more active man than yourself, and with one long accustomed to perils and dangers. Stand back, and answer me. Will you or will you not give up those papers by fair means, or must I take them myself?"

"I will never give them," replied the Earl; "I will never give them; though that vile and treacherous woman has not only betrayed my trust, but stolen from my private cabinet the key that you now hold; I will never give them; and if you take them, you shall take my blood first, and die for spilling it."

As he spoke, he placed himself, with his drawn sword still in his hand, between Langford and the small door in the wainscot.

Langford advanced upon him, but with the same degree of calm determination which, except during one brief moment, he had displayed throughout their whole conference. "My lord," he said, "you do the woman, Bertha, wrong. This key was not obtained from her. I beseech you to give way, for I am determined to use it."

"Not while you and I both live!" replied the Earl; and as he spoke, he made a sharp quick lunge at Langford's bosom. The other was prepared, however; his sword met that of the Earl in a moment, and parrying the lunge, he grappled with his adversary, and at the same moment wrenched the weapon from his grasp, and by an exertion of his great strength removed him from between himself and the door.

He had cast the sword he had mastered to the other side of the room, and the Earl seemed to hesitate for an instant as to whether he should spring forward to recover his weapon, or struggle with the prisoner to prevent him from obtaining the papers. He felt while he hesitated that the very hesitation was undignified. He felt too, perhaps, that either attempt would be vain; that he was in the presence of one superior to himself in bodily power, in activity, in energy; one equal to himself in courage, determination, promptitude; one who was what he had been when a youth, but with the grand superiority of mental dignity and conscious rectitude. He felt himself reproved and degraded but not humbled; and the natural movement proceeding from such sensations was to cross his arms on his broad chest, and stand with a look of dark defiance gleaming from beneath his long grey eyebrows; while Langford, taking the key in his right hand, and changing the sword into his left, stood, about to open the door which covered all those mysterious points of his history which he had so long concealed.

But, even then, his young companion paused. "Oh! my lord," he said, "I would fain have these papers with your own will and consent. Again, again, I ask you, now that you see I have the power to take them, will you give them to me? will you grant me that which is my right to demand? Oh! Lord Danemore, if you ever loved the race from which I spring—if ever human affection and natural tenderness affected your bosom—if ever you had sympathy with others—if ever the strongest passion of our nature touched your heart—I adjure you now, by the memory of the past, by the dark and awful circumstances of the present, by the frowning future, by the inevitable, interminable hereafter of weal or woe, to do that which you know to be right!—at this last, this fatal moment between you and me, to render justice to those whom you have wronged; to cast from your soul the burden of old guilt, and to make atonement for one out of the many dark deeds of the past!"

He gazed upon him sternly, fixedly, earnestly; and strong passion called up in the face of each a strange likeness of expression; but the whirlwind of their emotions was too strong for either to mark the clouds and shadows, the light, or the lightning, that passed over the countenance of the other. Urged into fury, thwarted, disappointed, foiled, the Earl had no longer any command over himself, and the only dignity that he could assume was that of disappointed scorn.

"Never, bastard!" he replied; "never! Take that which you can; secure that which is in your power! Fly, if you can fly! Use your advantage to the utmost, if it can be used; but I swear by Heaven and by Hell, by all that is sacred and by all that is accursed, to follow you henceforth and for ever, unto the gates of death; to devote life, and soul, and being, mind, and thought, and energy, corporeal power and worldly wealth and temporal influence, to your destruction; and never, never to cease, till the dark, dread, interminable gulf have swallowed up one or both."

Langford gazed at him with deep and intense earnestness; and while he did so, a thousand varied emotions, each painful but each different, flitted in expression across his countenance, and caused wavering irresolution to take the place of high and strong determination. As the Earl ended, however, the other looked at him for a moment fixedly, while the peer stood with his arms still crossed upon his chest, and a look of resolute, unchangeable purpose marked in every line of that dark but splendid countenance.

Emotions strong, but new and strange, overpowered his youthful adversary; and casting from him the sword which had successfully opposed him, and the key of all the treasured secrets of his opponent's eventful life, he sprang forward, as if with a sudden impulse which he could not resist, cast himself at the Earl's feet, and, looking up in his face, embraced his knees. The stern determination of the old man was shaken. Feelings equally new and strange took possession of his bosom also, and he strained his eyes upon the noble form of him who knelt before him, with sensations different from any that he had ever known in life.

At that moment, however, strange and unusual sounds made themselves heard from without. There were cries and screams, and the noise of many feet. Still kneeling, Langford gazed upon the Earl, and the Earl upon him; but ere one could ask the other what this meant, there was a violent rush against the outer door, as if by people propelled by terror. The bolts, the bars, the fastenings gave way, and half torn from the hinges, it burst into the room.

CHAPTER XXIII

We must go back for a few hours. The sky was without a star, and a dull heavy darkness brooded over the face of the earth, as a strong party of horsemen—whose numbers and appearance might well banish all fears, and laugh to scorn all the tales of highwaymen and footpads with which the county of —— then rang, took its way down the road which first led from the county town towards Danemore Castle, and thence passing under the walls of the park, proceeded to the little borough of Moorhurst.

The part of the road on which they were at the moment when we must first speak of them, passed between two high banks of sand rock, overtopped with trees and shrubs, so that if there had been any light in the sky it would have been shut out from that spot; and the person who rode at their head, and seemed to act as their leader, chose the gloomiest point for the purpose of causing the line to halt, and speaking a few words in a low tone to each of his companions. They answered in a whisper, as if the deep darkness and silence around had its usual effect in producing awe; and when each had listened and replied, their leader once more advanced to the front, and they recommenced their journey two and two. Descending slowly from the moors, they emerged into a more open country; and any one who had been by the side of the road might have counted their number as eleven, notwithstanding the darkness of the night, and might also have observed that, generally speaking, they were tall and powerful men, and sat their horses with a degree of ease and composure only to be acquired by long acquaintance with the saddle.

We have remarked before, that the country in that district is famous for little greens of an acre or two in extent, generally shaded by some tall elms, and often adorned by a bright gleaming pond. To one of these the party that we speak of had advanced; and though there was a cottage at the further side of the green, all was silent and still, when the word to halt was suddenly given, and the voice of the leader was heard in a low tone, saying, "Spread out to the right and left, under the trees. I hear a horse's feet!"

The evolution that he commanded was executed in a moment, with the most profound silence, each horseman separating from his neighbour and taking ground some yards to the right and left, without any of that pawing and prancing which give pomp and circumstance to many a military manœuvre. The proceedings of the leader himself, however, were even more remarkable; for, advancing perhaps twenty yards before the rest, he also quitted the road for the green turf, and then his dim figure was seen to dismount. The next moment, horse and man seemed to sink slowly down into the earth, and nothing but what appeared to be a small rise in the ground was seen through the darkness, marking the spot where they had stood.

While all this was taking place, the sound of a horse's feet beating the road with a quick trot was heard advancing from that side towards which the party had been going, and after a pause of about two minutes, a white horse, bearing his rider at a rapid rate, could be discerned entering upon the green. The horseman advanced some way, unconscious of the neighbourhood of so many others, but apparently not quite insensible to fear, as from time to time his head was turned to either side; and at length it would seem that he caught a glance of something unusual beneath the elm trees, for he suddenly pulled up his horse, and gazed anxiously into the gloom before him.

His eyes were keen, having been for some time habituated to the darkness; and becoming convinced that there was a considerable party assembled on either side, he was turning his bridle to gallop off on the same road by which he came, when suddenly what he had passed as a mere mound of earth and bushes started up into life, and his retreat was cut off by a man springing upon a horse which rose as if magically from the ground, and darting into the road before him.

"Stop!" cried a stern voice, while the gleam of something like a pistol in the hand of his opponent made the rider of the white horse recoil. He looked round, however, to see if there were no means of evading obedience to the command he had received; but by this time he found that he was surrounded, and that the way even to the low cottage by the side of the common was cut off. At the same time the command was repeated, "Stop, and give an account of yourself!"

The additional injunction, however, of "Give an account of yourself!" was rather satisfactory to the rider, who perceived therein a sort of police tone, rather than that generally employed by the worthies whom he most apprehended, and who to the word "stop!" usually added, "deliver!"

He replied, then, with a greater degree of confidence, saying, "I am a servant of the noble Earl of Danemore, and I am riding to the town of ——, by his orders, on particular business."

"Show me the badge upon your arm!" said the person who had first spoken; but the servant was obliged to acknowledge that he had come away in haste, and had not his livery coat on.

"You have some cords," said the same voice, addressing one of the other horsemen. "Tie him, and bring him along."

In a moment the unfortunate groom found himself seized, and his arms pinioned behind his back, while a still more disagreeable operation, that of tying his feet and legs tight to the stirrups, was performed by another of his captors, who dismounted for the purpose.

Not a word was spoken by any one but the leader of the party, and when he saw that the commands he had given were obeyed, he added, "Bring him up abreast with me?" and then riding on at the same slow pace in which they had been proceeding previous to the little episode which had taken place, he asked several questions of his captive in a low voice.

"We shall soon see," said he, "whether your account of yourself is true or not, for we are going to the Castle. Now tell me, how long do you say you have left it?"

"About half an hour, sir," replied the man, resuming a certain degree of courage on finding that he was not injured; "about half an hour, sir; and I can tell you that my lord will be mighty angry when he finds you have stopped me, and brought me back. He will make the house too hot to hold you, and the county too, that I'll warrant. You don't know whom you have got to deal with. He suffers no one to do anything but what he likes."

"Is the Earl of Danemore still up?" demanded the stranger, calmly, taking not the slightest heed of the other's intimation.

"Yes, that he is, and will not be in bed for these two hours, as you will find to your cost, perhaps, when he hears you have stopped me," answered the groom, firmly believing that what was awful to him must be equally so to every one else.

"Does he not usually go to rest sooner?" asked the stranger again. I understood that the whole household were required to be in bed by eleven, and I was afraid that we might have to rouse the porter to give us admittance."

"Ay, he generally does go to bed at eleven," answered the groom, "but he has not done so to-night. You will have to rouse the porter, however, and most of the other servants too; for old John came out, growling and swearing at me, in his shirt, when I made him open the gates."

"He must not swear at us, though," replied the other quietly, but in a tone which moved the groom's astonishment even more than anything which had passed before, so little reverence did his captors show either for the awful name of the Earl of Danemore or any of his dependants. As the other ceased, however, and did not resume the conversation, he had no choice but to accompany him in silence; and, followed by the rest of the party, they proceeded slowly on the road, which was evidently well known to the leader, now winding in and out amongst the high banks and woods, now crossing scattered pieces of the heath and moor-land, till at length they arrived at that spot under the walls of the park where, as we have mentioned in describing the forced journey of Langford, Danemore Castle, with its wide extent of park and woods, became first visible to the eye of any one travelling on the road from Moorhurst to the county town.

There the leader of the party halted, and suffering his hands to drop thoughtfully upon the saddle-bow, he gazed up towards the spot where the Castle stood. At that dark hour, however, nothing was to be perceived but the masses of tall trees with which the building itself was confounded in undistinguished shade, except, indeed where a single spot of light was seen gleaming like a beacon, marking that there was the habitation of some human beings amongst the dark and awful-looking blackness which the scene otherwise presented.

After thus gazing for a few minutes, the leader of the party turned towards the groom, and while he reined back his horse to the other side of the road, said, with something of a sneer, "We will save old John the porter the trouble of opening the gate for us." At the same moment, the well-trained horse which he rode, feeling a touch of the spur, started forward towards the wall, cleared it with ease, and horse and rider stood within the boundaries of the park.

"I can't leap with my hands and legs tied!" cried the groom, whose first feelings were those of an equestrian; "that's impossible; I shall break my own neck and the horse's knees."

"You shan't be required to leap," was the reply of the leader, from the other side of the wall; and then, turning towards one of his companions, he added, "You must manage to pull it down, Harvey."

"I will leap it first, however!" replied his companion, and away went a second horse and man over the wall. No sooner was this done than several of the other horsemen dismounted, and with short bars of iron, which each of them appeared to have slung at their saddle-bow, they set to work upon the wall of the park, and in less than a quarter of an hour the space of three yards was laid level between the road and the park.

The whole of the troop then passed in, taking the groom along with them; and, riding slowly up to a clump of old chestnuts at the distance of about three hundred yards from the terrace on which the mansion stood, they gathered themselves together in a group under the boughs, and their leader, advancing a few steps, again gazed steadfastly upon the Castle, whose towers and pinnacles were now to be more clearly distinguished rising here and there above the trees, and marking, with the straight lines of the older architecture, or the light tracery of the more modern and ornamental parts, the sky beyond, over which a pale gleam cast by the rising moon was just beginning to spread itself.

Gradually, as he sat there on horseback, the beautiful orb of night rose up from behind the trees, and with her peculiar power of dispersing the clouds and shadows that obstruct her way, she was seen struggling with and overcoming the vapours of the night; sometimes, like a veiled but still lovely countenance, beaming through a thin film of white mist which grew radiant with her radiance; sometimes hidden for a single instant behind a dark mass which swept over her with gilded edges; sometimes bursting forth from a dark cloud, with pure effulgence, like sudden joy succeeding despair.

As he sat there, with the varying light of the moon falling upon him, now casting his long shadow upon the soft green turf of the park, now leaving him distinct, and as it were magnified by the dim misty light, the powerful form of that horseman was scanned eagerly and apprehensively by the groom, on whose mind but little doubt remained in regard to the character and propensities of the party whose unwilling companion he had become. He thought he had never seen a more powerful frame, and in so thinking he was right; but the imagination of terror had had a great deal to do with the business, when he called him in his heart "the most ruffian-like fellow that his eyes had ever rested on."

After about ten minutes' contemplation, during which not a word was spoken by any one, and not a sound was heard but the low sighing of the wind through the neighbouring trees, and the scream of the screech owls which nested themselves in the old ivy of the Castle, the leader returned to his party, saying, "I would fain have that light put out first; but, however, we cannot stay wasting all our time here. Now, my good fellow," he continued, turning to the groom, "I want one or two pieces of information from you; but before you answer, you had better take into consideration that you are speaking to a person not willing to be trifled with; that if you do not answer straightforwardly and at once, your life is not worth five minutes' purchase; and that if you give me false information you will be as surely a dead man within two hours as you are now a living one. In the first place, then, inform me, in what part of the house do the servants sleep?"

"Why, up at the top, to the westward," replied the man; "that is where the serving men sleep; but there are others, such as the sewers, and the grooms of the chambers, who sleep at the top of Hubert's Tower. Then there's my lord's own man sleeps in his anteroom; but to-night there are two or three who were ordered to stay in the outer room where the prisoner is, in the old tower; that is to say, in what they used to call the haunted rooms, for they were always shut up, and nobody went in but my lord and Mistress Bertha, so that folks said that the ghost of the Countess used to walk there."

"So there are three men appointed to sleep there, are there?" demanded the other; "you are sure of the fact?"

"Why, no," replied the groom; "if you mean whether I am sure they were ordered to sleep there, I'm sure enough of that; but I am quite as sure that not one of them will do it; for I heard Will Hudson say that the Earl might skin him alive first. No, no; they'll none of them stay there after twelve o'clock at night, I'll answer for it."

"That is sufficient on that score," said the interrogator; "now tell me further, how many men in all may there be in the Castle?"

The groom paused for a moment, as if in thought, but then answered, "Some fifteen or sixteen that sleep within doors; but then there are all the grooms and horse-boys, and my lord's three coachmen, and the running footmen, who sleep at the stables, which you know lie out by——"

"I know, I know," interrupted the other. "Not more than fifteen or sixteen; fifteen or sixteen lackeys!" he continued, turning with a sort of contemptuous laugh to his companions; "it is scarcely worth while priming our pistols. Are there none of them sleep below?"

"Why, no; not by rights," replied the man, "except the porter and his boy; but to-night there will be Willy Hudson and the rest, who, I dare say, will come down into the corridor and sleep in the armchairs; and then, too, there is Fat Frank, who has got Silly John in charge, shut up in the dark room at the bottom of Hubert's Tower."

"Silly John!" exclaimed the other; "what does he do there?"

"Why, he would not tell, I hear," answered the groom, "who were the people whom he had seen bury my young lord under the beech trees by Upwater Mere, so my lord ordered him to be shut up in the dark room, without either meat or drink, till he did; and if he don't tell, hang me if he don't starve to death, for my lord's not one to go back from what he has once said."

As the man spoke, the person who had been thus questioning him moved his hand with a rapid and impatient gesture to the holster at his saddle-bow, plunged it in, and pulling out a pistol, thrust it into his belt. He muttered also a few words in a hurried tone, which could only be heard by himself; but then again, appearing to recover from some impatient feelings, he continued, "One word more, my good fellow. Is not the small wicket door, at the back of the western wing, very often, if not always, left open all night?"

The man hesitated, and showed evident signs of a disinclination to reply.

"It is, sometimes," he said at length, "but not always."

"I ask you," continued the other, "did you ever know it shut?"

"Yes, I think so. I don't know. I can't tell," replied the groom, with manifest hesitation, at what he felt to be betraying the way into his lord's mansion.

"He prevaricates," said one of the men behind; "he prevaricates; shall I blow his brains out, Captain?"

"Not yet," replied their leader, calmly. "Do you intend to answer, or not? Did you ever in your life know that door shut?"

"No. I didn't; no, I didn't," answered the groom. "It's always open; that's the truth."

"Very well, then," continued the other. "If I remember right, when one goes straight forward from that door, and then turns along the first passage to the left, it leads to the little hall, out of which a passage takes to the foot of the great stairs. Now, there are two other doors, one of which leads to the private staircase going to the Earl's apartments. Which of those two doors is it; the right or the left; for I forget? Your life is at stake," he added, in a warning tone.

There was a sound like the clicking of a pistol-lock behind him, and the man replied without the loss of a single moment, "It is the door to the left. I tell you true, upon my word."

"I dare say you do," replied the other; "if you don't, so much the worse for you. You will remain here till I come back; and you know what will happen to you if you have made any mistake in this business. Harvey, learn from him exactly the way to the room where the poor silly man has been put. You and Hardcastle must undertake to set him free; then join me with all speed at the point you know. You, Williams and Erith, stay with this man and the horses; and if you should have such reason to believe that he has told me a falsehood as to induce you to leave the spot, give him a couple of ounces of lead in his head before you go. You understand me. I know a word is sufficient with you."

"But, Captain," exclaimed the man whom he called Erith, "why should I not go with you? Curse me if I like to be left here, holding the horses like a groom. Why must not I go?"

"Because I appoint you to a post of trust and danger," answered his leader; "there is more to be apprehended from without than from within; judgment of what intelligence it may be necessary to give me, too, is wanted, and, therefore, I choose you. But to end all in one word, Erith," he added, seeing the other about to reply, "you must stay here, because I direct you to do so; I, who never yet found you unwilling to obey at once, in moments of action and peril!"

"That's the way you always come over me, Captain," replied his companion; "however. I suppose I must do as you bid me, having stood by your side in many a moment of life and death work."

"And always acted like a lion, where it was needful," answered his leader, holding out to him his hand, which the other grasped eagerly. "God bless you, Erith!" he added; "there is something tells me we shall not be long together. If we part for the last time to-night, remember that I love you, and that I think even now of the watch-fire of Kaiser-lautern, when, wounded yourself, you brought cup after cup of cold water to your wounded Captain's lips."

Thus saying he dismounted from his horse, and eight of his comrades followed his example. The well-trained beasts were then ranged in a line, and a single rope run through the bridles seemed all that was necessary to keep them together till their riders' return. One end of the rope was tied to a tree, the other to the last horse's bit; and after gazing for one moment more at the light in the window of the tower, across which a dark figure was seen to pass twice, the leader gave a signal with his hand. The whole party then began silently to descend the hill, with the exception of the two who had been appointed to remain with the horses and the unhappy groom, whose terror had now grown to such a pitch, that, had it not been for the lashings with which he was attached to his horse, he could not have sat the animal, although it remained as quiet and passive as if it had never known any other stable than that of a farmer's mule.

With eager eyes and a beating heart the man marked the party descend the hill, emerge from the shadow of the trees, cross the dewy grass, which glistened like frost-work in the full beams of the moon, ascend the opposite rise, and then take their way amongst the trees behind, towards the back of the building where they proposed to effect their entrance. It was certain that the property of his lordly master was at stake at that moment, and perhaps also the lives of several of his comrades; but yet the worthy domestic felt little or no agitation upon that score. All that affected him, all he thought of, as would too naturally be the case with most of the human worms which crawl about in this state of being, was his own situation, his own danger. He knew, he felt, that any misunderstanding of the directions he had given, or that anything going wrong in the arrangements of those who had compelled him to afford them intelligence, might be attributed to intentional falsehood or mis-statement on his part, and that a life which he valued just in proportion to its worthlessness, its inactivity, and its want of fine perceptions, might be taken from him on the slightest notice.

He regarded the party of nine, then, as they descended the hill, with feelings most strangely mingled and apparently contradictory; there was a hope for their success, which he trusted would free him from the painful situation in which they had placed him; there were sensations of dislike and enmity towards those who had stopped and made him a prisoner; there were feelings of anger in regard to the degradation of the Earl of Danemore, who had so long ruled paramount throughout the country round; and there was that longing desire which brutes as well as man feel, to witness everything of importance that is passing around them, especially when they are prevented by any cause from so doing.

His feelings, I say, were so mingled, that his whole capability of wishing was concentrated in one earnest desire to know the result, and to have, if we may use such a colloquial expression, "the matter out at once." There are times and seasons, indeed, when ten minutes of the past, ten minutes of anything that is absolutely certain, are worth whole ages of doubt, even though that doubt may not be mingled with any degree of apprehension; but in the present instance, personal terror added immensely to all that the unhappy man felt; and his thoughts of every dear relation of life which might be sacrificed, had ample room to torture his heart, while, silent and inactive, he remained upon the hill, watching the progress of those on whom depended his whole afterfate.

When they approached the side of the wood that swept round the esplanade, the straining eye of the captive could no longer distinguish them; and he waited eagerly, with his eyes fixed upon the building, as if he could gather all that was passing within those walls from the dull unmeaning face of the stone. For some time, however, neither sight nor sound gave him the slightest indications of what he longed to learn. It was like the cold outside, which we too frequently see in the world, covering a heart all agitation, anxiety, bitterness, and pain.

At length his feelings became insurmountable. There are degrees of terror which give courage: he felt that it would be a thousand times preferable to be amongst his comrades at the Castle, sharing their fate and mingling in their danger, than sitting there in perfect inactivity, waiting a result which he had no power to change; and he writhed with the bonds that confined him. As he did so, he felt that the knot upon the cords which tied his arms gave way in a slight degree—that he could loosen it still further by a great but silent exertion of his strength; and as he made that exertion, it slipped down to his wrists, over which it was easily passed.

The two men who guarded him were gazing as eagerly upon the Castle as he had been; and their minds were too full of the progress of their comrades to allow them to take any note of the slight movement he had made, so that, before they were at all aware of what he was doing, his arms were free. As silently as he could, he slipped one hand into his pocket for a knife to cut the cords which tied his legs, and he had almost accomplished that purpose also, while they still continued gazing at the Castle, along the windows of which more than one light was now gleaming. He felt that he could do no more without calling attention; but he perceived that what remained to do would be speedily done, if he could get away, and would not impede his progress as he went; and he gazed round upon the two who remained beside him, with a beating heart, longing to gallop down to the Castle as fast as he could, yet terrified at the idea of making the attempt. His hesitation was soon brought to an end, however, for, giving way to the impulse of habit, he put forward his hand, without thinking of what he was doing, and patted his horse's neck. The gesture instantly drew the attention of those beside him.

"What are you about there?" cried Erith. "He has got his hands free!"

The groom stayed to hear no more, but snatching up the bridle, he struck his horse hard and galloped down the hill. The report of a pistol rang in his ear the next moment, and at the same time a feeling as if some one had run a hot iron along his right cheek, followed by the trickling of blood, showed him that the robber's aim had not been far amiss. The slight wound only added wings to his flight, however, and the sound of a horse's feet following, urged him on still faster. It was—and he knew it—a ride for life or death; but fortunately for him his beast felt that it was speeding to its longed-for stable, and though the hoofs of the pursuer sounded close behind, the groom rather gained than lost ground in that headlong race.

CHAPTER XXIV.

FRANKLIN GRAY uttered scarcely a word as he led his men down the hill, through the deep plantations to the left of the castle, and to the small door which he was aware stood generally unlocked throughout the whole night. Not a human being seemed to be stirring in the mansion or its proximity; darkness, silence, and solitude, reigned in all the offices and courts; and the Robber laid his hand upon the heavy iron latch which was to give him admission into the interior of the building, without his approach having been perceived by any one.

He paused there for a moment, however, and spoke in a low tone to his band, saying, "Remember! to free this young gentleman is the first object. After that, take what may fall in the way, money and jewels; nothing heavy; nothing cumbersome. All the rest that is light in weight and valuable in quality, sweep off at once. What right has he to such wealth more than we have?" he added, in the tone of one who sought to justify, to himself and others, acts the justice of which he doubted. "He took many a thing from others with a strong hand, and he shall now feel the strong hand in turn. Your weapons, I know, are never unready; but use them not, unless we are compelled. As little bloodshed as possible! Remember, Harvey, the silly man, poor fellow!—then by the Earl's dressing-room up to the old tower! You may clear the dressing-room as you come, if you like. There are many jewels there."

Those he addressed heard his directions without reply, though swords were loosened in their sheaths, and the priming of some of the pistols examined or increased. Harvey, and one or two others, indeed, of the more experienced, seemed too sure of their preparations to need any investigation thereof, and, without touching their weapons, prepared to accompany their leader, with as much easy nonchalance as if he had been leading them to a ball-room.

Franklin Gray himself neither touched sword nor pistol, but there was no affected carelessness in his air. It was grave and stern, and full of thought, as it well might be when bent upon an errand in the course of which human blood might be spilt like water, without any of the exciting and animating spirit of martial enterprise which, under other circumstances, might have led him to tread gaily the path to tenfold dangers. He looked round at his companions, however, while the short and fluttered preparation was made; then laid his hand upon the latch, and the door opened easily to his hand.

All was dark within, and the hollow echo of Franklin Gray's foot, as he crossed the threshold, and strode on into the vaulted passage, was the only sound to be heard in the mansion. One by one the others followed, and leading them on through the dark corridors, without either hesitation or mistake, the Robber proceeded straight towards what was called the Little Hall, and pushed open a swinging door which lay between it and the passages communicating with the offices. As he did so, a bright light burst upon him, and dazzled his eyes, so long habituated to the darkness. He strode on, however, into the midst of the hall with a pistol in his hand; but the place was tenantless; and he found that the light proceeded from a large sconce over the chimney, and from a lamp standing on the table.

"This will light us on our way," he said, taking up the lamp. "That is the door, Harvey, which leads to the Earl's rooms above; when you have set the poor man free, come that way at once. In the end room of the suite you will find a door leading to a staircase between that room and the top rooms of the tower above. Follow the stairs and join me; but, remember, do not hurt the old man. Tie him, if he resists, but do not take his life, unless he tries to take yours."

Thus saying, he turned, and took his way through the passage that led towards the foot of the great stairs, which he found dark and solitary. There Harvey and his companion left him; and with the rest of his followers, now reduced to six in number, Franklin Gray ascended the steps, and entered the long corridor.

"Hark!" he whispered, after pausing for a moment; "hark! There are voices speaking beyond, and I think I see a light through the door. That chamber lies close at the foot of the stairs which we have to go up, and we must see what it contains, ere we proceed further. Follow me," he continued; and, advancing with a noiseless step, he pushed open the door, which was only ajar, and strode into the room.

There, seated round a table furnished with a large black jack full of strong ale, were, not only the three men who had been ordered to keep guard over Langford, but two or three of the women servants of the house, whom their male companions had prevailed upon to come and cheer the solitary hours of night with their presence, and to banish all fears of the ghost by numbers and merriment.

The sudden apparition of Franklin Gray and his followers, however, at once put an end to all glee. The men sat for a moment as if turned into marble with terror and astonishment, but the women, without waiting to see whether the object of their apprehensions was corporeal or incorporeal, fled with loud and piercing screams by the opposite door; and, as their retreat towards the great staircase was cut off, they had no resource but to rush up towards the chambers inhabited by Langford. No sooner was the example of flight set them, than the men hastened to follow it, with loud and terrified vociferations; and though Franklin Gray, irritated by the noise, vowed he would fire upon them if they were not silent, they continued their outcry as they rushed on before him up the stairs and through the outer chamber.

Without calculation or concert, it struck each of the terrified servants that they might make their way through the prisoner's room down into Lord Danemore's apartments, where they hoped to find new courage, or at least protection, from one to whom they had been accustomed to see all things yield in his vicinity. Each, then, rushed towards the door, and, when they found it locked, pushed against it with frantic vehemence. It shook—it yielded—the steps of the pursuers were heard at the top of the stairs—another great effort was made; and so sudden and violent was the rush, that the door gave way at once, and darting in, the terrified servants found themselves in the presence not only of Langford, but of the Earl himself.

"What is the meaning of all this?" exclaimed the Earl. But scarcely had the words issued from his lips, and before he could receive any reply, when the figures of several strange men, armed, and for the most part disguised, appeared at the door-way and gave him some intimation of the truth. No sooner did he behold this sight, than he sprang towards the door which led to his apartments below, unlocked it, and calling to his servants, "Follow me!" he darted down the stairs, leaving Langford to act as he thought fit.

Franklin Gray paused but for a single instant for the purpose of speaking a few hurried words to the prisoner, or rather spoke them as he passed; "Quick!" he cried; "take possession of the papers if you have not got them, and fly across the park down to Moorhurst, and thence to London, where use your advantage, and hire the most knavish, which means the best, of that great herd of knaves, called lawyers. I must after yonder old man, or he will get to the alarum bell, and have the whole county upon us."

"Stop, Gray, stop!" exclaimed Langford; "remember ——"

"I cannot stop! I cannot remember!" shouted Gray, sharply, in return, and, darting towards the door, he rushed after the Earl, followed by his band.

Langford, left alone, paused for a moment, as if to consider, and then took the same path that the rest had done. The stairs were all in darkness, but the lights from the rooms below, the noise of many voices, of trampling feet, and of evident contention, guided him; and, rushing on through the dressing-room, he came to the Earl's bed-room, where the old man, having snatched up what weapons he could find, with the terrified women clinging to his knees, and the three men armed in haste around him, now stood like an ancient lion brought to bay. With his white hair floating back from his face, and the fire of unquenchable courage flashing from his eyes, with a pistol presented towards Gray in one hand, and a drawn sword in the other, he leaned forward ready and eager for the unequal strife; while the Robber, with his band behind him, and his arms crossed upon his his broad chest, stood gazing upon the old peer with a look, stern indeed, but not devoid of admiration.

At the same time, in a detached group to the right, were Harvey and Hardcastle, the first of whom had his foot planted firmly on the chest of the Earl's Italian valet, who lay prostrate before him, while with his right hand the Robber pointed a pistol at the servant's head. Hardcastle from behind, with a short carbine raised to his shoulder, took aim at the Earl, exclaiming, as he looked towards Franklin Gray, "Shall I fire?"

Like lightning Langford sprang forward, grappled with Hardcastle, and threw up the muzzle of the carbine, which instantly going off, struck the fine gilded ceiling, and brought down a considerable part upon their heads.

"Hold! hold!" shouted Gray. "If any one stirs he shall die!"

I know you, mutinous traitor! I know you," exclaimed the Earl, gazing fiercely upon the Robber; "I have not forgotten you!"

"Nor I you, buccaneer!" replied the Robber. "But this is no time to call such memories to mind. Make no resistance, and you are safe."

But, even as he spoke, there came the rushing sound of many feet from the direction of the little hall below. The door to the left of the Earl was thrown open, and in poured a crowd of men, grooms, horseboys, running footmen, all armed in haste with whatever weapons they could snatch up, and led on by the very groom who had been left upon the hill.

Many of them were pale with terror, but the determination and courage of a few amongst them served to inspire the whole, and they poured on into the room to the number of twelve or thirteen men, jostling each other through the door, and gazing wildly round a chamber in which few, if any of them, had ever been before, and which now presented so strange and fearful a scene.

The eyes of Franklin Gray flashed as he beheld them, and Hardcastle, suddenly bursting from the grasp of Langford—for all this had passed in a single moment—sprang to the side of his leader, while Harvey, coolly firing the pistol at the Italian's head, followed his companion, and ranged himself with the rest. The unhappy valet started partly up from the ground, but ere he could gain his feet, fell back again, and writhed for an instant in convulsive agony, while the spirit quitted its frail tenement. Then all was still.

But matters of deeper interest to Henry Langford were going on at the other side of the room. Fury had evidently taken place of calmness in the breast of Franklin Gray, and the Earl's eyes were blazing with triumph and wrath as he found himself unexpectedly supported by so large a body of men.

"Now, villain! will you surrender and meet your fate?" the old man exclaimed. "Now surrender, or die where you stand, like a man! Out of the way, woman! why cling you there?" he continued, spurning one of the women servants with his foot, and striding over her, to approach nearer to the Robber. But at that moment Franklin Gray's arms were unfolded from his breast, the pistol in his right hand was raised in an instant—there was a flash—a report, and the Earl fell back. Consternation for a moment seized upon his attendants, and Langford's voice was heard aloud exclaiming, "If you have killed him, you shall answer for it with your life!"

But the Earl sprang up again instantly, crying, "'Tis nothing—'tis nothing but a slight hurt! Take that, villain!" and, in the very act of rising, he fired the pistol, which he had never let fall, into the midst of the group of robbers. He probably intended the shot for Franklin Gray, and there had been a time when no aim of his would have failed in reaching its object; but he was wounded and old, and the ball hit the man Hardcastle a few inches below the collar bone, and brought him to the ground with a loud unnatural scream.

All was now confusion; a number of shots were fired on both sides, till the pistols and carbines which had been loaded were discharged, and, betaking themselves to other weapons, the two parties mingled, and bloodshed, slaughter, and determined strife spread throughout the whole apartments. Some were driven back into the rooms beyond, and prolonged the struggle there; some died where they stood;

and some were seen to steal away wounded, or to fly as fast as they could with terror. Skill, however, and discipline were on the part of the robbers; and though they were inferior in number, the advantage was evidently on their side. Franklin Gray, with all the worst parts of his nature roused and fierce within him, commanded, directed, and fought, as if he had been in the field. His eye was on every part of the chamber in turn, and his voice was heard shouting orders to his different men, which, promptly obeyed, almost always brought success along with them. Two of the Earl's grooms, who thrust themselves between him and their master, fell by his hand, either killed or wounded, even while he was directing others. But while he still strode on towards the old peer, who struggled fiercely forward to meet him, he was encountered by one at least equal to himself.

With difficulty Langford had forced himself forward through the scene of strife and confusion that was going on. He spoke to no one, he assailed no one, though he parried more than one blow aimed at random at his head, for, though the lamp above their heads gave abundant light, the struggle and the obscurity caused by the smoke had got to that pitch that men scarcely knew who were adversaries or who were friends; but, with his drawn sword in his hand, he hurried on to the part of the room where he had seen the Earl, and now seemed to devote himself to his defence.

At the very moment when Franklin Gray was within another stride of the old peer, Langford thrust himself between them. But the Robber's blood was all on fire. "Out of my way!" he cried; "out of my way, or take the consequences!"

"Stand back!" cried Langford, in return, while his eyes too flashed with living lightning; "Stand back, or I forget all, and you die!"

"Out of my way!" again repeated Franklin Gray, and their swords crossed.

At that moment, however, the loud long peal of the alarum bell made itself heard throughout the whole Castle—rung with such violence and determination as speedily to rouse all the villages and hamlets in the neighbourhood. Franklin Gray heard the sound; and never in the moment of the strongest passion forgetting the judgment and the skill which had distinguished him in the army, even in the most unjustifiable enterprises, he glared for a moment upon Langford, unwilling to yield his victim, or to give up the strife; but then, as the knell sounded louder and more loud upon his ear, he turned to his nearest companion, saying, in a low voice, "Wilson, we must make our retreat. Tell Harvey to get the men together. We go by the same way that we came. Get hold of yonder casket, and see what is in that cabinet, while I and these good fellows screen you; and be quick, for we shall have the whole peasantry upon us! There is a tremendous smell of fire! Be quick—be quick!"

He spoke rapidly but calmly, glancing with his eye from time to time towards his antagonist. Although he felt very sure that Langford would not attempt to injure him, unless he pressed him, still he kept his blade playing round that of his opponent; and when he had done, he made a lunge or two to fill up the time, but evidently without any intention of wounding his adversary. Langford parried them both, and as rapid in his conclusions as Franklin Gray, he per ceived at once that the ringing of the alarum bell, which struck his ear also, had rendered the robbers apprehensive of their retreat being cut off, and now made them prepare to retire.

The Earl, however, fierce and implacable, rushed forward the more eagerly from the sounds he heard, and from the hope of taking or destroying those who had dared to assail him. With word and gesture he cheered on the men who still stood around him, and pressed forward upon the robbers, who were now ranging themselves in regular line, and slowly retreating to the doorway behind them. His men, however, were in general of the opinion that it is wise to make a bridge for a flying enemy, and they seconded his efforts but feebly, notwithstanding his reiterated commands and the fearful execrations which he poured forth upon their cowardice. Two or three, indeed, rushed forward with him, but they were driven back in a moment by the line of their adversaries, bearing with them some severe wounds to teach them more caution for the future.

They dragged back in their flight their more impetuous lord, and under cover of the smoke, which was now so dense as to render every object in the room indistinct, the Robber and his men reached the door by which they had entered, and began to pass it two at a time. As they did so, the eye of Franklin Gray ran over their numbers, and he suddenly exclaimed, "Halt! Hardcastle is down and dead; but where are Harvey and Doveton?"

"I am here," cried a faint voice, which proceeded from a man who was seen staggering towards them through the clouds of smoke. "Go on, Captain; never mind me. I will come after."

"We must leave none in the hands of the enemy," cried the Robber, starting forward, and taking the wounded man by the arm. At that moment, however, one of the grooms darted upon Doveton, and seized him by the collar, but as instantly fell back on the floor cleft nearly to the jaws by the heavy blade of Franklin Gray, who, while he was thus remorselessly sending the spirit of an adversary to its eternal account, was shouting out with anxious care for his companions—"Where is Harvey? I don't see Harvey!"

Such is human nature.

"I am here; I am here, Captain," cried Harvey, bursting into the room from the opposite door, and throwing down a man who stood in his way.

"Come quickly, then; come quickly!" cried his leader; "we shall scarce have time to retreat!"

"No, by ——, we shall not!" replied Harvey, rushing up to Franklin Gray, and speaking in a low tone. "We shall not, for the house is on fire in every part. I ran through there to see if we could get out by that staircase and the little hall, but the fire seems to have begun there; some of the men must have knocked over the sconce. Our only way will be up these stairs, down the others from the tower, and through the great gallery. But we must be quick, for the fire is running that way rapidly." He spoke quickly, but by this time there was no chance of his being interrupted, for the same tidings had just been communicated to the Earl and those who surrounded him, but not with the same clearness; and, horrified at the thought of the new kind of death presented to their eyes, the whole body of grooms and attendants had made a rush towards the ante-chamber and vestibule, hoping to escape by the same way that Harvey had attempted, but found impracticable.

The Earl followed them more slowly, and he might be seen once or twice to raise his hand toward his head, as if either faint from loss of blood, or giddy with the smoke and the fatigue.

Langford gazed after him eagerly, and when he saw him reach the door, and take hold of the lintel as if for support, he darted forward to aid him; but he was suddenly detained by a strong and powerful hand which grasped his arm, and turning, he beheld Franklin Gray and two of his men by his side.

"This way! this way!" cried the Robber, eagerly; "this way, if you would save your life and regain your liberty! This way, if you would recover the papers you have so long eagerly sought! The house is on fire, and everything will quickly be consumed!"

Langford hesitated; but when he turned again towards the Earl, the old peer had passed through the door, and was no longer visible.

"Quick—quick!" cried Franklin Gray. "Come you must and shall! Drag him along whether he will or not;" and, seized by both arms, he was hurried to the foot of the staircase leading to the tower. Some sudden emotion, however, seemed there to take possession of him, and make him throw aside all hesitation at once.

"My duty first," he cried, "and God's will for the rest;" and shaking off the hold of those who were hurrying him forward, he exclaimed, "Go on, Gray, and if I perish, forget that we have drawn our swords upon each other;—go on." As he spoke he turned with a rapid step, and retrod his way into the Earl's bed-room.

Gray gazed after him for a moment, with a look of stern sorrow and then said, "On, my men! He must perish if he will."

A number of voices assailed Langford as he entered the Earl's bed-room, exclaiming, "Not that way—not that way! the vestibule is all on fire! the stairs are down!" and men and women, rushing rapidly towards the other staircase by which the robbers had fled, passed him as he advanced, while the heat was becoming more and more intense, and the smoke almost suffocating.

"Where is the Earl?" he demanded of one of the grooms as he darted by him.

"I don't know," replied the man, with all the bitter selfishness of terror. "Gone to the devil, I dare say," and on he rushed.

But Langford, undismayed, strode forward—passed through the bed-room, and entered the ante-room beyond. It was now clear of all the crowd of attendants who had supported the Earl in his struggle with the robbers, but had fled in different directions from the still more appalling fate that now menaced every one within those walls. The fire was running round the cornices; the smoke was tremendously thick—the heat and smell of burning wood intolerable, and the rushing and roaring of the flames, as they seemed to revel with demoniac triumph in the passages beyond, was almost deafening to the ear.

Immediately under the lamp that hung from the ceiling, however, and leaning on a table of splendid mosaic work, which was soon destined to crumble into nothing under the jaws of the devouring elements, stood the Earl of Danemore, with the blood dropping rapidly from a wound in the shoulder and from another in the arm. There was a sort of fixed, stern, cold determination in his countenance, which had something awful in it, as, in that scene of terror and coming destruction, he stood without making one effort to save himself.

"Fly, my lord, fly!" exclaimed Langford, hurrying towards him; "this way is still clear."

"Sir," replied the Earl, calmly and coldly, "I cannot fly; I am old, and weak, and wounded, and I cannot fly. I have exerted myself somewhat too much in this little affray; my strength is expended, and I cannot fly. I may as well die here, as in the next room or the room beyond."

"God forbid that it should be so!" replied Langford, eagerly. "My lord, I can bear you forth; I am young and strong, unhurt and unfatigued. Let me—let me save you!"

"Touch me not, sir!" exclaimed the Earl; "touch me not! You have brought this thing upon my head. From the sight of that man's face, I know where you gained your information of my former life. He came to set you free. Touch me not! but go to join your fellows while you may. Here, with death hanging over me, and perhaps over you, I tell you I hate and abhor you, and will not have your support, even to save my life!"

"Say not so, my lord; say not so," replied Langford, casting himself on his knee before him; "let me entreat you—let me adjure you to accept my aid! Did you not see my sword drawn against him in your defence? Hate me, my lord, you may; injure me, you have; but you know not yet that I love you with a love that may change your hate into affection; and to show you what I feel, I swear that if you come not to safety with me, I will remain and die with you!"

The old man was moved. "This is strange—this is very strange!" he said; "but no!" he added, "save yourself, Monsieur de Beaulieu, save yourself; and, in gratitude for what you say, let us mutually forgive one another. For me, my hour is come; I know it—I feel it. My plans are frustrated and thwarted; the secrets of my early life displayed; the mansion of my fathers burnt to the ground! my son, my only son, dead by the hand of a murderer!—I am old, houseless —hopeless; why should I linger? I am companionless, childless; why should I live?"

"Not childless, my lord," replied Langford; "not companionless, if you will have it so. Your son, Lord Danemore, is dead, but not your only son. Your son is lost—but your eldest son is at your feet!"

"God of heaven!" exclaimed the Earl; "what do you mean? You are so like; yes, you are so like—"

"Yes, my lord—yes!" exclaimed Langford, "I know I am. I am like Eugenie de Beaulieu, your first, your only wife. I am her son! I am your child! But now let me save my father;" and he threw his vigorous arms around him.

The old man bent down his head upon his shoulder, and wept; but he resisted him no longer; and Langford, with a great effort, raising that still powerful form in his arms, bore him strongly onward through the bed-room, and the dressing-room behind it, to the stairs. It is true he felt that he carried a great and unusual weight; but there were those feelings within his bosom which made every muscle as strong as a band of iron, and he bore the old peer up the stairs into the chamber where he had been so long confined.

Until that moment, the Earl uttered not a word, and the tears rained heavy from his eyes; but then he raised his head, exclaiming, "Stop! stop! The papers, my boy! The papers!"

"Not for a world," exclaimed Langford; "if we have time, it is all that we shall have;" and on he hurried through the ante-chamber and down the stairs to the long gallery.

There was an awful sight before him. The rich carved oak wainscotting was all in flames. The invaluable pictures which covered the walls shrivelling and crackling with the fire. The armour and weapons, either of the chase or war, which had been piled up in the form of trophies between the panels, fallen from brackets that supported them, cumbered the floor in many places. The ceiling from above was dropping down with the heat, and in two places the flame might be seen forcing its way through the flooring from below, and curling up the wooden pillars which supported the roof. It was evident that the whole of the corridors underneath were on fire; and as Henry, bearing his heavy burden, strode on along the gallery, he knew not but that each step might precipitate both himself and his father into the gulf of death. His heart, however, was proud of its doing, and fearless; and if there was one feeling in his breast which was painful, it arose there only when the thought of Alice Herbert crossed his mind—when deep love and the memory of her affection came tender and unnerving upon him. For a single instant all the painful particulars of her situation, if he were lost to her, flashed across his mind, but he banished them in a moment, and summoned high resolution to his aid, knowing that he was acting as she would have him act—knowing that she would be proud and satisfied if she could see him at that moment.

Onward he went, rapidly but carefully. Twice he felt the flooring giving way beneath him, and twice by a longer stride he reached a spot where the beams were firm and unconsumed. The vast size of the gallery enabled him to breathe with greater freedom, but still he could not see clearly to the top of the great staircase, not only on account of the smoke, but on account of a shower of sparks which came down from a spot where the ceiling had fallen in.

The dust and mortar, even when he reached that place, prevented him from discovering what was the state of the flooring below; only two steps, however, lay between him and the head of the great staircase. If he reached it, he knew that he was safe, for it was of stone, and he strode on. The flooring gave way, however, at the first step, but he perceived it yielding before it was too late, and with a violent exertion sprang across the chasm. The effort was so great as nearly to have cast him headlong down the steps, but he caught the iron balustrade, and with a beating heart felt that he and his father both were saved.

"Thank God!" he exclaimed.

"Thank God!" rejoined the Earl; "I can walk now! I can walk well!"

But Langford still bore him on till they had reached the doorway, and passed out under the arch which projected beyond the building. There, relaxing his hold, he suffered the Earl to regain his feet; but, still supporting him by the arm, led him onward, after giving a moment to recover breath, towards a spot on the terrace where all those who had escaped from the fire, were assembled, and, as too usual on such occasions, were standing with inactive wonder and selfish thankfulness for their own deliverance.

Further on, indeed, there were two or three people engaged in raising with difficulty a long ladder towards the high tower where Langford had been confined. But a cry of "The Earl! the Earl!" which burst from the nearest group as the two approached, caused them to pause, and the woman Bertha, who had been directing their movements, ran up in haste. The Earl, leaning on the arm of him who had saved him, gazed up for an instant upon the splendid mansion of his ancestors, while in some parts wide black vacuities, fringed with fire, and in others a mass of flame and a blaze of light, crowned by a pyramid of red sparks and smoke, showed him the state of that building from the midst of which he had been borne.

The sight thus presented to his eyes, the memory of all that night's events, the sudden wakening up of old, and dear, but painful, associations, the renewal of feelings that had been extinct, and the struggle of wonder and uncertainty with joy and conviction, were overpowering to a frame weakened as his had been. He turned from the burning mansion to his recovered son; he gazed for a moment, earnestly, intensely, on his countenance, and then, casting his arms around his neck, he exclaimed, "It is—it is—my son! my child! my deliverer! But my eyes grow dizzy; my heart feels sick." And as he spoke, he fainted with the loss of blood and the manifold emotions which thronged into his heart.

CHAPTER XXIV.

"He acknowledges him! he acknowledges him as his own child!" exclaimed the voice of Bertha, who had run up in haste from the other group. "Bear witness all! bear witness every one! you Henry, you Jones, you Moreton; he acknowledges him as his son even at the moment of his death!"

"Hush! hush! he is not dead!" exclaimed the deep full voice of Langford; "he is but fainting from loss of blood. Some one seek a surgeon speedily. Give me something to bind up his wounds. Cannot some one fetch a cup of water?"

"He acknowledged him!" repeated the woman Bertha, whose whole mind seemed taken up with one idea; "he has acknowledged him; let every one bear witness. I knew it would be so; I knew it must be so. I knew that fate and inscrutable justice would work out their own way, though it were in darkness and in shadow. I knew that it wanted no mortal skill to direct, no mortal hand to help. Oh, thou," she continued, turning towards Langford, "thou who hast undergone the severe trial in thine infancy of evil fortune and adversity, thou who hast drunk the bitter cup in youth, now—now that the sweeter cup is presented to thee—forget not the lessons thou hast learnt, and show that thy heart has been softened, not hardened, by struggles early endured, and sorrows tasted in the brightest days of life; now show that thy bosom is as free, even when loaded with riches, as when lowliest fortune oppressed thee."

"I trust it may be so," replied Langford, quickly; "I trust it may be so; but nevertheless you mark not the Earl's condition. Quick, Mistress Bertha, quick! Surely some simples can be found to recall him from this state of insensibility. Seek them, I beseech you; seek them quickly, for it is terrible to think of losing a parent when one has so lately regained one."

"Fear not! fear not!" answered the woman, gazing upon the Earl; "he only faints. There is many a year's life yet within those old limbs. He was not saved from destruction to die at the moment when his dearest tie to the world was restored to him. But look not impatient, Master Henry; I will speed quickly to the rooms which are not yet on fire, although my keys have been stolen from me, and I know not where to find anything that I seek. Nevertheless, so be it; I go but to obey."

She turned as if to quit them; but Henry, and one or two of those who stood near, exclaimed, "Hold! hold! he is better; he opens his eyes. Bring us some water; that will restore him fully."

As they spoke the Earl did indeed open his eyes, and looked around him feebly. A few long strips of linen were procured, and made into bandages for his wounds. Langford, as we shall still call him, applied them skilfully and well; and some water was obtained, of which the Earl drank eagerly, for he was parched and thirsty with exertion and loss of blood. The deep draught seemed to refresh him much. and he raised himself up on his arm from the turf whereon they had laid him, making a sign for Langford and others to help him to rise entirely.

"You are better now," said Langford, eagerly; "you are better now. Let us bear you to some cottage in the neighbourhood, where the aid of a surgeon may be procured."

"I am better," replied the Earl, in a voice wonderfully firm; "I am better, my son; but there is much yet to be done. Raise me up. Stay; give me your hand, I can raise myself. How goes the fire? is the building all down?"

"Oh, mind not the building, my lord," replied his son; "mind not the building. Let us attend to your safety first. There will not be wanting means to raise Danemore Castle from its ashes again. No, my lord, no," he continued, seeing the Earl make an impatient sign with his hand; "the building is not all down; the whole of the right wing is free, and the people are bringing out everything valuable that it contains."

"But the tower, the tower," exclaimed the Earl. "Those papers, my boy, they must be preserved at all risks, otherwise your destiny will still be clouded. Lift me up, lift me up, I say."

With very little assistance he raised himself from the ground and gazed over the building, fixing his eyes eagerly on the old tower in which Langford had been confined. The fire, running along the corridors, had reached the first and second stories, and round the frameworks of the lower windows might be seen the long lambent flames curling like fiery serpents. But up above appeared the windows of the two chambers which contained matter of such interest to both the Earl and his son, through which shone forth nothing but the calm steady light of the lamps that had been left burning there—pouring forth a mild and tranquil lustre, high above all the fierce and eager flames below, like a gentle and virtuous spirit shining on in peaceful brightness amidst the fire, and flame, and smoke of the angry passions, and consuming strifes, and foul ambitions of the world.

"There is yet time," exclaimed the Earl; "there is yet time! Raise up that ladder," he continued, turning to those who had been placing it against the tower as a means for his own escape, but had now let it sink back again to the ground; "raise up that ladder. Why have you let it drop? There! Be quick! Place it against the furthest window to the east. Why do you not aid them?" he continued, turning to some of the servants who stood inactive. "By Heaven, I will have your ears slit, if you stand idly there!"

The men, reminded by the tone, of the fiery rule under which they had so long lived, sprang to obey; but notwithstanding all the eager haste with which he urged them on, to raise that tall ladder was a work requiring some labour and time, and, while they did it, the anxious eye of the Earl marked with apprehension the flames appearing, one after another, at the small loop-hole windows which lighted the staircase that led from the great gallery to the chambers above.

"Now, now," he said, in the loudest voice he could command, as soon as the ladder was fixed, "a thousand guineas to the man who will mount into that room, and with a pickaxe break open the cabinet door in the wall on the left hand, and bring me down safely the small iron case that is contained therein. A thousand guineas to that man, I say!"

"I will do it, my lord," cried a stout peasant, starting forth; "I'd go through fire, or water either, for a thousand guineas, for then I could marry Jenny Barker, and take old Hudson's farm. There's no pickaxe here, but here's a crowbar, which will do as well."

"Up, up then," cried the Earl; "a thousand guineas if you bring it down!"

The young man sprang up the ladder at once; but ere he had reached the top, the flames were seen bursting through the windows of the adjoining room, and every eye below watched his ascent with fearful interest. He went on boldly, however, and, reaching the top, contrived to open the window. He was seen kneeling for a moment upon the sill, and then sprang into the room.

A moment of anxious suspense followed, but then the small flickering point of the flame was seen curling round the wood-work of the casement through which he had just passed, and in another instant it burst forth in a volume. As it did so, a wild scream burst from the crowd behind the Earl, and a pretty country girl ran forward, wringing her hands. But at that moment the form of him she loved was seen emerging from the very midst of the fire. He planted his foot firmly on the ladder, and descended rapidly, holding a small case in his arms.

"He has got them!" cried the Earl; "he has got them!" and he turned towards Langford with a smile full of joy.

"He is safe!" murmured the girl; "he is safe!" and she burst into tears.

With haste so great as almost to be dangerous, the young man descended the ladder; but it soon became apparent why he did so, for the flames were seen curling about the upper rounds thereof, and just as he reached the bottom, the upper part, consumed by the intense heat, gave way, and the ladder fell, first against another point of the tower, and then with a crash to the ground. The young man, however, was safe; and, giving one pressure of the hand to the girl, who ran forward to meet him as he passed, he advanced directly to the Earl, and placed the small iron case that he carried in his hands.

It opened with a spring lock, and the Earl pressed it back eagerly.

Langford gazed, not without much agitation, for there before him, he thought, lay all that he had so long desired and striven to possess, the proofs of his mother's honour and purity, his title to great wealth, a noble name, and high rank, (not only in his own country, but in that which had in some degree adopted him,) and the means of showing, of proving, to Alice Herbert, that he had loved her, and sought her, with the high, pure, disinterested love of which she was worthy. He gazed anxiously, then, while the Earl pressed back the lock; but the old man's hands were still feeble, and it was with difficulty that he accomplished that object. He did so at length; the lock gave way, and the top flew open; but, to the surprise and consternation of both, the casket was void. Not a paper, not a trace of anything of the kind did it contain.

The Earl let it drop from his hands, and turned a glance of fierce inquiry upon the young peasant, exclaiming, "Have you opened it?"

"As I hope for salvation, my lord," exclaimed the young man, "I neither tried nor knew how to open it, but brought it to you just as I found it."

His anxious and terrified look, the sudden rush of blood to his countenance, his frank and ingenuous bearing, all confirmed his words, and left no doubt that he spoke the truth. The Earl then turned to his son, and gazed in his face with a look of deep and painful interest. Langford's brow was grave, but calm, and taking both the Earl's hands in his, he said, "Never mind, my lord; it cannot be helped; let us be satisfied with the good which has befallen us. This day I have gained a father, and you a son! It is enough! Let us not mind the rest."

The Earl cast himself upon his bosom. "You are my son, you are my son!" he said; I know and feel it, though there is much that I do not comprehend, there is much still to be explained. You are like your mother! Oh! too like your mother! Hating myself for having wronged her, I hated her because she was wronged; and yet, though it seem madness and folly to say it, I loved her still. But I knew not that she had had a son, or I would never have acted as I did act; I would never have wronged her as I did wrong her. A vague suspicion of the truth, a wild whirling phantom of the imagination, did cross my mind once in years long gone; and once, too, within these few days, when first I saw you in that tower. But why, why did she conceal it?"

"Because, my lord," replied Langford, "you had left her; you had taken from her the proofs of your marriage with her; you were upon the eve of marriage with another, a proud and princely dame of another land; and because her brother, my uncle, once your friend and companion, though he doubted not the tale that his sister told of her private marriage with yourself, and of your having obtained from her all the proofs of that marriage, upon the most solemn vow never to destroy them; though he doubted it not, I say, no, not a word of the whole tale, yet he insisted upon her concealing her situation and the birth of her child, for the sake of the honour of his family, at least till he could obtain from you the proofs of his sister's virtue. Nay more; when he found that, notwithstanding all his precautions, scandal had got abroad and was busy with her name, he forced her to quit her own land, to dwell in other countries, to assume another name, and to countenance the report of her own death. In every matter of fortune he treated her with noble and princely generosity; and in all points he was kind, except in one, where he was stern and inflexible. But I agitate you. You are not able to hear this tale now."

"Go on! go on!" exclaimed the Earl; "let me hear it all at once. Keep me not a moment in suspense."

"Well," continued Langford, "he educated me as if I had been his own child; but, as I was born in England—born within but a few miles of this spot—he caused me to be placed in the English regiments serving at that time with the troops of France. When of an age to judge for myself, he told me, with her consent, the sad story of my mother, which she had never told me——"

"What! then she lived!" exclaimed the Earl; "she did not die when I was told she died!"

"Oh no, my lord," replied Langford; "she bore deep grief for many a long and bitter year. Hers was a heart of much endurance, and though the disappointment of her first affection, the destruction of all confidence in ——"

"Hush! hush!" exclaimed the Earl, covering his eyes with his hands. "Hush, hush; I did her bitter wrong!"

There was a silent pause of several minutes, and then the old man asked again, "How long has she been dead?"

"Scarcely two years, my lord," replied his son; "and let me say, that even to the last, there was within her heart a lingering spark of affection toward him whom she had loved in early youth—whom she had loved alone."

"Bless her!" exclaimed the Earl; "bless her! Oh, could she but know that I weep for her even now!" and he did weep.

"But that, too," he added sadly, "is amongst the dark things of the irrevocable past. Oh! could but man remember that, though each act that he performs, each fiery passion gratified, each rash word spoken, each selfish wrong committed, may be blotted from his memory the next hour, like words written by the finger of a child upon the sea-shore sand; that, though his remembrance thereof may be but as a waxen tablet, on which each new impression effaces the last; could he but remember, I say, that there is a stern and adamantine record kept by fate, on which the lightest line, once traced, can never be effaced, which whole oceans of tears can never clear of one spot, nor the fiery longings of the repentant heart ever purify of one dark act done, human things would surely never give themselves cause to feel what I feel now, longing to pour out my blood like water, so that it could but recall the past."

There was another pause, and then the Earl continued, "Tell me more, my son; tell me more. You spoke of your uncle. He was a noble man, and generous. Though there have been harsh words and fierce acts pass between us, I loved him well: I love him even now."

"I was about to say, my lord," continued Langford, "that when I was of an age to hear and judge, he told me my mother's history, and my own condition. He told me that you had wedded another, and had a son on whom you doted fondly; and he showed me that there was no chance of your ever doing myself or my mother justice, if by so doing you were to wring your earldom and your rich estates from him, the child of your affection. He then proposed to me to make a sacrifice, and once more to apply to you for the proofs of my mother's marriage, entering into a solemn compact with you never to produce those proofs in England. Possessing them in France would not only have at once restored the honour of my mother, but would have rendered me heir to the Marquisate of Beaulieu, and to all the estates thereunto attached. But there arose a question as to whether my birth should be made known to you. My mother longed for it eagerly; for with a mother's fond affection she thought that there was something in your breast which would prevent you from utterly wronging your child."

The Earl stretched forth his hand and turned away his head, exclaiming, "She did me more than justice. My heart might have been torn with agony and shame, but I should have found no means to escape but in fresh crime, and might not have had the courage even to do partial right."

"So my uncle judged," replied Langford, "and he refused his consent to your being made acquainted either with my birth, or with my mother's existence. He offered you his solemn pledge, however, never to use the proofs, if you once yielded them, for any other purpose than to establish the fact of his sister's marriage, in France."

"And I refused him," said the Earl; "I refused him what he had every right to claim. But it is vain regretting; and he, too, is dead, bearing with him to the cold tomb a load of injuries, from him whom he once called his friend—from him whom he succoured in adversity, nursed in sickness. He, too, is dead, and with him likewise the past is beyond recall. But with thee, my boy, with thee it is not too late; and yet," he added, sadly, "those papers are lost which I promised never to destroy—which I guarded so carefully—the only proofs of that marriage—they are lost at the very moment that I find my son. Does it not seem as if fate were resolved to punish all my past deeds by stamping them with its irrevocable signet at the moment I first longed to recall them? What shall we do? How shall we act to prove the facts? Bertha you were present; you are the only one now left."

"Is it not enough that you acknowledge him?" demanded the woman; "are your laws in this land so hard that a man cannot do tardy justice when he longs to do it?"

"What is justice to one, might be injustice to another," replied Langford; "and if I am rightly informed, the title and estates must pass away to some far relative."

"A man I hate!" exclaimed the Earl, with a touch of his old fierceness.

But Langford interposed. "Oh, hate no one now!" he said; "but let us talk no more of these things; at least not now. You are faint, my lord, and I fear, much hurt; lean on my arm, and take this good youth's too, who, though he brought us but the empty casket, with the treasure gone, must not be unrewarded."

"The stables are not touched, my lord," said one of the grooms, advancing, and bowing low; "we can bring a carriage in a moment."

"Do so! do so, speedily!" replied Langford, and he endeavoured to lead the peer to some place of repose. But the old man seemed still inclined to linger and to inquire into the past, in the presence of the awful scene which was yet proceeding before his eyes. All that had been said, both by father and son, had been witnessed by a crowd of persons; but at first, the overpowering feelings of their hearts had withdrawn all attention from external objects, and neither had remarked nor remembered that there was any living soul present but themselves. Henry had awakened to their situation first, and he now strove to prevent the Earl entering further into the history of his past life, grieved and angry with himself for not having stopped him ere any ears had heard him charge himself with so many dark offences.

"We are surrounded by listeners, my lord," he said, in a low tone, seeing that the Earl was proceeding with the theme then paramount in his thoughts; "we had better pause till we are in private. There is many a keen ear around us."

"I mind them not!" replied the Earl, aloud, drawing himself up to his full height, but still leaning upon his son's arm; "I mind them not! I would have them know it! Who can say that I shall ever see to-morrow's sun? Hear every one, and bear witness, that I acknowledge this gentleman as my son; that I was fully and lawfully married to his mother, before his birth, in the church of Uppington; that by my hand the leaf was torn from the register which recorded that marriage; that the certificate thereof was taken by me from his mother; and that it, with the torn leaf and other papers, was kept by me, from that time to this, in the case which now lies empty there. Some one has stolen them in the horrors of this night; but for their recovery, I will double the reward I offered for the casket itself. Let every one remember the words that I have spoken. This is my legitimate son!"

The people around answered by a shout; but the heavy pressure of the Earl's hand upon his son's arm showed Henry that the exertion of speaking in so loud a tone had been too much for his exhausted powers; and he eagerly led him away towards a spot where he could sit down till the vehicle came to carry him to the neighbouring village. The old man seemed satisfied, however, with what he had accomplished, and gazing in his son's face with a smile, he said, "I have done my best towards one act of reparation. Oh, my boy, would that I could repair all!"

Langford said little in reply, but what he did say was kind and tender; and as soon as the carriage appeared; the Earl was placed in it, and conveyed to the house of the clergyman of the village, who gladly received his noble patron. Messengers were instantly sent off for surgeons, but ere they arrived, Langford, who sat by his father's bedside, saw with pain a bright red spot deepening every moment in the Earl's cheek, announcing, as well as his burning thirst, that strong fever was taking possession of him.

CHAPTER XXVI.

It is an awful thing to sit by the bed of sickness at any time; to see that strange and inexplicable thing, animal life, oppressed and beaten down like a crushed butterfly, waving its faint wings with the energy of suffering, but not the freedom of health; to mark the quick breathing, to gaze upon the anxious eye, to see the cheek, once florid, grown pale and ashy, the lip parched and dry, the thin nostril expanding for the insufficient breath, the hand suddenly blanched and grown meagre, the uneasy frame tossing with the dire combination of lassitude and restlessness; and to know that all these are signs of a spirit approaching that dread portal, which, if once passed, can never be passed again till the gates of life are thrown open for eternity!

It is an awful thing at any time! but when the being whom we see so situated is dear to our heart by the ties of kindred or of love, it is still more awful; and awful, trebly awful, is the scene, when the creature that lies weighed down by sickness before our eyes is both closely linked to our deepest feelings and tenderest natural affections, and yet loaded, even more than by the weight of malady, with faults and errors, and sins and crimes, which may render the dark passing of that fearful porch of death, the eternal separation from all who loved him on the earth.

The fire in Danemore Castle had burnt itself out. Part of the building had been saved, and remained uninjured. The servants had taken possession of it, and were using all means to prevent the fire from breaking out again. The greater part of the peasantry had returned to their homes, and few persons were seen in the park or on the terraces, but here and there a straggling group of idlers gathered together from the neighbouring country to gaze upon the scene of ruin and destruction.

He whom we have called throughout this book Henry Langford, had twice gone forth, at his father's desire, to see what was taking place without, and he now sat, in the cool grey of the dawn, beside the couch of the Earl, as he lay obtaining snatches of brief and troubled slumber. As Langford so sat, and gazed upon him, the natural feelings of a son's heart towards a father would have way. The blood of kindred stirred within him, and he felt that he was his son. But still as he gazed, the image of his dead mother rose up before his sight, and all the bitter wrongs that she had suffered made his heart sad, and brought the tears into his eyes.

He thought of her as he had known her in his youth, still exquisitely lovely, though touched by the withering hand of sorrow. He thought of her as he had known her in later days, fading rapidly away, like a flower broken and trampled under foot by some heedless passer-by. He thought of her as he had seen her on the bed of death, with every worldly hope at an end, and with no thought nor care but of the heaven to which her steps were bent, and of his own future fate and happiness on earth. Her words, almost the last which she ever spoke, still rang in his ears; the promise she had exacted from him, never to give up the endeavour to establish her honour and purity, and the injunction which she had likewise laid upon him, if his father ever did him injustice, to forgive and love him for her sake.

Henry felt that he did forgive him; but he felt, too, that there was another and a greater Judge whose forgiveness was needed; a judge not less merciful, indeed, but one not moved by human passions and affections; and as he thought of all that had been done by him to whom he owed his being—of all the dark deeds of other years—the fierce unruly passions which had remained unextinguished even to that very night, the scene of his father's suffering, the prospect of his death became awful, trebly awful to the eyes of his son.

The surgeon from the county town had been with Lord Danemore, had examined his wounds, and had pronounced that there was no immediate danger; but he had not in any degree assured the Earl's son that there was a prospect of his illness terminating favourably. He spoke as men are too apt to speak, with cautious consideration of his own reputation, more than with any regard for the feelings and anxieties of him to whom he spoke. Langford had gathered, however, that he judged unfavourably of his father's state. He dwelt upon the facts of the Earl being an old man—of his constitution, though strong, having been apparently severely tried in former years—of the event of all such wounds being uncertain—and of a great deal of fever having rapidly come on. He said nothing to mitigate these unfavourable circumstances, and Langford judged the worst. His feelings, then, when after the surgeon had left the Earl for a short time, and he sat beside him watching his fitful slumbers, were most painful; but they were destined to be more so ere long.

Scarcely had the sky grown yellow with the bright coming on of morning, when the trampling of many horses' feet below, and then the sound of persons ascending the stairs, called his attention. It had been the surgeon's express injunction that the Earl should be kept perfectly quiet; and as the sounds approached the chamber in which he lay, Langford started up and moved towards the door, in order to caution the new comers to make less noise. Before he reached it, however, that door opened, and five or six persons unceremoniously entered the chamber. The noise at once awoke the Earl, and, starting up on his arm, he exclaimed, "Who is there?"

"It is I, my lord; your lordship's very humble servant, Sir Thomas Waller," replied the first person who entered. "No sooner did I hear that your lordship's house had been attacked and set on fire, than I got on horseback with as many constables as I could gather together to come to your aid; and as my learned and worshipful friend and cousin, Justice Whistler, from London, the chief magistrate of police, happened to be lodging in my poor house at the time, I besought him to come over with me too."

"Whether in regard to the fire or in regard to the robbery," replied the Earl, cynically, "your coming is somewhat late; and as I am both wounded and in pain, and have the express orders of my surgeon to remain in perfect quiet, you will perhaps favour me by leaving me to repose; and another time, before you bring strangers into my room, do me the honour to inquire whether it is my pleasure to receive you;" so saying, he laid himself down again, and turned his back upon his unwished-for guests.

"This is a very extraordinary reception, indeed," said a portly, keen-faced personage, who had followed Sir Thomas into the room; "but, at all events, Sir Thomas, we must do our duty. My lord, I am sorry to trouble your repose."

"You must trouble it no longer, sir," said Langford, advancing towards him, "but have the goodness at once to quit the room."

The worshipful Justice Whistler—for he it was who had been speaking, calmly took a pair of spectacles out of his pocket, placed them on his nose, and gazed at Langford from head to foot.

"This is the young man, I take it, Sir Thomas," he said, turning to his companion· and, on a significant nod from Sir Thomas Waller, he proceeded, "You are the personage calling yourself Henry Langford, and stand charged, I find, with the wilful murder of Edward Lord Harold. On consulting with my good friend here on the subject last night, aided by the wisdom of Sir Matthew Scrope, I gave it as my decided opinion that you should be immediately committed to the county gaol, having been left too long already in circumstances which rendered it probable that the ends of justice might be defeated."

"What is this? what is this?" exclaimed the Earl, starting up.

"Nothing, my lord," replied the magistrate, "but that this young man stands committed upon a due warrant to that effect, placed in the hands of these officers behind me for execution."

"Do you know, sir," demanded the Earl, sternly—"do you know that he is my son?"

"We have heard something to that effect this night," rejoined the justice, in a sharp dry tone—he evidently having taken offence at the Earl's first salutation, and not having that reverence for his wealth and power which was felt by his neighbours in the country—"we have heard something to that effect this night; but as I observed to my good friend here, that only renders the matter more probable. That your lordship's illegitimate son ——"

"He is not my illegitimate son, sir," replied the Earl; "he is my legitimate child, by my first wife."

"It is very awkward, certainly," answered the imperturbable Justice Whistler; "but, nevertheless, my lord, we cannot help it. The law must have its course; and, as I said before, the charge is but rendered the more probable by the fact of his being your unacknowledged son. To get an obtrusive heir out of the way is no slight inducement; but besides all that, there is quite proof sufficient to justify his committal long ago. Here they are seen to draw their swords upon each other. The one rides away slowly up to the moor; the other gets his horse and follows him at full speed, just as night is closing in. The one is killed upon the moor, and his horse returns all bloody. The other does not get back till late that night, and then is in an evident state of agitation. A pistol shot is heard in that direction at the very time he is there, and at the very spot to which he is seen riding. My lord, the matter is quite conclusive; and though doubtless unpleasant, the young gentleman must to prison!"

The Earl gazed wildly but earnestly in the face of his son, with feelings which those who have read the steps he had taken to bring about the very result that now fell upon him like a thunderbolt may well conceive.

"I have done this!" he exclaimed; "I have done this! Oh, my son, I am your murderer!" and he turned away his head with an aguish shudder passing all over his frame.

Langford, however, hastened to console him. "Oh, no!" he said, grasping the old man's hand—"Oh, no! While you thought me guilty, you justly used all means to punish the supposed murderer of your son, but ——"

"You do not know," replied the Earl, with that withering expression of heartfelt anguish that nothing but remorse can give; "You do not know. I have pursued you like a fiend! Your blood will be upon my head—my own child's blood!"

"Not so, my lord; not so." replied Langford, again. "The worst will be but a few days' imprisonment. You know my innocence; I know it too, and know that it can be proved with ease. That which gives me the greatest pain at this moment, is to be deprived of the opportunity of watching by and attending you till you shall have recovered from your wounds. It grieves me—it is dreadful to me—to leave you to the hands of menials. My lord, there will be one comfort to me—one consolation in prison, which, as the first favour I have ever asked you, you must grant me. There is a lady in this vicinity, kind, and gentle, and tender; your son's promised bride: Mistress Alice Herbert, I mean. Will you let me sit down and write her a few lines, beseeching her, during my enforced absence from my father's sick bed, to attend him as if she were his daughter? I know that it will be an office which she will love to fulfil, not more for my sake than for yours. Pray let me do so."

The Earl's eyes had been cast down, and the thick eyebrows had gathered heavily over them; but he did not speak, for the knowledge of all he had done lay weighty on his heart, and took away all utterance. Sir Thomas Waller, however, took upon himself to reply. "Your writing, young gentleman, would be useless," he said; "for I am sorry to tell you that Sir Walter—who, though a hasty and passionate man, and sometimes very disrespectful to persons fully equal to himself, is a very good man, and much liked in the country—was arrested yesterday evening at the suit of the noble Earl here. Indeed, he would have been arrested in the earlier part of the day, but the country people rose and rescued him."

"This, too!" exclaimed the Earl, setting his teeth; "I have done this! I have done this!"

"Your worthy lawyer, my lord," continued Sir Thomas, whose mind was one of those shallow ones that cannot comprehend any deep and powerful emotion, even when they see its workings before their eyes; "your worthy lawyer, my lord, Master Kinsight, was very roughly handled by the people, and is likely to die."

"Curse him!" said the Earl, in a low, deep voice; "curse him! He is one of the vile instruments, the ready tools of wrong."

"May I ask you, sir," interposed Langford, with no slight anxiety now thrilling in his bosom—"may I ask you, who seem to know the particulars of the whole affair, what has become of Mistress Alice Herbert, under these distressing circumstances?"

"She chose to go with her father, I was informed," replied the Knight; "I dare say Master Bolland made her pay dear for permission to do so. He is not a man to grant anything without a consideration."

"And has worthy, kind-hearted, noble Sir Walter Herbert," exclaimed Langford, with the anguish of his heart making itself apparent in every feature—"has he fallen into the hands of that well-known, that infamous knave and peculator, whose very existence as an officer of the law, even though in the lowest grade of degraded offices, is a disgrace to this free country, whose acts make the capital of England notorious for monstrous injustice, and for the daily infraction of every social law, of every moral feeling, and of every sacred right? Has he—has he—simple, unguarded, plain, and true! fallen into the hands of one whose whole soul is fraud, corruption, perjury, and baseness? Yet how can this be?" he continued, after a moment's pause; "I myself furnished the money to pay this debt. I do not comprehend it."

"I have done this, too. I have done this, too," replied the Earl, in a tone of profound despondency. "I refused to receive the money! I seized upon it as the property of a felon. Bitterly, bitterly do these things fall upon my head; bitterly, oh, how bitterly, is the punishment of all coming upon me!"

There was a deep silence, for Langford's heart was wrung, and he could give him no consolation. After a moment or two, however, the Earl started up in bed, exclaiming, "This—this at least can be amended. This—this at least can be repaired. Give me the pen and ink; quick!"

He was obeyed immediately, and with a trembling hand he wrote a full acquittal of all debt from Sir Walter Herbert to himself, principal and interest—costs and charges; nothing was omitted.

"There," he said, putting it in Langford's hands—" there is the first act of atonement which I have been able to accomplish. Take it, my son; take it. The writing those lines has given me the first happy moment I have known for years. Oh, misery of violent passions indulged! thou fiery curse that makest even gratification a torment! Had I but known—had I but known what it is to refrain! Stay," he continued, as Langford was taking the paper, "stay. These wounds and this weakness have made my hand shake, and such men as now stand by us, cunning lawyers and wise justices as they are, may hereafter swear that the writing is not mine. Here, Sir Thomas Waller; here, worthy Justice Whistler, favour me by placing to this act the testimony of your hands."

"But, my lord—" exclaimed Mr. Justice Whistler.

"But me no buts, sir," replied the Earl, fixing his keen feverish eyes upon him; "I know what you would say; I know what your lawyer-like seeking for a flaw would suggest: that no consideration has been given, and that therefore the deed will not be legal. But I tell you, sir, that a consideration has been given; that the money in full was paid into my hand this morning, and will be found in my library, if that library has escaped the flames. Sign, sir, sign! that is all you have to do. Witness that this is my act and deed!"

The two justices put their hands to the paper; and, to render Sir Thomas Waller but simple justice, he did so freely and willingly enough; not so exactly, worthy Mr. Justice Whistler, who showed no slight disinclination and hesitation in even witnessing an act which might take a fellow creature from out of the clutches of the law. Twice, when he had got his hand to the paper, he withdrew it, and paused for a moment in thought, longing apparently to find some excuse or some motive for refusal. At length, however, he signed it; and the Earl gave it to Langford, saying, "There, my son; take it, and use it for your friend's deliverance."

"I beg your pardon, my lord," said the justice, again interposing; "but this gentleman will have no opportunity of acting in the matter. You had better trust it to me."

"Wonderful impudence!" cried the Earl. "What! give meat to the harpies! Out upon it, man! do you think I would trust you with any feasible means of hurting your fellow creatures?"

"My lord," answered the justice, sharply, "if I am to judge by your own words lately used, your sarcasm is as much applicable to your lordship as myself."

"You say true, man; you say true," replied the Earl. "But though I be a wolf, I will not trust a wolf; I know you all too well. My son," he continued, turning to Langford, "are they really going to take thee from me at this painful hour?"

"I fear, my lord, that such is really their purpose," replied Langford. "I will not insult these gentlemen by saying that they know me to be innocent, though I must say that they seem very willingly blind to innocence. But they are resolved to carry the matter through to the last, and, therefore, it may be well to bring this scene, painful and terrible as it must be to you, to an end as soon as possible."

"Stay yet awhile—stay yet awhile," cried the Earl, grasping the hand that he held out to him; "I feel that it is terrible to see you go, for, perhaps, my son, we may never meet again. We may never meet in this world. We may never meet in the world to come, that dark and awful world towards which I am speeding quickly—quickly!"

"Oh, say not so," replied Langford; "I trust—nay, I hope—I am sure—that my innocence will so speedily be made manifest by one means or another, that in a very few days, perhaps a few hours, I shall again sit beside you, and I trust then to find you better."

The Earl shook his head. "Too late found," he said; "too early lost. I now feel how I could love you. I see your mother's spirit shining out of your eyes. I see that spirit, which pardoned and gave way but too much, looking mildly upon me, who wronged both her and you so deeply; but it is all in vain." And as he spoke, he pressed his hands over his eyes; and Langford, willing to spare him any further agitation, took that moment to make a sign to Justice Whistler, signifying that he was ready, and turned towards the door.

The Earl heard his step, however, and exclaimed, "Oh, not yet— not yet!" but Langford opened the door, and called Bertha with a loud voice.

The Frenchwoman came immediately, for she was sitting watching in the neighbouring chamber.

"Look to my father," said Langford; "you who were a witness of my mother's marriage—you, who owe my race so much—you——"

"You," she interrupted, "you would say, you who have repaid their kindness so ill——"

"No," answered Langford, "such was not my thought. You, who have had a share in all the turns of my wayward fate, look to my father, now on his couch of illness; look to him, tend him well, and if you feel that you have injured me or mine, make up for it now by keeping his mind as free from all anxiety as may be, by shutting out all that can agitate or alarm him, by speaking cheerfully and hopefully of my fate, and by teaching him that there is much yet to be done on earth, much yet to be gained from heaven. Take this paper also. You will see its value at once. Find somebody—if there be such a being on earth—in whom you can place implicit trust. Send him to seek out Sir Walter Herbert, who is in the hands of the notorious, infamous John Bolland. Let him give the paper to Sir Walter himself, requesting him, from me, to send for some lawyer of high repute in London, and not to act himself in the matter. Tell him— tell Alice—not to fear for me, for, being innocent, my innocence **must** appear. They may aid me if they find means; but, at all events, I am safe in my integrity. But above all things, be careful to whom you trust the paper."

"I will," she answered, "I will; but you will soon be able to follow out these things yourself. I know it; I feel sure of it."

"So do I," replied Langford; "but Alice and Sir Walter must not languish till then. Now, gentlemen, there but remains to crave a father's blessing, and then I am ready. I mean to use no threat towards you, Mr. Justice Whistler, but the time may come when the share you have had in this matter will be fully inquired into, and the legality of your proceedings investigated and ascertained."

"I will look to that, sir," replied the justice, with a calm and sneering nod; "I have taken care of myself in more difficult circumstances than these, and, doubtless, shall be able to do so still."

Langford made no reply, but re-entered the room where the Earl sat gazing upon the door, and listening to the sound of his voice.

The young gentleman advanced direct towards him, and knelt by the side of his bed. "My father," he said, "give me your blessing."

The Earl turned away his head. "What, oh! what is my blessing worth?" he said; "but be it so. My blessing, the blessing of a father's fondest affection, be upon you. I have none now but you!"

"If you would render that blessing of effect," replied Langford, "remember that on your life and health my fate may greatly depend. Be careful, then; cast away from you every thought and every feeling that may injure or agitate you, and strive for life and health, if not for your own sake, for your son's. Now, gentlemen, I am ready."

The two justices and the constables accompanied him out of the room. "What think you of it?" asked Sir Thomas Waller, addressing his companion in a whisper as they went.

The London magistrate replied by a peculiar contortion of countenance, and then added, "We must make as good a case of it as we can, if it be but to bear ourselves harmless."

CHAPTER XXVII.

WE must now leave that part of the country to which we have so constantly adhered during the preceding portion of this true history, and lead the gentle reader with us along a road which, perhaps, he may never have travelled before, but which, if he ever have, he will doubtless remember at once, from the description we are about to give.

Setting off in a line lying north-west from the little village of Moorhurst, and proceeding over the wild heath to which we have so often turned our steps, one road leads, after various turnings and meanderings, of which our ancestors were undoubtedly more fond than ourselves, as the reader already knows, to the county town. But in one of these turnings the road effects an object very different from the usual one, of merely going out of its way, and branches off into a country road, taking the direction of various small and remote towns

Now, from the want of care and neatness with which this branch road was kept at that time, it would in all probability have presented a very much larger proportion of ruts and sand than the larger road from which it was derived, and would have required double the time to travel each individual mile along its course which was required upon its parent road, had it not been for one circumstance. That circumstance was an extraordinary development of a stratum of very hard stone in that part of the country, which, taking the place of the sand, just a quarter of a mile from the spot where the two roads separated, afforded—or, rather, might have afforded—equal pleasure and admiration to Mr. M'Adam, the geologists, and all the members of the stonoclastic race, if the period we speak of had not been before geologists were discovered, and when Mr. M'Adam was yet unborn.

On it, if horses had been in the habit of going as fast as they do now, a carriage might have been drawn at any given rate of velocity, till after the road had passed through two or three small villages and towns, and a space of about twenty miles, when it again got into the sand, and then plunged like an eel—which it very much resembled in some other respects—into a deep mud.

This state, however, lasted not long; but, issuing like a bittern from the morass, the road took its flight over the hills, which were low wooded and well cultivated for about twenty miles further, and then began to assume a wilder and more barren aspect, till at length, when their summits were crossed, and at the distance of about sixty miles from Moorhurst, they presented on their northern side a wide range of rough, chill, rocky country, covered only by short brown turf from which the sheep had much ado to nibble a scanty subsistence, and decorated alone by fine hawthorns and hanging birches, except where, in the deeper dells, the oak and elm had sought and found a friendly shelter.

Forges and foundries, and manufactories of various kinds, have since blackened and enlivened that part of the country; but at the period which I speak of, the great demon of civilization had not gone forth, with a smoky chimney in one hand, and a steaming kettle in the other, equalizing and vulgarizing the whole earth; and a tract of about forty miles in length, and from ten to fifteen in breadth, was left upon the side of those hills, if not without any sign of man's habitation, at least without any sign of his arts, except, indeed, the patriarchal one of sheep-feeding. Here and there, in the nooks and dells, indeed, an old farm-house, which perhaps might boast a few acres of corn land around it, showed the dwelling-place of the great sheep farmer, who, riding over the hills adjacent, might generally say, " I am monarch of all I survey." But these had never been many; and the loneliness of the situation, an increasing taste for towns and luxuries, and various changes in the state of society, on which it is not worth while to dwell, had diminished the amount of inhabitants to even a smaller number than it had once contained. Two farms had often been joined in one; some of them were untenanted, and encroached upon by their neighbours; some of the few houses that did exist were vacant, and some were tumbling down.

It is to a house in this district, about five miles from the spot where the road we have mentioned crossed it, that we must now bring the reader, begging him diligently to mark the outside of it, in the first place, seated as it is in a deep gap in the hills, sheltered on three sides by a grove of fine old elms, in the topmost branches of which innumerable rooks make the air musical with their sweet country sounds; the house itself placed upon a high bank, its small windows overlooking a little stream below; and the other side turning towards its farm-yard, with a cart-road, indeed, leading up to it, but requiring both very strong horses and very strong carts to undertake the rough and perilous ascent.

This house was not one amongst the uninhabited ones which we have mentioned, for at the period whereof we speak—namely, but a few days after the events had taken place which we recorded in our last chapter—the farm-yard might be heard ringing with several voices, and more than one horse stamped in the stables. Leaving the house, however, let us speak of one of its inhabitants. About midday a solitary personage issued forth from the gates, took his way into the deepest part of the grove, and with his arms crossed upon his broad chest, walked slowly up and down, bending the bitter brow, and gnawing the dissatisfied lip, while his eyes were bent on the dry leaves of the past year, in which his feet left deep marks as he strode along. After thus wandering in the shade for some time, as if the gloomy shadow was congenial to his feelings, he raised his brow, and looked up, seeming to seek higher associations in the sky above. Whether the feelings within his breast did become more free and clear or not, he then turned his steps to the hill-side, and climbed high up, gazing over the wild, waste prospect below, and pausing every two or three minutes, as if endeavouring to fix more distinctly some particular spot. Yet his thoughts were neither of the scene on which his eyes rested, nor of the cultivated country beyond, nor of the towns and villages, the haunts and resting-places of busy man, but, on the contrary, they were fixed upon the deep, dark recesses of an erring human heart—on the troubled world of his own bosom—where, as in the world covered by the deluge, the dove of peace found no resting-place, so overwhelmed was the whole by the waves of sin and sorrow and remorse. Upon that turbulent ocean, too, floated the wrecks of many bright things past—high feelings, noble aspirations, manly generosity, steady friendship, warm affections—and over it spread dark clouds of doubt and suspicion, and morose discontent, springing from self dissatisfaction and disappointment, and internal reproach.

Such was the state of mind of Franklin Gray as he strode along the hill-side, pondering the events of the last few weeks, and finding in all, matter of bitterness and regret. His feelings suffered some alteration, and turned to more material objects when he gained the summit of the hill. They did not exactly make themselves audible, but nevertheless to his own mind they clothed themselves in words, and the tenor of those words was somewhat to the following effect:—

"This is wild enough, and solitary enough, but nevertheless they will doubtless try to hunt me out here. So great an enterprise as this cannot, in this pitiful and servile land, pass without stirring up all the great tyrants of the soil to put down him who has dared to strip them of their ill-gotten wealth. Doubtless they will hunt me out even here; and by heaven I have a thousand minds to stay and dare them, and defend my mountains to the last. But then these fellows," he added, after some thought, " though brave and true in the moment of danger, now that we have divided the money, are all anxious to leave me, and hasten up to the great city, to spend it in rioting and luxury. Well, I must not blame them! I felt so once myself. But this land then must be no more for me; I must quit it, and take myself back again to those more ardent and free countries where I can roam at large, and where, with a strong hand and a stout heart, I can make the miser, and the extortioner, and the slave-master pay for his pitiful life at the price of gold. Yet this, indeed," he continued, "has been a glorious booty; what between gold and jewels, we have swept off a mighty sum, and my own share might well content me for the rest of my days. Why should I not cross the seas, and in some of those sweet valleys by the higher Rhine, pass through the calm close of a busy life in bright tranquillity.

And, as he thus thought, a vision of sweet and peaceful things, such as his heart had sometimes longed for but had never known, rose up before his eyes; and he pictured to himself sweet wanderings through fair scenes, with his beautiful Mona by his side, and his lovely boy growing up into proud manhood under his eye. But as he thought of Mona a sudden shadow came across him; it was a mood he struggled with, and would fain have conquered, but it was one unconquerable, for it was a part of his dark fierce nature; and after pausing gloomily for several minutes, and, casting his eyes down upon the ground, with his whole feelings changed in a moment by one gloomy thought, he burst forth aloud, "I love it not! She would not wrong me—I know she would not wrong me; but still she is too tender of him. If she give her heart's affections to another, if she even take from me the smallest portion of those feelings that once were mine alone, she leaves a gap, a vacancy, a break in that deep intense love which is enough, but not too much for love like mine. Shall I speak to her thereon? shall I tell her what I feel? Ay, and make her think me jealous," he answered, with a bitter sneer even at himself. "I jealous! jealous too of such a weak, pitiful, effeminate thing as that! No; she shall go on in her own way. She must have seen that I loved it not; she must have felt that it displeased me; and see it and feel it she shall still, but speak of it I will never. Doubtless she is there now, soothing him, tending his wounds, speaking to him sweet kindly words, and listening to his soft gratitude. I will go back and mar the sunshine;" and as he spoke, with a cloudy, moody air, he strode back again towards the house, passed through the farm-yard, and entered the door, which stood open.

Proceeding up a tall narrow stone staircase, he passed one of his men seated on one of the landing-places, at the last story but one, so as to prevent any one from ascending or descending without being seen. Franklin Gray was not one, even when the dark and debasing passions of jealousy and suspicion were roused within him, to commit a mean or a pitiful act; and he spoke loud to the man upon the stairs, and trod heavily up, so that his voice and his footsteps might give notice of his coming to those above.

When he reached the upper story, he opened a door before him, and entered a room, poorly and scantily furnished, where were two persons with whom the reader is already acquainted. The first—who sat near the door, with her small beautiful foot resting upon a rude stool, and her knee supporting an instrument of music, in shape much resembling a guitar—was that lovely being whom we have twice before had occasion to mention under the name of Mona, the wife of Franklin Gray. She was finishing a song when he entered—a sweet plaintive song, in the tongue of some distant land; and as he came into the room, her dark lustrous eyes grew still brighter, and were raised to his with a smiling and a happy look, as if she thought she was doing what would please him best, and that the well-known music would awaken some sweet thoughts in her husband's bosom. The stern unmoved gloom of his countenance pained but did not surprise her, for she was accustomed to his moody temper; and loving him at all times and in all states, attributed his ill-humour to things which had gone wrong in matters with which she had no concern.

The other person who tenanted that room was one whom we have lost sight of for some time. It was Edward, called Lord Harold, who now, very pale, and evidently but just recovering from severe sickness, leaned back upon his chair with his head resting on his arm, and the right side of the loose vest which he wore cut open and tied, so as to give greater ease and space to some wounded part beneath. So intently had he been listening to the music, that he scarcely heard the entrance of Franklin Gray, and a faint but expressive smile hung upon his pale lip, while the vacant gazing of his eye told that the melody had borne imagination on its wings afar, and that he was enjoying sweet fancies removed from all that surrounded him.

"I see," said Franklin Gray, looking earnestly at Mona, "that you have become his musician as well as nurse."

Mona started, and gazed inquiringly in her husband's face. "Did you not wish me to do so?" she said, with her sweet-toned voice and foreign accent; "did you not tell me to do everything I could to soothe him and restore him to health?"

"I did so," replied her husband; "and I see you do it willingly."

Mona gazed in his face with a bewildered look, as if she did not comprehend his meaning; for though his words were not ungentle, they were spoken in that tone which showed the feelings that prompted them to be bitterer than the expression. There succeeded a pause for one or two minutes; and Franklin Gray, moving across the room, cast himself into a chair near the window, and gazed out gloomily over the wide prospect that stretched afar beneath his eyes, diversified only by the slopes of the hills, without town or village, or hedge-row to mark man's habitation or his cultivating hand. As he sat there, he spoke not to any one, and the silence grew painful, till at length it was broken by Lord Harold, as we shall continue to call him.

"I am glad of an opportunity of speaking with you," he said, "for I want to know more precisely how I am situated. I have to thank you, I find—"

"For nothing, sir!" replied Franklin Gray; "I have done what I have done for my own pleasure and convenience, and you have to thank me for nothing."

"Such is perhaps the case, sir," replied Lord Harold, coolly; 'at all events, you saved my life when I should otherwise undoubtedly have bled to death upon the moor. You have since treated me kindly and skilfully, have nearly cured a wound which might have proved fatal, and have tended me with much attention. At the same time, from various events which have occurred, from my being brought forth across the downs and placed in a coach which carried me hither, as well as from having seen at all times an ill-looking fellow with a pistol in his hand sitting at the foot of the next flight of steps, when I crossed from one room to the other, I am inclined to believe that you view me in some sort as a prisoner."

"Doubtless the ill-looking fellow, as you call him," replied Franklin Gray, with a bitter smile, "may find many of the fair and the gay, in his own rank of life, who would think him fully as good-looking as Edward, Lord Harold. However, sir, I gather from your discourse, that you wish to learn whether you are to consider yourself as a prisoner or not. Now, as you acknowledge that you owe me your life, I do not think you can consider it a hard case, even should I, for my own convenience, keep you a prisoner for a certain time."

"Yes, I have, sir," replied Lord Harold; "for I suppose there is scarcely any Englishman who does not feel that liberty is preferable to life."

"Then perhaps the best way of settling it," answered Franklin Gray, sternly, "would be to shoot you through the head, and thus leave the account between you and me as it stood before."

But as he spoke, Mona had advanced gently to his side, and laid her hand upon his arm. "Oh, set him free!" she said; "set him free as soon as he is able to depart."

"What is it to you, Mona?" demanded Franklin Gray, turning sharply upon her; "Why should you wish him to depart?"

"It is much to me, Franklin," she answered; "very much to me; and I do wish him to depart, for you have twice looked cold upon me since he has been here, which you never in your life did before, and anything which causes such a change I wish instantly away; for you know, Franklin, that your kind looks to me are like the sunshine of my own happy land—sunshine that I have left far behind."

Franklin Gray was somewhat moved, and seeing that he was so, she went on, saying, "Oh, set him free, my husband! and if it be needful, make him swear that he will never betray your abode. I will be answerable for it, he will keep his word."

Franklin Gray had been moved for a moment, and he had also thought of setting Lord Harold free, or of only detaining him till all was prepared for executing his own purpose of crossing the sea and seeking other lands; but the last few words which his wife uttered hardened his heart in a moment.

"You will be answerable!" he exclaimed. "What have you to do with being answerable for him? No; I will not set him free? If you choose to betray your husband, woman, and open the doors to him whom it is needful to detain, you can do it when you like. I shall neither watch nor stop you; but the consequence be upon your own head."

Thus saying, he turned upon his heel with a frowning brow, and hastily quitted the room, after which his steps might be heard slowly descending the stairs. Mona sunk down into the chair beside her, clasping her hands together, and fixing her eyes upon the ground with a look of despair; for they were the first harsh words, the first unkind and ungenerous expressions, which had ever dropped from the lips of him she loved, from the day on which she had sacrificed kindred, and home, and fortune, and her native land, to follow his uncertain footsteps through the world. As she sat there, with that look of deep despondency, Lord Harold could not but feel admiration of her exquisite beauty mingling even with the compassion which he felt; and there was something of that admiration apparent in his look and manner, as he slowly rose from his chair and crossing the room, took her hand in his, saying, "He treats you harshly, lady."

But Mona, suddenly recalled to recollection by that action and those words, started up, and drew her hand quickly from him, gazing upon him with a look of anger and indignation. "Treats me harshly!" she said; "It is false! He is kindness itself; and he is right too! What had I to do meddling with his purposes or his will? I have been sorry for you, young gentleman, and compassion has led me to do a foolish thing, but I will take care so to offend no more;" and thus speaking, she left him, and hurriedly sought her husband below.

She found him in a lower room, gazing forth as he had done above, but the expression of his countenance was more sad and less fierce than before. Mona advanced towards him, but he heeded her not; she laid her hand upon his arm, but he did not turn his head. She was a creature of noble impulses, however, and where her heart prompted she would not be repelled. The tears, indeed, sprang to her eyes and ran over her cheeks, but still she cast herself on her husband's bosom, saying, "I have done wrong, Franklin; I should not have interfered where you thought fit to act. I was sorry for the young man, and I thought that he might have friends and relations, and perhaps a wife, that loved him as I love you, and I wished you to send him back to his happy home on that account. But I was wrong to speak of it at all, and still more wrong to speak of it before him. Forgive me, Franklin; I will not offend again."

Franklin Gray pressed her to his heart, and kissed the tears off her cheek; and—although the seed of suspicion and doubt, once sown in a soil so congenial to it as his mind, can never, perhaps, be wholly eradicated, take what pains we will—yet he was anxious to feel as he had felt, somewhat ashamed of having given way to such bitterness towards her who was associated with all the better spirits of his heart's dark tabernacle, and grieved to see the grief of one who had brought the only real sweet sunshine on his path that he had known through life. He pressed her then to his bosom, he treated her gently and kindly; and once more, to her powerful gentleness, the fierce and lion-like spirit of her husband was softened and bowed down.

She had not said one word of the dark shade of jealousy which had shown itself in Franklin Gray's first words to her. She was far too wise to comment on it, or to attempt to do it away by any eloquence but those of acts. She saw it plainly, however; she felt that what in her breast was but pity, had been misunderstood by her husband; and from a certain vague expression on Lord Harold's face when last he spoke to her, she feared that, with him, man's vanity had once more misjudged woman's best feelings. She blamed herself, however, more than either: "I should have known," she thought, "that man cannot see into the heart;" and from that hour she went near the prisoner no more. She gave no cause for so abstaining, and she took care that the woman who accompanied her should provide for his comfort as far as might be. It is the meed of such conduct, however, almost always to pass unremarked; the recompense, the success is in our own hearts. Franklin Gray saw that she was less with the prisoner than before, but he did not see that she was never with him at all.

CHAPTER XXVIII.

Having now exposed to view the state of mind of Franklin Gray, we must turn once more to Lord Harold, and display, in some degree at least, the feelings by which he was affected. His heart was one naturally kind; his impulses were in general noble and generous; but he had derived from his mother a strong degree of that quality which, more than any other of the human heart, lays our hearts open to evil passions, unless it be very early enlisted on the side of the good ones; I mean pride.

From his father, too, had descended to him various faults and peculiarities, which, if everything had gone smooth with him though life, might perhaps have remained dormant, or, under particular circumstances, might have assumed the aspect of virtues, when in fact they were much more nearly allied to vices. There was, when roused by anger or stimulated by hatred, a degree of remorseless determination about his character, very much resembling that of Lord Danemore. This had shown itself in a degree in his conduct towards Langford; but since that period all the bad points in his nature, which had been originally brought forth by his disappointment in regard to Alice, had been called into still greater activity by the wounds he had received, by the irritation of sickness, and by pondering in solitude and in a state of confinement, not only over the disappointment of his first and early love, but over the mortification which his vanity had received, and over the annoyance of having to remain at a distance from the scene of action, where he knew, from the few words which Langford had spoken to him, that great and important events were likely to be transacted.

Under these circumstances, a degree of angry irritation had taken possession of his mind; and even on the day when he was removed from the neighbourhood of Moorhurst he would have resisted, had his strength been sufficient to render opposition at all effectual. Besides his own weakness, however, there was about Franklin Gray a tone of command and authority, a decision, a breaking forth of powerful intellect, which had the effect of producing, as the first impulse, an inclination to obey in all that surrounded him; and Lord Harold felt that power, and was angry with himself for feeling it.

He had determined, then, even before the period of the interview which we have just described, to seek his liberty by any means; and had the Robber at once granted him what he sought, had he either soothed or reasoned with him, the whole current of the young nobleman's feelings might have been changed, and he might have learned to admire those very qualities which now, arrayed as they were in opposition to his wishes and obnoxious to his pride, not only excited hatred, but created a stern and bitter determination both of taking vengeance, which he called "inflicting punishment," and of triumphing over the pride of one whose mental powers overawed him, which he called again "doing justice."

As he sat and listened to the brief discussion between Franklin Gray and the beautiful creature that pleaded for his liberty, his determination became more strong, his purpose more decided; and though, to do him but justice, vanity did not speak, and he entertained no definite thought of striving to raise into warmer feelings the compassion which he had excited in Mona's breast, and of thus striking the Robber in the most vulnerable point, he could not, as we have before said, help feeling a sensation of admiration mingling with his gratitude, and sentiments rising up in his bosom which might easily have become dangerous and evil.

The degree of scorn also which mingled in Franklin Gray's tone in speaking of and to himself had neither escaped his attention nor passed without producing its natural effect; nor did the sudden coldness which came over Mona diminish at all the strength of his determination to seek for vengeance in the shape of justice.

His first purpose, then, was to obtain his liberty as soon as possible. The wound he had received was not otherwise dangerous than from the great loss of blood it had occasioned; and he felt that he was every day and every hour recovering strength, which would soon enable him to use any means he thought fit for regaining his freedom. In order to do so, however, it would be necessary, he saw, to engage the co-operation of some one; and as the compassion of Mona Gray was already enlisted on his side, he determined, in the first place, to induce her, if possible, to aid him in escaping. Nor did the consideration that by so doing, he would render her a party to the execution of his second purpose, at all deter him, though that second purpose was, instantly to take measures for apprehending her husband and bringing him to the scaffold, having seen enough during his confinement to remove all doubts from his mind as to the real occupation and pursuits of him into whose hands he had fallen.

During the whole of that day and the next, the absence of Mona Gray rendered his design abortive. He looked for her coming in vain, though he often heard the sounds of her voice speaking to her husband, or singing to her child. She never approached the rooms to which he was confined; and though the woman who attended on her, came frequently to see that everything was done which could ensure his comfort, Lord Harold feared to trust a menial, and consequently still remained in expectation of the other at length appearing. When, towards the close of the second day, however, he found that his anticipations were not fulfilled, he ventured to ask of the woman, "Why does not your mistress ever come to see me now? Will her husband not let her?"

"Oh no," replied the servant; "for he is out the greater part of the day; but she is going out with him just now herself, and will be out all night, I hear."

Lord Harold took two or three turns up and down the room with a sufficient degree of agitation to attract the attention of the woman, who asked in a peculiar tone, if she could do anything to serve him?

"If you could go down," said Lord Harold, "and ask your mistress to speak with me for a few moments before she goes, you would very greatly serve me. Do it privately!" he added.

The woman nodded her head, and left him. She returned in a few minutes, however, alone, seeming to have met with a different reception from her mistress to that which she expected. "She says she cannot come," replied she, to Lord Harold's eager questions. "If you want anything, she bade me tell you to speak with Captain Gray himself, who will do anything you may desire that is reasonable."

"Pray go down to her again," said Lord Harold; "tell her it is with her I must speak. That I beg, that I entreat of her, by all the kindness that she has shown me, to come and speak to me, if it be but for one minute."

"I don't like to go any more," replied the woman; "she answered me quite crossly, and the Captain himself is there, sitting at the further end of the room reading, with his brow as dark as that great black hill, which looks as if it never saw the sun."

Lord Harold pulled a ring from his finger, which was the only thing of value on his person that had escaped the hands of Wiley and Hardcastle, and held it out towards the woman. "Will you do what I ask you," he said, "and have this for your reward?" She was not proof against the temptation; and murmuring, "He cannot eat me, if I do whisper again to his wife," she left the room and descended the staircase.

In a shorter time than before, she returned, however, and with a still less satisfied countenance, saying, "She says she will not come. She bids me tell you she will not come; and I'm to bring her no more such messages, which I'm sure I would not do for twenty rings; for there he sat while I whispered to her, and though he was so far off that he could not hear a word, he looked up from his book and stared at me as if his eyes had been swords to run me through."

Lord Harold turned away, mortified. "It may be the worse for all of us," he said to himself; "it may be the worse for all of us. There, woman, there is the ring I promised you; take it."

With a brightening countenance she received the gift, which was perhaps more than she expected, as she had failed in her errand; and then, descending the stairs, Lord Harold heard her stop a moment, and apparently speak with the man who kept watch below.

"That must be my next resource," he said to himself; "that must be my next resource. Perhaps I shall succeed better there."

He then gazed for some time from the window, laying out his plans in his own mind, and feeling that, though still somewhat weaker than he had hoped and expected to have been, he must take advantage of the temporary absence of Franklin Gray, lest such another opportunity should not occur again speedily. The windows of the room in which he was, looked out over the high bank which we have mentioned in describing the house, so that, in addition to the three stories below him in the building itself, there was at least a perpendicular descent of forty feet between him and the road. To let himself down from the windows, therefore, was utterly hopeless; and nothing remained but to bribe the man who guarded him, if such a thing were possible. How that object was to be effected, was the great difficulty, for he had been stripped of everything upon him when he was stopped upon the moor, except the ring which he had given to the woman; and a man of the class to which he who kept watch below pertained, was not likely to take promises for payment.

While he still gazed and revolved all these matters in his mind, he saw Franklin Gray and his wife habited, like two of the higher class of peasantry, and mounted on two strong horses, ride slowly down the road, and take their way across a track which lay between the upper hills and the flatter country below. He watched them for some time as they rode along, and shortly after, he saw two other persons issue forth and take a different direction. During a few moments their departure was succeeded by some loud talking and laughing in the house itself, which soon ceased, however; and shortly after, the voice of the man at the foot of the stairs was heard calling aloud, as if to the female servant, "Come up here, Harriet; come up here, and chat to us a bit. Curse me if I'm not lonely. Bring the child with you, if you don't like to leave it."

"Now is my time," thought Lord Harold; "doubtless they are all out but these two, and I may deal with them without interruption." He accordingly advanced to the door, and, opening it, walked out to the head of the stairs. The sound of his step, however, instantly attracted the attention of the man below, and he started up with the pistol in his hand, exclaiming, "What do you want?"

"I want to speak with you, my good sir," replied Lord Harold.

"Well, what is it?" rejoined the man, in a surly tone; "speak! I can hear!"

"That will scarcely do," said the young man; "if you like to come up here, I can speak to you at my ease, for I have a good deal to say, and much that may be to your advantage."

The man hesitated, but then replied, "I can't come now, for I've called to Harriet to come and talk to me, but I will come by-and-by."

"Come now," replied Lord Harold, "and bring the woman with you."

"Oh, oh! is that it?" said the man; "well, go in; I will come."

Lord Harold felt that he was treated with scanty ceremony; that he, the eldest son of a proud and haughty peer, in the midst of a free land, without any imputed guilt, or any liability in the eye of the law, was held as a prisoner, and treated with degrading familiarity by a low and probably guilty being. Nevertheless, he had an important object before him, and a moment's reflection taught him to master all feelings of irritation, and, according to the somewhat sordid view of our great philosopher, submit to indignities that he might rise above them.

He strode up and down the room once or twice, and then listened for the steps that he hoped to hear coming. For some time, however, nothing struck his ear but the low murmur of voices from the story below, in which he could distinguish the treble tones of the woman and the deeper ones of the man, and he judged, and judged rightly, that they were in earnest consultation in regard to himself. Nearly a quarter of an hour elapsed before the discussion ended, and they then entered together; the woman with a bolder and freer air, as one who had already taken two or three steps in the course which they both saw was about to be laid before them; the man with a look half sullen, half shy, as if he still doubted and hesitated at a leap which he felt morally convinced he should ultimately take.

Lord Harold paused, and gazed upon them both for a moment, calculating what should be the tone and manner which he ought to employ towards the persons before him; and after a moment's consideration he determined to act that part which was most congenial to his own nature, not alone because he felt that he should act it better than any other, but also because he gathered from the man's countenance in an instant that he was one of those low and grovelling animals who would take advantage of the least condescension—who might be overawed, who might be bribed, by those he felt to be above himself, but who would harden himself in opposition or raise the price of his services extravagantly to any one who descended to his own level, or who seemed to need his assistance so much as to court it at the expense of degradation.

Lord Harold accordingly threw himself into a chair, and gazed full in the man's countenance with that look of haughty consciousness which was in some degree natural to him; and when he saw that he had beaten down his gaze, he demanded, in a very different tone from that which he had used before, "I suppose, sir, you know who I am?"

"Why, yes," replied the man; "I have heard that you are the son of that old Lord ——."

"That is enough!" interrupted Lord Harold; "knowing then who I am, you must at once see that being kept here in this state is disagreeable to me. Besides which, important business requires my presence at home."

"Ay, that it does, if you knew all," muttered the man between his teeth.

Lord Harold continued, without taking any notice of what he said: "You must very well know, also, that anything which I promise, I will execute fully."

"Ay, that's what I don't know," replied the man; "that's just what I was talking to Harriet here about; for I know nothing of you; and it's just as likely as not, that if I were to let you out this very night, instead of doing anything that you said you would, you might take and hang me for my pains. No, no; a bird in the hand is worth two in the bush."

Lord Harold again felt angry and indignant; but he would not give way to feelings which might in any way interfere with his plans; and, though his nostrils expanded and his lips quivered, he mastered himself in a moment, replying, "So you and Harriet have been settling the whole business for me, and have doubtless saved me a world of trouble, for you have most likely made up your minds as to whether you will do what I require or not."

"Why, I think not," replied the man, somewhat staggered by the cool and decided tone in which the prisoner treated the question; "I think not; but that depends upon circumstances."

"On what circumstances?" demanded Lord Harold, shortly.

"Why, you see the matter is this," answered the man; "as far as I can judge, we shall all separate in ten days or a fortnight, for every one is wanting to go his own way. Now, you see, if the Captain—that is Captain Gray—were going to remain in England, I would as soon try to let you go as I would to jump out of that window, being as sure of getting an ounce of lead in my brains before the month was out if I did the one thing, as I should be of breaking my neck if I did the other. But then, I've a pretty rare inkling that the Captain and his lady are going across the seas; so that if you can make it worth my while in ready money to hide myself away for a fortnight till they are off, we may very likely come to terms."

"Ready money I have none," replied Lord Harold.

"Ay, that's what I was saying," interrupted the man; "I knew very well that Hardy and Wiley left no more money in your purse than there is in a dog's side-pocket. So I don't see——"

"But I do," replied Lord Harold. "As far as I can judge, from the direction which the carriage took that brought me hither, from the time occupied in the journey, and from the aspect of the scenery round, we are now somewhere in the Chalden hills, and the town of —— cannot be far distant."

"Some fifteen miles," replied the man; "at least, so Harvey told me the other day; I have not been there myself."

"It cannot be much more," said Lord Harold; "for I have hunted over all these wastes many a time, and I know the town well; for therein, as it is a seaport, lives a rich merchant and banker of the name of Drury, whom I have often employed in buying fine objects of the arts—pictures, and statues, and such things, from Italy. He has even now in his hand a sum of near three hundred pounds belonging to me, sent him to make such purchases; and, if you will engage this night to set me free, I, putting full confidence in your word, will write an order upon him for the money. You can send it by a messenger on horseback, who may easily be back before nightfall; and then, dividing the amount between you and your friend here, you can open the doors for my escape."

"It's a pretty sum," replied the man; "but let us have a little talk together, Harriet," and, drawing her to the further corner of the room, he consulted with the woman in a low voice for several minutes.

Lord Harold watched them eagerly, and, as they conversed, he could see the deep colours and shadows of strange and bad passions rise in the countenance of each, but especially of the female servant. At length, however, they grew calmer; their course seemed determined, and they returned, the man taking upon him to speak, as before.

"What you offer, my lord," he said, "does not exactly suit us. We could not send to the town, as you mention, without being discovered; for it is a small place, and Captain Gray has gone there himself to-day, to see about a ship, I fancy. His wife too, pretty Mistress Mona, would go with him; and altogether he is in a fine humour, and when that is the case, he has more eyes and hands than other people. However, as you showed you would trust us, we will trust you. Of course, you have got some banker in London, and if you have a mind to double the sum mentioned, and give us an order upon London, Harriet and I will be off together, and let you out, too, this very night. But you must swear to us that the money shall be paid, and that when we go to get it, we shall not be dogged, and that you will not appear against us in any way, and that if ever we are in trouble, you'll lend us a helping hand, bearing witness that we let you out."

"I pledge you my honour," replied Lord Harold, "most solemnly and most distinctly, not only never to injure you in any way, but to bear witness, should need be, that you both served me faithfully in my need. The sum you demand you shall have; and now nothing remains but to get me pen, ink, and paper, that I may write my order upon the banker in London."

"That will soon be done," replied the man: "for there is nobody in the house but ourselves, and we can do what we like. Come along, Harriet; I hear the child crying. I will be back again in a minute."

"Now," thought Lord Harold, when they had both left the room, "this man will betray the master who trusted him, disobey his commands, and, by letting me out of his hands, put his life at my disposal, without even binding me by any promise not to bring him to justice; and this woman, trusted by a kind and gentle mistress with the care of her sweet child, will leave that child helpless, while she schemes things that may destroy the happiness of father, mother, and child for ever. Such is fidelity in this world! Whom shall we trust?"

As he thus thought, he might feel a momentary touch of shame at using such tools and yet so critically examining their actions; but he felt no shame in owing his life to Franklin Gray, and then, because the Robber detained him for a few days longer than it suited his pleasure, deliberately resolving to bring him to the scaffold, veiling the darker features of such an act under the shining guise of justice. So human passions contrive ever to conceal their real nature from the eyes of those who entertain them.

In a few minutes the man returned with pen and ink, and paper; but before Lord Harold's hand could draw the order, the woman followed into the room, carrying the child in her arms, and saying, "Be pleased to make it half for him and half for me, for though he promises to marry me, I like to have something in my own hands."

The woman was young and pretty, and the man only laughed, replying, "You're right, Harriet, you are right. If every woman was as careful as you, there would be fewer faithless lovers in the world." The matter was arranged as she proposed; and as soon as it was concluded, Lord Harold demanded, "What is to prevent us executing our scheme now? Why should we not set off at once?"

"Only because we should be caught and brought back again in five minutes," replied the man; "and while you might risk a bullet or two, I should certainly get my brains blown out. Why, there is Harvey and little Bill, and all the rest of them, gone out with their carbines turned into birding pieces, for the purpose of seeing what game they can get upon the hills. They are scattered about all over the place, and we could not go half a mile without the risk of meeting some of them. Besides, there's that young devil, Jocelyn, lurking about in some of the dells, trapping wheatears and such things, and we must take care to blind him, for he's all eyes and ears together. No, no; one of them has promised to come back to take my place in a couple of hours; then I'll go out as if to sport, and mark out our way across the country. I shall come on again to watch about ten o'clock at night, and then, depend upon it, they'll all be drinking as hard as they can drink, till they go to bed. Most of them will be drunk; and, when they are all fast asleep, we can do what we will, for Franklin Gray won't be back till noon to-morrow, so you and I, and Harriet here, can take horses and be off."

"And what will you do with the infant?" demanded Lord Harold, looking to the woman.

"Oh, it sleeps all night," she replied, "when once it's put off; they'll find it in the morning, and feed it till its mother comes back."

Lord Harold shut his teeth tight, but there was no remedy for it, and he made no comment. He could not help doubting, however, whether the order he had given upon a London banker would be very safe in the hands of this faithful couple, who might or might not make use of the paper, and yet leave him as much a prisoner as before. As he had given them the drafts, however, he felt that it would be impolitic to demand them back again, and consequently, after arranging all the minor particulars of their plan, he suffered them to depart, carring with them the unconscious child whom they had brought to witness the betrayal of its parents' trust.

The rest of the day passed over to Lord Harold with no slight impatience and anxiety. In somewhat more than the two hours, which the man had mentioned, several of the gang were heard to return and relieve the guard, who was found sitting at his post below. The voice of the woman, too, could be distinguished, caroling at her work, as gaily and lightly as if there had been neither vice, nor guilt, nor folly at her heart; and from time to time, the young nobleman could hear her talking to the child as tenderly as if she had been its mother. "Strange and contradictory human nature," he thought, "which can reconcile all these most opposite things;" and, as do most people who comment upon the actions of others, he forgot to look into the contradictions of his own bosom.

Seldom had Lord Harold seen the sun go down, with such anxious feelings as he then experienced. The voice of the boy Jocelyn was heard below, but the few sounds to be distingushed in the house showed that the greater part of the gang were still absent. Speedily, however, others were heard, and then came several more, laughing, talking, and singing; and the woman, when she brought him in lights, said, "They are all come back, and are soon going to supper."

The noise, after a short interval, increased rapidly, and it was evident that wine began to do its work. The rattling of dice was heard; then many a merry song—some appropriate enough to the calling of those who poured them forth, some as opposite as it was possible to imagine. Hour after hour passed by, and Lord Harold fancied that the revel would never end; but gradually the sounds became fewer as one after another of the party fell asleep under the influence of wine, or retired to rest, from weariness. At length, after one more general burst of merriment, the whole of the band seemed to betake themselves to repose. Steps were heard in different directions, a voice here and there speaking to a companion, the dull end of some drowsy ditty hummed amidst hiccups, as the half drunken reveller stripped off his clothing, and then all was silent throughout the mansion.

"Now," thought Lord Harold, "I shall soon see whether they will keep their word with me;" for he could not shake off from his mind an impression that they would prove as faithless to him as they had done to Franklin Gray; and, as nearly an hour elapsed after all was quiet, without his seeing anything of any one, he became more and more convinced that it was as he had suspected. He was mistaken, however; for at length the door of his room slowly opened, and the man, putting in his head, beckoned to him to come out.

Lord Harold had been long prepared, and he instantly followed the footsteps of his guide, who led him silently down the stairs to a wide, deep, porch doorway, where the woman Harriet was in waiting. Not a word was spoken by any of the party, and the man then took his way across the court-yard towards a long range of stabling and outhouses, which in former times had sheltered many an honest and modest farmer's gelding, but which now contained not a few of those animals which have established for themselves an impudent reputation under the title of "a highwayman's horse." The man raised the latch, and pushed the door, but it resisted his efforts, and, with a voice full of dismay and bewilderment, he exclaimed, " Hang me if Harvey hasn't locked the stables!"

Lord Harold made no reply, but waited to see what expedient he would propose, and very soon found that it was one to which he was not at all inclined to submit, namely, that of returning to the house and taking their chance of another day.

"No," he said, in a low tone; "no, my good friend! I have determined to make my escape to-night, or not at all. I am out here with you and this good lady, and nothing shall make me go in again. If there are no horses to be found, we must go on foot."

"But suppose I say you shall go in again," replied the man; "what then?"

"Why then," replied Lord Harold, "I shall take care to make my refusal in so loud a tone that some of the good people who are asleep there shall hear it, and come down to find you and this fair lady so far upon your way, with an order upon my banker in your pockets."

The man stood and glared at him for a moment, as if he would have shot him where he stood; but at length he said, with a slight stamp upon the ground, "Well, it's no use; I suppose we had best take our way off on our own feet, if we cannot get four legs to carry us. One must risk something in this world; and perhaps, after all, the clatter of those horses' feet might have roused some of the fellows above. Come, Harriet, my lass; you must try what you can do for a forced march."

Thus saying, he led the way out of the court-yard, and bent his steps straight against the side of the hill. He seemed to bear no malice towards Lord Harold for having forced him to the decided step he had taken; and when they were at a sufficient distance from the house to permit of his speaking aloud without risking anything, he said, "I found out this morning, while I was exploring, that if we take this way over the hill, between those two high knolls, we shall get into a little lane on the other side which leads down to a village some ten miles off. Now, we shall get there, I dare say, before daylight, though it is tough work walking up this hill, and there, I don't doubt, we may get horses to take us on. If so, we part there, my young lord; for it won't suit me to travel with lordship any longer. I and Harriet will go on to London as fast as we can, and I dare say you will be able to make your way without us."

"That I shall, easily," replied Lord Harold, "even if I go as far as that with you; but most likely I shall stop before that."

The truth was, that Lord Harold began now to feel that he was much feebler than he had supposed; and although they had not gone at this time above half a mile since they first set out, it was with difficulty that he kept up with his two companions. They showed him some degree of kindness and consideration, however, slackening their pace for his convenience, when they found, on looking back towards the house they had left, that no light nor any other sign whatever announced that their flight had been discovered. A strong effort of his determined nature enabled the young nobleman to do more than many persons would have effected in his situation, and he succeeded in crossing the summit of the hill, and descending so far on the other side as to arrive at the end of the wooded lane of which his guide had spoken. There, however, he was obliged to declare that he could go no further; and the reply of the man was, "Well, then, we must leave you; for of course we can't stop here; for, to say the truth, I would rather meet the devil himself than Franklin Gray after what has happened."

"Go on; go on!" replied Lord Harold; "go on, and take care of yourselves. I will rest here for an hour or two by these trees, and then doubtless shall be able to go forward very well by myself."

"Mayhap you would like a pistol, however," said the man, putting one into Lord Harold's hand; "I always find them convenient;" and, without further adieu, he left the young nobleman, who seated himself under one of the trees, with the darkness of the night around him. The other two went on; and in a moment after the woman's voice was heard in a loud laugh, which Lord Harold doubted not was in some way at his expense.

CHAPTER XXIX.

"LET us do everything formally," said Sir Matthew Scrope to Sir Thomas Waller, when the latter returned from the expedition which we have already recorded to Danemore Castle, at about eleven o'clock in the day. "Pray, let us do everything formally, or we may get into a scrape. Indeed, what you tell me about this young man being the Earl's son makes me afraid we have got into a scrape already. Ha! Mister Justice Whistler; is it not so? ha!"

"What is life, my dear sir," said Justice Whistler, who was somewhat of a wag, and generally displayed his talent for raillery upon any one he saw in mortal terror or great anguish of mind—such as young prisoners brought before him for capital offences, and their friends or relations; "what is life, my dear sir, but a succession of scrapes? We get into a terrible scrape when we enter it, surely, and an awful scrape in going out of it. Then, between, there is love and matrimony, two other sad scrapes; beside all the others, such as the present, which we fall into between infancy and dotage. The great art of life is to get out of our scrapes cleverly. Now, let us see how you will manage to get out of this; ha! ha! ha!" and he laughed most uncomfortably close to the ear of his two fellow justices.

Sir Matthew Scrope was evidently in great anxiety respecting the result, and bitterly regretted that a rooted disinclination to rise by candlelight had prevented him from going over to Danemore with his colleague Sir Thomas Waller, whom he looked upon as a rash young man, though he was at least fifty-eight years of age. He had been in very great apprehension before, lest it should ultimately prove that the personage whom he at first determined to be undoubtedly guilty, should prove entirely innocent; and the extraordinary consequences of hearing that the Earl acknowledged him, not only as his son, but as his legitimate son, were, that he speedily not only began to doubt whether the prisoner was guilty or not, but whether he, Sir Matthew Scrope, had ever thought him guilty; and he might very soon have worked himself up into the belief that he had always maintained his innocence, but had been overruled by Sir Thomas Waller.

The latter worthy knight was a man of courage of a certain kind, that is to say a sort of chameleon courage, which took its colour from whatever was next to it. As long as he had remained by Mr. Justice Whistler, the cool, self-possessed resolution of the London justice, who knew better than any man living how to carry through what is called an unpleasant piece of business, had kept him up, and bold measures were all that he thought of; but the timid apprehensions of Sir Matthew Scrope damped his fire most amazingly, and when he found the London justice admit calmly that they were in a scrape, the fire went out altogether.

Both the country justices, being men of vivid imaginations, instantly set to work to picture to themselves all the evil consequences which might ensue from the *faux pas* they had committed; and a sort of nervous twitching came over Sir Matthew Scrope's whole person, which afforded Mr. Justice Whistler much internal satisfaction.

"Nay, nay, my good friend," exclaimed Sir Matthew; "these are no joking matters; and the only thing that it seems needful to do now is, to see how we may best retreat from this business quietly."

"Retreat from it! exclaimed the London magistrate; "nonsense. Face it out boldly. The man is just as innocent of the murder as you or I; but what matters that? Do your best to prove that he is guilty; then there will be always so fair a case against him that you will be justified in all you have done; and the more vigorously you act against the Earl's own son, the more credit you will get for the impartial administration of justice."

But such bold counsels were not for Sir Matthew Scrope; and Sir Thomas Waller, whose courage was just now lukewarm, was more inclined to timidity than anything else. "Let us discharge him at once," he exclaimed, "and be civil to him."

"Nonsense, I say again," replied Mr. Justice Whistler. "What! discharge him without cause, after having dragged him away from his dying father's bedside this very morning. Would you make fools of us all!"

"No, no; that will never do," said Sir Matthew Scrope; "but, nevertheless, let us do things formally. Let us have the young gentleman up for examination; let us be civil to him, as Sir Thomas says. Perhaps something may come out in his re-examination which may show his innocence."

"If it do not come out, you will squeeze it out, that is clear," rejoined Justice Whistler; "but the man stands committed, the warrant is made out, and there is nothing to be done but to send him to the gaol. I am sorry I did not send the constables on with him at once."

"I am very glad you did not," said Sir Matthew. "As to the warrant, it is but a bit of parchment, which will shrivel up in my kitchen fire in a minute; and so we will have him up into the justice-room to re-examine him before we send him—"

"Back to his father," said Justice Whistler, supplying the words, and shrugging his shoulders. "Well, if you will act in such a way, I suppose I must help you to do it gracefully. Let us go to the justice-room. Call the clerk. Leave the whole business to me, and do not be afraid. Whatever you may hear or see, I will get you out of the business—and in your own way," he added, seeing his fellow justices hesitate.

"Well, well," replied Sir Matthew Scrope; "if in our own way that will do; but let me beg of you, Mr. Justice Whistler, not to plunge us further in the mire than we are at present."

"A capital simile," muttered the London justice between his teeth, as he led the way to the justice-room, which communicated by a long passage with the mansion of Sir Matthew Scrope.

The clerk was then called, the magistrates took their stations in formal array, the table was diligently strewed with papers, and an order was given to bring in the prisoner.

"Ahem!" cried Sir Matthew Scrope, as Langford appeared between two constables. "Ahem! ahem!" said his fellow justices; and Sir Thomas Waller, who now—like a tennis ball, which, having been struck in one way by the hand of a strong player, is met by his opponent's racket, and is driven further back in the opposite direction—was inclined to go further than any of his colleagues, according to the new impulse which he had received, added, with a simpering smile, "Pray, be seated, sir. Ahem! You rascal, why don't you give the gentleman a chair?" and he bent his brows as frowningly on the constable as if he had committed petty larceny at least.

Langford was pale, and his features somewhat worn and haggard, with all the anxiety, agitation, and distress of mind which he had gone through, within the last week; neither was his heart well at ease when he regarded either his father's situation or his own at that moment, and felt that his recovered parent might remain in sickness and in anguish, and even pass the gates of death, without the consolation of his son's presence; while he, perhaps, manacled and treated like a common felon, was detained in the solitary wretchedness of a prison upon the charge of murdering his own brother. Nevertheless, a faint smile came over his lip at the somewhat burlesque exhibition of Sir Matthew Waller, and it instantly flashed across his mind that something must have occasioned a change in the worthy justice's feelings towards him, both from the sudden alteration and great embarrassment of his manner. He threw himself into the chair, however, that was placed for him, and leaning his elbow on the table, gazed upon the magistrates, thinking, "What next?"

"You stand before us, sir," said Mr. Justice Whistler, in a pompous tone, "accused of the murder of Edward Lord Harold. Ahem!"

There was something in the man's whole manner that roused Langford's indignation and contempt at the same time; and he replied, with his lip curling and his nostril expanding, "I *sit* before you, sir, committed on that charge; at least, if I believe what you told me not above three hours ago."

"Circumstances may have occurred since, sir," said the justice, with a mysterious look, "to make us take a more favourable view of the case, and we have consequently determined to re-examine you."

"Sir, I am tired of re-examinations," replied Langford. "You informed me that I was committed: under such circumstances, I am not disposed to answer any further questions, or to be re-examined at all."

Mr. Justice Whistler looked at his two companions, and both the knights looked at Mr. Justice Whistler, for Langford's renitency threatened to keep them exactly in the disagreeable position in which they had placed themselves; but after a moment's pause he added a few words, which, like the sound of parley, gave hope of entering into some capitulation. "Pray, sir," said the prisoner, "what are the circumstances which induce you to take a more favourable view of the case?"

"Nay, young gentleman," said Mr. Justice Whistler, with a benign and yet dignified look, "you cannot expect us to give you such information. That would be defeating the ends of justice; but if you think fit to answer the interrogatories which shall be addressed to you, and if your replies coincide with the information which we have received, the result may be very much in your favour."

Langford paused for a moment ere he replied. He was naturally extremely anxious to free himself as soon as possible, but yet he felt a degree of indignation at the conduct that was pursued towards him which overcame every other feeling; and at the same time he began to perceive that the worthy justices were very doubtful as to their own proceedings, so that he was not without some expectation of their setting him free at once if he avoided any further reference to that journey to the moor, which he could neither explain nor account for, without inconvenience and danger to himself and others; he, therefore, once more refused to submit to any interrogation.

"All I shall say," he continued, "is, that I am, as you well know, perfectly innocent; that I never saw the unfortunate young gentleman of whose death I am accused, after I parted with him in the Manor park at Moorhurst; and that there is not the slightest evidence to show, that though he drew his sword upon me, I ever drew mine upon him. I shall reply to nothing more."

Mr. Justice Whistler whispered eagerly to Sir Matthew Scrope. "There is nothing for it, I tell you," he said, " but to send him to prison, and make out the best case against him you can. You see he will give us no opportunity of letting him go. Your risk will be much greater in the one case than in the other."

Sir Matthew Scrope turned very pale, for the alternative was certainly somewhat disagreeable; and his eyes wandered with an anxious vacancy from the countenance of the London justice to that of the prisoner, and then again stole round to the face of Sir Thomas Waller, without finding any resource in the expression of either of the three. Sir Thomas Waller, on his part, being of a more irritable and less lamb-like disposition than his worthy colleague, was getting somewhat excited, or rather into a state of irritable despair, which inclined him to side with Mr. Justice Whistler, and take the leap before him, even at the risk of breaking his neck.

At that moment, however, while the justices were in this state of anxiety and embarrassment, a constable made his appearance at the doorway, closed the door gently behind him, and, walking slowly up the room, communicated something to Sir Matthew Scrope, which was instantly transmitted to the other two magistrates, in the same low tone in which he had received it.

"Oh, send him away; send him away," said Mr. Justice Whistler. "Bid him come another time."

"He's a most respectable man," said Sir Thomas Waller; "perhaps he might help us in this business."

"Why, your worship," said the constable, in a low tone, "I understood him to say that it was something about this very business he wanted to tell you."

"Show him in, then; show him in!" said the large round voice of Mr. Justice Whistler; and in a few minutes a small neat dapper man was ushered into the presence of the three magistrates, dressed in a plain suit of black silk, who was greeted by the two country magistrates as Master Evelyn.

With a quick, short step he advanced to Sir Matthew Scrope, took him by the button, led him into the recess of a window at some distance behind the other magistrates, and spoke to him for a few moments with rapid utterance, but in a low voice. Most men have seen the sun come from behind a cloud; but the glorious visage even of the great orb of day, when it bursts forth from that vapoury veil, is scarcely more radiant than became the countenance of Sir Matthew Scrope while listening to the words of Mr. Evelyn, the attorney.

"Hist! hist!—Sir Thomas!" he exclaimed; "Your worship. Master Whistler!" and with dignified grace he beckoned them up to the place of conference. Mr. Justice Whistler, as he listened, laid his finger solemnly upon the side of his nose, and then, making a sign to his colleagues to be silent, returned to his seat, and said in a full round voice, "Mr. Evelyn, be so good as to introduce the witnesses."

"What is coming now?" thought Langford, as he heard the direction given, and he turned to look towards the door, while the London justice, with an air of perfect self-composure, took up some of the papers from the table, and seemed to study them attentively, as if perfectly indifferent to the next act of the drama.

Langford still kept his eyes upon the door, however, not a little anxious to see who were to be the witnesses for or against him; and certainly his surprise was not slight when he saw Sir Walter Herbert enter the room, with Alice, pale and evidently much agitated, leaning on his arm; and a woman servant, whom he had often seen at the Manor House, following close behind.

He started up with an impulse that he could not resist, and sprang forward to meet her. Had he kept his seat. Alice might have gone through the scene very well, for, though agitated in a very great degree, she had taken much pains to nerve her mind, in order calmly to perform the part assigned to her; but the sudden start, the joyful smile, the radiant look of happiness with which Langford sprang forward to meet her, quite overthrew her equanimity, carried her away altogether, and she suffered herself to sink forward in the arms he held out to her, bursting into a violent flood of tears.

Sir Matthew Scrope, who was naturally not without a feeling heart, was affected at what he saw, and Mr. Justice Whistler amused. "No private communications between the witness and the prisoner," said the latter, with a broad grin; and though Langford turned round towards him with a heavy frown gathering on his high forehead, he went on in the same strain. "Pray, separate them, Mr. Evelyn. Pray, separate them, Sir Walter Herbert, else we shall have evident collusion, and be obliged to refuse the evidence!"

Langford removed the arms which he had at first clasped warmly round the beautiful form of his promised bride; and Alice, while she wiped away the tears with one hand, placed the other in that of her father, and advanced towards the table.

"Well, madam," continued the justice, "what is it that you have to say upon this subject? I understand it is something of great importance."

"I trust it may prove so," replied Alice; and indeed I should think it would prove of the greatest importance. What I have to say is this, that in the course of last night I myself distinctly saw Edward Lord Harold alive."

"And are you ready to swear to this, madam?" asked the justice.

"Quite ready," replied Alice.

"Then be so good, madam," he said, "as to detail all the circumstances."

Alice immediately complied; and with distinctness and precision, which called a compliment from the lips even of Mr. Justice Whistler, she narrated every event of the preceding night which related to the matter in question. She told, glancing timidly at the cause of their journey at that late hour, how the carriage which contained herself and her father had been stopped, they themselves obliged to alight, their own horses turned loose, and others put to; and she went on to say, that when the party which had dispossessed them took possession of the carriage, she had distinctly seen Lord Harold, whom she had known from her childhood, assisted to the carriage by two men, and placed therein, together with other persons. She further said, that she had called her maid to witness what was going on, and she had consequently seen the whole, of which she would give her own account. The maid was then called forward, and corroborated in every respect her mistress's statement. She knew Lord Harold perfectly well by sight; had known him from the time he was a boy, and could not be mistaken. She had seen him distinctly by the bright light which was then in the sky, and which she had since heard proceeded from the burning of Danemore Castle. She had heard his voice, and recognised it, as well as his person, so that there remained no earthly doubt upon her mind that he was still alive.

"Well, then," exclaimed Mr. Justice Whistler, "such being the case, of course, where nobody has been killed, nobody can be the murderer. We have therefore nothing further to do but to discharge the warrant against this gentleman, and set him at liberty. We have heard in romances, and such trash, of gentlemen being liberated by fair ladies, but I must confess I never saw it before till this day. However, we must, as I said, discharge the warrant; though, if I am rightly informed," he added, with what he intended to be a pleasant and meaning smile to Langford—" though, if I am rightly informed, almost as many aliases should have been put into the description of this honourable gentleman as into that of any person brought to the Old Bailey."

Langford looked grave, for his feelings were very much mingled. He was rejoiced, undoubtedly, at his liberation; he was rejoiced to hear that the man of whose safety he had himself given up all hope, was still living; he was rejoiced that Alice Herbert should have been the means of restoring him to freedom; but still he saw many a difficulty and many a pang before him; and with a generous heart and mind, he grieved for the sake of his younger brother, as well as for himself, that he had not known of Edward's safety before, when he might have taken means to soften everything that was now likely to

15

be harsh and painful both to the Earl and to himself, as well as to him who had so long looked forward with a feeling of perfect certainty to the enjoyment of high rank, commanding station, and one of the most splendid fortunes in the country.

He could now do nothing; the Earl had so loudly proclaimed the secret of his birth, had acknowledged him before so many persons, that no means of breaking or softening the matter to him who had hitherto been called Lord Harold now remained; and even with regard to the Earl himself, all that Langford could hope for was, to have the opportunity of communicating the facts to him in the first instance, and of concerting some means with him for taking the sting out of his offence. Such were the feelings which were busily crossing his bosom while the magistrate spoke, and for the moment, they produced a look of serious thought, almost of sadness, which surprised even Alice Herbert. The next moment, however, his countenance was all clear; and taking her hand in his, he thanked her a thousand times, feeling, with true love's sweet deception, as if his liberation were entirely owing to her exertions.

"Oh, dear Langford!" she said, "indeed, you owe me nothing. I wish it had been in my power to do anything to free you sooner, not only from imprisonment, but from a horrid accusation, which was even worse. But this has been all accident; and though it has made me very happy, I have had no merit therein."

Langford thanked her still, however, and thanked her eagerly; and then turning to good Sir Walter Herbert, he shook him warmly by the hand, thanking him too, and asking him if he had yet received the paper which the Earl of Danemore had sent that very morning. He found, however, that such was not the case; and that Sir Walter Herbert was then waiting with Alice to tender bail for his appearance; Bolland and his follower never yet having reached the county town to which the good knight and his daughter had bent their steps after having been left without their carriage.

The tale of their adventures instantly roused the peculiar genius of Mr. Justice Whistler, who had that very morning, on his way back with Langford, investigated accurately the whole history of the attack upon Danemore Castle, and who now, furnished with a clue by the account of Sir Walter Herbert, resolved to remain in the county, and to pursue the robbers till he had brought them to justice, though he vowed that his presence was daily needed in London. On this sage determination he proceeded to act, and as soon as Bolland appeared—which he did in somewhat rueful plight about the middle of the day, having remained tied to a tree during the whole night—Mr. Justice Whistler sought to engage him in the scheme, well knowing that never ferret traced the windings of a warren with more supple ingenuity than the sheriff's officer would trace the track of a fugitive.

It was with difficulty, however, that Bolland was persuaded to undertake the task, for the warning voice of Franklin Gray rang in his ears; and though he longed to be revenged for the cold night he had passed upon the moor, yet he had a great reverence for the Robber's threats, having remarked that they seldom went unexecuted. He was at length, however, persuaded; and as soon as Sir Walter and his daughter, accompanied by Langford, now at liberty, had taken their way back, with hearts greatly relieved, towards the scenes where first they appeared before the reader's eyes, the London magistrate and his new ally, with the two country justices, as slow hounds behind them, proceeded to hunt out tidings of Franklin Gray and his party. They were soon at fault, however; for though the marks of wheels and horses' hoofs could be traced from the spot where the carriage had been taken from Sir Walter Herbert as far as the road continued sandy, the nature of the soil soon changed; hard rock succeeded, and all such marks were lost. At the same time, it was found in vain to question the cottagers and townspeople, for all declared that if such a party had passed at all they had passed in the night, when heavy sleep had closed each ear and shut up every eye.

CHAPTER XXX.

It is probable that very few persons in the world, were the choice left to them, would prefer that any mixture whatsoever of pain should chequer the happiness which they covet. But yet have we not all felt, have we not all at some time owned, that the mingling of a slight drop of acid in the sweet cup of enjoyment gave it a zest which prevented it from palling on the taste.

Seated beside Alice Herbert, in a vehicle which had been hired at the county town to convey them back to their own dwelling, a vehicle the external appearance of which none of those it contained even saw, Langford gave way to joy, not unmixed, indeed, but only so far touched with care and anxiety as to bring out the brighter points in the more striking relief. As far as he could, he cast from his mind every memory of evil: he thought of that which was pleasant and gladdening in his fate alone, and suffered the memory of past discomforts and pangs, or the apprehension of difficulties and dangers in the future, to come across his mind but as vague shadows, like distant clouds upon the edge of the horizon, which the wind might or might not bear away, but which at all events did not serve to obscure the sun that shone in the zenith.

He had, indeed, infinite cause for satisfaction. He had a thousand motives for joy, and even for triumph. That which had been for many years the first, the great object of his existence, was now accomplished, and accomplished, though not without pain, and difficulty, and danger, still without one action which he could look back upon with sorrow or with regret. He felt that, though he had been tempted to do things which he would afterwards have repented, he had resisted the temptation, and had struggled nobly as well against himself as against the injustice of others.

Whatever might result from the circumstances in which he was placed, he had succeeded in that great object of clearing his mother's memory from a stain. The Earl, in the presence of many witnesses, had more than once acknowledged the marriage which for eight-and-twenty years he had concealed and denied; and Langford doubted not that the same good providence which had led him so far through such tortuous paths to success, would accomplish the rest in good time, nor leave unfinished the work begun. It was a blessing, too, when he gazed on Alice Herbert, the beautiful and the beloved! to feel that the only stigma upon his name, which even the eye of prejudice could have seen, was removed, and that her father's views of illegitimate birth would not in his case mingle any degree of pain with that approbation which in other respects he had given so joyfully.

He sat beside her, then, giving way to the extreme of happiness; and, strange to say, the love which in their last meeting had been new and timid in the hearts of both, had now, by the events of deep interest, by the dangers, by the sorrows, by the anxieties which they had passed through together—by all the various circumstances, thoughts, and feelings in which the fate of each had been associated with that of the other, been taught to feel like old and tried affection, had lost much of the shyness of novelty; and Alice allowed the hand which he had taken, to rest in his, while on their onward journey he told as much of the strange tale of his past life as he could do without embarrassing the story with the names of others whose fate was yet uncertain, but might be affected by the very share they had taken in all that had passed regarding him.

He mentioned not the name of Franklin Gray, but he took his own history far back, and told her and her father that long ago, in the days of the civil wars, many an Englishman, driven forth from his native land, had sought refuge in France; that many of them, broken in fortunes, and bankrupt even of hope, had become mere adventurers, and had established for their countrymen the reputation of bad and reckless men.

He went on to tell her that one of these exiles from their native land had been kindly received and nobly entertained by a family which had long been more or less connected with England and English people. He was of a daring and adventurous nature, and had sought his fortune, before he came to France, in still more distant countries; but there was something in his whole demeanour, in the high education which he displayed, in the noble feelings which often burst from him, even in the very faults and untamed wildness of a nature spoilt by indulgence, which confirmed his account of his own high rank, and the large possessions of his dead father in the island of his birth.

That man, he said, was now the Earl of Danemore; and then, in the graces of youth, he found no great difficulty in winning the heart of Eugenie de Beaulieu, whose feelings in his favour were first excited by compassion, and ended in admiration and in love. They parted, but it was soon to meet again. Her brother had been forced to join the army then warring in the Low Countries. Her uncle had been sent to England on one of the brief embassies which from time to time marked the broken intercourse between the great usurper Cromwell and the legitimate monarch of France. The aunt of Eugenie de Beaulieu, having accompanied her husband, had sent over people in whom she could confide, to bring her niece, who had been left almost unprotected in France during her brother's absence, to the British capital; but the death of Cromwell, and the uncertain policy of his weak successor, had thrown the whole country into confusion ere she arrived. Eugenie was followed by her lover, and never reached the dwelling of her uncle in London. Ere she arrived at that city she had consented to become a wife; and her husband, having been discovered as an adherent of the house of Stuart, was soon after obliged to fly and leave her. What he meditated, what he purposed by such an act, his son now touched upon but slightly; but he was obliged to tell how, by threats as well as by entreaties, the Earl had forced her, who had been his bride but a few weeks, to give into his hands all the proofs of their private marriage, promising by everything he held sacred never to destroy them.

The next part of the story was a painful one, and was also passed over lightly: how his mother returned to France, and did not find her husband where she expected to meet him; how she was forced to communicate her situation to her brother; how her brother doubted and feared, but at length believed her tale; how he cast all thoughts aside but that of doing justice to his sister; how he traced out her husband, and eagerly, perhaps fiercely, demanded that he should do her right. How, in short, two high tempers went on to words which could not be forgiven; how they fought, and how both had nearly died where they stood. So went the tale.

The husband, carried from the field, was not heard of more for nearly two years, when he suddenly re-appeared in England, claimed and received his honours, titles, and estates, and wedded into a rich and noble house. His first and deserted wife, forced by her brother to countenance a report of her own death, brought forth a son in secret; and the rest of the tale, as it was told to Alice Herbert, the reader must have already gathered. There was a part of it, however, which was not told then, and which will be noticed, perhaps, hereafter; but it was a part which involved the whole history of those steps which had been taken for several years to regain from the Earl the proofs of his first marriage; and it touched upon so much that was painful, and so much which might be imprudent to speak, that Langford was not sorry when he found that the many questions of Alice and Sir Walter, their many exclamations of pity for his mother's sorrows, and interest in her fate, the long explanations and minute details which he had to give, and the various episodes and collateral anecdotes which were required in such a history, told to such listeners, had occupied the time till they had nearly reached the spot where he had left his father, and he was compelled to leave his tale for the time incomplete.

Anxious in every respect to return to the side of his sick parent, Langford gazed up at the windows of the house where he lay, as the carriage rolled heavily into the court before the old parsonage. All was still, however; and a careless horseboy whistled in the yard while he thrust the straw on one side. Langford questioned him regarding his father's health; but the lad knew nothing on the subject, but that "there had been a rare coming and going, and seeking for the doctor, who had gone to see Betty Hinton, who had been scorched while seeking to pilfer something from the fire at the Castle."

Sir Walter Herbert and the Earl's son, however, both felt that the boy's account gave a bad augury; and the Knight and his daughter remained in a vacant room below, while Langford ascended the stairs. He found some of the Earl's attendants in the outer room, and from them he learned a confirmation of his fears. His lordship, they said, was much worse, and had become so about an hour before. The doctor, they added, was then with him, as well as Mistress Bertha and the rector; but they could say nothing further as to his condition.

Langford hurried on, with a sweet hope that his presence might soothe and cheer. He opened the door cautiously; but the face of the old peer was towards it, and the bright, fevered eye was fixed upon him instantly. With much pain, however, Langford saw that his appearance seemed to agitate rather than to calm; the lip quivered, the brow knit, and tossing round upon his other side, he turned his face to the wall. His son, however, divined at once the cause of this change, and shaped his course accordingly. Moving gently forward, he advanced to the bedside of his hurt father, and sat down, while Bertha gave place, and the rector bowed low to his patron's son.

"How fare you now, sir?" demanded the young gentleman, "I hope better, for I bring you good news."

The Earl, however, occupied with his own thoughts, did not seem to attend to his words; "No!" he cried, casting himself round again in the bed, and grasping Langford's hands; "No, I will not disown thee—my gallant, my noble boy! No; I will not recall my words, be the consequences what they may! Your voice sounds in my ear like your poor mother's, when first I heard it in youth and generous-hearted innocence; it sounds soothing, and not reproachful; and I say it again, you are my son! She was my wife! Let them do what they will—let them say what they will—so it is, and shall be denied no longer; and yet, poor Edward!—think of poor Edward! He is living, you have heard? he is living! The joy of those sudden tidings had well nigh killed me; but the pangs that came after have gone further still. Think of poor Edward!"

"I have thought of him, my dear sir; I have thought of him much and deeply," replied Langford; "but indeed there is no cause for your present agitation—"

"No cause!" exclaimed the Earl, with his old vehemence breaking forth even then; "no cause, do you say! Why, do I not, by the very act of acknowledging you, bastardize the boy that has lain in my bosom, that has dwelt with me through years which would otherwise have been solitary? Do I not take the wrong from your mother to put it upon his? Do I not deprive him, by a word, of station, rank, and noble name? Do I not proclaim myself false—a breaker of all vows? Oh! young man, young man, you know not how this proud hard heart is wrung and torn at this moment! Say not a word; say not a word! I know that it is by my own follies; my own crimes, if you will. I know what you can say; I know all that you can say; that your mother, as noble and as virtuous as his, bore her sorrows through a long life, raised no loud murmur against him who had injured her, and died forgiving him who had embittered her existence; that hers is the just right; that hers was the first claim; that the real wife lived in sorrow and under reproach, and died in misery and despair; that the false wife lived in honour and in high esteem, and died in the arms of her son, and of him she thought her husband; that it is time now, even now, to make the atonement! I know it all, and the atonement shall be made; but neither tell me that there is no cause for agitation, nor utter one reproach in the voice of her who never reproached me."

"Far from it, my lord," replied Langford, as soon as the Earl would let him speak; "far from it! I seek not in the slightest degree to utter a word that comes near a reproach; and though I know you must be pained and grieved by much that has occurred, there is still, I trust, cause for nothing but joy in the tidings we have heard of my poor brother's safety. In the first place, my lord, the papers which are necessary to establish my claim as heir to your estates and title in England have not yet been found, and may never be so; nor do I at all seek to deprive my brother of that to which he has through life looked forward. Were they found to-morrow, as long as he lived I should conceive myself bound by the engagement which I and my uncle both entered into formerly, never to make use of those papers in England, but to employ them solely for the establishment of my legitimacy in France. No one in this country, but myself, knows, or should ever obtain proof from me, of the period of my mother's death; and consequently, as that event might have taken place before your marriage with another, that second marriage will remain valid in England, to all intents and purposes. I say, that such shall be the case, even should the papers be found. Should they not be found, your own solemn declaration, upon oath, together with the testimony of Bertha here, a born subject of France, will be sufficient fully to establish my legitimacy in that country, and to restore to me my uncle's title and estates, which have passed away to others. Such being the case, I say again, there is no cause for anything but joy in the tidings of my brother's safety. If you desire it should be so, he even need never know that you were united to his mother while mine was still living. I pledge myself, upon my honour, never to tell him, and in no respect to seek to wrest from him the estates or honours he would have derived from you. Shall it be so?"

The Earl gazed at him for several moments, with a countenance over which the shades of many passions came flitting like figures across a glass. He hesitated; he doubted; he admired. But his was not a nature to remain long in uncertainty. Keen, eager, fiery in all his determinations, he strode at once to his object, and when his resolution was once taken, he could trample upon his own heart when it lay in the way, as well as upon the hearts of others.

"No!" he exclaimed, at length, in answer to Langford's question; "no; it shall not be so! I will do justice, even at the last hour. I will do justice, let it cost me what it may. No! noble, and generous, kind-hearted, and true as you have shown yourself, worthy child of her that I wronged, true descendant of a noble race, upon whose fame and honour I brought the first imputation, I will not take advantage of your too generous kindness; I will not screen myself from the consequences of what I have done, by withholding from him who saved his father's life, at the very moment that father was doing him the grossest injustice, the rank that he will honour nobly, the wealth that he will rightly employ. No; though I break my own heart by what I inflict upon his, Edward, when he returns, shall know all; shall know how well and nobly you have acted; how ill I have acted towards both; and then if, while you forgive and soothe, he in the bitterness of his heart should curse the father that has wronged him, let him do it; I say, let him do it."

Langford was about to reply, but the surgeon interposed, saying, "Indeed, sir, though it may be very necessary that such important matters as those on which you have been speaking should be settled in some manner, it is absolutely necessary to make all discussion upon the subject as short as possible; for, if prolonged, the consequences must necessarily be of the worst and most serious nature."

"Far be it from me to prolong them," replied Langford; "let the matter rest as it is, my dear father. Let us take no steps whatsoever, nor discuss the matter in any shape, till your health is returned, and then—"

"Do not deceive yourself," said the Earl; "do not deceive yourself, my son. From this bed I shall never rise again! The day is past, the night is coming. The fire is burnt out, and there lingers but a spark behind. The oil in the lamp is exhausted, and though the flame may flicker up yet once or twice, it soon must sink and be extinguished. Henry, I feel that I am dying! It is not these wounds that have killed me, but the long intense struggles of a fiery and uncontrollable spirit have at length beaten down the bars of the fleshly prison that once strongly confined it, and it is now ready to take wing and fly to other lands. We will discuss the matter, as you say, no more; but my hours are numbered, and ere I die I must act. Where is that man Kinsight, the lawyer? Why did he not return to me last night? Let him be sent for instantly, for I must take those measures, both to place your birth beyond all doubt, as far as yet lies in my power, and to provide amply and nobly for the son I have wronged. But alas, alas! have I not wronged you both? you first, and him last, both deeply, terribly, equally! Where, I wonder is that lawyer? I wonder why he came not last night?"

"I fear, my lord," replied the surgeon, "that he will not be able to attend you, for I find that he was very severely handled by the people yesterday evening, in an attempt to execute a writ upon Sir Walter Herbert, so that he has been in a state of insensibility since yesterday about five o'clock, till this morning, and is not likely, it would seem, to recover."

"Retribution!" said the Earl; "retribution! Though it sometimes comes slowly, it is sure to come at last, and then comes altogether. This was my doing too, though by his prompting. However, be it as it may, retribution has fallen upon us both. But somebody told me that Sir Walter was arrested last night nevertheless, and I sent a release, that he might be set free."

"I have found no one," said Bertha, who had remained standing behind—"I have found no one to whom I would trust so important a document. You told me," she continued, turning to Langford, "to give it to nobody but one on whom I could implicitly rely, and I have thought over all the persons I know—over all the persons I have ever known, and cannot remember one who deserves such a name."

"You are bitter," said Langford, "but not just, Bertha. However, set your mind at ease, my dear father; Sir Walter Herbert is at liberty, and in this house, waiting anxiously to hear tidings of your health. His daughter is with him, too; and she thinks that, if you would permit her, she could, by that care, and kindness, and tenderness, which are parts of her nature, greatly soothe and comfort you."

The Earl shook his head; and a smile, faint indeed, but still the first that had crossed his countenance for a long time, hung upon his lip during a single instant. "You are a lover," he said; "but nothing can soothe or comfort me more in life, Henry. Yet I would fain see Sir Walter Herbert. I am in the course of atonement, and I must atone to him, too, in words as well as deeds."

"Indeed, my lord," said the surgeon, "the fewer that you see—"

"Sir, I will have it so!" exclaimed the Earl, turning upon him with a frowning brow. "Let me not be tormented by opposition even at my last hour!" And with a firm and imperious voice he directed Bertha to invite Sir Walter and his daughter to his chamber.

They came speedily, and no trace of any feeling but that of kind and generous compassion was to be seen upon the countenance of Sir Walter Herbert, when he entered the presence of the man who had inflicted so much pain and anxiety upon him.

The Earl gazed for a moment in his face, as if to see what expression it bore, in order to form his own demeanour by it; and then held out his hand to him frankly. "Sir Walter," he said, as the old knight advanced and took it, "I have done you wrong; I have acted ungenerously towards you, as well as towards many others. Do you forgive me?"

"From my heart," replied Sir Walter Herbert; "but let us not think of anything that is painful, my good lord. I trust that you have not been seriously injured in the course of this sad business, the details of which I know but imperfectly."

The Earl shook his head at the expression of such a hope, but he made no reply; and merely demanded, turning to Bertha, "Where is the paper?" When it was put into his hand, he continued, "I intended this to have reached you early in the morning, Sir Walter. Take it now. It is but an act of justice; and anything that might be considered wanting by your lawyer to put it into due form, had better be mentioned to me soon; for I am going a long journey, Sir Walter, and would fain leave nothing incomplete that I can set to rights. Mistress Alice," he continued, turning to the fair creature who stood timidly a step behind, in a scene so painful and so unusual—"Mistress Alice, sweet lady, come hither, and speak to an old man ere he dies."

Alice approached quickly to his bedside, and taking her hand, he gazed up in her face, saying, "Lady, to you I have acted doubly ill, for in my demeanour towards you lately I not only forgot what was just and right, but what was courteous also; and yet I am going to ask a great and extraordinary favour of you. When you are the wife of this my son—which God grant you may be, and soon—try, if it be possible, by kindness and affection during the whole of the rest of his life, to make up to him for the want of a father's love, and a father's care, during the adverse period of his youth."

Alice blushed deeply, but she replied, "Indeed, my lord, I will; and I also have a favour to ask of you. I see that you are ill. I know that you must be suffering. My father, thank God, needs not my care nor help. Let me stay with you, I beseech you, and be to you as a daughter until you are better, which I hope and trust will be sooner than you expect."

"Hope nothing, young lady," replied the old nobleman; "I do not deceive myself. Nevertheless, you shall stay, if you so will, because I know that it may be a satisfaction to you hereafter, and to him, my son, even now. Yet it is cruel to inflict upon you, so young, so tender, and so well assorted to sights of hope, and joy, and life, and expectation, scenes of sickness, and suffering, and of death. Yet if you will, it shall be so."

Alice turned a little pale, but still she firmly pressed her request;

while her father and her promised husband gazed upon her with looks of love, and tenderness, and approbation. "Mistress Bertha," she said, after again repeating her wish to remain, "you will let me share your cares, and with a little instruction from you I doubt not to prove skilful in my new employment."

"More skilful than I am, lady," replied Bertha; "for I was never made for soothing or for tenderness. I seek it not myself when sickness or when pain seizes on me, and I am not fitted to give it to others. Nevertheless," she added, in a lower voice, "you may perhaps find a moment to teach that dying man to prepare for the world to which he is speeding. I have lived long enough in this land, which I once thought given over to perdition, to believe that salvation may be found by even those who do not believe all that the Church of Rome would have them. Seek a moment to speak to him, young lady; seek a moment to point out to him that all the earthly compensation he can now make is nothing when compared with the faults he has committed. Tell him he must find an atonement, that he must seek for an intercessor; and show him that that intercessor cannot be gained but by full faith and trust in Him."

"I will," replied Alice. "Indeed, I will lose no opportunity;" and she kept her word. At the reiterated request of the surgeon, the chamber was soon after cleared, while a lawyer was sent for from the county town to supply the place of the Earl's own attorney. No person was left in it but one; and the task of sitting by the sick man's side was fulfilled by Alice at her own choice.

Sir Walter went on to the Manor House, promising to return ere night; and Langford sat in a chamber below, consulting with the rector and others concerning the best means of tracing out his lost brother. But in the meanwhile Alice, watching by the Earl, while he strove ineffectually to gain even a brief interval of sleep, pondered in her own mind how she might accomplish the great object she had promised to attempt; how she might even touch upon a subject from which, but a few moments before, when mentioned by the rector, she had seen the sick man start away with impetuous vehemence, apparently judging that all appeal to Heaven's mercy was too late, and determined not only to brave fearlessly once more death which he had so often tempted, but to encounter unshrinkingly the "something after death" which he believed his own acts to have loaded with all the wrath of Omnipotence.

After tossing for a long time, with great restlessness and apparent pain, sleep fell for a few minutes upon the Earl's eyes; and, when it was over, though it had lasted so short a time, he turned to Alice with a smile, saying, "Oh, how blessed a thing is sleep! Could heaven itself be sweeter than slumber after restlessness and agony?"

"Oh, yes," replied Alice, "I think so; for here, rest requires labour, or fatigue, or pain, to make it sweet: there, the enjoyment must be pure and self-existing, requiring no contrast. However, we know little of such subjects. God grant that we may all know such a state hereafter."

The Earl gazed thoughtfully in her face for a few minutes, and then said, "Alice, do you think that those who meet in the same place hereafter, will each know the other?"

"Oh, doubt it not!" cried Alice, eagerly; "doubt it not! It were sin to doubt it. Heaven could not be heaven without those we love."

"Then, Alice," cried the Earl, with his brow darkening and his eye straining upon her—" then, Alice, what would it be to meet, with all one's crimes laid bare, a long, long train of those we have injured or oppressed—the slighted, the broken-hearted, the wronged, the insulted, the slain! Could hell itself be worse than that?"

"But," said Alice, eagerly—"but to those whom God has pardoned, who shall impute wrong?"

The Earl started up, and leaning on his elbow, grasped her hand. "Is there, Alice," he cried—" is there pardon for such as me?"

"There is pardon," she replied, "for every sinner that repents and puts his trust in Him who alone can save. Such were His own words; and, oh! let me beseech you," she cried, and she cast herself upon her knees beside his bed—"let me entreat you to hear them. I am young, unlearned, inexperienced, but yet His words need no learning to expound; His doctrine is clear; His promises are addressed to the spirits of every one. Oh, hear them, my lord: hear them, for my sake, for Henry's sake, hear them."

"I will," answered the Earl, sinking back upon the pillows. "From your lips, Alice, I will; but not from his who gives them forth by rote. Speak, Alice; speak, my child, and I will listen. There is one thing that I now know, and to know that much, I feel, is something already done. It is, that never man yet lived who had greater need of intercession than myself. Speak to me, then; read to me; and though I promise nothing further, though I say not that I will have faith, though I say not that I will hope, yet I will listen to every word." He did listen to her when he would have listened to no one else, while she, with a beating heart and timid earnestness, went on in her new task. How she fulfilled it we need not dwell upon. What was the effect cannot be told, for the Earl made neither comment nor reply; but when the door opened, and they announced that the lawyer Evelyn had arrived, he pressed Alice's hand affectionately in his own, and said, " I thank you, Alice; from my heart and soul, I thank you."

CHAPTER XXXI.

"Good news, Master Justice; good news!" said John Bolland, entering the room of the small inn, where Mr. Justice Whistler sat sipping a bowl of fragrant punch with his two brother magistrates, about two days after we last left him; "I have found out our man, and nothing is wanting but good courage and plenty of people to take him and the greater part of his gang."

"Sit down, Master Bolland; sit down, and take a ladleful," replied Justice Whistler. "By your leave, Sir Matthew; by your leave. Now, Master Bolland, now tell us all the facts. To speak truth, I am in no condition to move far to-night, though I have courage enough to take the great prince of thieves himself, were it needful; but there is a certain feeling about my knees which speaks a too great pliancy. This punch is potent, Sir Matthew; very potent; but the upper story is quite clear. So pray, Master Bolland, sip, and recite."

"Why, I have but little to say, Worshipful," said Bolland, who saw that the punch evidently had produced a not infrequent effect upon all three. "The only matter is, I have found out where this worthy Captain Gray and his band have housed themselves; that is all."

"And where may that be?" demanded Mr. Whistler. "Pray, where may that be, my dear Bolland?"

"Why, over the hills, beyond Badeley," replied the officer; "the further particulars I will keep till to-morrow, as you cannot set out to-night; though, to say the truth, every moment lost is likely to lose us our man. He'll not stay there long, depend on it. They'll be just like a covey of partridges at sunset, flitting about from place to place before any one can come near them."

"But tell me all the particulars," cried Justice Whistler; "for if need be, I will go this minute."

"And so will I," shouted Sir Matthew Scrope, who in his cups grew mighty valiant. "And so will I, I swear!"

Sir Thomas Waller had proceeded a step beyond the other two, and he could only stare. But even the proposal of Sir Matthew was more than suited the purposes of John Bolland and his friend Mister Justice Whistler, who had agreed long before to share the profits of the matter, which were likely to be considerable, between them. Each hoped, also, to gain a certain share of honour and credit by the joint management of the affair, which honour and credit were somewhat necessary to both to lacker over certain flaws in their reputation that were becoming rather too apparent.

It may seem a strange paradox, perhaps, to say that Mr. Justice Whistler was as sober when he was tipsy as when he was not, but such was the case with all the upper man; the drunkenness began at the knees with him, and went downwards, leaving the brain quite as clear and shrewd as usual, with the only difference that his manner was a little more jocular—his pomposity somewhat higher flavoured. On the present occasion, one glance from the eye of Bolland towards Sir Matthew Scrope reminded the London justice of their arrangements, and he instantly changed his tone.

"No, no, Sir Matthew; we cannot go to-night," he said. "We will hear what Bolland has to say; we will ponder on it on our pillows, and act to-morrow. Let me help you, Sir Matthew. Generous punch never yet harmed any man but a flincher. Sir Thomas, your glass is empty. Master Bolland, join us. You see I do not spare myself;" and he filled himself out a ladleful, nodding to Sir Matthew Scrope, and drinking to the health of his fair niece.

The additional burden thus poured upon the mental faculties of Sir Thomas Waller was quite sufficient to send him quietly under the table; and Sir Matthew Scrope, who likewise did justice to his glass, was reduced to that state at which eloquence, however unruly, finds utterance difficult. Mr. Justice Whistler, perceiving the effect which the last cup had produced, nodded to Bolland, and said in a half whisper, "Now for his nightcap! Perhaps, Sir Matthew," he added looking at the knight with a compassionating air, "perhaps we had better not drink any more, though the bowl is not yet empty. I am not at all drunk myself, though I fear for your head to-morrow, Sir Matthew. I thought you had been stronger men in these parts. Why, with the help of Master Bolland, we have not finished the—"

"Sir, sir," hiccupped Sir Matthew Scrope, "I am no more drunk than you are. I can take another glass very well. Ay, two. We will never leave the bowl unfinished."

Mr. Justice Whistler might, perhaps, upon another occasion, have found some degree of pleasure in prolonging the yearnings of Sir Matthew Scrope for the liquor of his heart, for all the minor sorts of tormenting were generally sweet pastime to him, but at present he was too deeply interested, to pursue anything but the straightforward course; and when he saw that opposition had sufficiently roused the drunken energies of his fellow magistrate, he suffered him to drink his punch in peace, and fall back into his chair in the soft embraces of the son of Lethe. No sooner was this accomplished than he looked upon Bolland with a triumphant smile. He had himself, indeed, in no degree, flinched from the potations he had inflicted upon his two fellow-magistrates, but he was very well aware of his own calibre, foresaw the result, and knew the remedy. A slight additional weakness of the knees was all that he had to anticipate; and though he felt morally certain that, if he rose from the table and attempted to make his exit by the door, it would cost him five or six efforts before he could shoot the arch, he knew at the same time that there were restorative means to give back vigour to the sinews of his lower man, and to enable his whole body to recover that just equilibrium of which the potent punch had deprived it.

"Bolland," he said; "Bolland, I'm in no condition for riding just yet, but half an hour will set the whole matter to rights. Have these two clods carried home, and make pretty Sally, the black-eyed barmaid, bring me a large basin and a ewer of water. Then quietly steal into the kitchen, and tell the cook to do me a good rump-steak, and bring it up piping hot, with some sliced onions. I dar'n't move from the table; for unless I were cautious, cautious—cautious, Master Bolland, I should be at my full length on the floor in a minute."

Bolland did as he was bid; and as, in those days, there were attached, as indispensable appendages to the inn of every county town—especially, if a club of magistrates held its meetings thereat—certain sturdy fellows, both ready and willing to carry away the bodies of such as fell in their contest with good liquor, three or four personages were soon found to bear off Sir Matthew Scrope and Sir Thomas Waller to their respective homes. Betty also soon appeared with the basin and ewer, as the magistrate had directed, and Mr. Justice Whistler, taking off his wig, caused a deluge of the pure cold element to be poured over his naked head, which bent humbly before the hand of the practised barmaid.

When his face was well dried, and the wig replaced, he looked up in the face of Bolland, who had just returned from his errand, with a smile of satisfaction, saying, "I think I could do it now, Bolland; I think I could do it now. But I won't try till I have put the beefsteak upon the top of the punch. In the meantime, give me the whole particulars of this grand discovery you have made. Where is this man to be found, and how have you found him out? for we must be sure of what we are about, before we stir an inch."

"Oh, for that matter, I am quite sure," answered Bolland; "for I had it this very morning from a sheep-drover whom I met just under the hills on this side, and who gave me a long account of this strange gentleman coming with half a dozen or more men, and taking the sheep-farm that he described, without inquiring into anything, as another man would have done. I asked him if he had seen this strange gentleman. He said, 'Oh, dear, yes; twice, walking about the hills in a melancholy kind of way, with his arms crossed upon his chest.' And then the fellow went on, and painted him like a picture. I got the whole account of the place exactly, too, so that when we get to the little town of Badeley, I can lead you at once to the spot."

"How far is it, Bolland?" demanded Mr. Justice Whistler.

"Some fifty-five miles, I hear," replied the officer; and, thereupon, the justice shook his head, exclaiming, "Too far for one night's ride. Too far; too far. It would make my old bones ache."

"I did not know your worship had any bones," was the quaint reply. "However, it is too far for me, also, for I have ridden nearly forty miles this morning, and I am neither a post, nor a post-boy."

While they were yet discussing the matter, a savoury odour was smelt even through the double doors of the club-room, and Mr. Justice Whistler interrupted Bolland's eloquence by exclaiming, "Ha! here comes the rump-steak. It will set all things to rights presently; and in the meanwhile you go and get two strong horses ready. Find out what constables you can rely upon for a long journey, and have everything prepared for our departure."

To the few questions which Bolland now asked, he gave the clearest and most precise answers; and when the worthy officer returned, after fulfilling his mission, he found the dish which had contained the beef-steaks void of its contents, and Mr. Justice Whistler walking up and down the room as steadily as ever.

"I have only got two constables," he said, "who were willing to go; all the rest were either drunk, or in bed, or did not like the job, and would have run away and left us at the bounds of the county."

"Two are quite enough," replied Mr. Justice Whistler. "We can get plenty more at the nearest town. These people here are all in a fit of fright at the strange doings that have been taking place near them. Better have some folks that are ignorant of the whole business. Now I'm your man, Master Bolland. Are the horses ready?"

Bolland answered in the affirmative; but, before he followed the justice into the court-yard of the inn, he swallowed what remained of the bowl of punch, thinking that such encouragement was well adapted to a long cold ride and a dangerous enterprise.

Mr. Justice Whistler now consulted gravely with Bolland in regard to the road; and, taking one of the constables for their guide, they determined to proceed about thirty miles that night, and accomplish the rest upon the following day. They were, however, deceived in regard to the distance. At the end of thirty miles, they found no town, nor place of repose of any kind, and they were, consequently, obliged to ride on till they got on the first soft slopes of those wild hills which we have elsewhere described.

Mr. Justice Whistler began to grumble seriously at the length of way; Bolland declared that he was nearly knocked up; and one of the constables avowed that he saw the grey streaks of the morning resting on the tops of the hills, which would serve at least to show them their way, for they were at this time immured in the darkness of high hedges and narrow wooded lanes. At that moment, however, a loud voice before them called, "Stop!" and Bolland, at once recognizing the voice of Franklin Gray, turned his horse's head, and galloped off as hard as he could go.

The rest would most likely have followed his example, had not the same voice vociferated, "Stop them there, Harvey! Do not let them go!" and four or five men, leaping their horses over the hedge, cut off the retreat of Mr. Justice Whistler and the constables, while one of them fired a pistol down the lane after the retreating figure of Bolland, which was followed by a sharp, sudden cry. But the horse's steps were still heard galloping onward. The flash of the pistol had afforded sufficient light, however, to show Mr. Justice Whistler that resistance was vain, though he was a courageous and determined man, and would have made it gallantly if there had been even a hope of success. Such not being the case, however, he determined rapidly what to do, but determined, unfortunately for himself, upon wrong grounds.

Remembering nothing but the awe with which his name and presence inspired the petty plunderers of the metropolis, he resolved to announce himself and all his terrors in good set form, and to endeavour to frighten from their purpose those who stopped him. In the meanwhile, however, the leader of the party threw back the shade of a dark lantern, and poured the light thereof full upon the justice and his followers, and he demanded, "What are you doing here at this hour? What is your name, and what is your errand?"

"Let me pass, in the King's name, I command you," said the justice. "My name is Whistler, and I am one of his Majesty's justices of the peace for ——."

"Oh, you are Mr. Justice Whistler, are you?" replied the other. "Worthy Mr. Justice, who are those two men behind you? They seem not of your own condition."

"We are only two poor constables from the town of ——," replied the men, choosing to speak for themselves, and in a humbler tone than that which the justice had thought fit to use. "We are two hard-working men, with small families, and are forced to do our duty."

"These are not any of those we sought," said Franklin Gray to one of his followers. "Let these two poor fellows go; but strip me this justice here to his skin. Take every sous he has in his pocket, and then tie him to a tree and give him a hundred lashes with the stirrup leather, as hard as you can lay it on. I will not take his life, though I should like to give him one lash for every false and villanous act he has committed, for every innocent man he has sent to prison, to the stocks, the pillory, or the parish beadle. One lash for each, however, would cut him to pieces; so give him a hundred, and let him go."

The commands thus issued were punctually obeyed; and while the justice shouted loudly under the infliction, which was administered in the neighbouring field, Franklin Gray went on addressing the man Harvey, sometimes commenting upon what was going on near, sometimes speaking of other subjects.

"They know we are on the look-out," he said; "and they will not stir so long as that is the case. How the beast roars! Yet you say they must be in this neighbourhood, for you traced their footsteps clearly. Those fellows love flaying a justice in their hearts; I can hear the lashes they give him even here. But we had better ride home now, and change our quarters soon. There, there, that will do."

There, my men, stop. You will kill him, if you don't mind. Put his vest upon his fat back, turn his face to the horse's tail, and send him cantering down the lane."

Every tittle of Franklin Gray's commands was executed to the letter; and Mr. Justice Whistler, still writhing with the pain of the stripes he had received, was partly clothed once more, and set upon his beast again. His face, however, was turned in the contrary direction to that which it usually assumed in relation to the animal that bore him, and his feet being thrust through the stirrups, a few smart blows were added to send the charger off. Happily for the preservation of the justice's equilibrium, the horse was weary, and, even in its most frisky moods, was a quiet, good sort of beast; so that, after having jolted him in a hard trot for about three hundred yards, it began to slacken its pace, gradually dropped into a walk, and finally stopped to crop a scanty breakfast from the herbage by the side of the road.

Mr. Justice Whistler did not neglect to seize such an opportunity, and carefully descending, for in his bruised condition every step was painful, he remounted according to the usual mode, and, with a somewhat splenetic jerk of the bridle, made his beast abandon its poor meal, and proceed on the road before it. That road, indeed, was as unpromising to a man in his condition as any road could be; for his first necessity was now repose and food, and as it was the very way by which he had come, no one could be more certain than himself that there was no house, village, or anything in its course for at least ten miles. When he had gone about one, however, a small country road was seen leading to the left, away over a low hill; and Mr. Justice Whistler paused, and gazed, and pondered.

The darkness of the night had now fled, the dull streaks over the eastern hills had changed into gold and crimson, and the clear, cool fresh light of morning was spreading over the whole prospect. The hills rose up and shone in the coming beams; but a faint grey mist lay over the lower grounds, marking out each wooded slope, each wave in the fields, and each hedgerow, in long-defined lines across the view. The hill over which the country road that now attracted the errant justice's attention ran, was, as he sagely judged, fully high enough to conceal a farm, a village, a town—nay, a city itself, should need be—on the other side; and along the sandy road itself were to be traced various marks of cart wheels of no very remote date, and the prints of horses' hoofs more recent still.

Such a sight was wonderfully cheering to the justice, who instantly turned his horse's head up the lane, and pursued it perseveringly, though the high and manifold trees in which it embowered itself, soon cut off all further prospect. A quarter of an hour's riding had not yet brought him to anything like a house; but the joyful sound of some one whistling broken snatches of a favourite village song set his heart at rest. The crack of a whip, too, and the rattle and clatter of harness, were soon heard; when lo! the road suddenly turned to the left round a steep bank; and a little village green, with its pond affording much matutinal enjoyment to a party of ducks, and its clump of tall elms, ready to give shade when the sun rose high, presented itself to the eyes of Mr. Justice Whistler as one of the pleasantest sights he had ever seen.

To the right was a small farm-house, from which probably proceeded those sounds of early labour which had given the scourged magistrate encouragement on his way; but exactly before him, on the other side of the green, appeared the grey village church, with its yews and its little enclosure, where rested the dead of many a gone year; and, what was more to the purpose of the justice, a neat and rather large white house, in a pretty garden enclosed by low walls, which were chequered with flints, and guarded by broken bottles from the predatory feet of apple-loving boys. The justice at first thought it was too good a house for the parsonage; but seeing no other abode of the kind near the church, and looking at the air of comfort and wealth about the village itself, he judged that it must indeed be the dwelling of some rector well to do, and therefore straightway rode up to the gate to make his piteous case known. Those were hospitable days, and such circumstances as his, he well knew, would find instant compassion and relief; but, as the occasion was urgent, it was no slight satisfaction to him to see the gates into a stable-yard already open, horses in the court bearing signs of having come from far, and one regular domestic, with one personage, half groom half plough-boy, busily engaged in the duties of the stable.

"Why, here's another, Bill!" cried the rustic as the justice approached. "I think it rains strays just now."

To the inquiries of Mr. Justice Whistler, the servant replied that the house was the rectory of the Reverend Mr. Sandon—that the rector was up, and talking in the parlour with two gentlemen just arrived. A second glance at the horses confirmed Mr. Justice Whistler in the opinion which he had at first entertained, that they had been his companions on the road during the greater part of the night; and on being ushered into the presence of the owner of the house, he found him listening to the two constables' tale of woe.

The rector was a quick, sharp-nosed, reddish-faced gentleman, extremely well to do in the world, yet active, vigilant, shrewd, inquiring: the good things of life having had no effect in producing sloth or indulgence. He was a worthy man in the main, more charitable both in thought and deed than he suffered himself to appear, and not by many degrees so avaricious as some of his refractory parishioners wished to prove. He was up early, to bed late; took great care of his farm and of his flock; spared no one's vices or follies in the pulpit, and required that his dues should be paid, if not rigorously, at least exactly, dispensing that money for the benefit of one deserving part of his flock which he derived from another.

On seeing the apparition of Mr. Justice Whistler clad simply in his vest, and that not very well buttoned over his protuberant stomach, the rector stared for a single instant in silence; but the next moment, though he could not repress a slight smile which came upon his lip at such a strange apparition, he resumed his courtesy, and, advancing towards the stranger, said, "I presume I have the honour of seeing Justice Whistler; at least, so the account of these good men leads me to imagine; and most happy am I to see him alive and well, for, knowing the desperate character of the men into whose hands he had fallen, I was apprehensive of the result."

"Alive, sir, alive," said the magistrate, impatiently, "but not well, by no means well: half-flayed, scarified, basted with stirrup leathers till there is not an inch of the skin on my back without a wound, nor a bone in my body that does not ache. I have come, sir, to claim your hospitality—to seek a few hours' repose—to obtain some refreshment, and to get some soft appliances to my back; after which, God willing, I will raise the hue and cry through the country, and tuck that fellow up as high as Haman, or my name's not Whistler."

"You shall have all that my poor house affords, to make you comfortable," replied the rector; "and after you are refreshed, perhaps I may be able and ready, more so than you expect, to aid in your very laudable design of ridding the country of the band of ruffians who have lately taken up their quarters upon the verge of these two counties."

"I am pleased to hear it; I am pleased to hear it!" exclaimed Mr. Justice Whistler; "but just now my back aches so portentously, I am so wearied and so hungry, that I can think of little but a flagon of mulled ale and a toast, a soft bed, and four or five hand-breadths f old linen to my back."

"All that you shall have, sir," replied the rector; and, though there was just that degree of pain in the countenance and the whole movements of the justice which excites one almost as much to merriment as to compassion, the worthy clergyman kept his countenance very well, and with kindness and alacrity ordered everything that was necessary for making the suffering man more comfortable. The mulled ale and the toast were brought, and a small cup of metheglin was superadded to give the whole consistency, as the magistrate observed. After that, the broad magisterial back was dressed by a staid but not unskilful housekeeper; and, tucked up in a comfortable bed, Mr. Justice Whistler soon forgot in the arms of slumber the woes and the adventures of the preceding night.

CHAPTER XXXII.

WHILE Mr. Justice Whistler and his colleagues had been proceeding in their examinations, and the events we have just narrated had been taking place in a distant part of the country, the days and nights in the little village of Danemore had been spent in the slow and wearing anxieties of watching the progress of sickness towards death. Alice Herbert remained almost constantly with the Earl, at his own earnest wish, and Sir Walter Herbert coming over from the Manor House early every day, spent the greater part of his time with Langford, in all those various occupations of which the circumstances in which they both stood furnished an abundance to fill up the time.

The Earl of Danemore lay upon his bed of sickness, and hour by hour showed as it went by, that it would be the bed of death also. It was not, indeed, that his wounds were mortal, for no vital part in all his frame had been touched; but he received those wounds, not only as an old man in whom the loss even of a portion of that strange red current that flows within our veins, dispensing life and vigour, is not easily restored; he received them also as one on whom strong and ungovernable passions had already wrought most powerfully, and on whom also the same intensity of feeling was still destined to work, though excited by better causes, and a better purpose. Weakened by great loss of blood, exhausted by fatigue and excitement, but little was wanting to bring fever in the train of corporeal injury; and the energetic eagerness with which he applied his mind to everything connected with Henry Langford, only served to increase his irritability, rather than to lead his mind to calmer and more tranquillizing subjects. He felt that his days on earth were numbered: and that feeling begat in him an anxiety to make up for the evils he had inflicted, which tended to shorten those few hours that remained to him.

The difficult and painful situation in which he was placed also; the necessity of sacrificing one child to another; the struggle to do justice to one for whom he felt deep gratitude and esteem, when opposed by the claims of old affection and long-nourished tenderness; the knowledge that disgrace would fall upon his name, and, like the yellow lichen on a tombstone, would live and flourish, and render indistinct every record of his life, when all below had mouldered away into dust; all joined together to make him feel most poignantly and bitterly that the last dark hour of life, when the bright sun that has lighted us through the morning of our youth and the mid-day of our manhood, and even shone warmly on the evening of our decline, has gone down behind the horizon, leaving but a few faint rays in the sky behind, is not the time to seek our way back into the right path which we have abandoned in the splendid noon of our existence; and that even if we do regain it at last, it must be by plunging into the thorns and briars of grief, regret, and remorse, without hesitation, though with difficulty and agony itself.

It was not that even in those last hours of his life the Earl of Danemore looked upon death with any feeling of terror. Such sensations were not within the grasp of his nature; he knew not what fear meant. He might see and know that there was danger in this thing or in that; he might fix his eyes even upon death itself, and the retributive future after death; but still while gazing on the frowning brow of fate, and comprehending all which that dark inevitable countenance menaced, he strode on undaunted, and said, even to Omnipotence, "Strike!"

No! it was not that anything like fear affected him; but weakened in body and wearied in mind with a long struggle against many internal adversaries, he listened to the voice of conscience and of equity, making itself heard through the medium of a judgment naturally strong and acute—making itself heard not the less distinctly in the silence of exhausted passions, because in former times the small still voice had been drowned amidst their contending fury.

He felt what it was right to do, and he strove now to do it, however difficult, however painful his own acts might have rendered the task—however fatal to his corporeal frame might be the efforts that he made, and the anxieties he suffered. For the greater part of one whole night he remained eagerly dictating his will to the lawyer Evelyn; providing for his younger son, but endeavouring to strengthen in every way the claim of the elder to his title and estates. He made a solemn declaration of his marriage too; named the day, the spot, the clergyman who had performed it, with scrupulous accuracy; pointed to the woman Bertha as the only surviving witness, and related how the leaf on which the marriage had been inscribed had been cut from the register, and how he had forced his young and unhappy wife to give up to him the certificates she had received of their union. He spared himself, in short, in nothing; and again and again he asked eagerly if that declaration and the woman Bertha's testimony would not be sufficient.

The lawyer shook his head doubtingly. The marriage, he said, had been denied for so many years; the woman, too, was an alien and a Roman Catholic, against whom prejudices then ran high. The question involved an ancient peerage and immense property; and, in short, there was every reason to doubt whether the young gentleman's title could be sustained, unless the papers were recovered. If the register itself were not in existence, and the marriage had never been denied, the case might easily have been made good; but, with no trace of such an act in the existing register, and no absolute publication of the marriage, he had many doubts.

"But there is a trace!" exclaimed the Earl vehemently; "there is a trace; there is the leaf cut out. Send for the register! Let it be brought here immediately!"

"We can do that to-morrow, my lord," replied the lawyer.

But the Earl would not be satisfied till a servant was despatched for the record on which so much depended. It was brought to him by the clerk of the parish of Uppington, during the grey daylight of the next morning, for the very vehemence of his nature had taught every one through the country round to yield instant, and now habitual deference to his wishes. On examining the book, however, he found nothing but disappointment. When by large bribes he had induced the low-minded but cunning priest, who then held the living, to cut out the leaf, he had enjoined him strictly to leave no trace whatever of the transaction; and so nicely had the removal been accomplished, that no eye could detect the place where the vacancy existed.

Again his own acts fell upon his own head; and the Earl felt as if it were ordained by retributive justice that he should go down to the grave leaving the fate of both his children still entirely in doubt. The idea took possession of him, and it weighed him down. Often he asked if any news had been heard of his son Edward; and when the reply was made that none had been received, he exclaimed, "Of course—of course! Nothing will be known of him till I am dead."

As the third and fourth days went by, his mind began to wander, and that most painful of all states to see, delirium, came rapidly upon him. He raved of his first wife, his Eugenie, the only one whom he had ever loved, and yet the one whom he had most deeply wronged. He called upon her to return to him, to bring her boy to his father's arms; and then again he went over some bitter quarrels, where it was evident that her firm sweetness had but served to aggravate his fiery wrath. It was a scene most painful to behold, and yet Alice Herbert, tending him as if she had been his own child, beheld it all, and with sweet and thoughtful tenderness did much to soften and tranquillize the mind of him who suffered, as well as the feelings of him who stood by with a wrung heart, witnessing a father's agony and a father's remorse.

To the eyes of Langford never did Alice Herbert, in all the bright flush of health and happiness, as he had at first beheld her, look so lovely; never did she seem to his heart—even when she acknowledged the love that made him happy—so dear as now; while somewhat pale with cares and anxieties lately suffered, and fatigues daily undegone, she stood, by the pale light of the shaded lamp, with calm sorrow and apprehension in every line of that fair face, watching the death-bed of his father, and soothing the last hours of him who had caused her so much pain. He felt from his heart that a common exaggeration of affection was, to her at least, well applied, though he would not himself apply it; and he listened well pleased, when Bertha, after watching Alice long, with the usual dark and stern expression, at length exclaimed, "Thou art certainly an angel!"

Towards the evening of the fifth day there seemed a slight improvement in the condition of the Earl. He slept for an hour or two in the course of the evening. His mind was more collected: he recognised his son, and Alice Herbert, and her father, at all times; and although his words occasionally wandered and his eyes looked wild, yet there were evident promises of returning judgment and returning strength; and both Alice and Langford hoped—and in a degree trusted because they hoped—that the Earl might yet regain his corporeal health, and that his mind, like the air when purified by a thunder-storm, might rise freed from all the vehement passions which had worked up the tempest that had hung around the last few days.

Nevertheless, the vital powers were evidently diminished in a terrible degree; and the eye of the surgeon at once perceived that the sleep he enjoyed was the sleep of exhaustion; that feebleness, and not returning health, brought repose; and that, although that repose might perhaps produce the only favourable change which his situation admitted, there were a thousand chances to one against its restoring him to health.

It was on that very night that a messenger arrived from a village at a considerable distance, eagerly asking to speak with the Earl of Danemore, and on being questioned by Langford, he at once informed him that he came to bear the Earl tidings of his son Lord Harold's safety, as well as a note under the young nobleman's own hand, with which he had been entrusted. Some discussions ensued between the rector, Sir Walter, and Langford, as to whether it would be expedient, in the Earl's state at that moment, to communicate the intelligence which had just been received.

Sir Walter, who had seen less of the world than his young friend, and had examined much less deeply that which he had seen, eagerly entreated Langford to communicate the tidings to the Earl directly, declaring that the news of his son's safety must necessarily act as the best remedy which could be applied to his case. The good knight spoke from the impulse of a fine and generous mind, practically unacquainted with evil, and with all the complicated and even opposite impulses which the existence of evil in the human mind must necessarily produce. The rector urged the same course through mere ignorance, for he was a man of no strong sensations himself, and those which he did possess were merely the animal ones. To hear of a son's welfare, he felt in himself, must—separate from all other things—be a joyful event; and he was incapable of weighing or judging, or even comprehending the various circumstances which might render that which was in itself joyful, most painful and agitating.

Langford, however, knew better. He had discovered before this time, many of the deep, peculiar points in the Earl's character, and he knew all the particular details of his situation which might make the certainty of his brother's life and speedy return a matter of apprehension, care, and emotion. Both his companions, however, so strongly urged him to communicate at once the tidings to his father, that he felt he could not and he ought not to withhold them.

He cared not, it is true, what others would think of his conduct; but it might, perhaps, be a weakness in Langford, that—knowing well, by early experience of the world and all the world's baseness, the many turns, the subtle disguises, the strange masquerading tricks which selfishness will take to deceive, not only the natural and habitual egotist, but the kindest and the most liberal of men, where any dear interest, or prejudice, or affection is at stake—he was as much upon his guard against himself as if he had known himself to be ungenerous; and was always more willing to take the opinions of others in a matter where his own interest might be risked, than on subjects where self was totally out of the question.

In the present instance, it was clear that the life or death of his brother might make the greatest difference in the Earl's views and feelings; and although he knew himself too well not to be sure that the consideration of such a difference would not influence him in the slightest degree in withholding or communicating the news he had received, yet he yielded to the opinion of others against his own judgment, when he would not have done so had his own interests been in no degree implicated. He only demanded that Sir Walter himself should communicate the tidings; and he warned him, when he agreed to do so, that the effect might be more powerful than he expected.

Sir Walter, though he totally misunderstood the view that Langford took, and the fears which he entertained, acted, from natural goodness of heart and sensibility of feeling, exactly as his young friend could have desired, only apprehending that the joy would be so great as to perform the part of grief itself.

Although he had resolved at first not to do so—lest his very presence might excite in the mind of his dying father those painful combinations on which his thoughts had evidently been wandering during his delirium—Langford followed Sir Walter into the room, and stood at a little distance behind, listening, with a heart whose accelerated beatings told even to himself how deeply he was interested by the words in which the worthy knight clothed his communication.

"I have got what I trust may be pleasant news for you, my good lord," said Sir Walter, as he seated himself deliberately in the chair by the Earl's bed-side, affecting the greatest possible degree of composure and tranquillity as he did so, and banishing every appearance of haste or excitement from his manner.

"What is it?" demanded the Earl, turning round towards him as quickly as he could; for he no longer started up with that vehemence which he had displayed but a few days before. "What is it? Are the papers found? For ever since Eugenie—but I wander—I wander. I feel that I wander; that I have been wandering for many days. But go on, go on. I am more collected now. What of the papers? It was about them you were talking, was it not?"

"No, my lord," replied Sir Walter; "we are not talking about the papers, but of something which, if I judge rightly, may prove of as great interest as even their recovery—I mean that of your son. We have heard some tidings of him, my lord."

"What are they?" demanded the Earl. "Speak! What are they?"

"They are all as favourable as you could desire," replied Sir Walter, in the same calm manner. "We have heard that he is rapidly recovering, and has escaped from the hands of the people who detained him." And seeing that the Earl listened without reply, he added, "We may, I trust, soon expect him here."

Lord Danemore pressed his thin white hand—through the blanched and shrivelled skin of which might be seen protruding the large bones and joints which had once marked his extraordinary strength—upon his eyes, and remained for several minutes in deep thought. He then withdrew his hand, and turning to Sir Walter Herbert, he said in a low voice, "It is a terrible thing, Sir Walter; it is a terrible thing not to be able to thank God for the recovery of a son that we love—not to know whether we desire to see him before we die, or not."

"It is, indeed, a terrible thing, my lord," replied Sir Walter; "but I trust that such is not your case, and that your son's coming will give you unmixed pleasure."

"Far from it," replied the Earl, gloomily. "He will have to hear sad truths; to undergo mortifications the most bitter to a proud nature like his. He will have to hear of his father's faults and crimes, he will have to learn that, instead of vast wealth, a noble name, and a high rank, he has no inheritance but that of an illegitimate son; that he has no name; that he has no station; that he has no rank; and all this the consequence of his father's faults. I know him, Sir Walter Herbert; I know him: and there is too much of my own blood in his veins for me to expect that he should do anything, in the bitter disappointment of a proud spirit, but curse him who, for his own gratification, and in the indulgence of mad and headlong passions, brought shame and sorrow and disgrace upon him. My own blood, I say, will cry out against me in his heart. He will curse me, as I would have cursed my father had he so acted. He will look down upon me as I lie here like a writhing worm, and he will think that it is only because my corporeal vigour is at an end, and my strong heart weakened by abasing sickness, that I do those acts of justice which I had determined on long ere I knew these wounds to be fatal: which I had determined on as soon as I found that he whom I had wronged, that he who had borne with me so patiently, that he who had defended me, and rescued me from death, was my own child, the son of her I early loved. He will misconceive, he will misunderstand it all. I know his heart, from my own; and I know that in my meeting with him under these circumstances all will be dark, and stormy, and terrible. I feel not even sure that it will be better for him to live rather than to die, as we supposed he had. I feel not sure that death would not be preferable to the feelings he will have to endure. He will not bear the crossing of his high fortune meekly. He will strive against it; he will strive to prove the words false that take from him his high station, even though they are spoken by his father. He will contend for the rank and fortune and place which he has so long expected, even with his brother. Through life he will go on in bitterness and disappointment. His heart will henceforth be full of gall, and his lip breathing curses. It would have been so with me, and why should it not be so with him? He is my own child, the inheritor of my nature, if not of my name."

It was evident that he was exciting himself to a dangerous degree by the exaggerated picture which his imagination drew; and Langford could not restrain from advancing, and trying to soothe him.

"My dear father," he said, "if such be really Edward's character—though I think you judge of him and of yourself too harshly—how much better it will be to take the middle course that I have proposed; to conceal from him the period of my mother's death; and never to let him know that the marriage to which he owes his birth was an unlawful one. Willingly I offered, and willingly I repeat the offer to do more, and abandon to him altogether the rank and station which he has held in England, the estates which are attached to the title of our ancestors, and content myself with justifying my mother's fair fame to her kindred in another land, and with claiming there the fortune to which I have a right through my noble uncle."

"You are all your mother!" exclaimed the Earl, gazing upon him. But then other feelings seemed to rush across his mind; the expression of his countenance changed, and he exclaimed, "What! would you have me afraid of my own son? Would you have me dastardly conceal the truth from him, for fear of his anger? No, no; he must hear it. It may be bitter, but he must hear it. Bitter things are good for us sometimes. But from whose lips shall he hear it?" he added after a moment's pause. "Not from mine, Henry; not from mine, for I feel that the hour is drawing nigh! I shall never see him more in life. I feel that there is a chill hand upon me: surely it must be the hand of death!"

It was so, for from that moment the Earl rapidly sunk. His senses did not leave him again, however, and from time to time he spoke to those around him. He expressed neither hope nor fear in regard to the future. The only words, in fact, which he uttered at all, referring to the awful consideration of a future life, were spoken about an hour after the conversation had taken place which we have just detailed. He then beckoned Alice to draw nearer, took her hand affectionately in his, and as she bent down to listen, he said, " I owe you much, sweet lady—much for all that you have done for me; but more than all for the endeavour to give me such hopes and expectations as may best soothe and cheer this last dark hour. Whether such hopes are to be realised I soon shall see, and as far as bitterly repenting everything I have done amiss, I have followed the injunction to the letter. But alas! Alice, if it be necessary to the repentance you speak of, to bow down in terror as well as remorse, that—struggle for it as I may—I cannot accomplish. I can repent, but I cannot fear. I am ready to meet my doom, whatever it may be, and to endure it to the utmost. Nevertheless, to you I owe deep thanks, and you have them. Now leave me, sweet lady. Farewell, for the last time! I would not have you see me die."

His words had turned Alice deadly pale, and Langford, taking her hand, led her from the room. She found relief, however, in tears. She then strove to read, but she could not; and she sat waiting in the rector's parlour, with a heavy heart, till she heard footsteps moving down the stairs. Her father and Langford then entered the room.

The latter was pale and grave, but calm and firm; and sitting down by Alice's side, he laid his hand upon hers, saying, "Thank you, my beloved Alice, for all that you have done to soothe the death-bed of my father."

It was enough, and Alice again burst into tears; but the next moment a servant entered the room, asking the two gentlemen if they knew where he could find the rector.

"He is up stairs, in the chamber of death," said Sir Walter; "but you had better not disturb him at present."

"Why, sir, I must disturb him," said the man; "for there is a gentleman waiting, who came down two or three days ago, in a coach with only two horses, and who has been hanging about here and up at the Castle ever since, though nobody knows who he is. He desires to speak with my master immediately. He has inquired every day if the Earl were still living, but would not give his name nor tell his business. So I must disturb my master."

"Do so, then," replied Sir Walter; and the man quitted the room.

CHAPTER XXXIII.

THE words which the servant had spoken, in announcing to Sir Walter Herbert the arrival of a stranger, had made but little impression either upon the worthy knight or on the son of the deceased nobleman; and, after a broken conversation, in which pauses of deep and solemn thought constantly interrupted their discourse, Langford was begging Sir Walter to convey his daughter from that melancholy house to her own happy home, when the rector entered the room, bringing with him a person unknown to any one present.

"I am forced to intrude upon you, sir," said the clergyman, addressing Langford, "as this gentleman who has just presented himself has come on business in which you are deeply interested."

"It is an unpleasant moment, sir," replied Langford, "for me to enter upon any business at all. I am occupied with very gloomy thoughts and very painful feelings, and I could wish that the business, whatever it is, might be postponed till to-morrow."

"I am very sorry, sir, both for your sake and my own, that cannot be," replied the stranger, advancing.

He was a man about the middle age, tall and well made, though meagre, courtly in his personal appearance, and bearing in his whole demeanour the stamp of gentleman. Nevertheless, there was something repulsive in his aspect—something cold, and cynical, and dry, which was smoothed down, indeed, by courtesy of manner and personal grace, but which, nevertheless, tended to make Langford the less inclined to enter into any conversation with him at that moment. The stranger, however, went on, and the next few words he uttered were sufficient to show him to whom they were addressed that he must meet the subject at once.

"It will, perhaps, sir," the stranger said, "be satisfactory to you to know, in the first instance, who it is that is forced to intrude upon you, which our worthy and reverend friend here has forgotten to mention. My name is Sir Henry Heywood; I have the honour of being second cousin to the late Earl of Danemore, and in default of his son

Lord Harold, who, there is good reason to believe, I find, is dead, am heir to the title and estates of the late peer."

There was something in the manner of his announcing himself—the tone, the demeanour, the look—that galled Langford not a little, and made him assume a cold dryness of manner which was not natural to him. To the stranger's announcement, then, he only replied by drawing up his head and demanding, "Well, sir, what then?"

The shortness of this reply seemed to puzzle Sir Henry Heywood a good deal, for he paused a moment or two before he answered, and then begun with some degree of hesitation: "Why, sir, under these circumstances," he said at length, "during the absence and probable death of Lord Harold, I am the only fit person to take possession of the late Earl's papers and effects."

"I do not feel quite sure of that," replied Langford, in the same tone.

"Pray, then, sir," demanded Sir Henry; "if you consider yourself a fitter person than I am, and the question be not an impertinent one, will you inform me who it is I have the honour of addressing, for this excellent divine has given me but vague information upon the subject?"

The question somewhat embarrassed Langford, for he had determined to wait for his brother's return ere he took any step whatsoever in regard to asserting his rights as the eldest son of the late Earl, and to be guided entirely by the frame of mind in which he found that brother at the time. He determined, therefore, to evade it as far as possible for the moment, and consequently replied, "The character in which, sir, I should oppose your taking possession of the papers of the late Earl, is that of one of his lordship's executors; and in order to satisfy yourself that I am justified in assuming that character, as well as my friend here, Sir Walter Herbert, and the worthy rector himself, who are the only persons named, you have nothing to do but consult with Mr. Evelyn, the lawyer, who drew up the Earl's will four or five days ago, and will inform you that such is the case. He is now, I think, in the next room, writing. Let him be called in."

"That is unnecessary; that is unnecessary," said Sir Henry Heywood. "Of his lordship's will, at the present moment we are supposed to know nothing; and I must contend that I, as the next heir, in default of Edward Lord Harold, am entitled to take possession of the papers, especially as there is every reason to believe that I am at this moment Earl of Danemore."

"There is every reason to believe the contrary," replied Langford, growing provoked; "and great reason to believe also, that you never will be so. If you are at all acquainted with the handwriting of the gentleman you call Lord Harold, you will recognise it in that note, which was received from him not three hours ago, informing his father that he was not only alive but at liberty, and rapidly recovering from the injuries he had received."

Thus saying, he threw down the note on the table before him, and after eyeing it with a cursory glance, the countenance of Sir Henry Heywood fell amazingly; nevertheless, he replied in the same bold tone, "I am extremely happy, sir, to hear that such is the case, but this does not in the least prevent me from insisting on my right till Lord Harold appears."

Langford was about to reply, perhaps angrily, but Sir Walter Herbert interposed, saying, "It seems to me, sir, that you are pressing forward a very painful discussion at a very painful moment, and I really do not understand what is your object in so doing."

"Why, I will explain my object in a few words, sir," replied the other. "There is a gentleman, I understand, who has of late set up some chimerical claim as eldest son of the late Earl of Danemore, in which it seems that he has persuaded the Earl to concur—"

Langford's cheek grew very red, and his lip quivered; but Alice, who was sitting by him, laid her hand upon his arm, and looked imploringly up in his face.

Langford bowed his head with a smile, saying, in a low tone, "Do not be afraid, sweetest; these matters are not decided by the sword."

In the meanwhile Sir Henry went on, saying, "Under these circumstances, sir, I think it absolutely necessary that the papers of the Earl should be placed in safe keeping, for we have seen too much lately, in the various plots and contrivances of the last reign but one, of how papers may be manufactured or altered to suit certain purposes."

It was Sir Walter Herbert's cheek that now turned red, and he replied somewhat sharply, "Sir, your imputations are of a character— But it matters not," he added, interrupting himself. "I will not be provoked to forget my age or my station. The late Earl of Danemore has appointed three respectable persons, of whom I perhaps am the least worthy, to act as his executors, and take possession of all his papers after his death. The testimony of Mr. Evelyn to that effect will be sufficient, till we have an opportunity of reading the will, which was given by the late Earl into that gentleman's keeping.—Do not interrupt me, sir! But in order to satisfy you completely till the will is read, I am perfectly willing, and doubtless the two other executors are so also, to permit of your putting your seal in conjunction with ours upon all the effects of the late Earl. Does this satisfy you?"

"Why, I suppose it must," replied Sir Henry; "although," he added, giving a bitter and angry glance towards Langford, "I am sorry that I cannot get this gentleman to put forth his claims and acknowledge his purposes boldly and straightforwardly."

"My not doing so, sir," replied Langford, "proceeds, I beg to inform you, from sources and considerations which have no reference to you whatsoever. If there were not such a worshipful person as Sir Henry Heywood in existence I should behave exactly as I do now. The matter remains to be settled, not between me and you, but between myself and another."

"It may do so," replied Sir Henry Heywood, "or it may not."

"But I say, sir, *it does*," replied Langford, frowning.

"You misunderstand me, sir," replied the other, with the same dry courtesy. "I do not mean to impugn your word in the least. I have no doubt that you are perfectly a man of honour and integrity. All I meant to say was, that, after all, Lord Harold may never appear. However, I am bound to take care of my own rights, and from those rights neither frowns nor high words will move me. In the meantime, I accept the terms proposed. We will both put our seals upon all cabinets and private receptacles of the Earl's papers, either till his son Edward appears, or till the will is opened, and persons lawfully in power take possession thereof. I seek nothing but what is straightforward and right, but I am firm in pursuing that which I do seek."

"After all, the man is right," thought Langford to himself, for he was one of those marvels that can acknowledge an adversary right; "he does it in a disagreeable and harsh way, it is true, when a few sweet words would have honeyed the thing over, and made it palatable instead of bitter. Nevertheless, he is right, and we must not quarrel with the manner."

"Well, sir," he continued, aloud, "I am ready to proceed with you in the matter you propose. We will, if you please, take the lawyer with us, and my worthy and reverend co-executor will probably do me the favour to accompany us. Sir Walter, I think, will trust to my accuracy; for, if I am right, he ordered his coach to convey himself and his daughter home, and we need not detain him."

"Alice will go home with her maid," said Sir Walter; "I have much to speak to you about to-night, Henry, and many things to settle here; therefore, if the good doctor will give me lodging for one night more, I will remain."

The rector expressed his satisfaction; but Langford looked out of the window upon the sky to mark how far the sun had declined, for, after all that had happened during the last few weeks, he could not part with the only being that he loved deeply upon earth, even upon a short but unprotected journey like that before Alice Herbert, without feeling something like the apprehensiveness of strong affection steal over his heart. The plan proposed by Sir Walter, however, was followed. Alice took her departure, and, to save the reader any unnecessary doubt, we may say she arrived in safety.

The four gentlemen then called in Mr. Evelyn, the attorney, to whom Sir Henry Heywood thought fit to be very condescending; but he found Mr. Evelyn as short and dry as even he himself could have desired, in one of his own shortest and dryest moods. The lawyer said, when he was informed of their object, that there was not the slightest necessity for any one to seal up the papers, except the executors, as he had the will in his pocket, and their names were endorsed upon it, so that the persons appointed could be ascertained at once, without the indecency of opening the paper within an hour of the testator's death. Langford, however, to save any further discussion, informed him that it had been so arranged; and, in the first place, notwithstanding all the many painful feelings that were busy at his heart, he accompanied the others with a firm step into the room where his father's body lay.

Sir Walter Herbert cast down his eyes, and would not look upon him as he entered. The rector, on the contrary, took a quick glance to see how he bore it; but all was firm and calm—sad, but self-possessed; and while the others proceeded to their task of sealing up several cabinets which had been brought from Danemore Castle after the fire, Langford advanced to the side of the bed of death, by which, as was then customary, stood a light on either side, and gazed upon the countenance of him who had just departed.

All was calm and still on that face where so many fierce and violent passions had displayed themselves through life. All was peaceful, tranquil—even happy in the expression. The muscles which had habitually contracted the brow were now relaxed, and the deep wrinkle between the thick eyebrows was obliterated. The closed eyelids veiled the quick, keen, flashing eyes which had now lost not only the blaze of passion but the lustre of life; and the lip which had quivered with a thousand emotions in a moment—which had now curled with bitter scorn—now been raised with hasty indignation—now been shut with suppressed passion—and now been drawn down with stern determination, was motionless, meaningless. The only expression that it bore, if it bore any, was that of gentle and quiet repose—an expression which is so consonant to the features of a child, that in infants we trace it alike in sleeping, in waking, and in death; but which is seldom, if ever, seen in sleep upon the countenance of the aged; though it is sometimes assumed by them in waking life, when a natural placidity of disposition overcomes cares, infirmities, anxieties, regrets, and all the heavy burden of years; and is often, very often seen when the hand of the eternal tranquillizer, death, has stilled the fiery passions into his deep, unbroken repose.

Langford gazed long and wistfully; and, at length, the finger of Sir Walter Herbert, laid gently on his sleeve, made him start; and, turning round, he left the apartment, with a deep sigh that thus should have ended a life full of mighty energies and noble capabilities, which might have been devoted to the accomplishment of a thousand great and magnificent things. The whole party thence proceeded to Danemore Castle, and went through the same process of sealing up all the private cabinets and chests which could be found. Few, indeed, were there still in existence, for the greater portion had been kept in that part of the building which was burnt; and, though Sir Henry Heywood showed an inclination at first to make himself sure that all had been consumed beyond the line marked out as that of the fire, he was very soon satisfied by nearly breaking his neck down a flight of stairs that seemed tolerably steadfast till he set his unlucky foot upon them.

This being done, and Sir Henry quite assured that the other parts of the Castle were not practicable for human feet, a low and formal bow separated the two parties, and the expectant heir of the earldom retired to the small village public-house, where he had put up on his arrival, and immediately sent off for shrewd lawyers to advise with him in the circumstances in which he stood.

As the others returned on foot towards the Rectory, Sir Walter took the arm of Langford in one hand, while he gently grasped that of the lawyer, Master Evelyn, with the other, saying, in a low and kindly tone, "We must lose no time!"

"Certainly not, Sir Walter," said the lawyer; "we must lose no time, indeed; for opponents, you see, are in the field quickly."

"But," said Langford, "perhaps—"

"There is no 'perhaps,' my lord," replied Master Evelyn, interrupting him, but with a civil and courteous tone, and a deprecatory bow; "I know quite well what you would say: that perhaps your mind is not made up how to act; but all which I mean to urge is, that it is necessary to be fully prepared to act in any way that you may think fit at a moment's notice. Here is your father's declaration in regard to his marriage, drawn up and sworn to. It is now expedient to take the declaration of Mistress Bertha, and swear her thereunto before the magistrates, as well as to employ every means of obtaining further proof and information. You may act afterwards as you think fit."

Langford readily agreed that the lawyer was in the right, although he felt a repugnance at that moment to follow, with even apparent eagerness, his claim to the heritage of him who was just dead. He returned, however, to the Rectory, where Bertha had still remained, and she soon appeared in answer to his summons.

There were traces of tears upon her cheeks; and when Langford, speaking some soothing and consoling words, explained to her his object in sending for her, she replied, "You have done well, sir. You have done well; for I feel that I shall not live long; and what I have to say had better be rightly taken down. I feel that I shall not live long, I say, because, for the first time for thirty years, I have shed tears. It is a weakness that I did not expect to fall upon me again; but now that the last of those who have been connected with my fate is gone into the tomb, I feel that the time is come for me to take my departure also; and these tears, I suppose, are a few drops of rain ere the dark night sets in."

"I trust not, Bertha," said Langford, kindly. "I trust not, indeed. The last being connected with your fate has not departed; for surely my fate has been strongly and strangely connected with yours, and I have so much to thank you for, that I would fain show my gratitude, and make the last days of your life pass happily away."

"You have, perhaps, something to thank me for," replied Bertha, 'but more to blame and hate me for. But you know I am not a person of many words; and if I am to tell all that I know of you and yours, let me do it now, and as shortly as may be."

"In the first place," said Mr. Evelyn, "we had better send for another magistrate; the lady can make her declaration in the meanwhile and swear to it afterwards."

"Do not call me the lady, Master Lawyer," said Bertha, with her usual cold sharpness; "I am no lady. I am Bertha, the housekeeper. But send for what magistrate you like. I will say nothing that I will not swear to."

A messenger was accordingly sent off for Sir Matthew Scrope, and in the meanwhile Bertha went on with her tale.

"I was born on the beautiful coast of Brittany;" she said; "my father was a small holder under the Lords of Beaulieu, his mother's ancestors," and she pointed to Langford. "The chateau stood upon a high rock, crowned with thick woods above the sea; for in those sweet shores the green leaves dip themselves in the green waters. At fifteen years of age, I went to attend upon the Lady Eugenie—his mother—who was some two years older than myself. The Lords of Beaulieu were fathers to all beneath them, and she was as a sister to me. She found out that even at that early age I loved, and that there was little hope of him I loved ever being able to win my father's consent, for my father was wealthy for a peasant. She told her father and her brother, and prayed their help; they gave it; and so well did they do for my happiness, that ere two summers were over, Henri Kerouet was the prosperous owner of a small trading ship. My father's consent was given, the day was appointed, and two days before, I saw from the windows of the castle my father, my two brothers, and my lover, put out to sea in a fine boat, to buy things at Quimperle for the wedding. I watched them from the windows of my young mistress's room with the eyes of love, and saw them skim for half a mile over the waters, as if it had been a thing of their own;

but then, I know not how or why, the sail flapped upon the water, the boat upset, and all that were in it disappeared. One of them rose again for a moment, and clung to the side of the boat. I think it was Henri; but ere my screams called attention, and other boats could put off, his hold had given way, and he too was beneath the waters.

"There is in every woman's breast a history; and this is mine. I had but one brother left; every other relation was gone, and he I loved also. My heart was shut up from that hour, never to open again. My young mistress was all kindness, and tenderness, and benevolence; she kept me with her, she strove to soothe and to console; but she had soon need of consolation and soothing herself, for her father died suddenly as he sat at breakfast beside her, and she remained an orphan in the castle of her ancestors for several weeks, till her brother, who was with the army, could obtain permission to return to his estates. When he did come, he brought with him one whom I remember well, as he then crossed the threshold, in all the graces, the powers, and the fiery passions of youth; one whom you have all seen bent and worn by age and care, and by the punishment of those passions indulged; one who lies within a few steps of us even now, in the cold and marble stiffness of death, with all the stormy impulses of his nature passed away. He was then like a fiery warhorse, full of beauty, and strength, and danger, for there was nothing on earth that he dared not do; there were but too few things, also, which, with such a mind and such a body, he could not accomplish. He loved my mistress, and my mistress loved him, ere many weeks of his sojourn with us passed away.

"He brought with him a boy of some twelve or fourteen years old; a gay, wild, fearless creature like himself; the son, as I understood, of a poor but noble gentleman, who had placed him as a page, to learn from infancy the art of war, with the young lord. This boy would often sit and tell me of wild scenes which had taken place in the civil strifes of England, and sometimes would glance at stranger and still more terrible things in western lands, where they both had sojourned long. This Franklin Gray it was who first called my notice to the love that was growing up between the two; and I saw how strong it was, though there was nothing avowed as yet between them.

"The time came for the young Marquis to return to the wars. The English Lord was to return with him, and still nothing was spoken of their love, at least so far as I could learn; but on the day when they were about to depart, the young foreigner turned to my mistress, in her brother's presence, and said, 'Lady, I have a parting present to make you. You have applauded and admired my gay young page. In the present beggary of my fortunes, I can do but little for him; I pray you to take him to your service, and when he is old enough, let your noble brother do what he can to promote him in the career of arms. Till then, as he is of gentle blood, he may well serve a gentle lady.' He spoke gaily, and as it seemed freely; but I could observe a peculiar expression on his face which gave the words more meaning; and there came at the same time the blood, like a rising rebel, into my mistress's cheek, telling that she comprehended him well.

"It had been arranged that while the Marquis was absent, she should proceed to England, to join her uncle, then on a political mission in London, rather than remain in solitude in France. A vessel was engaged, and in a few days, after she had parted with her brother and her lover, she embarked, with myself, the boy Franklin Gray as a servant, and the priest. We met with foul weather, and the ship with difficulty reached a port upon the coast of Cornwall, where we landed; but there, upon the pretext of fatigue and illness, she determined to remain some days; and on the first night of our arrival she despatched the boy Franklin Gray to London, both to announce her safety to her uncle, and, as it proved, to communicate with one who in disguise had returned to his native land, at the risk of life, for the purpose of meeting her.

"As soon as the boy was gone, she told me all; how they loved, and how their love had been told, and of the impossibility of his asking her hand at that time, while in exile and in poverty, having nothing but his sword to depend upon. When the boy returned, she seemed a good deal agitated; and, as when once she had given her confidence it was extreme, she told me that she had received messages from the Earl begging her to follow a particular course in her journey, in order that he might see her, if but for a moment, by the way. She shaped her course accordingly, and passed through the very scenes where now we are; and at the little town of Uppington, not ten miles hence, she was met by the Earl. He had obtained—Heaven know how! for I do not—a considerable sum of money, which raised high his hopes and expectations. He pressed her to be united to him immediately in private. Love was strong and eloquent in her breast, and she consented. She exacted, however, that their marriage should be solemnized according to the rites of his faith and the laws of his country, as well as according to her own.

"The good weak priest who accompanied her was easily induced to perform the ceremony of our church, and the Earl had now wealth sufficient fully to bribe the priest of that village; but as it was determined that in a very few days she should go on to join her uncle, and double the quickness of her journey to make up for the lost time, I only, and one of the servants, were admitted to be present as witnesses to a marriage which was to be held strictly secret. I saw them married by the rites of both churches; and my mistress, for her honour's sake, demanded and received from both priests, certificates of the marriage. The day before that on which she was to have set out, news arrived of the death of Cromwell, and the rumour that all was in confusion through the country across which we had to pass. The tidings did not make them very sad, for they were in their first happiness; but the boy Franklin Gray was again sent to London, in company with our good weak priest, to see her uncle, and ask whether she should come on. At the end of a week, the boy returned alone. Her uncle had quitted London in haste, and the poor priest had been involved in a tumult in the streets, had been recognised as belonging to the Catholic Church, and had been murdered by the brutal populace. For him she grieved sincerely; but it seemed to me that she was not very sorry that a fair excuse was given her for remaining with her husband, and sharing his fate, whatever that fate might be.

"She soon experienced, however, the sad lot of those who cast themselves upon the mercy of man. He was violent—rash—hasty. There were matters grieved him deeply. The sum that he possessed was drawing near to a close, and he wished much it was evident, ere two months were over—I do not say to annul his marriage, for I believe, nay, I am sure, he loved her still—but to have it concealed for the time. He urged her then to return to her brother, showing her that he could with difficulty support her, even if he were not himself by chance discovered by lingering in England; and he framed for her a plausible story to account for the period of her absence, which in times of such danger and confusion might easily be done.

"She refused, however, firmly, though mildly. She said, that though, so long as it merely referred to concealing her marriage, she was willing to do all he wished; nevertheless, when it could no longer be concealed but by a falsehood, she would yield no further; and nothing should ever induce her to tell her noble brother a lie. Anger and fury on his part succeeded. I and the boy Franklin were in the room; and the Earl, when he found that passion could effect nothing, turned to me, thinking that I might persuade my mistress to consent. She had that morning given me some offence; for I had ever been idle and vain, and my terrible fate had not cured my follies, though it had embittered my heart. I did not try to persuade her, but I said maliciously and falsely—for I knew better—that I thought she was very wrong not to do as her husband told her.

"She gazed upon me with surprise and indignation; but the boy Franklin burst forth, exclaiming, 'She does very right not to tell a lie for any one:' and the Earl in his passion struck him to the ground.

"The boy instantly drew his dagger and sprang upon the Earl, but he wrenched it from his hand in a moment, and putting him forth from the door, returned laughing, moved to merriment, even in the midst of his anger, by the youth's daring. With him the storm for a time passed away; but from that moment my mistress seemed to look upon me with contempt. I felt that I merited it, and hated her the more. All her good deeds, all her kindness towards me, were forgotten; and a few hasty words which she spoke the next morning, in her indignation at my conduct, became like poison, and rankled in my heart. Thus passed two or three more days; and I laid a scheme which succeeded but too well. I looked at the Earl often as I passed him, seeking to draw his attention, and make him speak to me upon the matter of his dispute with my lady. At length, one day he did so, and I hurriedly and basely advised him to obtain from her by any means the proofs of her marriage, and then let her refuse to go back to her brother for a time if she dared. My mistress came in as we were speaking, and looked surprised, but said nothing; and the Earl followed my advice. He tried many methods to arrive at his purpose; but it was in a moment of love and affection that he induced her to give him up the certificates, the attestations of myself and the other servant, and all the proofs of her marriage, upon the pretence that he would keep them more securely. A doubt, however, seemed to cross her mind, even when she was placing them in his hands, for she asked him to swear most solemnly that he would never destroy them; and I remember particularly, that when he said he would swear by everything he held sacred, she insisted upon his adding that he swore upon his honour as an English gentleman.

"When he had got the papers, however, and he knew that he could compel her to do whatsoever he liked, his love and his tenderness seemed to return in full force, and the idea of parting with her at all was evidently hateful to him. At length, however, necessity compelled him to propose it again; and once more, high words and angry discussion ensued; and then it was that all the smothered feelings which she had been long nourishing towards myself burst forth. She accused me of alienating her husband's affection. She called me base—ungrateful—criminal. She told me to quit her presence, and never re-appear in it again; and I did quit her, determined to return to France, and obey her to the letter.

"How the matter would have ended between herself and her husband, I know not. had not other circumstances intervened; for, with all his violent passions, he certainly loved her still, deeply—tenderly—devotedly. But news was suddenly brought him that his real name and character, which he had concealed, had been discovered, and that warrants were out for his apprehension, as what they called a Malignant. He returned to the house for a few minutes after receiving these tidings, informed his wife what had taken place, took a tender and affectionate leave of her, and besought her to hasten to France with all speed, where he would join her ere ten days were over. The spot was named, the time fixed, and I saw him press her warmly to his heart as they parted.

"He then spoke to me for a moment, and, bidding me forget all that had passed, enjoined me to remain with and console my mistress. I refused at once, sternly and bitterly, to do so; and as he had no time to lose, and found my determination fixed, he only further asked me to let him know without fail where I established my abode, that he might show his gratitude for my services in brighter days, and do away the evil feelings between my mistress and myself. I told him that he would always hear of me at the house of my brother, and he departed. He was scarcely gone when I too left the house, and found my way back to France alone, but took care not to revisit the place of my birth, believing that a bad name had gone there before me. What happened to my mistress then I do not know; but I heard that, keeping only the boy Franklin Gray to attend upon her, she had sold all her jewels—"

"We had better not admit anything into the declaration," said Mr. Evelyn, "except what you personally saw or knew, my good lady. Indeed, as it is, only parts of the declaration can be used."

"I am neither good nor a lady, Master Lawyer," replied Bertha. "But to go on with what I personally know—about a year and a half after, or perhaps two years, a letter reached me by a circuitous route from the Earl of Danemore, telling me that the restoration of the Stuart family to the throne of England had restored him to his native land and all his honours, and that if I chose to come to England, and occupy that post in his household which I lately filled, I should spend the rest of my days in comfort and peace and honour. I agreed to do so, for where I then was, I was very miserable; and I set out for England. When I came into his presence, however, he scarcely knew me; for when he had last seen me I had been a blooming—perhaps a handsome girl; and in that short space, grief, anxiety, and self-reproach had made me, with very little difference, what I now am. To my surprise, however, I found that his house was occupied by a noble and beautiful bride; and when he told me, I gazed in his face with wonder and apprehension. He understood my looks, and with that stern, determined air which was so natural to his countenance, he told me, in a few short words, that when he had returned to France, being hopeless and nearly destitute, he had not sought out his wife as he had promised, trusting that she would go back to her brother and conceal her marriage, as he from the first had wished. The Marquis de Beaulieu had sought him out, however, and covered him with reproaches: they had fought, and both had been severely wounded. 'I then,' he added, 'went into other lands; but suddenly found that the king had been restored. I returned to my native country, but speedily perceived, that though I had sacrificed everything for my sovereign, I could regain my honours, but could not regain one half of my estates without using the influence of another peer, all-powerful with the king. To him I applied, and he proposed to me a marriage with his daughter. I might have resisted the temptation if I had never seen her; but she is young, beautiful, fascinating. I married her, and regained all.'

"'And the Lady Eugenie,' I cried; 'the Lady Eugenie?'

"'She is dead,' replied the Earl; 'I have now obtained certain information that she is dead; but I cannot say,' he added; and he grasped my arm tightly while he spoke—'I cannot say I am sure that she was dead before this second marriage was contracted; and now, Bertha,' he continued, 'now, swear to me, by everything you hold sacred, never, till I permit you, to reveal to any one the fact of my former marriage; and if you do swear, you bind me to you for ever!' I did swear, for we both thought that she was dead; and I kept that promise inviolably. But I asked him, before I took any vow, if he had kept his, and preserved the proofs of his first marriage; for, at first, I thought he wished to entangle me by an oath, when his real wife was still living; and I had repented enough already what I had done against her. He told me that he had, and showed them to me in the chamber where they were preserved: and again he swore never to destroy them, though her death, he said, might well free him from that promise. But I saw then, and I have seen through his life, that he felt, as well as I did—that there was a fate attached to those papers which would one day change everything.

"He then brought me to the presence of his lady, to whom he had announced my coming. When the door opened for me to enter, and she knew who it was, she turned towards me, as I thought, coldly and somewhat sullenly; but the moment after, she looked surprised. She had expected to see a young and handsome girl; but she saw a lean and sallow woman, and all doubts of me and of her husband, if she had entertained such, vanished. She became as kind to me as the first day of spring, though she was often haughty and cold to others. She trusted me in everything, and I learned to love her well. I loved her better, far better, than the mistress I had at first served; but there was still something wanting in the latter attachment. I believe it was the freshness of early feelings; the freshness that never comes again. However, after I had been in England for some ten years, and one son of the Earl and his Countess had been born and died, and the second supplied his place, being then but a sickly child himself, I remained behind for a short time in London after they had quitted the court to come down into the country. In about ten days I followed, and travelling slowly, stopped one night at a little inn in the town of Stockbridge.

"It was night; and, after having supped, I went along the passage towards my bed-room, when, as I passed a door that was open, I heard a voice that almost made me sink into the earth. It was that of the Lady Eugenie; and, as I passed by the door, I looked in without wishing to look, and I saw her there, sitting speaking to a servant, pale and worn, but scarcely less beautiful than ever. I was fool enough to faint; and when I revived, I found myself in her chamber, with herself and her woman bending over me. At first I thought she did not know me, so terribly was I changed, and so little did she seem moved by the sight of one who had injured her; but when I was quite well, and thanked her in the English tongue, and was about to leave her, she said. 'No; stay a moment. Leave us, Marguerite;' and I trembled so that I could not move. The girl went away; and then she said, 'You are terribly altered, Bertha; but I have kept you to say, that if sorrow for anything you ever did against me be the cause of that sad change, console yourself. I have long ago forgiven you. Nay, more; I have often thought I did you some injustice.'"

"Then you positively saw the same lady with your own eyes," said Mr. Evelyn, "whom you had seen united to the late Earl before the death of Cromwell, ten years after he had married another person?"

"I did," replied Bertha. "But it is useless now to detail all that passed between us. I found that her brother had compelled her to assume another name, and to spread a report of her own death. That after her return to France she had borne a son; this gentleman present, the true Earl of Danemore—"

"You mistake," said Langford; "I was born in England, in the very town where my father's marriage was celebrated with my mother; for she was resolved, she has often told me, that I should lose none of the privileges of an Englishman by being born in a foreign country, and she crossed the seas to England a month before my birth, in order that her child might first see light in the native land of his father. I have the certificate of my birth duly attested."

"All that, she told me," answered Bertha; "and I meant but to say that the child was born some months after her husband had left her. The boy was with her then, and I saw him; and I am ready to swear, though changed now from a youth to a man, that this is the same person. She strove eagerly to persuade me to give her an attestation of her marriage, under my hand; but I would not do it, for I had vowed not. She asked anxiously after the papers, too, and if I knew whether they had been destroyed; but I assured her that her husband had kept his word. I told her even where they were placed; and I assured her that if ever fate so willed it that the obstacles which then existed to the open establishment of her marriage should be removed—and I felt that they would be—I assured her, I say, that I would then aid her to the very best of my power in obtaining the result she wished. I promised her even then to do all that I could, without breaking my oath, to console and comfort her; and I told her, without, however, telling her the whole truth, that her husband fully believed her to be dead.

"We women derive comfort from strange sources often; and that thought that her husband believed her to be dead, and had acted as he had acted under that belief, seemed to console her more than anything that I had said. She wept bitterly; but the tears were evidently sweet ones; and when we parted, she made me promise to write to her frequently, and give her news of him whom she still dearly loved. I did write to her frequently, and she to me; and I told her everything that passed, which could give her any pleasure to hear. After her death her son wrote to me; and though for some time past he has not told me his movements, yet when I heard from accidental report that for two or three summers a gentleman had been wandering about the neighbourhood, attracting the attention of many by his gracious manners and his kindly heart, I felt sure that it was the son of Eugenie de Beaulieu, led on by the hand of fate towards the destiny that awaited him."

Thus Bertha ended her history, which had occupied some time in the narration; and when it was done, both Langford and Sir Walter pondered for several minutes over the tale just told. The first who broke silence was Mr. Evelyn, who though but a country attorney of those days, was superior both in knowledge and in mind to the generality of his class.

"Though, undoubtedly," he said, "there is sufficient matter to bear us out in making a vigorous struggle to recover your rights, my lord, yet I very much fear that, without the documents which afford the only real legal evidence of the marriage, we should be defeated. The leaf has been taken so nicely out of the register that we can draw no conclusive inference from that fact. And yet," he continued, as if a sudden thought struck him—" and yet there may be means of proving that a leaf is really wanting. Of that, however, more hereafter, for we cannot be at all secure without the papers."

"Should I make up my mind," said Langford, " to enter into the struggle at all, I think that I shall be able ultimately to obtain them; but in the meantime—"

He was interrupted, however, by the entrance of the rector's servant, who announced that a gentleman had just arrived, demanding to speak with the Earl of Danemore, and on being told that he was dead, had appeared in what the man called a great taking.

"Is he gone?" demanded the rector.

"No, sir," replied the servant. "When I told him the Earl was dead, but that a number of gentlemen were in the parlour talking the matter over, he said that he should like to speak with them, as he had news of great importance to communicate from Lord Harold."

"Pray let us see him," said Langford; and the rector, bowing his head, told the servant to give the stranger admittance.

CHAPTER XXXIV.

Before we follow any further the proceedings, however important they might be, which were taking place at the village of Danemore, we must return to several of the personages concerned in this history, whom we have now quitted for somewhat too long a period. In the first place, we must give due consideration to Mr. Justice Whistler, whom we last left fast asleep. Whether he dreamed at all or not is difficult to say, but if he did, it is certain that his dreams must have been of prisons and the gallows, for such were the very first thoughts that presented themselves to his mind when he awoke after a nap of between five and six hours.

It is probable, indeed, that he would not have roused himself near so soon, but for an extraordinary trampling of horses and the sound of manifold voices, which, ascending from the court-yard below, caused Morpheus to flap away upon his soft wings, and leave the worthy magistrate with his eyes and ears wide open, wondering what could be the matter. He started from his bed instantly, and advanced to the window, the curtains of which had been drawn to keep out the sun; and putting forth his head above the court-yard, he perceived a number of persons collected together, habited principally like sturdy yeomen and farmers. Each had his horse with him, and all seemed to be well armed; while the two constables who had followed the worthy magistrate in his nocturnal expedition were seen in the midst of the crowd, bustling about with a look of importance. Now Justice Whistler was a man of rapid combinations, and he instantly divined what was the occasion of the meeting; but he was a cautious man too, and he loved to have his own conclusions confirmed by the testimony of others. He consequently protruded his head still further from the window, and, catching the attention of one of the constables, demanded, in somewhat of an impatient tone, "What is all this about, sirrah? What are you going to do?"

"We are going to catch the thief, your worship," replied the constable; "and all these good gentlemen are going to help us."

"On no account! on no account!" exclaimed the justice from the window. "What! without me? I tell you if that fellow were hanged without my help, I would hang myself."

"Why, we thought as how," replied the man, "that your worship had been so well basted already, that you might likely not wish for any more of it."

"Out upon you, fellow!" said the justice, "I'll baste you, if you do not mind. Go, and beg Mr. Rector directly, to stop but for ten minutes; and I'll be ready to go with him. If any man were to lay a hand upon that fellow Gray before me, I should hold myself but half a man and no gentleman. Go, and tell him so, sirrah!"

While the man proceeded to obey the commands he had received, Mr. Justice Whistler hurried on his garments, wincing desperately, every now and then, as a sudden turn made him aware of the deficiency of skin on some part or another of his back. At length, however, his toilet was accomplished as far as it could be; that is to say, his vest was put on, for neither coat nor cloak had been left to him; and with a rueful face he was obliged to descend with his sturdy arms only decorated by the wide white sleeves of his shirt.

Guided by the sound of voices he found his way to the rector's parlour, and, opening the door, presented himself to the eyes of the more select party therein assembled. It consisted of three or four of the principal farmers or small landed proprietors in the neighbourhood, together with the rector himself, and a young gentleman, who instantly, by the entire difference of his mien and demeanour from those of the persons by whom he was surrounded, attracted the attention of the worthy magistrate. He was tall and well proportioned, though somewhat slightly made; but he was extremely pale, so much so, indeed, as to have the appearance of ill-health. He was only armed with an ordinary sword, which might perhaps have befitted a country gentleman in those days, but did not harmonize with the striking and distinguished appearance of the personage who bore it. But while there was something about the corners of the mouth which implied a certain degree of indecision of character, there was a quick dash in the eye, and lines and furrows upon the brow, that seemed to contradict the other expression, and gave a look of stern determination even approaching to fierceness. The appearance of the justice in his shirt sleeves, joined with the account which had been previously given of his adventures of the night before, for a moment relaxed the countenance of the young gentleman we have mentioned, and, sitting by a table on which various refreshments were laid out, he gazed upon Justice Whistler with a smile.

"My dear sir," exclaimed the magistrate, addressing his host— "My dear sir, how could you think of going against this scoundrel without me? I would not have had it done for a thousand pounds."

"Why," replied the rector, "we judged that your worship was so tired and injured that it would have been cruel to disturb your repose; and as I had yesterday morning gone round the country, and appointed all these worthy people to meet here, for the purpose of taking as many as we can of this gang of villains, I could not very well delay."

"What! then you had determined to go against them before I came?" cried the justice, hewing himself off a large slice from a cold sirloin that graced the table. "How was that? How was that? I understood they had only been in this country some few days, and they cannot have committed many depredations."

"Yes; but my noble young guest here, the Lord Harold," replied the rector, "only escaped from their hands the night before, and arrived at my house yesterday morning. We consulted together what was to be done, and determined on the steps we have taken."

"My Lord Harold!" cried the justice; "my Lord Harold, I give your lordship good morning, and very happy I am to see you alive, for we have had many doubts on the subject; and I have had more to do with your concerns of late than perhaps you are aware of."

"I am afraid my father must have suffered much anxiety on my account," said Lord Harold, with a somewhat cold and stately air; "but I sent off a letter yesterday morning, the very first moment that I had the means of doing so, to inform him of my safety. Had the messenger not arrived when you left that part of the country?"

"Not that I heard of, not that I heard of, my lord," replied the justice. "My good lord, your father, indeed, had much anxiety; and, for the matter of that, other people too; for there was a certain young gentleman taken up, and accused of having murdered you. He remained for several days in confinement, which seemed to chafe his proud spirit very much."

"Pray who was that, sir?" demanded Lord Harold.

"Why, he calls himself Captain Henry Langford," replied the justice; "but you may doubtless know more of him by some other name."

Lord Harold's brow grew as dark as night, and bright red spots came into his cheek as he replied, "I have heard of him, and seen him, and have also been informed that he takes the name of the

Chevalier de Beaulieu. But perhaps you have had an opportunity of investigating more fully who he really is?"

The justice, however, saw that Lord Harold was utterly unacquainted with all that had taken place during his absence; and, as there was a great deal that he himself could not explain clearly, while everything that he could explain was anything but agreeable, he determined to leave the task to others, and was meditating how to evade giving any reply, when the rector came unexpectedly to his aid, by saying, "I beg pardon for interrupting you, gentlemen; but allow me to remind you that time wears. It is now near one o'clock. We have fully fifteen miles or more to go, and it may be necessary not to fatigue our horses before we arrive at the point of our destination. By your leave, therefore, I think we had better postpone all explanations."

"One more cup of this excellent ale," exclaimed the justice, "and then I am ready. I hope the rascals have got my horse saddled. Pray, your reverence, make inquiry."

"But, my dear sir," said the rector, "how can you manage to go without a coat? I am afraid, too, that none of mine would fit you—not even one of my loose riding coats, for I am a spare man, and you are ——"

"Fat! you would say," added the justice. "Yes, I am fat, sir; that is to say, fattish; and how to do without a coat I know not; but go I will. Is there not a fat person in the neighbourhood that would lend me a jerkin?"

"Why, your reverence," said one of the farmers, who had hitherto stood aloof, but who now advanced towards the rector, "there's Farmer Balls, down at the Pond Gate; his coat would just do. He weighs full one and twenty stone. His coat would surely just fit his worship."

"I could get into it, at least," said the magistrate, "for I only weigh nineteen, so there are two stone to spare, which makes more difference in a coat than in a load of hay. So run, my good sir, or send some one, and beg Farmer Balls to lend Justice Whistler a coat for a few hours. Hark ye! hark ye! not his Sunday's best, for we have dirty work to do, and there is no need to spoil it."

The coat was soon procured; and Mr. Justice Whistler, having mounted with the rest, set out at the head of the procession, which consisted of nearly thirty persons, having Lord Harold on one side of him, and the reverend rector on the other. The justice took the place of leader as a sort of right, which was tacitly conceded to him by all the rest, more out of respect for his portly person than from anything that they knew of his character or abilities.

Lord Harold, however, soon began to appreciate his ready shrewdness, for as they moved onward at a slow trot, he put several questions to him with regard to their future proceedings, resolved, if he found any occasion to be dissatisfied with the other's arrangements, to take the matter into his own hands; for the stern and harsh determination which he had formed in regard to Franklin Gray had not at all given way since the period of his escape.

The plans which the justice proposed however, the shrewdness with which he put all his questions regarding the exact situation of the house, and the rapidity with which he received and comprehended every explanation given, soon convinced his young companion that they could not be in better hands. It was accordingly determined that, as soon as they reached the top of the hills at the point where they could first see the house, the party should divide, and one body, under the direction of the rector, should sweep round through a hollow in the hills, while the other pursued the road by which Lord Harold had made his escape, so as to approach the abode of Franklin Gray on both sides at once. By this means no one could quit the house without being seen by one or other of the parties, and the possibility of the robbers effecting their escape by one side of the building while the assailants forced their way on the other was guarded against. In making these arrangements, and in giving directions to all the various personages of which the troop was composed, the time was passed, till they emerged from the woods, lanes, and cultivated grounds on the first slopes of the upland, and began to take their way over the soft short turf, which was only varied by the innumerable scattered stones that covered the higher ground on that side.

Lord Harold—though it must be acknowledged that he thought, and with bitter pleasure, more of the capture of Franklin Gray than of any other thing on earth—had determined to pass the rest of their march, after every arrangement had been fully made, in learning from Mr. Justice Whistler all that had taken place during his absence from Danemore Castle, some vague reports of extraordinary events having reached him even there, though the news which now travels by a steam carriage then went by the waggon.

On putting his very first question, however, he perceived that the keen, hawk-like eye of the justice was fixed upon a particular spot on the hills, over whose soft green bosoms the sunshine and the shade were chasing each other quickly, as the wind blew the light clouds over the sky. The effect was beautiful but dazzling; yet still the justice kept his eye fixed on that particular spot at the distance of about two miles before them, and made no reply whatsoever to the young lord's interrogation.

Lord Harold, who was in no very placable frame of mind, repeated his question in a sharper tone; but the magistrate instantly exclaimed, without taking any notice of him, "Yes, yes; I see it move! Do not you, parson? Look ye there, up in that hollow which the shadow is just leaving. I have been for this ten minutes trying to determine whether that is a man on horseback or a hawthorn tree. It is a man, I'm sure! I saw it move this minute, a bit to the left, so as to get a better sight of us."

"There is a hawthorn tree there," said the rector; "I know it of old. But you are right, you are right! There is something moving from behind it. It is a horseman indeed, evidently watching us. See, he is cantering up the hill. I am afraid this bodes disappointment."

"There is another on the top of the highest mound," cried Justice Whistler; "they have a terrible start of us; but never mind. We must not fear breaking our horses' wind. We must gallop as hard as we can go; and now there must be no thought of going round by the hollow as we proposed. The only plan is to make for the house as fast as possible. Don't you say so, my lord?"

"Most assuredly," replied Lord Harold; "there are women and children also to be moved, which must take them some time. It cost them nearly an hour and a half to get ready when they came hither, for I was with them, and saw all their proceedings."

"Set spurs to your horses, then, gentlemen!" cried the magistrate, aloud. "Master Constable, ask some of these good yeomen to lend me a pistol. They can muster a brace for me amongst them, I dare say. Some of them seem to have three or four."

But leaving the constable to bring him the weapons afterwards, he himself spurred on without any delay, while Lord Harold and the rector accompanied him at full speed, and the officers and farmers followed quickly, gaining, by the rapidity of motion and the excitement of the sort of race they ran with each other, a good deal more courage and enthusiasm than they had probably set out with. At this eager pace they reached the top of the hill, but were obliged to ride some little way to the right before they could get a sight of the house. When they did so, however, though nothing was seen of it but the chimneys towering up above the tall trees, every one instinctively pulled in his bridle rein, with somewhat of an awful feeling at his heart.

The house lay at the distance of about two miles and a half, but the air was clear and pure, and every curl of the thin blue smoke, as it rose peacefully over the trees, might be traced by the eye till it mingled with the atmosphere around. After a moment's silence, the constable rode up, and put the pistols into Justice Whistler's hands; but at that very instant a body of horsemen was seen passing over the slope beyond the house, and then giving rein to their horses, and galloping away as hard as ever they could, over the open downs beyond.

Man is undoubtedly a beast of prey; and, in the present instance, no sooner did the posse who followed the justice, the rector, and the young nobleman, see a body in flight before them, than those who had been most timid and fearful of leading the way, were all setting off at full gallop in pursuit of fugitives whom there was little or no chance of overtaking. It was with the utmost difficulty that the fat but powerful voice of Mr. Justice Whistler, the shriller tones of the rector, and the deeper but feebler sounds of Lord Harold's voice, each exerted with the utmost force, could induce these hot pursuers to halt and receive orders ere they departed.

When they were at length brought to pull up their horses, however, a few words between their three leaders seemed to settle their arrangements, and Mr. Justice Whistler raised his voice, exclaiming, "Constable Jones!"

But no one came forward, he having pronounced the name at random, and there being no Constable Jones amongst them, "The youngest constable," he cried again; but thereat his own two followers, with three or four others, spurred forward from the crowd; and fixing upon the one who appeared the most intelligent of those who had come with him, he said, "Take that man, and that man, and that man, and that, and gallop after those fellows as hard as ever you can go. Remember, your business is not to come up with them till you have got a sufficient force, but to raise the whole country as you go along by the hue and cry, commanding all men, in the king's name, to follow and assist you. Keep them in sight as far as possible, but at all events keep above them on the hills, and drive them into the populous country. There you may follow them by the tongue as well as here by the eye. Now off with ye, quick! We will come soon after, when we have run through the house."

The men obeyed, though their worthy leader twice showed an inclination to doubt whether this person or that was the man whom the judge had appointed to follow him. But Mr. Justice Whistler cut him short sharply, and having seen him depart, turned to Lord Harold, saying, "Now, my lord, I think with you that we had a great deal better go down to the house, and examine what it contains, before we pursue these men, having set our hounds upon the track. But as this reverend gentleman says nothing, and seems to think otherwise, pray satisfy him in regard to your reasons, to which I will add mine."

"Why," added Lord Harold, hesitating, "why, I think—that is to say, I saw nothing but men in the party that went away. Now there is a woman and a child, and if you take them, depend upon it, the chief bird of the mew will hover near, and be caught at last."

As he spoke there was a deep and burning spot came up into his cheek, which showed that there were feelings of shame and remorse, glowing like coals of fire at his heart, even at the moment that the baser spirit triumphed, and bowed his words and actions to its will.

Mr. Justice Whistler, however, did all that he could to make the matter smooth to him. "Spoken like a true falconer," he cried; "my lord, you take my trade out of my hands. We are fully justified in bringing our bird back to the lure. However, there is no time to spare. Let us ride on as fast as possible;" and so saying, he put his horse into a quick pace, and, followed by the others, dashed down the hill at a rate which scared many of the younger and more active of the party.

We must now, however, leave all the busy actors we have brought upon the scene, and, quitting hounds and huntsmen, and the gay and merry chase, turn to the dark and solitary lair where the quarry lay, fully conscious of pursuit, in order to explain the motives of that sudden flight which had been observed by the pursuers from the hills above.

CHAPTER XXXV.

THE escape of Lord Harold, and the flight of one of their companions with the woman-servant, had thrown the little band of Franklin Gray into consternation and terror when it was discovered on the following morning. Harvey, however, who assumed the command during the absence of their leader, instantly took measures for tracking the fugitives, and, by no other guide than the footmarks upon the sandy parts of the road, traced the course of all three exactly to the spot where Lord Harold had been left sitting under a tree by his two companions.

From that point all traces of those two were lost; but a shepherd, who had seen the young nobleman, weary and exhausted, in the morning, and had conducted him to a small village, hidden amongst the beeches to the left of the spot, gave still further information; and leaving men to keep a strict watch upon the place to which the fugitive had been brought by the peasant, Harvey returned, with very unpleasant sensations, to meet Franklin Gray, and gave him an account of the evasion of the prisoner. He doubted not, indeed, that having thus tracked him to his place of repose, they might be able to lay hands on him again, for he never calculated upon the young nobleman doing what in fact he already had done—taking a single hour's repose, and then speeding on as fast as possible to the house of the nearest magistrate, which was that of the gentleman with whom he was found by Justice Whistler.

As Harvey returned, he perceived Franklin Gray and Mona riding leisurely up the hill towards the house, and spurring forward at once, he told the whole of his disagreeable tidings without any concealment. The robber instantly turned his eyes upon his wife, and bit his lip hard; while she, innocent of all share in what had occurred, but feeling herself an object of suspicion and jealousy, turned very red, and then very pale, and trembled violently.

"So, I am betrayed!" said Franklin Gray, "betrayed by those I trusted! Harvey, I think you are faithful to me!"

"Indeed I am, Captain," replied the other; "and so are all the rest, except that fellow who is gone, and whom I always thought was a low scoundrel, unfit for the company of gentlemen. They are all faithful to you, Captain, depend upon it."

"On what can we depend in life?" asked Franklin Gray, bitterly "Friendship turns to hate; love betrays us always; gratitude was never anything but a name; and honour is now a shadow! On what can we depend? Let us come in, however, and consult what may be done. Action has been through life the principle of my being; and I will not yield to circumstances even now."

So saying, he led the way to the house; but he said not one word to his wife, either as they went or when they arrived. The boy Jocelyn, however, was in the court-yard, holding the infant in his arms, who seemed well pleased with his new nurse. But Mona, the moment she had set her foot to the ground, sprang forward and caught the baby to her heart, exclaiming, "and did she leave you, my sweet babe? Cruel, cruel woman! She never had one, or she could not have left you;" and dewing its smiling face with tears, she ran away with it into the house to hide the emotions she could not restrain.

Had Franklin Gray witnessed that meeting between mother and child, the dark suspicions that had fully taken possession of his mind might have been banished at once; but he was talking with Harvey at the moment, and remembered nothing but the many whispered messages which he had seen brought by the maid from the prisoner above on the preceding day; and keen and bitter were the feelings at his heart. He went on speaking with Harvey, however, as if occupied with ordinary business.

"If he have not quitted the village before this time," he said, "he will most likely not quit it till night, knowing that we shall be waiting for him. But at all events the horses must have some rest and food. I rather think that, as far as insuring our own safety goes, Harvey, we might as well let him journey on his way, for depend upon it by this time he has given full information of everything concerning us to the people where he has stopped. However, I am determined, if possible, to have him in my hands again. In the first place, to punish him for what he has done; in the next place, to find out the truth of some matters in regard to which I am not at ease."

He spoke calmly; there was no heat, nor haste, nor agitation in his tone. On the contrary, it was unusually slow and distinct; but there was a knitting of the dark heavy brow, a setting together of the white teeth between every two or three words, which made Harvey, bold man and daring as he was, shrink, as it were, within himself, at signs of deep and terrible passions, the effects of which he knew too well.

"Perhaps," continued Franklin Gray, in an easier tone, "the possession of this young lord's person might be made, too, a sort of surety for the safety of the band. There is a ship, I find, sails for the port of St. Malo in four days; and I have made such arrangements that I can have what space in her I like. I should wish our brave fellows to keep around me till that time; when those who like to go with me can; those who love this cold land can remain. But if we get hold of this pitiful boy, I shall deal with him as a hostage, and make his life the price of no step whatsoever being taken against me and mine."

With such objects in view, and believing that Lord Harold still remained at the village to which Harvey had traced him, the arrangements of Franklin Gray were soon made for proceeding in a few hours to the spot in person. In the meanwhile he entered the house, and held his infant child for several minutes in his arms, gazing on its face in silence. He gazed, too, for an instant upon his beautiful wife, with a cold meditative look, and without proffering a word; then gave her back the child, and walked out across the hill, marking with a soldier's eye every peculiarity of the country, when he did look upon it, but in general bending his eyes down upon the ground, and communing with his own sad heart, and muttering to himself as he strode along.

When the appointed hour was come, he was in the court-yard and his foot in the stirrup; but his after proceedings on that night require no long detail. Some information which he gathered, both from the men whom Harvey had left to observe all the movements in the village, and from some persons who passed, led him not only to believe that Lord Harold was undoubtedly there, but that the young nobleman had gained tidings of the close watch that was kept upon the place. The night was spent in watching, and in vague councils held with Harvey and others, in the course of which Franklin Gray did not display that firm decision which had ever previously characterized his actions. He now thought of taking the rashest and the boldest steps, of attacking the village itself, and carrying off Lord Harold by force; then, again, he seemed inclined still to watch, though the night had so far waned that it was improbable any movement would take place; and again he was for giving up the pursuit altogether.

In such infirm purposes passed the night, till the sound of horses' feet revived expectation; and the appearance and flagellation of Mr. Justice Whistler afforded a pleasant episode for the robbers to break the tedium of their dull night's work. As soon as that was over, Franklin Gray turned his steps homeward again; but feeling a conviction that the peasantry of the neighbouring districts would soon be moved against him, he took the precaution of placing two of his band, whose horses were in the freshest condition, on two points, where they could communicate by signs with each other, and see over the whole country below.

He then returned straight to his dwelling; but there had come a recklessness over him, a sort of moody and splenetic demeanour, which was remarked by Harvey and all his companions. He who usually laughed so seldom, now recalled the affair of Justice Whistler more than once with somewhat wild and fitful merriment; but then the moment after he would fall into deep stern thought, answer any question that was put to him in an absent if not in an incoherent manner, and would frequently break forth at once upon topics totally distinct from those which might naturally have occupied his mind.

When he arrived at home—at least that temporary kind of home which was all that his wandering life ever allowed him to know—he was met at the door by his fair wife Mona, who gazed timidly up in his face, to see whether his feelings were softer or happier than they had been. It was an agreeable surprise to her to find that he took her by the hand, and gazed on her with a look of admiration and love. The only words he spoke, however, were, "You are fair, my Mona; fairer, I think, than ever, to look upon. Where is the babe?"

She led him to see the child sleeping; and as Franklin Gray bent over it, and gazed upon the calm and placid face of infant slumber, a bright drop fell from his eyes on the cheek of the child, and woke it from its rest. It held out its little arms to him at once, however; and taking it up, and pressing it to his bosom, he carried it to the window, and gazed forth upon the wide world beyond. Mona had seen the drops which fell from her husband's eyes, and she saw, too, his action towards the child, but she would not interrupt the course of such feelings for the world, and only saying in her heart, "He is softened," she hastened to seek some apparent occupation, while her soul was busy with the joy of renewed hopes.

That joy was soon clouded, for again over Franklin Gray came that same fitful mood, which tenderness for his child had for a moment interrupted. He said nothing harsh, indeed; he showed no sign of unkindness; and no word announced that the dark suspicions and jealousies which he had before entertained still remained as tenants of his bosom. Often, indeed, he fell into deep stern fits of thought, and would rest for more than half an hour in the same position, with his head bent forward, and his eyes fixed on one particular spot of the ground. Then, again, he would start up, and, especially if he found Mona's eye resting upon him, would break forth in gaiety and merriment, tell some wild tale of laughable adventure, or sing a broken part of some cheerful song.

Mona, however, was not to be deceived by such signs; and they were all painful to her. That he whom she had never known to be merry, even in his brightest days, should so suddenly, after deep gloom, break forth into gaiety, was quite enough to show her that all was not well within; and watching him with the anxious eyes of deep affection, she strove to do and say all that could soothe and calm, and console and cheer him. Sometimes her efforts would seem successful, sometimes not. Sometimes he would gaze upon her with looks of deep and earnest love; sometimes would start away when her hand touched his, as if it had been a serpent. All and everything she saw was matter of deep pain and anxious thought to Mona Gray.

When the hour of dinner came, she strove to tempt him to his food, but he would scarce taste anything except wine, and of that drank more than usual. It seemed not to excite, however, but rather to calm him. His manner grew more consistent; sadder, but more tranquil; and leaving his companions still at the table, he led his wife away to the chambers they usually inhabited, and sat down and spoke with her rationally on many things. There was an occasional abruptness, indeed, in his speech, and a rapid transition from one thing to another, which still alarmed her, but she consoled herself with the hope that the fit was passing away, and that all would be better soon.

At length he said, "Come, Mona, come! While I take the child upon my knee, you sing me a song. Who knows if I shall ever hear another?"

Though her heart was sad, she made no reply, but hastened to obey; and she chose such words and such an air as she thought most likely to soothe him. Both were sad, but through both there ran the bright glimmering of hope; a cheerful note every now and then mingled with the more melancholy ones, and promises of future happiness blended with the sadder words of the lay.

The music still trembled in the air, when Harvey suddenly entered the room, and approaching his captain, whispered a word or two in his ear. Franklin Gray instantly started up, with the dark cloud upon his brow which usually gathered there in moments of determined action.

"The time is come!" he exclaimed. "Harvey, I will speak with you and the rest. Mona, take the child. I will be back in a few minutes."

He then followed Harvey out of the room; and from that moment his whole demeanour was calm, collected, and firm. "Have all the horses saddled quickly," he said; "each man collect everything valuable that he has. Each man, too, have his arms all ready for action at a moment's notice! Did you say, Harvey, that they had both come over the hill?"

"No; only one," replied Harvey; "but he came at such speed that there can be no doubt the other will soon follow. We shall doubtless have to stand to our arms soon, Captain, I suppose?" And as he spoke his cheek was a little paler than ordinary; but there is such a thing as the emotion of strong resolution, and it may blanch the cheek, though in a slighter degree than fear.

"Perhaps so, Harvey," answered Franklin Gray; "but we shall hear;" and as he spoke he advanced to the window, and having satisfied himself by one glance, he turned back to Harvey, saying, "The other is coming too. We shall know more anon."

The first of his watchers, who had been left on the other side of the hills, had by this time nearly reached the house, and in a minute or two after he entered the room where Franklin Gray and Harvey, with the rest of the band who were not occupied in preparations, waited his report. "Well," said the Captain, "what news, Miles?"

"Why, I am afraid they are coming up in great force, Captain," he answered. "I could only see them draw out from the end of the lane upon the hill side, but there seemed a good many of them. I did not move a step, however, till I saw Doveton begin to canter away, then I thought it right to come on and give you the first tidings. He will be here soon, and render you a clearer account."

"You did quite right," replied his leader. "If we had all to deal with such as you, my man, we should do very well." The man looked gratified; but Franklin Gray went on: "Come, Harvey; we will go out into the court. We shall be nearer the scene of action," and he walked deliberately out into the court-yard, where the horses were now all brought out and ranged in line.

"Mount, my men!" he cried; "mount! We shall soon have Doveton here. Miles, that pistol will fall out of your holster. Don't you see the lock has caught on the leather? You hold my horse, Jocelyn! Harvey," he continued, speaking to the man apart, and pointing to the boy; "do you think if we were obliged to make the best of our way off, and this youth were left behind—this mere child, as you see he is—they would injure him?"

"Oh, no," replied Harvey, "certainly not. They might take him away, but we could soon find means to get him out of their hands again."

"So," replied Franklin Gray, "so. But I hear Doveton's horse's feet clattering down the road as hard as he can come;" and in a minute or two the man he spoke of rode into the court-yard, with his horse foaming from the speed at which he had come.

"I am glad to see you are ready, Captain," he exclaimed; "for depend upon it we shall have sharp work of it. There must be at the lowest count forty of them coming up the hill, and all seemingly well mounted and armed, for I looked at them through the spy-glass you gave me, and I could see them all as plainly as if they were at the other end of the table."

Franklin Gray mused for a moment, and then demanded, "Could you see who it was that led them on?"

"Why, there were three rode abreast," said the man, "and I could see them all plainly enough. The one on the left was a man in a black cassock; but I don't think I ever saw him before. The middle one was a fat heavy man, who, I rather think is the justice whom we flogged last night—only in the darkness then I didn't well remark his face. But the third one, on the right hand, is certainly that lord you had up here for so long: that Lord Harold."

The cloud grew doubly dark upon Franklin Gray's brow, and putting his hand to his throat, he loosened the laced collar of his shirt. "Fully forty men, you say?" he demanded, thoughtfully. But then added, without waiting for reply, "Harvey, you are not mounted! Quick, quick, into the saddle! Miles and Doveton, put yourselves upon the left. Now, Harvey, mark well what I have to tell you! Lead those men out, and take at full gallop across the hill to the right. If you keep Elsland Peak always a little to the left, you will come to a hollow; and if you ride up it as fast as you can go, long before any one can overtake you, for their horses are not used to this work like ours, you will have reached a spot where the slope divides the hollow into four, and all four lead away to the beech wood, where you may disperse, and set chase at defiance. Arrange your plans amongst yourselves as you go; and now lose not a moment, for they must be over the hills by this time."

"But yourself, Captain," asked Harvey, anxiously; "yourself, and the lady, and the little child? I will never leave you here alone."

"Do not be afraid Harvey," replied Franklin Gray, with a stern smile; "I will take care of them and myself, depend upon it!"

"But I do not like this plan at all," cried the man. "What! to run away and leave my captain behind me, at the mercy of these fellows that are coming up! I do not like it at all, Captain Gray. This will never do."

"You surely would not disobey me in a moment of danger and difficulty like this!" said Franklin Gray. "No, no, Harvey, you are too good a soldier for that! But to satisfy you, you shall see that I provide in some degree for my own safety. Jocelyn, take my horse down into the narrow part between those two sheds, and hold him there, whatever you see or hear, till I come to you. In the first place, open those two other gates at the bottom of the court, and when you are holding the horse, keep as far back as possible, that nobody may see you! Now, Harvey," he added, "you see and are satisfied. Lead the men out as I have commanded. I trust their safety to you!"

Harvey looked down and bit his lip, hesitating evidently for a moment as to whether he should obey or not. At length he looked steadfastly in Franklin Gray's face, and held out his hand to him, with a melancholy shake of the head.

"God bless you, Captain Gray," he said; "I obey you even in this; but I am very much afraid that you are not quite right in your plans. I am afraid, I say, that you are acting under a wrong view; and I wish to God you would think of it before it is too late. Well, well; I will go—God bless you, I say. Come, my men, let us march;" and so saying he led them all out of the court-yard.

Franklin Gray saw them depart with stern, unmoved composure; then advanced to the gate himself, and while their horses were heard at the full gallop proceeding in the direction which he had pointed out, he himself gazed up towards the other part of the hills, and saw a strong party of horsemen crowning some of the summits. He then spoke another word or two to the boy Jocelyn, returned into the room where he had conferred with Harvey, and paused with his arms folded on his chest, pondering gloomily for about a minute.

His next act was to cast himself into a chair, and cover his eyes with his hands, while his lip might be seen quivering with agonizing emotion. It lasted scarcely a minute more, however, and rising up, he struck his hand upon the table, saying, "Yes, yes; it shall be so!"

He then took a brace of pistols from the shelf, loaded them carefully, and placed them in his belt; after which he proceeded to a closet wherein were deposited several other weapons of the same kind; chose out two with much deliberation, looked at them closely with a bitter and ghastly smile; and having loaded them also, he locked the door of the house, and returned to the room where he had left his wife.

The same dark smile was upon his countenance still, but he said as he entered, "I have been away from you long, fair lady, but it was business of importance called me. Now we will have another song, but it shall be a gayer one than the last."

Mona sang, but it was still a sad strain that she chose; and Franklin Gray, with his head bent down, and his ear inclined towards her, listened attentively to every note. When it was done, he caught her to his breast, and kissed her repeatedly, saying, "They are very sweet. Is there no poison in them, Mona?"

"None! None! Franklin," she replied. "If any poison has reached your heart, it has not been from Mona's lips."

Franklin Gray turned away, and muttered something to himself, but Mona did not hear that the words were, "Would it were so!"

"Play upon the lute," he continued sharply; "let us have the sound of that too;" and again she did as he bade her, though by this time there was a sound of heavy blows, as if given by a hammer below; together with the trampling of horses' feet, and voices speaking.

"Those men are making so much noise I can scarcely play," at length, she said, "and the poor baby is frightened by it. See, he is going to cry!"

"Play, play!" said Franklin Gray, soothing the child with his hand, as it sat close to his feet; and Mona again, though with a trembling hand and anxious heart, struck the chords of the instrument. At that moment, however, there was the rush of many feet along the passage; and the next, the door of the chamber flew open, and seven or eight persons rushed in.

Though Mona had not remarked it, Franklin had drawn some of the benches and tables across the room when he first entered, in such a manner as to form a sort of barricade; and the moment the door burst open he started upon his feet, and levelled a pistol towards it, exclaiming, "Stand!" in a voice that shook the room.

The first face that presented itself was that of Lord Harold, and though his nerves were not easily shaken, yet the tone and gesture of Franklin Gray caused him to pause for an instant, of which the Robber at once took advantage.

"Lord Harold," he exclaimed, "you have come to see your handy-work, and to receive its punishment. I saved your life. You taught my wife to betray me!"

"Never, never!" shrieked Mona, falling on her knees before him.

"Never?" exclaimed Franklin Gray. "False woman! did you think I could not see? Lo! pitiful boy, here is your handywork, and here your punishment!" and turning the pistol at once towards her, he discharged the contents into her bosom. She fell back with a loud shriek, and Lord Harold in an instant sprang across the barrier; but ere he could take a step beyond it, a second pistol was aimed at his head, and fired by that unerring hand which seemed only to gain additional steadiness in moments of agitation or of agony. Bounding up like a deer from the ground, the young nobleman was cast back by the force of the shot at once upon the table over which he had leaped; he never moved again; there was an aguish quivering of the limbs, and a convulsive contraction of the hand; but, as in the case of Wiley, the shot had gone straight into the brain, and consciousness, and thought, and sensation, were instantly at an end for ever.

The rest of the Robber's assailants shrunk back with terror; and Franklin Gray, with a fierce triumphant smile, gazed at them for an instant, while, casting the weapons he had used to such fatal purpose on the ground, he drew a third from his belt, and exclaimed aloud, "Who will be the next?"

Borne back by the fears and pressure of his companions, with great difficulty Justice Whistler struggled through the doorway into the room again, but he did so with a bold and undismayed countenance, and, pistol in hand, advanced towards the Robber. But an object had attracted the attention of Franklin Gray, and he was bending down towards the floor.

The infant—the poor infant—had crawled towards its mother, and the fair small hands were dabbled in her blood. The Robber snatched the child up to his bosom, and giving one fierce glance towards the only one who remained to assail him, he exclaimed, "Fool! you are not worth the shot;" and thrusting the pistol into his belt again, he sprang towards the window, which was wide open.

Though embarrassed with the child, he had passed through in a moment, but not before Justice Whistler, shouting loudly, "He will escape! he will escape!" had pulled the trigger of his pistol at him with a steady aim. Loaded, however, by hands unused to such occupations, it merely flashed in the pan; and though he instantly drew forth the second, and fired, it was too late; Franklin Gray had passed, and was dropping down to the ground below.

"Stop him! Stop him!" exclaimed the justice, springing to the window, and overturning chairs and tables in his way. "He will escape! He will escape! Stop him below there! Run down, you cowardly rascals! Run down, and pursue him in every direction! By ——! the fellow will escape after all!" And after gazing for a single instant from the window he rushed out of the room.

On the side where Franklin Gray sprang to the ground there was not one of the party who had come to take him, all, except those who had entered the house and learned the contrary, believing that he had fled with the rest whom they had seen traversing the hills, and all being busy in examining the Robber's abode, the courts, the stabling, the harness that had been left behind, with open-mouthed curiosity.

The voice of the justice, indeed, called one stout farmer round, and he instantly attempted to seize the stranger whom he saw hurrying forwards towards some sheds at the other end of the building, but, though a burly and a powerful yeoman, one quick blow from the Robber's hand laid him prostrate on the earth, and springing past him, Franklin Gray reached the spot where his horse was held.

The boy Jocelyn had managed skilfully, constantly avoiding the side from which a sound of voices came. But now the quick and well-known step called him forth in a moment; the fiery horse was held tight with one hand, the stirrup with the other; and by the time Justice Whistler, with the troop that followed him, came rushing forth from the door, Franklin Gray was in the saddle; and still bearing the child in his arms, he struck his spurs into the horse's sides, and galloped through the gates.

Two of the farmers who had remained on horseback without, had seen him mount, but not knowing who he was, had not attempted to interrupt him. The appearance of their companions in pursuit, however, instantly undeceived them, and they spurred after at full speed. On went the gallant charger of Franklin Gray, however, faster than they could follow; and when they had kept up the race, at about twenty yards behind him, for nearly a quarter of a mile, the one nearest exclaimed aloud, "I will shoot his horse."

The words must have reached the Robber's ear; for instantly his charger slackened its pace, and the pursuer gained upon him a little; but then Franklin Gray turned in the saddle, and with the bridle in his teeth stretched out his right hand towards him. Next came a flash, a report, and the farmer tumbled headlong from the saddle severely wounded, while Franklin Gray pursued his course with redoubled speed.

Almost all the rest of the party who had come to take him were now mounted and in full pursuit; but his greatest danger was not from them. A little above him, on the hill, and nearly at the same distance from the house where he had dwelt, were seen, when he had gone about a mile, several of the party who had been sent to follow his band. The sight of a horseman in full flight, and many others pursuing, as well as the gestures and shouts of those below, made them instantly turn and endeavour to cut him off. On that side, as he was obliged to turn to avoid both the parties, the pursuers gained upon him, and, as if by mutual consent, they now strained every nerve to hem him in.

There was, about half a mile further on, a chasm caused by a deep narrow lane, between banks of twenty or thirty feet deep, descending from the top of the hills; and those above him on the slope, having already passed it once that morning, strove to drive him towards it, their only fear being lest those below should not act on the same plan. Franklin Gray, himself, however, took exactly the course they wished, and as, bearing down from above, they came nearer and nearer to him, they laughed to see him approach at full speed a barrier which must inevitably stop him. They urged their horses rapidly on, lest he should find some path down the bank into the lane; and nearer and nearer they came to him as he bore up towards them. They were within fifty yards of him when he reached the bank, and so furious was his speed that all expected to see him go over headlong.

But no! The bridle was thrown loose, the spur touched the horse's flank, and with one eager bound the gallant beast cleared the space between; and though his hind feet, in reaching the other side, broke down the top of the bank, and cast the sand and gravel furiously into the lane below, he stumbled not, he paused not, but bounded on, while the rashest horseman of the party pulled in his rein, and gazed with fear at the awful leap that had just been taken. A part is still pointed out on those hills where the top of the bank above the lane exhibits a large gap; and the spot is still called the Robber's Leap to the present day.

Every one, as we have said, drew in their horses, and some rode to and fro, seeking for a passage down into the lane; but, in the meanwhile, Franklin Gray was every moment getting further and further out of reach of pursuit.

When Justice Whistler, who came up as fast as his horse would bear him, arrived upon the spot, he saw at once it was too late to pursue the fugitive any further, and he exclaimed, "Give it up my masters; give it up; he has escaped us for the present, but we shall get hold of him by-and-bye. A man who gets into a scrape like this never gets out of it without a rope round his neck. Let us return to the house and conclude our examinations there; though a terrible day's work it has been, for, if my eyes served me right in the hurry, there is that poor young gentleman as dead as a stone, and the woman, who seemed a beautiful creature, too, no better."

Thus saying, he turned round, and rode back towards the house, while those who followed, and who had not been present at the events which had taken place within the building, eagerly questioned such as had witnessed the fearful scene. While they listened to the details, magnified as they might be, perhaps, by fear and the love of the marvellous, a gloomy feeling of awe fell over the whole party; and they gazed up towards the house as they approached it with sensations which made the blood creep slowly through their hearts.

Such feelings were not diminished by the sight of their wounded companion, who had received Franklin Gray's fire in the pursuit, and who was still lying on the ground, supported by one of his friends who had remained behind, and bleeding profusely from the right breast. Several alighted, and aided to carry him towards the house, while Justice Whistler and one or two others rode on, and proceeded at once to the room where they had first found the Robber.

There were sounds of many voices within, for six or seven of the party had remained behind, together with the good village rector, Dr. Sandon; and when the justice entered the room he found it occupied by three groups, the nearest of which consisted of two or three farmers, gathered round the head of the table, and gazing curiously at the object which it supported. A little further on was one of the constables, holding firmly by the collar the fair curly-headed boy called Jocelyn; while still further on was the rector, kneeling on the ground, and surrounded by the rest of the farmers and yeoman.

The magistrate advanced direct to the table, and saw that the object of the farmers' contemplation was the dead body of the unhappy Lord Harold, which was now stretched out, with the limbs composed, and stiffening into the rigidity of death. Too much accustomed to such sights to be strongly affected by them, the justice passed on, shaking his finger at the boy Jocelyn, and saying, "Ah, you little varlet, I shall deal with you by-and-bye."

"He's a funny little rascal, your worship," said the constable. "He ran up the hill so fast that nobody could catch him, till he got to a place where he could see the whole chase, and there he stood, and let himself be taken as quietly as a lamb, though I told him he would be hanged to a certainty."

The justice looked in the boy's face, and saw the tears streaming down from his eyes. One of the redeeming qualities of Mr. Justice Whistler was his love for children; and the boy's affliction touched him. "Poh! poh! you foolish lad," he cried; "they'll not hang such a child as you. Whip the devil out of you, perhaps; but don't cry for that."

"I'm crying for my poor mistress," said the boy; and the justice then advanced in the direction towards which Jocelyn's eyes were turned, pushing two of the farmers out of his way who obstructed his view of what was taking place. He found that Mr. Sandon was kneeling by the side of Mona Gray, and supporting her lovely head upon his arm. Her face was deadly pale, her lips blanched, her eyes closed, and the long black lashes resting upon that fair cheek: while the dark hair, broken from the bands that had confined it, hung in glossy confusion to the ground. The blood which had been flowing from a wound in her bosom was now stanched; and the clergyman, sprinkling cold water in her face, was at that moment endeavouring to bring her back to life; but the countenance was so like that of a corpse, that the magistrate immediately demanded—"Is she not dead?"

"No, no," said the clergyman, in a low voice. "Don't you see she breathes: she has twice opened her eyes."

In a moment or two after she unclosed them again; but those

bright and lustrous eyes were dimmed with the grey shadows of approaching dissolution. She feebly lifted her hand, and putting it to her bosom, drew forth a small crucifix of gold, which she pressed earnestly to her lips. New strength seemed to be acquired by the very effort; and gazing wildly round her on the strange faces that filled the room, she made an effort to speak. At first no sound was heard; but the next moment she distinctly uttered the words—"Is he safe? Has he escaped?"

The boy Jocelyn caught the sounds—burst away from the constable who held him—broke through those that stood around, and cast himself down on his knees beside her. "Yes, Mona, yes!" he cried; "he is safe! He has escaped! I saw him leap the gap myself, and none was brave enough to follow him. He is safe, and the baby too!"

Mona Gray raised her eyes, as if seeking the heaven to pour out her thankfulness; but the next moment, by another great effort, she said, "Jocelyn, if ever you see him again, tell him that Mona did not betray him in deed, or word, or thought. Tell him it was her last asseveration."

As she spoke, she pressed the crucifix again to her lips, and then murmured forth some sounds in a language that was not understood by any one present. She then closed her eyes, but still from time to time uttered a few words in the same tongue and in a low tone.

At length they ceased. The hand that held the crucifix to her lips sunk a little lower on her bosom—the other dropped motionless by her side—there was a slight gasp, and a shudder, but neither groan nor cry, and the breath stopped for ever.

Several moments elapsed before any voice broke the deep silence which that sight had produced; and the first words that were spoken were by the clergyman, who said, "God have mercy upon her."

She was then carried into the room beyond, and laid upon her own bed; and Justice Whistler returning, despatched messengers to the next town to summon the coroner with all speed.

His design, however, of apprehending Franklin Gray was by no means abandoned; and he endeavoured, skilfully enough, to make use of the simplicity of the boy Jocelyn for that purpose. After talking with him for some time in rather a kindly tone, yet asking him a great many questions in regard to his connection with the robbers, and attempting apparently to ascertain whether the boy had taken any share in their exploits, he said at length, "Well, my good boy, since such is the case, and you had nothing to do with them, but merely minding your master's horse, and the commands of the lady, you are pretty clear of the business; and, indeed, I do not know what to do with you, so you had better go home to your friends, if you've got any."

"I would rather go with you, sir," said the boy, "if you would take me with you. You seem good-natured, and I should like to serve such a gentleman as you; and if you did not choose to keep me on, I could serve you along the road."

The suspicions of the justice were excited, and he asked, "Why, which way do you suppose I am going, my man?" And then added, keeping his eyes fixed upon the boy's face, "I am not going back over the hills; I am going on to the town of ——, to seek out this master of yours."

The boy's countenance appeared to fall; and Mr. Justice Whistler convinced by what he saw, that Franklin Gray had most likely taken his way back over the hills, and that the boy knew it, left him in the hands of the farmers, and took the constable aside.

"Keep an eye upon that youth," he said. "Don't seem to restrain him at all; and if he says he will go back to his friends, let him go, but watch every step that he takes. If he says, however, that he will go with me, look to him well every step of the way; for I judge by his manner that he knows his master has gone over the hills, and wishes to be carried back with us for the purpose of rejoining him."

The man promised to obey punctually; and the justice, returning to the boy, spoke to him once more, as if in passing, saying, "Well, my good boy, you shall do just as you like. Upon second thoughts, I am going back to Moorhurst and Uppington; and you can either go away by yourself, and find out your friends, or you can come with me, and I'll feed you well by the way. Think about it, and let Master Constable know."

The boy's face brightened in a moment, and he said at once, "Oh, I will go with you."

There was much to be done, however, before the justice could set out, and it was nearly dark ere, leaving the scene of so many sad and horrible events in the hands of the officers of the county, he took his way back over the hills with the reverend gentleman, who once more invited him kindly to his house.

All the farmers accompanied them. No one choosing to separate from the rest at that hour, with the knowledge that Franklin Gray and his band were free, and in the vicinity. The boy Jocelyn, mounted behind the constable, was carefully watched, but he showed not the slightest inclination to escape, and when he arrived at the parsonage, ate a hearty supper in the kitchen, and fell asleep by the fire-side.

He was roused about eleven o'clock to accompany the constable to a garret chamber which had been prepared for them, and in five minutes he was asleep again; but when his companion woke an hour or two after daylight on the following morning, no Jocelyn was to be found, though the door was still locked, and the room was in the third story. There were found, indeed, the window partly open, the traces of small feet along a leaden gutter, the branch of a tall elm, which rested against one corner of the house, cracked through, but not completely broken, and the fragments of glass at the top of the wall neatly and carefully pounded into powder with a large stone.

These were the only traces of the boy's flight that could be discovered; but these were quite sufficient for Mr. Justice Whistler; and after chiding the constable severely for sleeping so soundly, he turned to the clergyman, saying, "It is very evident that this man is still in the neighbourhood, and is on this side of the hills. Let me beg you, my good sir, to keep a good watch in every direction till I come back, which will be to-morrow evening. I think it better, now, to go on myself, in order to see old Lord Danemore, who lies dangerously ill, and to break to him the news of his son's death, which, if I judge rightly, may, at the present moment, be a matter of the greatest importance to him and many others."

The justice breakfasted, and then proceeded on his journey.

CHAPTER XXXVI.

We must now return to the conversation which was going on at the Rectory of Danemore between Mr. Evelyn, Sir Walter Herbert, and him whom we shall still call Henry Langford—in the fear that he should never establish his claim to any higher title; and the reader need scarcely be told that the interruption which took place therein was occasioned by the arrival of Mr. Justice Whistler, bearing with him the sad account of all that had occurred in consequence of the expedition which he himself led against Franklin Gray.

Putting down his hat upon the table, the leather band of which was dripping with some rain which had now begun to fall, he declared that he believed such events had never happened before in any civilised country; and he related with no inconsiderable degree of real feeling the death of poor Mona Gray. For a time, sensations of awe, and grief, and astonishment, suspended every other feeling in the bosoms of his hearers; but he himself, who had cast off the first impression under the influence of a good night's rest, and a long heavy ride, recalled the rest of the party to other thoughts, by making Langford a low bow, and saying, "Under existing circumstances, I suppose I may congratulate you, sir, upon your undisputed succession to the title of Earl of Danemore."

Langford replied that he certainly intended at once to assume that title, though, he believed, it would not be undisputed; and Mr. Evelyn, who had a great inclination for doing business under all circumstances, immediately proceeded to take into consideration the change which the news they had just received might produce in Langford's position. Judging that it might be as well to engage the activeness of Mr. Justice Whistler in their service, at least as far as seeking for the lost papers was concerned, he opened the matter to that respectable magistrate, and held out to him such cogent inducements for exerting himself to the utmost in the business in hand, that the justice, though he represented the importance and necessity of his presence in London, agreed to leave all business there to his colleagues, and devote himself to the object in view.

Langford heard this arrangement without saying anything, and without giving any encouragement to Mr. Justice Whistler to remain; for, in truth, he had his own views upon the subject, and had already determined what course to pursue, feeling perfectly sure that the lost papers were in the possession of Franklin Gray, and that any efforts of Mr. Justice Whistler for the recovery of those papers would retard, if not utterly prevent, the attainment of their object.

He took care therefore to give no hint either of his own purposes, or his suspicions as to the hands into which the papers had fallen, but at once turned to another part of the subject, saying, "In the first place, Mr. Evelyn as it is my full intention to deal openly and straightforwardly in this business altogether, I think it may be necessary immediately to send a line to Sir Henry Heywood, informing him of the terrible fate which has befallen my unhappy brother, and begging to meet him here, to confer more fully on the subject tomorrow morning."

The note was accordingly written, and sent; and Sir Henry, who fancied himself considerably nearer to his object in consequence of the death of Lord Harold, returned a gracious answer, and appointed ten o'clock on the following day for the conference. Sir Walter Herbert then proceeded to Moorhurst; but although Langford felt a longing desire to pass one more evening of tranquillity with her he loved best, in the library of the calm old Manor House, he would not quit the sad dwelling where the body of his father lay, but remained there during the night.

By ten o'clock the next morning Sir Walter had returned, and the arrival of Sir Henry Heywood soon followed. He was now, however, accompanied by a lawyer, and on his entering the room, Langford immediately, in plain and courteous language, and few words, announced to him the situation in which he stood, as son of the late Earl of Danemore, by his private marriage with Eugenie de Beaulieu.

Sir Henry Heywood had not lost his time since his arrival in the neighbourhood of Danemore Castle, and by one means or another had collected a very accurate knowledge of Langford's situation, and the points in which his claim was strong or defective.

"Sir," he said, in reply, " what you have just asserted may be, and, indeed, very probably is correct. You are a likely young gentleman; bear a strong resemblance to the late Earl, and so forth. I have nothing to say against the fact of the Earl being your father, or of your mother being a very virtuous lady; but all I have to say is, that such assertions are good for nothing in law without proofs of the fact. If you will do me the honour to show me the registry of your father's and mother's marriage, a certificate to that effect from the hands of the clergyman who married them, the attestation of the proper witnesses, or, in short, satisfactory legal proofs, I shall make you a very low bow, and congratulate you on your accession to the title of Earl of Danemore. Till then, however, by your leave, I shall assume that title myself, and acting as heir to the late peer, take possession of everything to which the law gives me a claim."

"In regard to taking possession of anything, sir," replied Langford, "be my claim what it will, I think you will find yourself barred by my father's will."

"Then let it be produced, sir--let it be produced," said Sir Henry Heywood, with some degree of irritable sharpness. "We have heard a great deal about this will: let it be produced."

"Certainly, sir," replied Mr. Evelyn; " here it is. But before it is opened, we will call in, if you please, the witnesses who heard every word of it read over to the Earl, and who saw him sign it. I think that his chief servants should be present."

What he suggested was agreed to. The small room of the Rectory was nearly filled; and while Langford, with feelings of deep grief, perhaps we might even say despondency, sat at the table shading his eyes with his hand, and Sir Henry Heywood, seated on the other side, shut his lips close, and looked full in Mr. Evelyn's face, the lawyer, after all due formalities, proceeded to read the will aloud.

In the first place, it ordained as private and speedy a burial of his body as possible. In the next, it provided liberally for all the servants.

It then went on to leave to his son Edward, heretofore erroneously called Lord Harold, a large independent fortune, which was to revert, in case of his death without issue, to the person whom next he named; that person was his eldest son, Henry, by his first wife, Eugenie de Beaulieu, whom he had married privately the year before the Restoration.

Under the skilful management of Mr. Evelyn, nothing had been left undone to show that Langford was the person to whom he alluded, and to render the wording of the Earl's will the most solemn acknowledgment of his marriage and declaration of his son's legitimacy. With all these precautions, the Earl went on to leave to him every part of his vast fortune not otherwise disposed of; noticing the estates attached to the title of Earl of Danemore only as coming to him of necessity. The three executors were then appointed, as had been before announced, and the will terminated with the signature.

The reading of this document called forth a burst of angry vehemence from Sir Henry Heywood, which might have proceeded further had it not been repressed instantly by a murmur of indignation which ran through all present.

Langford, however, himself, was the coolest of the party, and as soon as the reading of the will was concluded, he said, "Sir Henry Heywood, in the present state of feeling experienced by all parties, the less discussion that takes place, of course the better. You are now satisfied as to who are the executors; but I think it will be better, till after the funeral is over, to remove none of the seals which have been placed; and I doubt not that this reverend gentleman, and Sir Walter Herbert, will agree with me in that view. You will, of course, be present at the funeral; and I doubt not that on that sad occasion we shall all meet more calmly. For the present, I wish you good morning;" and so saying, he bowed and quitted the room.

Sir Henry Heywood remained, and would fain have entered into the discussion of many points, both with Sir Walter and Mr. Evelyn, but neither were at all inclined to gratify him in that respect; and he retired, declaring that he would certainly attend the funeral; but that before that time he would have such legal authority from London as would enable him to maintain his just rights against any conspiracy which might be formed to oppose them. Sir Walter Herbert coloured, and raised his head at the word conspiracy, with signs of ill-repressed indignation; but Mr. Evelyn laid his hand upon his arm, saying, "He is a disappointed man, Sir Walter, and has privilege of angry words."

On the measures that were taken by Sir Henry Heywood we will not dwell; nor will we pause, even for a moment, on the melancholy ceremony of committing to dust the bodies of the Earl of Danemore and his younger son. Langford, although between him and the dead there existed none of those endearing ties which gather round the heart in the tender intercourse of early years, though his affection towards them was not, like the rich shells which we find embedded in the coral rock, joined to the things it clung to by the accumulated love and associations of years, still could not help feeling deeply and painfully as he laid the father and the brother in the grave, and took the dark farewell of his last earthly kindred.

Sir Henry Heywood had by this time learned so far to restrain himself that nothing disagreeable occurred; and from the vault the whole party turned their steps, not to the Rectory, but to one of the large saloons which had remained unconsumed in Danemore Castle. The two noted lawyers were found waiting for the baronet, who immediately addressed himself to Langford, demanding if he distinctly understood him to lay claim to the earldom of Danemore.

"Distinctly, sir," replied Langford.

"Very well, sir. Then—" interrupted Sir Henry.

But the other waved his hand, and went on, "I do most distinctly lay claim to that earldom, sir; but as I wish to do nothing whatsoever that can be considered unfair towards you, and shall in a few days be able to produce the only papers which seem necessary to convince you of my right—having at this moment a certain knowledge of the person who has taken them—I shall leave the executorial duties under my father's will entirely to my excellent friends, who, well advised, will deal with you in all justice and kindness, I am sure. I myself am bound upon important business, and therefore you will excuse my presence any further. I trust in two honourable men, all whose actions I know will bear the closest inspection; and I shall feel satisfied with and ratify everything that they shall do."

A word whispered in the ear of Sir Henry Heywood by one of his lawyers, made him start a step forward ere Langford departed, and say, "Doubtless, sir, we are to expect on your return the production of the papers; and of course you will be willing to submit them, as you do the conduct of your friends, to the closest inspection?"

"Quite," replied Langford, with a calm smile, so slightly coloured by contempt that none but an eager and well-qualified appetite could have detected the admixture. "Whether I bring back the papers or not, Sir Henry, depends upon fortune; or, rather, I should say, upon God's will. You judge rightly when you think I go to seek them; and that I go to seek them where they are to be found, I am quite certain. My chance may be to find them, or not. I give you good-day."

Leaving Sir Henry Heywood to follow what course he thought fit, and Sir Walter Herbert with the rector, guided by Mr. Evelyn, and an old, calm, thoughtful, experienced, little-speaking lawyer from London, to deal with him as they judged advisable, we shall trace the course of Henry Langford, who now, followed by two servants, one attached to Sir Walter Herbert, and the other an old and faithful domestic of his father, the late earl, took his way abruptly from Danemore Castle, but not in the direction which the reader may imagine. He rode at once across the country to the little village of Moorhurst; and passing over the bridge—because the shortest way, though the park, under lately existing circumstances, had been closed—he approached the Manor House; and leaving his horse, with orders not to unsaddle him, in the court-yard, he hurried through the house in search of Alice Herbert.

He found her without much difficulty; and sweet and tender were her feelings on that first meeting, alone, and altogether to each other, after a long period of distress and anxiety, and the obtrusiveness of a thousand anxious and busy cares. He told her that he could not go away upon a journey of some distance and of much importance without seeing her—without bidding her farewell for the time. He told her again and again how deeply and how passionately he loved her. He pressed her again and again to his heart, in gratitude for past kindness, in the ardour of present affection, in the longing apprehension of parting. He took, and she granted, all that a noble heart could wish or a pure heart could yield; and then, springing upon his horse, he once more pursued his way towards the spot which the tale of Justice Whistler had pointed out as that where Franklin Gray was likely to be met with.

He left the village, with the Rectory of Mr. Sandon, far to the left, about an hour before sunset; and then inquiring his way to the nearest farmhouse—for there were neither railroads over deserts, nor hotels upon mountains in those days—he prepared to repose for the night ere he pursued his inquiries on the following morning. The people of the farm were kind and civil: and, though it put them somewhat out of their way to receive a guest with two servants and three horses, when they expected no such thing, the matter was readily arranged, and Langford soon found himself sitting at a pleasant country table, whereat ten or twelve people were enjoying themselves after the fatigues of the day.

Langford made himself friends wherever he came, by the urbanity of his manners; generally ruling as much as he wished in all circumstances, by appearing, like the ancient Greek, to yield and to respect. In the present instance he was received with great gladness, and was enabled to gain information of everything that was passing throughout the country round, by the very fact of his making himself at once at home amongst the people, as we have said he did, and by seeming to share their feelings, which soon proved the means of sharing their thoughts. The whole tittle-tattle of the neighbourhood was now detailed to him, and he heard every particular of the death of his brother. The stopping of Mr. Justice Whistler, and his scourging with the saddle-girths and stirrup-leathers, were also told him, with many other interesting details, which seemed to have made a deep impression upon the laughter-loving hearts of the honest villagers.

Langford himself was, in comparison with his ordinary moods, sad and gloomy, as he well might be, not so much from anticipation of the future as in reflecting upon the past, and upon all the deeds, wrongs, and sorrows whereon that inevitable past had set its seal for ever; and as he approached the spot where his brother had fallen, the despondency that he felt was of course not diminished. Without asking any direct questions concerning Franklin Gray, Langford obtained tidings which made him hesitate in regard to his further conduct; for in answer to his inquiries as to whether any of the robbers had been captured, the honest farmer—who had been one of those that went out against them, and therefore took a personal interest in the whole affair—informed him that the band had certainly dispersed, each man, it was supposed, taking his separate way back to London. Such was the opinion pronounced by Mr. Justice Whistler, the farmer said; and Langford now learned, for the first time, that the worthy justice had returned to the scene of his former adventures, and was eagerly aiding the local magistrate in the pursuit of the robbers.

He feared, then, that Franklin Gray might thus have been driven from the neighbourhood; but after some reflection, an impression took hold of his mind—probably springing from traits of the Robber's character which he had seen and marked in better days—that Gray would linger, for a time at least, round the spot where his unhappy wife was interred; and Langford consequently proceeded at once to the little solitary burial ground in which she lay. To it was attached a small church, situated at a great distance from any other building, high upon the side of the hill, and offering once in the week some means of religious instruction to the inhabitants of that wild tract. He easily found the grave of poor Mona Gray, for no one had been buried there for many months but herself, and every other grave was green.

The sight of that grave, however, confirmed him in the hope of soon finding Franklin Gray, for at the head were strewed, here and there, some wild flowers, evidently lately gathered. Justice Whistler, with a heart hardened by intercourse with evil things, did not comprehend the character of the Robber as Langford did, and never dreamed that he would linger near the spot where the wife whom he had himself slain with such determined premeditation, slept her last sleep.

Leaving his two servants to watch in the churchyard, Henry Langford rode up to the top of the hills, and continued his course along the ridge towards the sea; but ere he had gone half a mile, he saw something move in one of the deep, shadowy indentations of the ground, and riding quickly down, he pursued the object as it fled before him, taking advantage of everything which could conceal it in its flight, doubling round every tree and bush, and plunging into each deep dell. But Langford caught sight of it sufficiently often to feel sure that it was a human being, and he gained upon it also as it led him back in its flight towards the churchyard.

There, however, he lost sight of it again; but the moment after, a faint cry met his ear, and a shout; and riding on fast. he found the boy Jocelyn in the hands of his two servants. The boy was evidently in great terror; and the sound of another voice behind him, when Langford spoke as he came up, made him start almost out of the hands of the men who held him. The sight of Langford's well-known face, however, instantly made his countenance brighten; and when that gentleman spoke kindly to him, and bade the men let him go, the boy came up towards him, bending his head, and looking gladly in his face, as a favourite dog that has been lost for several days, runs up, fawning, but yet half frightened, towards its master, when it returns.

"Well, Jocelyn," said Langford, gazing at him, and marking his soiled clothes and pale and haggard appearance, "you seem not to have fared very richly, my poor boy, since you got away from Justice Whistler. Did you find out your master?"

The boy looked timidly at the two men who stood near, then hung down his head, and made no reply. Langford bent over him, and said in a low voice, "Do not be frightened, Jocelyn. I am seeking no ill, either to yourself or your master. Come with me on the hill side, and tell me more. We will leave the men here."

"You must leave your horse behind, then, also," said the boy, in the same low tone, "if you want to see the Captain as you used to do; for he will never let us find him if he sees any one coming on horseback."

"'That I will do willingly," replied Langford; and throwing the bridle to one of the men, he bade them remain there till he returned.

Holding the boy Jocelyn by the hand, he then went out upon the hill side, questioning him as they walked along, with regard to Franklin Gray; but before he would answer anything, the boy made him again and again promise that he would not betray his master. When he was satisfied on that point, he gazed up in Langford's face, with a look of deep and anxious sadness, saying, "Oh, you don't know all, Captain Langford! You don't know all!"

"Yes, my good boy, I do," replied Langford; "I have heard all the sad story of the people going to attack your master in his house, and his fancying that his wife had betrayed him, and shooting the person he loved best on earth."

"Ay, poor thing, she is happy!" said the boy; "I am sure she is in heaven, for every day since they laid her in the churchyard, I have strewed what flowers I could get, upon her grave, and they do not wither there half so soon as they do anywhere else. But I am sure it is better for her to be there than to see her husband in such a state as he is now."

"What do you mean, Jocelyn?" demanded Langford. "Grief and remorse for what he has done must, I dare say, have had a terrible effect upon your master; but you seem to imply something more. What is it that you mean?"

"Alas," replied the boy, "he is mad; quite mad. That is what made Harvey and the rest leave him, for they found him out after he got away and joined him again; but, both for his sake and their own, they were obliged to separate, when they found what state he was in. But I am sure he had been mad some time before, for the day after that wicked man made his escape, who brought all the people upon us. I saw him on the hill fire one of his pistols in the air, as if he had been shooting at something, though there was nothing to be seen: and when he had done he looked at the pistol and said, 'You are not so dangerous now.' But now he is quite wild, and you must take care how you go near him, for it is a thousand to one that he fires at you, and you know he never misses his mark."

"Whereabouts is he?" demanded Langford. "I wonder he has not been discovered."

"Oh, he is two or three miles off, at least," replied the boy; "in the rocky part of the hills near the sea. He comes here about night, when he goes to the grave in the churchyard, and moans over it; but then before daylight he is away again."

Langford and the boy walked on, but the two or three miles he spoke of proved to be fully five, and during the last mile the scenery became wild and rugged in the extreme. The turf, which had covered the hills further inland with a smooth though undulating surface, was here constantly broken by immense masses of rock, sometimes taking the form of high banks and promontories, with the tops still soft and grassy; sometimes starting abruptly up in fantastic groups out of the ground, like the rugged and misshapen columns of some druidical temple. Here and there a few scattered birch trees varied the scene, and near a spot where a spring of clear water broke from the ground, and wandered down in a stream into the valley, some fine oaks had planted themselves, sheltered by a higher ridge of the hill from the sharp winds of the sea.

As they came near this spot, the boy Jocelyn gave a long low whistle, more like the cry of some wild bird than any sound from human lips, saying, after he had done so, "He is often about here at this hour."

No answer was returned, however, and they went on for nearly another mile, which brought them to the high rocks that encircled a bay of the sea. "I should not wonder if he were here," said the boy; "for I sometimes catch fish for him there, and there are more berries upon the shrubs that grow half way down than anywhere else."

"Good God! Is that the only food that he obtains?" demanded Langford.

"He has had nothing else," said the boy, sadly, "since Harvey and the rest went away. Look! There he is!—just below us. Hush! Do not let us go quick!"

Langford laid his hand upon the boy's arm, and detained him, while he gazed down for two or three moments on the unhappy man who had once been his companion and friend in the stirring days of military adventure.

It was a terrible sight! The sun was shining brightly, though over the deep blue sky some large detached masses of cloud were borne by a soft and equable but rapid wind, throwing upon the green bosom of the water below, and the rocks and hills round about, deep clear shadows, which, as they floated on, left the objects that they touched brighter than ever in the sunshine, like the shadows which doubt or suspicion, or gloom, or the waywardness of the human heart, will cast upon things in themselves beautiful, and which, when the mood is gone or the doubt removed, resume at once all their splendour. Part of the steep close by Franklin Gray was covered with bushes, mingled with some taller trees, and over these the shadow of a cloud was flying, while he himself sat in the full light upon a small projecting piece of the rock.

Tenderly folded to his bosom, he held his infant with both his arms; and, swaying backwards and forwards, while his eyes wandered wildly over the waters, he seemed endeavouring to rock it to sleep. A little further up, his horse, his beautiful grey, of which he had been so fond, cropped the scanty herbage, with the bridle cast upon his neck; and hearing the approach of strangers even before his master, he raised high his proud head, and gazed eagerly around.

"How does he feed the child?" demanded Langford, in a whisper.

"With berries, and anything he can get," replied the boy; "he never lets it be out of his arms but to crawl round him for a few moments on the turf."

"This is very terrible, indeed," said Langford; "but he sits there on such a fearful point of the rock that you had better go forward yourself, in the first instance, and tell him that I am here. The least thing might make him plunge over."

"It would not surprise me at all," replied the boy, "for where he goes I am sure I would not go, and yet I can climb as well as any one."

Langford then withdrew for a few yards, and the boy again uttered his low whistle, which was immediately answered. After pausing for a moment or two to give him time to reach his master, Langford again advanced, and saw the boy in eager conversation with Franklin Gray, whose eyes were now bent upon the spot where he stood. Satisfied that he was prepared for his coming, Langford descended with difficulty the precipitous path which led to the shelf of rock on which he stood; and Franklin Gray himself took a step or two back from the edge, and came forward to meet him. Holding the child still to his bosom with one arm, he at first held out the other to his old companion; but the next moment, as they came near, he drew it suddenly back, gazing upon him with his bright flashing eyes, and exclaiming, "No, no! This hand killed your father and your brother, and you must pursue me to the death!"

"No, Franklin," replied Langford, in a calm and quiet tone; "I pursue you not with any evil intent towards you. What you say is true; that hand did slay my brother, and aided, perhaps, in taking my father's life; but that hand too aided and supported my mother; and my father, not many days before his death, made me promise that I would not seek for vengeance upon you. He said that he had wronged you in early years, and that it was fitting your own hand should punish him."

"He did—he did wrong me!" cried Franklin Gray. "To him I owe all that is evil in my nature. He had me kidnapped when I was a boy, and would have fain followed the sweet lady he had deserted. He had me kidnapped, and carried me away into the south, and made me familiar with blood; and when I fled from him, he pursued me as if I had been his slave; but I escaped. And now, Henry, tell me what you seek with me! If you come not for vengeance, what is it you come for?"

"I came," replied Langford, "from a personal motive; but I did not expect, Franklin, to find you in this state, and the thoughts of myself are swallowed up in pain to find you thus."

"What! you mean I am mad!" burst forth Franklin Gray. "It is true, I am mad, madder than any that we used to see nursed by the Brothers of Charity at Charenton. But what matters that? Every one else is as mad as myself. Was not she mad to let me think that she had betrayed me? Was she not madder still to send me word when she was dying that she had not betrayed me, and to pile coals of fire upon my head? Was she not mad to die at all, and leave me with this infant?" and sitting upon the ground, he looked earnestly upon the face of the child, which his vehemence had awakened up from its sleep.

After pausing for a few minutes, and pressing his hand tightly upon his brow, he turned to Langford more collectedly, saying, "You told me you came here from a personal motive. What was it? Speak quickly, while my mind will go straight, for my brain is like a horse that has just gone blind, and wavers from one side of the road to the other." And he laughed wildly at his own simile.

"The motive that brought me, Franklin," replied Langford, "was to obtain from you the papers which you know I have been so long seeking to possess. My mother's marriage, it seems, cannot be proved without them."

Franklin Gray started upon his feet, and gazed with wild surprise in Langford's face. "I have them not," he exclaimed; "I never touched them. Did you not take them? It was your own fault, then; and they were burnt with the house. We rushed out as fast as we could go. I know nothing further."

That he spoke truth was so evident, that Langford instantly determined to say nothing more on the subject, though the disappointment caused him a bitter pang. But it was useless to enter into any explanations with the unhappy man before him; and with the usual calm decision of his character he determined at once to apply himself, as far as possible, to see what might be done to relieve and comfort him. If he remained in England, his life would inevitably be sacrificed to the law, notwithstanding his manifest insanity. He himself, under such circumstances, could not even intercede in his favour, and the only hope of saving him from public execution was to induce him to fly to France, and by giving notice of his condition to some persons of influence there, to obtain admission for him into the institution which he himself had mentioned—namely, that of the Brothers of Charity at Charenton, who devoted themselves to the care of persons in his unhappy situation. All this passed through his mind in a moment, and he replied to Franklin Gray at once, "Well, if it be so, it cannot be helped; but now, Gray, to speak of yourself. You must be aware that you are here in a very dangerous situation, surrounded by people who are pursuing you for the express purpose of bringing you to the scaffold. Would it not be much better for you to fly to France?"

Franklin Gray gazed in his face for a moment or two, then looked up to the sky with a sort of half smile. "It would be better," he answered, at length; "it would be better, and my passage is even taken in a ship which is to sail, I think, in two days. But what am I to do with the child?"

"Oh, I will provide means for its joining you," replied Langford: "it shall be well taken care of."

"I have got a little boat, too, down there," said Gray, in a rambling manner, "which would carry me to the ship in no time."

Langford looked at the boy Jocelyn with an inquiring glance; but the youth shook his head, murmuring, in a scarcely audible tone, "There is no boat."

Franklin Gray was evidently occupied with other thoughts. He put his hand again to his head, and then, turning to Henry Langford, he said, "Henry, we are old companions, and I will take you at your word. Promise me, as a man and a soldier, that this babe shall be well taken care of till he joins me. It is a sweet creature, and seldom, if ever, cries. You will use it as your own, Henry, in every respect as your own?"

"I will, indeed," replied Langford; "I will, indeed; but let us think now how you can best be got off to the vessel."

But Franklin Gray went on thus:—"And poor Jocelyn, too," he said, laying his hand upon the boy's head; "you will be kind to him, and breed him as a soldier?"

"He had better go with you, Franklin," replied Langford.

"No," answered Franklin Gray, "No; I shall be better alone;" and at the same time the boy whispered to Langford, "Humour him; humour him. I will find means to follow him closely."

"Will you promise that, too?" demanded Franklin Gray, but instantly went on without waiting a reply—"Then the baby, too, Henry; you will be very kind to it, and tender, and love it very much? See, it smiles at you. Take it in your arms."

Langford took the child as he held it out to him. Franklin Gray bent down his head and kissed it; then laid his two muscular hands upon Langford's shoulders, and gazed gravely and solemnly into his eyes.

"Henry," he said, "your vow is registered in heaven!" and before Langford could answer him, he shouted exultingly, "Now I am free! Now I am free!"

With a sudden spring forward he reached the ledge on which he had lately stood, and without pause, or thought, or hesitation, plunged at once over into empty air.

The depth below might be near two hundred feet, and the water of the sea washed the base of the rock. It was in vain that Langford himself sought, and, with the aid of his servants and some people that they brought to his assistance, spent the whole of that evening in endeavouring to find the body of Franklin Gray. It was not till nearly ten days after that some fishermen found a corpse, with marks of much violence about it, showing that it must have struck upon the rocks at the bottom of the water, lying on a sandy spit that ran out from one of the points of the bay. The clothes proved it to be that of Franklin Gray; but nobody took any pains to identify it as such. A verdict of found drowned was returned by the coroner's jury; and it was buried, at Langford's expense, close to the side of Mona Gray, in the churchyard on the hills.

The road which Langford pursued, on his way back, was that which passed over the moor, as we have before mentioned, near the spot called Upwater Meer, and thence descending the hill, separated into two branches, at a point where, on the one hand, the remains of Danemore Castle, with its wide park and deep woods, were to be seen at the distance of about four miles, and on the other appeared the graceful little spire of Moorhurst Church, with the manifold roofs and chimneys of the Manor House, peeping out of the trees some way in advance.

When Langford reached that spot, which was at the period of the evening when the shadows begin to grow long, but before the sun had lost any of its power, he paused and gazed for several minutes upon the mansion of his ancestors; saying to it in his own heart, "Farewell for ever. The things which were to have given you back to me, with all the honours and pride of high birth and long ancestry, are lost beyond recall. But never mind. It may be better as it is. I shall escape the temptations of high estate. Alice will not love me less; and though it may cost Sir Walter's heart a pang that the legitimacy of my birth is not clear to the eyes of all men, he himself will not doubt it. It may cause mine a pang, too, that even a shade should rest upon my mother's name; but I have done all that could be done."

Such were his thoughts, though not, perhaps, his words, as, after gazing for some time upon the castle, he turned, and directed his horse's head towards Moorhurst. On arriving at the old Manor House, he looked up with pleasure to see the smoke curling above the trees, the lattice windows wide open to give admission to the sweet fresh air, and all bearing that air of comfort and cheerfulness which it used to do.

There were several persons, not servants, lingering about in the court-yard, however. There was a look of some vexation in honest Halliday's face as he gave Langford admission, and some strangers were in the hall. The events of the last few weeks had brought an apprehensiveness upon Langford's heart which sorrow can do even to those who are steeled against danger; and he asked at once if anything were the matter.

"Oh, no. His worship and Mistress Alice are both quite well, sir," replied Halliday, divining Langford's feelings at once. "It is only that they have brought a poor fellow up before Sir Walter, charged with stealing, who I am sure never stole; and that Sir Henry Heywood, or Lord Danemore, as he calls himself—I hope he'll have to uncall himself soon—is pressing to have him sent to prison at once. Mistress Alice is up in the village. I am glad she is away, poor thing."

Langford went on into the library, and, passing without much notice a group of persons around the prisoner at the end of the long table, he advanced to Sir Walter, who was sitting with Sir Henry Heywood at some distance, with a table before them, and some books. The Knight and the Baronet both rose on seeing Langford; the one to grasp his hand; the other to make him a more cordial bow than hitherto.

"Pray, sir, may I ask," he said, immediately, with a certain anxious quivering of the lip, but with perfect civility, "if you have been successful in your search?"

"I have not, sir," replied Langford, honestly; "I have not found what I sought."

"Then I presume, sir, that you are not disposed to pursue further your claims in this matter?" rejoined the other, in a hesitating manner.

"You are wrong, sir," replied Langford; "I shall pursue it upon such proofs as are in my possession. If it were but for the purpose of clearing my mother's fame, I would do so, even if there existed no chance of my recovering my right."

"It is a noble feeling, sir," said Sir Henry, with an urbane smile; "but perhaps there may be a method of compromising this affair. Allow me one word with you;" and so saying, he drew Langford aside into the recess of one of the windows. "For my own part," he continued, "I am not ambitious. I am a widower, and shall certainly never marry again. I have but two daughters—you are a single man—"

"But one engaged to be married very shortly," replied his auditor, making him a low bow; and Sir Henry went back to Sir Walter Herbert, saying, in a fierce and impatient tone, "Let us proceed with the business before us at once, Sir Walter. I say the man must be committed, and I call upon you as a magistrate to do so."

"I do not see the case as you do," answered the good Knight of Moorhurst; and as he spoke, Langford approached the table also, and, raising his eyes to the prisoner, at once recognised the poor half-witted man, Silly John Graves. Though surprised and grieved, he said nothing, having learned in a hard and difficult school to govern his first emotions. Standing beside Sir Walter Herbert, however, and feeling that internal conviction of the man's honesty and truth which is gained, not alone from great and significant actions, but from small signs and casual traits, which betray rather than display the heart, he determined to interpose in the poor man's defence, and not to suffer the overbearing vehemence of Sir Henry Heywood to crush the calm simplicity of truth, as overbearing vehemence so generally does in this world.

"Why, Sir Walter Herbert," exclaimed Sir Henry Heywood, in the same sharp tone, "has not the man been found carrying out of Danemore Castle a valuable cup and silver cover? Has he not been taken in the very act?"

"I took nothing but what was my own,' said Silly John, gazing upon Sir Henry Heywood with a shy look, which mingled in strange harmony terror, and contempt, and hatred; "I took nothing but what was my own, or what ought never to have been there, or what no one there had a right to."

"What, then," exclaimed Sir Henry Heywood, "you took more beside the cup?"

"Ay, that I did," replied Silly John; "I took the cup because Mistress Bertha brought it to me full of wine on the night I was shut up there, in the dark hole under the tower; and she gave me the cup and all, and said I might keep it; and then the fire came, and I lost the cup; and so, whenever I was well enough of the burns and the bruises, I went back again to seek it, and to take my own."

"Send for Mistress Bertha," said Sir Walter, speaking to one of the attendants at the lower side of the room; "She is now in the house, which is fortunate."

Sir Henry Heywood gnawed his lip, but, as if to fill up the time, he asked the prisoner, looking keenly at him, "You acknowledge you took other things out of the Castle before you were caught. What were they, and what right had you to them? You will see, Sir Walter," he continued, "that whether Danemore Castle belongs to me, or to this other gentleman who claims it, it is absolutely necessary that we who dispute the property, and you who are executor to the will, should investigate accurately, and prosecute vigorously, every one who abstracts anything from that building. I ask you again," he added, addressing the half-witted man, "what it was you admit taking, and what claim you had thereunto."

"More claim than you can show," answered Silly John; "for I had some right, and you have none. And worse than a fox you are, for a fox only seeks a young bird out of the nest; you seek nest and all. Every one knows I never told a lie in my life!"

"Ay, that we do!" cried some voices at the end of the library; but at that instant Sir Henry Heywood exclaimed, "Silence there! how dare you disturb the court?"

"By your leave, Sir Henry," said Sir Walter Herbert.

But at that moment the woman Bertha entered the room, with the same cold, calm, and dignified air which had become second nature with her, and gazing round with a look of inquiry, she demanded, "What is wanted with me? Who sent for me?"

The next moment, however, her eyes fell upon the half-witted man, as he stood at the bottom of the table, and clasping her hands together with emotion, such as no one present had ever beheld her display on any previous occasion, she exclaimed, "Good God! is it possible? Art thou living? or art thou risen from the dead? I thought thou hadst been burnt to ashes in Hubert's tower, which fell amongst the first that went down. I dared not even mention thy name, for thy confinement there, and the dreadful fate that I thought had befallen thee, were too terrible, were too awful for thought even, to rest upon! But now thou art come to life again to bear witness of the truth—and yet," she added sorrowfully, "they will not hear his testimony, for they will say he is mad—that he has been mad for years!"

"Never you fear that, Mistress Bertha," said the half-witted man. "The foxes let me out before they set fire to the house; and I never forget anything; so, while they were fighting and tearing each other to pieces, I went and fingered—what do you think?"

"The papers! the papers!" exclaimed Bertha, almost screaming with joy.

"Ay, even so," said the half-witted man, thrusting his hand into his breast. "I found the key upon the floor of the room, and I opened the hole in the wall, and took them out."

"What right had you with them?" thundered Sir Henry Heywood, who had sat by, no unconcerned spectator of the scene. "What right had you with anything in that place? You confess robbery!"

"What right had I with them?" exclaimed Silly John, with a wild laugh. "Why, you are as foolish as if you had been born before Noah's flood! Wasn't there the leaf of the register which they cut out of my own register book just about the time I first went mad, when I was usher of Uppington Grammar School, and clerk of the parish? and did not that make me madder than before? Who had any right to the leaf but I?—and there it is!" and he spread out upon the table an old yellow leaf of paper, written over both sides with pale ink, and bearing the traces of many foldings.

"It is a falsehood! a forgery!" exclaimed Sir Henry Heywood. "It is got up for the occasion! It is a conspiracy! Let me see the sheet!" and he started forward to snatch it up from the table; but at that moment Mr. Evelyn, the lawyer, stepped in before him, and laid his hand firmly upon it.

"By your leave, sir," he said, "this valuable document is fingered by nobody. Do not bend your brows on me, sir. I am firm! Clerk, take up the document, and be you responsible for it. If Sir Henry chooses to bring this business into court, he may; but if he will take my advice he will listen to a few quiet words. While thinking that my noble client and patron, the young Earl of Danemore, here present," and he pointed to Langford, "would certainly obtain this same document from another source, I busied myself eagerly to obtain every collateral testimony which could prove the identity of the leaf that had been so nicely extracted from the register; and I have here, under my hand, the certificates of five marriages which took place in that same year in the parish of Uppington, which are not now to be found in the volume of the register, but which will be found, I will answer for it, in the leaf that is now produced. This will be confirmation, beyond all doubt, if it be so. Clerk, compare the papers!"

"Oh, but that is all nonsense, Master Turney," cried Silly John; "there's no need of comparing anything. Was not I clerk of the parish myself, and witness of the marriage? And besides, here's the certificate of the marriage in the Rev. Jonathan Whattle's own hand. Anybody in the place will swear to the drunken parson's handwriting. The only difference was, that it was more crooked and shaky when he was sober than when he was drunk; and here's my own handwriting to it, as I used to write in those days. God help me! I've nearly forgotten how to write now. And then there's Mistress Bertha's there; her hand is to it too, and a Frenchman's hand that was with them at the time. I remember very well. And here's another paper besides, written in a tongue I don't understand, which is all the more likely to prove a matter of moment. God help us all! we're as blind as kittens of three days old, and can tell nothing of what will happen at the end of the nine."

"Sir," said the clerk, who had been busily looking over the papers, "I find all these extracts placed at intervals in the leaf of the register before me. There are nine or ten others, too, which could doubtless easily be traced. Shall I send for the register of Uppington to compare the book and the leaf?"

"It is unnecessary, sir; it is unnecessary," said Sir Henry Heywood, making a virtue of necessity. "My Lord the Earl of Danemore, I congratulate you on your unexpected accession to such honours and so much wealth. That you have cast me out from them I forgive you. Disappointed I must feel; but that disappointment, believe me, proceeds more from affection for my two poor girls, whose inheritance will be but their father's sword, useless in their hands, and their mother's virtues, which God grant may adorn them always, than from the loss of rank and wealth to myself. Sir, I give you good morning, and leave you."

"Stop a moment, Sir Henry Heywood," said Langford; "a word in your ear before you go." That word was spoken in a moment, but Sir Henry Heywood's face was in that moment lighted up with joy, and grasping Langford's hand in both his own, he exclaimed, "Indeed! indeed, my Lord, you are too generous!"

"Not so, Sir Henry," replied Langford; "for the present, adieu. We will meet to-morrow at Danemore Castle, and all shall be settled entirely. Sir Walter," he added, in a lower tone, "there is some one whom I would fain see, in this moment of joy and agitation, before I say a word more to any one."

"She must have returned by this time," said Sir Walter. "Let us go!"

They went out, and proceeded to the ladies' withdrawing-room, where they found Alice, with her beautiful eyes raised anxiously towards the door. As soon as she saw Langford, she sprang up to meet him, with the whole pure unrestrained joy of her heart beaming forth upon that lovely face.

"Alice," said Sir Walter, with a touch of his kindly stateliness, "this is the Earl of Danemore!"

"Your own Henry, ever dearest Alice," said Langford, casting his arms round her; and then, while he held her to his bosom with one hand, he extended the other to Sir Walter. "Most excellent and generous friend, I have never yet asked your consent with my own lips. Do you give her to me? Will you part with this great—this inestimable treasure?"

"I will give her to you, Henry," replied Sir Walter, "with all my heart and soul. I will give her to you, but I will not part with her. I must have a garret in the Castle, my dear boy! There, there; I give her to you. She is yours. God's blessing and her father's be upon your heads!"

So saying, he clasped their hands in each other's, and they were happy.

THE END.

www.ingramcontent.com/pod-product-compliance
Lightning Source LLC
Chambersburg PA
CBHW032059220426
43664CB00008B/1071